In the Margins of Deconstruction

In the Margins of

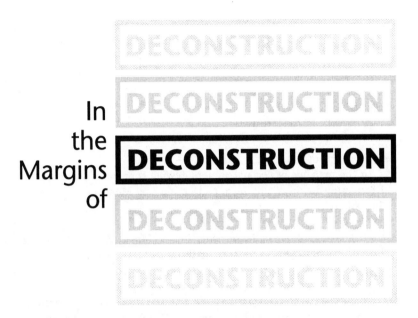

DECONSTRUCTION

Jewish Conceptions of Ethics in Emmanuel Levinas and Jacques Derrida

by *Martin C. Srajek*

Duquesne University Press
Pittsburgh, Pennsylvania

Library of Congress Cataloging-in-Publication Data

Srajek, Martin C.

   In the margins of deconstruction: Jewish conceptions of ethics in
   Emmanuel Lévinas and Jacques Derrida / by Martin C. Srajek. —
   1st pbk. ed.
      p. cm.
   Originally published: Dordrecht; Boston, Mass.: Kluwer Academic
   Publishers, ©1998, in series: Contributions to phenomenology.
   Includes bibliographical references and index.
   ISBN 0–8207–0312–5 (pbk.: alk. paper)
      1. Lévinas, Emmanuel—Ethics.   2. Derrida, Jacques—Ethics.
   3. Ethics, Modern—20th century.   4. Ethics, Jewish—History—
   20th century.   I. Title.

   B2430.L484 S73 2000
   194—dc21   99–053427

Published by
DUQUESNE UNIVERSITY PRESS
600 Forbes Avenue
Pittsburgh, Pennsylvania 15282

First paperback edition, Duquesne University Press, 2000.

Printed in the United States of America.

For Noah and Jacob
whose beauty surprises me every day

and

For Leslie
whose love means more than I could say

CONTENTS

Acknowledgments xi

Introduction 1

ONE The Text
Reading and Revelation 27

Introduction: The Text as *"Espace Vital"* 27
Levinas's Concept of Subjectivity 29
Midrashic Ethics 50
Humans as the Irruption in Being 55

TWO The Absolute
*Cohen, Rosenzweig, Levinas: Infinite
Ethics* 57

God as Infinite 58
The Modern Jewish Tradition 61
Emmanuel Levinas 77
Conclusion 82

THREE Agency
Ezekiel: Fragmented Subjectivity 90

The Language of Constitution 91
The Prophet Ezekiel in the Writings of
Levinas 95
The Prophet Ezekiel in the Thought of
Cohen 103

From Fragmentation to the I/Thou 106
Fragmentation and Completion 107

FOUR   **Community**
       Phenomenology of the Face **110**

Towards a Community of the Face 111
Husserl's European Scientific Community 113
Levinas's Critique of Traditional
    Phenomenology 118
Face-to-Face: The Grounding Aspect
    of Community 130

FIVE   **Transition**
       Judaism as the Matrix Between
       Levinas and Derrida **140**

SIX   **The Text**
      Pure Presence and the Task of
      Translation **151**

The Text and the Meaning of Presence 151
Husserl's Infinite Task 154
The Ethics of Babel 172

SEVEN   **The Absolute**
        Apocalypse: Epistemological Exile
        vis-à-vis Truth **181**

Apocalypse and Absolute 181
Kant's Distinguished Tone 196
The Apocalyptic Aspect in Kant's Approach 199
Apocalypse and Prévenance 202
The Hermeneutics of Exile in Levinas and
    Derrida 205
The Ethical Significance of the Apocalyptic
    Discourse 208

EIGHT   **Agency**
        Differentiality and Negativity **212**

Apocalypse as the Critique of Negativity 212

Negative Theology in Jewish Thought 214
Derrida and Negative Theology 223
Negative Theology and Speaking About It 228
Différance and the Discourse on Truth 234
Apocalypse and the Ineffable Name of God 238
Cohen and Derrida: On the Possibility
    of Theology 244

NINE **Community**
*Différance as Messianism, Khora,
    and Minimal Community* **246**

Deconstruction as Description and
    Prescription 246
Messianism 250
Khora 261
Community 267
Deconstructive Practice of Halakhah 283

Conclusion 285
Notes 297
Works Cited 349
Index 360

ACKNOWLEDGMENTS

This book has been in preparation for a long time. The list of people who participated in its genesis is too long to be replicated in its full length. I will only mention a few and assure those who are not mentioned that their thoughtfulness and support is very much appreciated. Since the book started out as a dissertation I am indebted to all the people that helped me along in that process. Thanks go to Tom Dean who introduced me to Derrida, Levinas, and other postmoderns, and to the members of a seminar on Hermeneutics of Suspicion he taught in the fall of 1987. They first brought up the idea of understanding deconstruction as a *Jewish* philosophy. Thanks go to Gibson Winter who never stopped asking me what the ethical content of deconstruction was and to Joe Margolis whose ability to see loose ends in any argument kept me on my toes. Thanks to Bob Gibbs for taking me on by referral and for knowing my manuscript enough to like some chapters and not like others, and for introducing me to Edith Wyschogrod who became not only a formidable reader of my dissertation and later manuscript but also a much appreciated source of support, ideas, connections, and suggestions for how to begin my career as a scholar of religion. Last, but by no means least, I am infinitely thankful to Norbert Samuelson my advisor and friend for providing me and other students with an academic refuge, i.e., a place where academic discourse could thrive, for making me feel that Jewish philosophy would be accessible to me the non-Jew, and for agreeing to be my advisor.

Aside from the committee itself I feel that perhaps the most powerful and academically fruitful influence on my work came from the various reading groups of which I have been a part since I began graduate school. I want to thank Uwe Ritter, Michael Simon, Gereon Kopf, Sandy Brainard, Marga Kasper, and Todd Lekan for making philosophy and religion an experience of friendship, slow meticulous readings, and, literally, nightlong discussions. My appreciation and gratitude goes out in particular to Tom Downey without whom I would have never understood that philosophy is always good news and bad news, who read through my manuscript and parts of it uncounted times, and whose french roast coffee never failed to perk me up when exhaustion was about to get the better of me.

Lastly, there are relatives that should not be forgotten. Mary Anne and Donald Crowley, Lauren and Michael for continual encouragement, my grandparents for providing me with the occasional pecuniary gift, my parents Uwe and Hannelore Srajek for believing in me even though I am 5,000 miles away from them, and to Katia for being my sister. Most of all thanks to Leslie, my wife, whose readings of my manuscript (and encouraging notes in the margins) improved my style, and whose steadfast love for me became the most reliable emotional support throughout the last eight years.

INTRODUCTION

Although this book is a study of the work of Emmanuel Levinas and Jacques Derrida, it would be mistaken to refer to it as a comparison. The book develops a framework which might aide the reader of Levinas and Derrida in determining the scope and significance of their respective projects as far as a discourse of the sacred is concerned. It does so by emphasizing their status as philosophers whose thought correlates but does not compare.

Within this correlation, without obscuring either their differences or similarities, we can see a common framework that consists of the following elements. First, it is clear from what and how Derrida and Levinas have written that the general import of their work lies in the area of ethics. However, in many ways it would be justifiable to say that their work is not about ethics at all. Neither of them proposes a moral theory; neither is interested in discussing the question of values vs. social norms, duty vs. virtue and other issues that might pertain to the area of ethics. To be sure, these issues do come up in their work, yet they are treated in a peculiarly different way. For Derrida and Levinas, ethics is not so much an inquiry into the problems of right and wrong but an inquiry into the problem of the ethical constitutedness of human beings. It is the question of *the* ethical that they raise and attempt to elicit from the realm of philosophical thought. In other words, rather than asking what we should do these philosophies ask who we are.

Is this a withdrawal from ethics? Is it the silent admission that ethics has failed and that it is impossible to come up with a universally applicable system of rules and laws that will aide us in improving the world? I think that one will have to say "yes" to these questions, at least initially. Both philosophers withdraw from a presumptive type of ethics that assumes a certain knowledge of the good and can thus deploy a structure in which a notion of improvement is derived solely from what is defined as the good. Structures are difficult because they inevitably turn into strictures, i.e., they tend to marginalize and reduce the very real and very material problems with which ethics is concerned. In popular discussions on the issues of postmodernity, it is often held that in order to avoid such presumptive ethics we have to abstain from approaches to the problem that in some way attempt to think the absolute, i.e., the good. If we give up the penchant for comprehension of the absolute, it is claimed, then we will be able to avoid marginalization and reduction and finally view the problem in its real breadth and scope. Yet, I have not heard of or seen any attempts by Levinas or Derrida to avoid the absolute absolutely. Quite the contrary, their work strikes me as a struggle to find a liberating way to think the absolute that will not result in the proliferation of structures. In short, there is a good way to think the good, and Levinas and Derrida are trying to find out what that way might be.

This gets us to the second element that, I think, is formative in Derrida's and Levinas's work. It is the element of a particular anti-essentialism. Both thinkers share the belief that the problem of ethics is in part a consequence of how we think and talk about the absolute. They qualify anti-essentialism as pertaining to how we think and talk about essences, i.e., how we approach this problem of essence theoretically. Anti-essentialism, then, does not mean that Derrida and Levinas are against essences but, to be precise, that they are against essential*ism*.

To say that they are against essentialism is a very crude way of putting a delicate problem into words, for their claim is that any word or thought about something already constitutes such an "ism." This means that there is a certain anti*ism* in anti-essentialism which only gets us further away from the problem of ethics. I would therefore prefer the term "suspicion" in order to describe the ways in which Derrida and Levinas deal with this problem. This term in its literalness already gives us some clue as to what the approach might look like. When we "suspect" we are engaging in an activity of looking under something. We do not just approach a problem from the surface; we also turn it over and consider it from those angles under which it is usually not considered. This is by no means an exclusion of the surface, rather it is a way of saying that the surface itself points to something beyond itself (or better underneath itself) that needs to be considered as well if one wants to get a better picture of the dimensions of the problem.

Both Levinas and Derrida recognize that suspicion can be best implemented if we develop a particular attitude toward the absolute. Clearly, this attitude cannot just consist in stating the absolute as if it were an object. That would be absolut-*ism*. Their attitude amounts to a certain rhetoric, i.e., a certain use of language, that both philosophers have developed in order to talk about the absolute without falling into the trap of "*ism* ology." For Levinas, this rhetoric consists in the relentless effort to serialize the finite language that we use including its finite meanings in order to show its hollowness, openness, or fracturedness all laced with the infinite. The absolute in his thinking shows itself as that hollowness, i.e., as the infinite in the finite. Every attempt to express this fact will end up with the same result, viz. finite words inside of which the infinite dwells.

Derrida's rhetoric can be described as the juxtaposition of negativity and positivity. With respect to every statement we make, every word that is said, Derrida applies a logic that simultaneously affirms and negates that which is said. From the perspective of logic, language is a succession of explicit affirmations and implicit negations. Every word in a sentence constitutes an affirmation of itself and the meaning it carries as well as a negation of everything else (i.e., it points to what it is not). Derrida, like Hegel, assumes that affirmation and negation can both be applied to the same word. Traditional logic would rule out this case because it is a contradiction in terms. Yet, Derrida believes that in so doing he brings binary logic (i.e., a logic that assumes that "a≠b" is true) to a suspension and instead claims that a doubling of "a≠b" as both true and not true is a much more accurate way of describing reality logically. The consequence of such a logic is not chaos or paralysis but rather a focus on something that lies between the yes and no of traditional logic. This is where Derrida locates the absolute. Similar to Levinas, the discovery of this absolute and its transformation into language brings back the same situation in which a yes or no decision is demanded. This in turn will have to be suspended once again by comprehending the affirmative and the negative, not as two contradictory claims about one and the same thing, but as two claims which, in their juxtaposition, can point to that which lies between them and thereby iterates the absolute.

There is a third element that demands consideration in positioning Levinas's and Derrida's projects. This element is the question of how far their work can be related and connected to modern Jewish philosophy. This is a tricky question because with it one runs the risk of stereotyping philosophies or philosophers simply for the sake of making them cohere with each other. In particular in the case of Derrida the question is difficult to decide. Nonetheless, the language that he uses, the breaking up of traditional binary logic, and his occasional yet very explicit references to Judaism and his own Jewishness suggest that there are connections, even if these connections were not initially intended. The question is less difficult for Levinas because he identifies himself as a Jewish philosopher and is regarded as such within the French intellectual community. In considering the connections with modern Jewish philosophy, it would be appropriate to think of Levinas's philosophy as a backdrop for the thought of Derrida which illuminates some of the moves of the latter, without, however, simply labeling them as Jewish.

The most important discovery with respect to both thinkers is their very intimate intellectual connection with the neo-Kantianism of Hermann Cohen and the Marburg School. Cohen's correlational and differential approach, although discussed explicitly only in chapters II and VII nevertheless forms the backbone of this book. In particular, it is Cohen's work on monotheism and the logic of correlation on which I will be drawing many times throughout this text. Around the figure of Hermann Cohen I have arrayed the medieval philosopher Moses Maimonides, as well as some of Cohen's contemporaries and followers such as Franz Rosenzweig, Walter Benjamin, Alfred Schütz, Edmund Husserl, André Chouraqui, and Edmond Jabès. It is in the shadows and areas of light cast by these philosophers that Derrida and Levinas are writing. And although it might be especially problematic to say that Derrida is doing Jewish philosophy, it can be said that some of the premises of his thought are mediated by Jewish philosophy and give a certain character to his work that it otherwise would lack.[1]

In addition to these specific common elements in the thought of Derrida and Levinas, a few general remarks about the purpose of deconstructive readings may be helpful. I will then undertake a short exposition of Derrida's and Levinas's biographies in order to determine more clearly the locus of their philosophical approaches.

I think it would be wrong to judge the work of Levinas and Derrida as in-conclusive and possibly unserious. I am committed to this point, because my project is, in part, to show that even the thought of the early Derrida (I here am referring to pieces in *Writing and Difference, Of Grammatology*, or the essay "Différance," etc.) is more than just an exhibition of a somewhat bizarre, bordering on the perverse, playfulness that legitimates itself through recourse to the assumption that nothing in this world happens outside the realm of signification; and, since signification always involves ambiguity, this world is founded on ambiguity, rather than on certainty. To be sure, this is a very Derridean line of argumentation and it does have its place. But the question is, where does it have such a place, and, a fortiori, if such a place of playfulness is found, does that entail the immediate and absolute displacement of ethics?

The first part of the title of this book "In the *Margins* of Deconstruction . . ." is based on the assumption that deconstruction has its own, sometimes autobiographical, margins which, although never fully comprehensible, are inscribed into the theory that we know as deconstruction.[2] It is based on the further assumption that those autobiographically based margins are woven in with another less idiosyncratic and more universal type of marginality inherent in deconstruction as it has been adopted in academia. The margins of deconstruction have been mostly overlooked since deconstruction became "en vogue" in academia.[3] I claim that those margins are of theo-logical as well as of ethical significance. The problem, however, is that a period of rather crude readings of deconstructive texts has contributed to the exact mistake that Derrida never tires of exposing: Deconstruction itself is read as only saying what its surface says rather than reading and looking for what it does not say, what is somehow hidden inside of its own text. Those things that it does not mention, or, if it does, those things which seem to surface only in rather vague forms, are the questions of truth, God, origins, ends, etc. They are, in other words, questions about absolutes. Deconstruction shies away from absolutes. It is a shyness reminiscent of the way baroque music is composed: playful and arabesque, but also disciplined and planned and always with the allusion to something in the background that is larger, transcendent, and thus not palpable. Thus, one would ultimately have to say that it is not shyness as much as a respectful distance that deconstruction keeps from those absolutes. This is the main thrust of Derrida's critique of Levinas in "Violence and Metaphysics." It is Levinas's perhaps unconscious attempt to achieve an epistemological fraternization with the absolutely other that evokes Derrida's indignation. Talk about the absolute other is absurd since it denies, as part of its own adjectival qualification (absolute), what is immediately affirmed in the succeeding noun (other): it denies a relationship with the same. In saying what he is saying, Levinas only reaffirms the senselessness of speaking about absolutes. They cannot be conceptualized and words are, thus, most inadequate to aide us in their understanding.

This complex situation also warrants a couple of comments about the style one chooses to write about deconstruction. A meta-discourse on deconstruction does not have to follow the stylistic blue-print of a text by Derrida. In attempting such an echoing, the secondary text would necessarily fall into a pattern of responding that would precisely not let the original text stand as other, as it is. Furthermore, though the writing in this text might appear linear at times, and thus strangely unqualified to speak about Derrida's texts, it is just this juxtaposition of the linear with the arabesque, of straight text with deconstructive analysis that will yield the most insightful results about the writing of Derrida. Lastly, the absolute that both Derrida and Levinas write about is reticent and ephemeral in all texts not just in the linear texts of traditional philosophy. Even for the masterful writings of Derrida and Levinas the point of writing cannot be to write the perfect text in which the absolute will not hide its face again. Rather, the point is that writing means to be engaged in it as an infinite process. Writing about the absolute, then, can never, must never, come to an end!

If absolutes can only be grasped in their marginality or ephemerality with respect to what is actually said or written, where is the place that the ethical can occupy? Is the ethical itself part of a realm of ephemeral, marginal concepts? Would Derrida thus tune in with those who lament the disappearance of the ethical in an increasingly violent world? Can the ethical disappear at all?

It is my conviction that both Levinas and Derrida are intent on showing that the ethical is precisely de-scribed (i.e., unwritten)[4] by that peculiar relationship with an absolute that cannot be said or otherwise conceptualized. I am persuaded to think that for both philosophers this relationship is unavoidable, despite its nonconceptualizable character; it is a given cipher of what it means to be human. This means that, although the world can turn into an increasingly violent and "mensch"-defying place, the ethical cannot disappear. Consequently, responsibility will persist as well as a demand to actualize that responsibility. The question is, however, if it will foster "Menschlichkeit." But to show this is the work that needs to be done in the main body of this book. For now I would like to return to the question of biography and its relationship with the issue of margins as it is brought up by Derrida and, in a varied form, also by Levinas.

For the work of Derrida and Levinas, the term "autobiography" cannot just mean that somehow they are writing about their own lives. Although this might indeed be the case, I would like to push for a reading of this term that illuminates more of the scope of deconstruction. The term auto-bio-graphy brings to light three different aspects: that of the self (αυτος), that of writing (γραφειν), and that of life (βιος). I understand this term as the expression of an hyperbolic function in which αυτος represents the asymptotic limits of the function of βιος which in itself has to be written, i.e., represented by way of a γραφειν. The term auto-bio-graphy by itself, then, is already an expression of the theme of both Levinas's and Derrida's thought, viz. the question of how absolutes can be seen to position themselves over against ones own attempts to represent and describe them. Biographical description, then, has the function of showing the hyperbolical relationship that exists between life and self. The quality of this relationship itself can serve as a model for a better understanding of the function of absolutes with respect to the question of ethics.

In addition to this more structural need for auto-bio-graphy, it will become clear that, in this context, biography will also serve to shed some more light on the question of Derrida's and Levinas's expression of and relation to Judaism. We will see that their lives diverge quite a bit on that issue and thus come to understand that the relationship to Judaism that nevertheless exists must be treated more as a methodological issue than as one of sociological dimensions.

Derrida was born in El-Biar, Algeria, on July 15, 1930.[5] He spent his childhood and part of his young adulthood in Algeria and moved to France proper at the age of nineteen, in 1949, shortly before the first unrest break out that, in the end, proved fatal for French domination of Algeria. Little has been made public by Derrida about those first nineteen years of his life. But the things that have become known are, I think, relevant to his ethnicity and consequently to his philosophy. In an interview with the *Nouvel Observateur*[6] Derrida, when asked about that time, answers with hesitation: "Ah, you want me to tell you things like 'I-was-born-in-El-Biar-in-the-suburbs-of-Algiers-in-a-petit-bourgeois-Jewish-family-which-was-assimilated-but . . .' Is this really necessary? I just couldn't do it, you'll have to help me . . ."[7] With some help from his interviewer, Catherine David, he continues to describe some images of his childhood. Times in Algeria were rough and constantly changing during his childhood. World War II begins when he is nine years old and that event already precipitates the

> rumblings of the Algerian War. As a child, I had the instinctive feeling that the end of the world was at hand, a feeling which at the same time was most natural, and, in any case, the only one I ever knew. Even for a child incapable of analyzing things, it was clear that all this would end in fire and blood. No one could escape that violence and fear, even around it . . .[8]

Of all the upheaval going on at that time Derrida most remembers "those racist screams that spared no one, Arabs, Jews, Spanish, Maltese, Italians, Corsicans . . ." He goes on to describe how, from 1940 on, it was especially the fate of the Algerian Jews that inscribed itself in his mind. Jews were persecuted in Algeria, despite "the absence of any German occupier." Schools expelled Jewish students and teachers without explanation. The French government maintains the racial laws for the first six months after the war was over, and no one was willing to risk speaking up for the Jews. Derrida himself "skipped classes for a year."[9]

As a consequence of these events Derrida began to feel excluded from the French and Jewish communities and started to withdraw from both. For a while he "naively thought that anti-semitism had disappeared"[10] but realized that it remained for everyone else. His desire to be integrated into the non-Jewish community was accompanied by a heightened awareness of their racism while simultaneously his impatience with various forms of Judaism grows as well. "From all of which comes a feeling of non-belonging which I have doubtless transposed . . ."[11]

In the interview with Engelmann[12] Derrida's response is much more ironic and dismissive of the question about his Jewish roots. Perhaps it is the systematical rather than historical character of the question that causes his dismissiveness. Derrida is asked to comment on the influence of the Talmud on his writing as was asserted earlier by some American commentators. Derrida's response, "Man kann sich viele Wege ausdenken"[13] (One can speculate in many ways), makes this assertion seem like a rather frivolous idea. In mimicking the possibilities that others might come up with, he ironically remarks that he does not know the Talmud, but that perhaps the Talmud knows him, perhaps as a type of unconscious. But he says he never learned Hebrew and, probably because of his own doing, was never educated in a properly Jewish sense. He closes his remarks on this topic by musing that some remnants of his Jewish childhood, however, might have persisted, since he only came to France when he was nineteen.

In the interview with Kearney[14] Derrida volunteers a third variant of the influence of Judaism on his thinking. He locates the question on the borderline between Greek and Hebrew thinking and claims that "though I was born a Jew . . . the ultimate site of my questioning discourse would be neither Hellenic nor Hebraic if such were possible."[15] He furthermore explains his attachment to the philosophy of Levinas as based on the latter's interest in phenomenology, especially in the question of the other.

In that part of Levinas's work, he argues, "the Judaic dimension remained at that stage a discrete rather than a decisive reference."[16]

Derrida's various accounts of Jewish influence have to be considered from different angles in order to gain some clarity and insight into the impact of his Jewishness on deconstruction. The first point that can be made unhesitatingly is that Judaism did have an impact on Derrida's life. We have evidence from the interview with the *Nouvel Observateur* to support this thesis, but one can formulate rather generally that even the fact that Derrida has been frequently confronted with Judaism as an interpretive framework for his own work reinforces the impact of Judaism on him. This latter point should not be disregarded since it might account for many of the explicit turns to Hebrew thinking in Derrida's more recent work. The second and third interview, however, emphasize Derrida's shallow Jewish education. He does not know the Talmud, he does not know Hebrew, etc., and therefore is understandably hesitant to consider himself a *Jewish* philosopher. Yet, what we do get in the third quote is something that is very much in line with the experiences described in the first. Here Derrida describes how he felt displaced between the French ("which they used to call 'the Catholics'"[17]) and the Jewish community; philosophically, the issue reappears, this time as the question of Greek vs. Hebrew thought. And Derrida's diagnosis of his own position is interestingly similar. He belongs to neither tradition, he is displaced, and instead positions himself on the edge between them.

The next important stage of Derrida's life is the environment that he lives in after his move to France. Soon after the move he enrolls at the École Normale Supérieure — in part inspired by the "success story" of Albert Camus to whom he is introduced through a radio broadcast on philosophy. He decides that he wants, "as they say, 'to write.'"[18] Through the influence of Sartre, however, Derrida begins to develop an interest for Husserl, Heidegger, and Blanchot next to more literary writers such as Joyce, Artaud, Bataille, and Ponge. In several ways, therefore, the scenery is set for Derrida to become what we now know him to be: namely, a philosopher with a very pronounced literary interest, a philosopher who is willing to go as far as saying that the distinction between literature and philosophy is arbitrary and not valid.

Aside from marking the beginning of his professional career, Derrida's entrance into the university also invokes a very significant turn towards the politics of the university and everything that is attached to it. In "Time of a Thesis: Punctuations"[19] he describes how his entrance into the university implied the almost never-ending delay of the presentation of his thesis, since from now on his intellectual work was in a very "peculiar" way connected with "the university milieu, with cultural, political . . . representations, [in which] are located some of the most serious, the most pressing, and the most obscure responsibilities facing an intellectual."[20] His first attempt at writing a final thesis (which was later abandoned) with the title "The Ideality of the Literary Object" "reinforced the questions that had started to grow, fostered by the milieu of the university. The relations between philosophy and literature, science and literature, politics and literature, theology and literature, psychoanalysis and literature,"[21] and an increasing awareness of the peculiarity of his own position vis-a-vis the established sciences "made it clear to me that the general turn that my research was taking could no longer conform to the classical norms of the thesis."[22] The direction that his research takes is one that in many ways defies the rules and discursive procedures that a university sets for its students and faculty. His texts begin to work subversively. Surface and sub-surface seem to interact in ways that had become un-presentable, etc. In 1968, then, without explaining what he really means by it, Derrida says that "something I had been anticipating had found its confirmation at that time,"[23] he is more than ready to distance himself from the university.

What Derrida must have seen happening at that time is not easily explained. A generation of young people, mostly students, who had long ago become frustrated with the bigotry of the preceding generations and had turned to Marxism in the shape of Leninism and Maoism in order to find a better, more suitable model after which to live their lives, now had to realize that Marxism, both in its Leninist and in its Maoist expressions, was least of all a political paradigm for a humane humanism. An increasing awareness spread that, independent of the political color that one chooses, one will always again end up with the problematic of institutions, centers of power, majorities vs. minorities, oppression, torture, injustice, and all the other phenomena that go along with the accumulation of power.

> The reproductive force of authority can get along more comfortably with declarations or theses whose content presents itself as revolutionary, provided that they respect the rites of legitimation, the rhetoric and the institutional symbolism which defuses and neutralizes whatever comes from outside the system. What is unacceptable is what, underlying positions or theses, upsets this deeply entrenched contract, the order of these norms, and which does so in the very *form* of works, of teaching or of writing.[24]

This really seems to be the "essence" of Derrida's approach. The inertia, gravity, and immobility that characterizes politics, and in particular university politics, is visible precisely in the work that is produced within the frame of the university. The form of an essay, a paper, a dissertation, but also that of a normal speech, all have this one thing in common: that they locate somewhere within themselves the center of truth and power. The centers of the different works that are produced within the university are connected, and together they produce the structure of power and of utter disregard for what is marginal.

This theoretical point marks biographically the inception of a project that America has heard of only little. Under the acronym GREPH (*"Groupe de Recherches sur l'Enseignement Philosophique"*) Derrida started to plan and work toward a new university model that would specifically address the above-mentioned issues of power and, even more specifically, research the collaborative role that traditional philosophy has played in the

formation of the traditional university structure.[25] The questions that this group of teachers and philosophers raise, mainly
in the form of a think-tank, concern the fact that "philosophical
teaching could not be separated . . . from all the other cultural,
political and other contending forces in this country and in the
world."[26]

Influenced by his work with GREPH, as his general discom-
fort within the university rises, Derrida decides that vis-a-vis
the results of his own research concerning the possibility, meaning, and consequences of asserting truth within a closed system
it would be best for him to prepare himself for a "new type of
mobility" that would confront the immobility of the university
in a new and more effective way. Structurally, this type of mobility takes the form of the denial of the possibility of saying
something about something which "I began by saying that it
was as if I was bereft of speech."[27] in order to illuminate the
strategic value and position of a formally negative way of expression. This negative way of expression is not equal to saying
nothing. It is saying it all, yet in ways that unbalance the object
of which such a negative something is said. The idea behind
this strategic move is that whatever is said about something in
an affirmative, positive way will do nothing but enhance that
something in its central and powerful position. Only a strategy
that circles, rather than charges, the center of power will create
enough force to make the powerful tumble.

The biography of Emmanuel Levinas shows, aside from the
difference in age, many parallels with that of Derrida. Levinas
is born on January 12, 1906, in Kaunas, Lithuania.[28] Lithuania
was, then, part of the tsarist empire as well as the focal point of
a very rich Jewish tradition which has been developing since
the early eighteenth century and which, in opposition to Poland
(for example), could be maintained because of its "proximity to
Prussia and trade connections with the West and with Russia"[29]
Lithuanian Jewry witnessed the partitioning and ensuing ex-
tinction of Poland starting in 1772, and the concomitant decline
of Polish Jewry into either a poor city worker population or a

dispersed community in the country side. One of the characteristics of Lithuanian Jews was their tendency not only to speak Yiddish, like the Polish Jewry, but also to share in the Russian orientation towards France and thus be conversant in French as well as Russian. Lithuanian Jewry was thus looked upon much more favorably than those in other parts of the Russian empire.

After the assassination of Tsar Alexander II, however, a wave of anti-semitic pogroms in Russia began which, with varying force, continued into the twentieth century. In 1905, the year before Levinas is born, Tsar Nicholas II, who was largely responsible for the rise of anti-semitism after Alexander II, was forced to grant the Duma (parliament). This, however, did not improve the situation of the Jews. Immediately after the establishment of the Duma, another wave of pogroms started that involved active street gangs — the so-called Black Hundred — and a completely passive police-force.

The situation in all parts of the Russian Empire became increasingly unstable and unsafe for Jews. Many of the cities were repeatedly targeted by the Black Hundred and similar groups. Levinas and his family therefore move to the Ukraine where they remained during World War I and the Russian Revolution. Between 1918 and 1920 however, pogroms began in the Ukraine as well. In the course of those latter events, the Russian revolutionaries also abolished the Jewish communal institutions (kehillot) in their entirety.

It is not surprising that, against the background of these events, Levinas decided to leave Russia and move to Strasbourg. From his dedication in *Otherwise Than Being or Beyond Essence* however, it is clear that he comes from a family with a history of rabbis[30] and, thus, that he is familiar with the Jewish tradition in ways that Derrida can never claim for himself. In 1923, at the age of seventeen, Levinas became a student at Strasbourg University where he studied under Blondel, Pradines and Hering and also became acquainted with Maurice Blanchot. During the academic year of 1927/28 Levinas studied in Freiburg with Husserl and Heidegger. This year also marked the appearance of *Being and Time*, the book that Levinas called a shock to the academic community.[31]

Upon his return to France, Levinas moved to Paris in 1930 and started writing his dissertation, *La theorie de l'intuition dans la phenomenologie de Husserl*. He liked France very much and was naturalized in 1931, surprised, as he puts it, about a "people which one could belong to through sympathy as well as heritage."[32] Levinas's studies were interrupted by World War II. He joined the French armed forces in 1939, became a war prisoner in 1940, and was transferred to a labor camp for Jewish prisoners. After WW II, Levinas's interest in Jewish education increased and he became director of the *Israelitische Lehrbildungsanstalt für den Westen*. In the process, he began to concern himself more and more with questions of Zionism and the global situation of the Jews. After the publication of *Totality and Infinity* in 1961, Levinas received an invitation to The University of Poitiers, then, in 1962, to the University of Paris-Nanterre and in 1973, his final call, to the Sorbonne. He became emeritus in 1976.

The position of Levinas's philosophy vis-a-vis the philosophy of Derrida is, I think, less difficult to determine than is generally assumed. On the surface not much more can be said about the relationship than that Levinas was a senior philosopher when Derrida arrived on the scene. At the time Derrida attempted to write his thesis, Levinas was already forty years old and had, at least within France, an established record as a philosopher and writer. Derrida is quoted as saying that the influence of Levinas on his own thought, which is undoubted, has nothing to do with the former's Jewish roots, but everything to do with his interest in phenomenology and, a fortiori, the phenomenological possibility of otherness. At this early stage of Derrida's academic career he was probably more eager to read Levinas's phenomenological writings than his Jewish work. Simultaneously, however, Derrida reveals in this statement how Levinas's influence developed within the French intellectual community. Only now, at a point where Levinas's Jewish writings have become interesting to a wider academic public, does his earlier work, specifically his writings on Edmund Husserl, regain in interest precisely for their probable Jewishness.

I am persuaded to think that an analysis of the relationship between Levinas and Derrida can only partly come out of the coincidental parallels between their biographies. Both, separately, come to philosophy from a perspective that is colored by their own life-experience. In addition, Derrida reads Levinas and vice versa; they talk, exchange opinions, question each other, etc. But it seems to me that it goes too far to describe this relationship to the point where it seems that there is only one person, *Levinasderrida*, indistinguishable as separate entities, and somehow symbiotically related as two stages of one intellectual journey.

The format of this book is, besides other things, an attempt to make clear the distinctness of Levinas's and Derrida's thinking. It was for this reason that I refrained from including into the title something like the "development from Levinas to Derrida," "connections," "parallels," etc. While it is clear to me that similarities can be found between the two thinkers, much can only be explained by looking at the philosophical sources that informed their writing and thinking.

The philosophy of Hermann Cohen is such a source, although neither for Levinas nor Derrida can the case of a clear dependence on Cohen be made. Clearly, both know who this Jewish neo-Kantian philosopher is. But there are only a few explicit references to Cohen in either of their writings. Yet, and this is the claim that this book attempts to make, Cohen's correlational model resonates in Levinas's concept of the infinite as the in-the-finite. Similarly, Derrida's term "différance" is a very clear and almost unequivocal rendition of Cohen's correlational method in relation to its mathematical description as an asymptotic function. But Cohen also cannot be regarded as the original source of such thinking either, even if Derrida's and Levinas's dependence on Cohen were beyond all doubt. From a certain angle, Cohen's philosophy is nothing but an extrapolation of Kantian philosophy. Kant's Ding-an-sich already raises the question: How exactly does the Ding-an-sich relate to the world of phenomenal being? Hegel tried to obliterate the difference completely. But was it not Descartes who, two hundred years earlier, posed the question: How can the idea of the infinite be known by a finite being unless the infinite itself had put the knowledge of that idea into that finite being? This intellectual lineage and genealogy could be pursued without ever finding a beginning or an end. The fact that both Levinas and Derrida are thinking and writing about the same issues is less founded on the fact that they share this lineage (of which utilitarianism is as much a part as is pragmatism) than it is founded on their similar biographical experiences combined with a certain academic context to which they grew accustomed.

Their biographies, however, are marked, at least in part, by the fact of their Jewishness and the fear, persecution, hatred, and exile which they had to confront because of that heritage. In reading their texts we have to remind ourselves continually of the perennial societal ostracism to which the two thinkers were exposed in order to understand the connections with the philosophy they write that centers around absence, the no-place ("non-lieu"), exile, etc. It is to be aware that, to some extent, thinking is a social construct that does not occur in a vacuum but reveals its genesis as the interaction between the individual and the world surrounding it. Deconstruction has cleared the way for an understanding that finally permits the collapsing of such boundaries as the private and the public, the academic and the nonacademic, theory and praxis, etc. It did so in favor of an understanding that grasps the intricate relationship that exists even between the most radical of opposites.

Obviously, the type of argument that is needed to sustain this point in all its depth and complexity is not only philosophical but also sociological in character. Yet, as mentioned earlier, this book will not help us much further with regard to the latter. However, it would be negligent to read these philosophers of utter transcendence without realizing that somewhere in their lives such transcendence must have its "Sitz im Leben." This is not a simplistic point, but it is a simple one; one that gets glossed over far too often. If we only pay attention to the academic side of philosophy, and do not also deal with how the people who teach and write such philosophy live it themselves, then we contribute to the naiveté with which decades of philosophers have read people like Heidegger, de Man and others. There are exceptions, to be sure, and both Levinas and Derrida, according to my reading, belong to that category. But their critical stance toward philosophy's imperviousness to the thought of the ethical cannot simply be explained as a better intellectual grasp of the philosophical material. It is clearly also a reading that was and is informed by the type of vigilance that derives from understanding the intricate relationship between one's own life and one's thinking.

Understanding and acknowledging this relationship between practical and conceptual life cannot only help us transcend the paralyzing forces inherent in thought alone, but it can also empower us to understand the valuable complexities of the thought of Levinas and Derrida who, to many — from a merely philosophical view point — barely make sense. In an interview with Richard Kearney Derrida says:[33] "I concede that the style of my questioning as an exodus and dissemination in the desert might produce certain prophetic resonances . . . The fact that I declare it 'unfortunate' that I do not feel personally inspired may be a sign that deep down I still hope . . . It means that I am in fact still looking for something . . . Perhaps my search is a twentieth century brand of prophecy? But it is difficult for me to believe it." Derrida's difficulty in believing in the possibility of his prophetic mission is understandable and realistic. What counts in this context is the mere fact that he decides to connect the style of his philosophical discourse with his own personal hopes. It is the experience of their own marginalization that compels them to write philosophies of obsession and subversiveness. Thinking, and this is an important realization never too old or obsolete to be repeated, is connected to and dependent upon the material givenness of our lives. Thinking reinforces and reflects on what life has presented to it. That is to say that thinking can never truly confront us with the other, it can only distance and result in highly sophisticated theories and systems. But the other, the new, that which our thinking has not yet transformed into theory, comes from elsewhere. There can be no topology for such a place. It can neither be talked nor thought about. Here lies one of the crucial issues with respect to Derrida's relationship to Jewish thought and Judaism.

More than the details of biography and ethnicity, it seems that it is the question of ideology that decides these days on the question of Derrida's Jewishness. The ideological question put before Derrida and others is: Are you for or against Hegel? It would lead too far in this context to explore historically why the "Hegel-question" has become the "tertium comparationis" regarding Jewish identity. It is obvious, however, that to a large extent Hegel's own anti-Jewish perspective on the progression of philosophy has contributed to this problem. In his writings on Judaism and Christianity he propounds the idea that by way of its radical monotheism Judaism is an alienated religion. It is so dependent on the absolute difference of its God from the world, he asserts, that it makes this insurmountable difference into the core of its account of how the world is and should be constituted. Aside from the extremely dismissive way in which Hegel talks about Judaism in these essays, it is the very vision of a good infinite, i.e., an infinite in which the nonidentity of identity and difference will finally come to rest, that has been construed as Hegel's anti-Judaic attitude.[34]

There are, in other words, two criteria to the "Hegel-question" with respect to being Jewish or not: First, it is the question whether one thinks lowly of Judaism, as did Hegel, because Judaism is about the belief in the oneness and uniqueness of God. Secondly, it is the question whether the person in question believes in the final overcoming of all difference, including the one between the world and God. While the latter can be construed as indirectly anti-Jewish the former is a direct attack on one of the tenets of the Jewish religion: its monotheism.[35]

The Hegel-question has been put before Derrida from various angles. The reasons for this development have largely to do with Derrida's response to Levinas's first major work[36] *Totality and Infinity* which is very critical of Levinas's methodology, although, I would claim, not of the project itself. Very briefly, Derrida's critique of Levinas centers on the latter's attempts to *articulate* the difference between the world and the absolutely other. In Derrida's view language itself is a system of signs that presupposes sameness. The terms "other" and "same" presuppose and agreement that contradicts the absolute disagreement between the world and God which Levinas claims for monotheism. Derrida has subsequently been confronted with the Hegel-question because his critique of Levinas has often been perceived as a critique of difference in the style of Hegel.

It seems to me, however, that such criticisms of Derrida are superficial, for they align Hegel's questioning of difference in general with Derrida's questioning of language. Hegel, really did want to overcome difference; he wanted the good infinite instead of the bad one. Derrida, however, leaves that question unanswered and instead focuses on the aggressive potential inherent in language to forge an agreement between two or more terms that should be understood as radically distinct from each other. Derrida does not critique the radical difference itself but the language that we use (are forced to use) in order to express it. With few exceptions,[37] the distinction between a critique of difference and between the language of difference has not been perceived with the necessary acuity, thus resulting in a wholesale dismissal of Derrida's work as relativistic at best or immoral at worst.[38] This book is dedicated to pointing towards the many forms that the thought of the absolute takes in Derrida's work, while simultaneously emphasizing the methodological precautions that Derrida takes in order to suspend the violence of language that reduces the other to the same.

Neither Derrida's nor Levinas's life will find much more

mentioning in this book. This work was not meant to expound and elaborate on their respective life-stories which would, to be sure, be an interesting enterprise in itself. Rather, I have chosen to compile for both some central concepts and ideas in order to elucidate how a postmodern approach can also be an approach that is fundamentally concerned with ethics. — Concerned not with its impossibility but with its very possibility.

The burden of proof lies with Derrida, not with Levinas. The latter has established his case again and again and one cannot write about Levinas without touching on the question of the ethical and ethics. Derrida on the other hand, is hardly known to ever write about ethics. And if he does, he will not do so explicitly, but rather from an angle that is both elusive and allusive. He hints at it but also avoids it simultaneously. And out of a wealth of roughly three hundred essays that were written on Derrida and his work since 1963, only four question him explicitly on this matter. The question of ethics has been shunned in Derridean circles. The reasons for this are (1) Derrida does not really seem to be interested in it, so that there is an embarrassed silence among his commentators about the obvious but unaffordable lacuna in the thought of this incredibly influential thinker. But (2) what is even worse is the fact that many of Derrida's readers fail to see the intricately involved and careful way in which Derrida does indeed tackle the problem of the ethical and ethics. They deem it sufficient to raise Derrida's well-known a-foundationalism as an argument or corroborative point for a philosophy that can dispense with ethics.

My argument is that, although Derrida's thought may rightly be called a-foundational, it cannot be called anti-foundational. The foundation, the ground, the origin, or the telos all are of indispensable value and meaning for the type of thought that Derrida has pushed forward into the realm of public (philosophical) discourse. They are so precisely for their dispensability, for their double-edgedness or maybe their multi-edgedness. They have become *the* central concepts that organize his thought and especially the critical impetus of his attack launched against the stasis of Western philosophy. The question, I think, that leads us through his writings is not whether there are foundations or not, but how we think of foundations. Foundational thinking is a thinking that believes in the eternal persistence and durability of a foundation and that will hold those foundations up against anything or anybody who attempts to shake them. A-foundational thinking is a thinking that has begun to understand the temporal character of foundations, yet, at the same time, recognizes the importance of foundational thinking for the proliferation of thought and action.

Derrida's thought is an attempt to be loyal to both the foundational and the anti-foundational approach. It is an attempt to think through the relevance of the concept of foundation for a thinking that can never reach, but also never dispense with it. This kind of thinking, for epistemological, but also for ethical reasons, will admit its powerlessness regarding the creation or solicitation of a real foundation, while at the same time also admit its eternal infatuation with the possibility of a foundation. This epistemological reasoning relies on the simple observation that thinking is temporally bound and thus a genetic, proliferate thing that cannot be understood properly through the pattern of a static, foundational thought. But, also for epistemological reasons, this thinking will reveal its drawnness to a limit that it cannot ever reach. This kind of thinking will, for ethical reasons, reconcile itself to a position that acknowledges the temporal character of all ethical thinking. It will thus recognize the differences in ethical reasoning that occur throughout the world and throughout the ages as genuine to the ethical project itself. However, the acknowledgment that such a project does indeed exist is already an indication of the eternal commitment that this kind of thinking also has to true justice, i.e. a state where the ethical will have been achieved fully. This kind of thinking is deconstructive thinking.

I am suggesting that deconstructive thinking is informed by the concept of a limit-function in which the limit is the ideal to which deconstruction will always be committed, while the function itself is representative of the struggle in the actual world to reach this limit. It is the concept of the limit which, in my mind, constitutes the intersection of the thought of Derrida and Levinas with Hermann Cohen. Neither Derrida nor Levinas have studied Cohen extensively. Yet, indirectly, through the work of philosophers like Husserl, Bergson, Heidegger, Rosenzweig and others, his thought has exerted a tremendous formative power on them.[39]

Cohen's work is characterized by the intellectual struggle for a concept that would allow him to understand ideal limits in their connectedness to the actual world. Only if we can logically comprehend the connection between infinite and finite, God and world, eternal and ephemeral, will we also be able to understand how we, as part of the finite, ephemeral world are nevertheless aware of and informed by "the other side," so that we can understand the intricate inter-action that takes place between the two sides of those odd couples. They are odd in the literal sense; they are never even. Their secret lies in a radical nonreciprocity, an unevenness, that guarantees the direction of a movement that leads towards, but never to, the limit. This nonreciprocity, however, has important consequences for the possibility of agency or subjectivity. The subject is no longer understood as a free entity which rules with infinite power over the world and its own goals, but it is instead reclaimed as an entity that is infinitely susceptible to the power and pull of a limit towards which it is drawn and whose presence it can investigate at any given point without, however, being able to represent that presence.

Both parts of this book are conceived along a fourfold scheme of Text, Absolute, Agency, and Community. This framework provides a certain amount of continuity to the work of Levinas and Derrida without, however, claiming to compare their respective thought in all respects. In Part I, I develop Levinas's notion of a reading that provides a space, an *"espace vital."* Chapter 1 looks at Levinas's concept of the text. It shows how Levinas combines midrashic ethics, i.e., an ethics of reading and interpreting Scripture with the shattering of the subject as an epistemological category. In Chapter 2, I will discuss the logical implications of Levinas's concept of the Absolute. In particular this chapter analyzes how Levinas's concept of the finite in the infinite relates to Cohen's method of correlation. Chapter 3 is a study of agency and the paradigmatic role that prophetic thought plays in Levinas's thought. In the figure of the prophet Ezekiel we find combined Levinas's notion of a hollowed out or shattered subject, an other who commands me what to do, and a God whose authority consists less in commanding me directly than it does in reminding me of my responsibility towards the other, my neighbor. Chapter 4 is an attempt to show how Levinas notion of the face-to-face encounter is the keystone of his approach to the question of the community. It situates Levinas's thought within the framework of phenomenology without throwing out his own, very serious concerns about the phenomenological method. This is done through a study of Levinas's notion of the face-to-face encounter from the perspective of the biblical פנים אל פנים as well as an analysis of Husserlian terminology and thinking in Levinas's thought with respect to the notion of the face.

Between parts I and II a transition takes place which is meant to shed some further light on the problematic of the relationship between Levinas and Derrida. The transition deals mainly with Derrida's second long essay on Levinas "En Ce Moment Dans Cette Ouvrage Me Voici," and focuses on the questions that Derrida himself asks in that piece. One of these questions is the problem of the economy of the gift and the logocentrism involved in responding to Levinas or anybody else in general. Another question that Derrida tackles in this essay is that of Levinas's style and the strategies that are involved for Levinas to talk about the wholly other while knowing that the wholly other cannot be thematized at all. The transition, then, is meant to show that first of all, Derrida's response to Levinas must never be read as a response, and, second, that his concern is nevertheless with the question of how to talk about the absolute rather than a wholesale rejection of such a project. Part II, again, is divided into the four parts of Text, Absolute, Agency, and Community. It contains four chapters on the thought of Derrida focusing on the question of subjectivity and its drawnness to a limit which it will never fully reach. Chapter 1 is based on an analysis of Derrida's early piece on Husserl ("Speech and Phenomena"), an elucidation of how truth as the transcendental condition for human thinking is nevertheless obfuscated by the problematic that language itself, and a fortiori languages, is always already an indication of the distance that we hold from truth. Given such distance and the concomitant need for translation, the realization is again that truth is infinitely removed from the realm of human discourse, yet close enough to always function as a limit for that discourse. Chapter 2 is an analysis of the relationship between humanity and truth as the absolute limit of knowledge. This chapter shows how Derrida uses the differential/apocalyptic model in order to show how humanity's striving for truth, along with the concomitant failure to ever know truth, is a transcendental condition of human thinking. Chapter 3 develops the ways in which it is possible to speak and act vis-a-vis the thematic of absolute truth. It establishes Derrida's rejection and recognition of negative theology both as a valid discourse in and of itself and also as a methodology that is useful for the deconstructive project as well. Chapter 4 is the attempt of a summary of the three preceding chapters from the perspective of time (which is the issue of messianism in Derrida's work), space (which is the issue of khora) and the community (the issue of social nonreciprocity).

ONE

The Text

Reading and Revelation

INTRODUCTION: THE TEXT AS *"ESPACE VITAL"*

On the first two pages of his essay "Revelation in the Jewish Tradition,"[1] Levinas discusses two of the most striking aspects of the Jewish religion's relationship to revelation. For one, he says revelation is the impact of an exteriority on an interiority; it is "the abrupt invasion of truths from outside,"[2] triggered through the opening and reading of a book or a couple of books. Moreover, this revelatory reading generates more than just new interpretations and aspects that were inherent in the text; the *act of reading* creates an *"espace vital,"* a space in which the Jewish people may live. This term is Levinas's translation of the German *"Lebensraum,"* a term used also by the National Socialists to justify the invasion of Poland, Czechoslovakia, etc. but also to legitimize the extermination of the Jews in concentration camps. Levinas seems to be saying that reading provides a whole people with that kind of space which other nations have only been able to acquire through expansionist warfare. It would be negligent to underestimate the materiality which is designated by the term *"espace vital"* in this context. The Jews are a people whose existence is synonymous with the words "exile" and "dispersion," yet Levinas claims that they have found, and always had found, a perfect plane of existence within the texts and subtexts of scripture and the long list of its traditional commentaries. He goes even further and asserts that this *espace vital* would exist for the Jews even if the relationship with these books was one not of repeated reading but of continuous forgetting, or of memorizing merely some impressions and feelings. In other words, the mere chronology of events that one would normally just call sacred history has always been *espace vital* for the Jews.

Levinas's insistence on the vital aspects of the book underline the increasing significance that Scripture has had for the Jews since the destruction of the second Temple in 70 C.E. The destruction of that sacred space demanded the finding of a new sacred space, one that was preferably more flexible than a temple, more appropriate for people in exile (and thus with no permanent home) and, above all, less susceptible to physical destruction. Rabbinic Judaism, as it developed in the first three centuries after the destruction of the second Temple, is an attempt to do exactly that. The sacred space of the Temple had turned into the texts of Scripture creating the new, infinite, space for interpretation. This interpretative space became the new textual Temple in which God was to be worshipped.

The emphasis on text as space has certain consequences for the act of reading and interpreting, which we will look at in more detail later. Suffice it to say here that a reading that recognizes space as its guiding metaphor will in all likelihood be more interested in the spaces and interstices created by the text. It will often look at those things that a text does not explicitly say. The absence that is present through what is not said implies more space. And if Levinas's thesis is right, such an absence must then also contain more vital space for the Jews.

The main concern in this chapter is the relationship between ethics and the study of the Torah. How does midrashic inquiry into the texts of the Torah, God's living word, replicate Levinas's theme of an ethics which is grounded in a recognition of otherness that precedes subjectivity? In order to answer this we will have to look at some of the sources of Levinas's understanding of the subject, and we will have to get a clearer idea of how the text is positioned between subject and God. We will then, in a last step, see that it is precisely this position that gives ethical value to Midrash, viz. as an ongoing interpretation of God's command to love one's neighbor. This chapter will therefore be divided into five parts: 1. Levinas's concept of subjectivity over against Kant, Hegel, Husserl, and Heidegger; 2. the subject and the text; 3. the text; 4. the text and God; 5. midrashic ethics. These five parts are arranged in such a way that we will start by looking at Levinas's general view on subjectivity (part 1) before we can analyze the actual textual levels (part 2–4) and finally close with a more general part on midrashic ethics (part 5). At the end of this chapter we will have begun to see how Levinas understands the text as the site of the material epiphany of the other with transcendence to God. We will see that the text functions as the site at which the reader encounters a unique structure of command and obedience in relation to the task of interpretation which turns the site of reading and understanding into the site of ethics.

LEVINAS'S CONCEPT OF SUBJECTIVITY

Before we can proceed to look more closely at how Levinas works Jewish textual theory and practice into his system, we must first explain the hermeneutical situation which allows for reading sacred texts as *"espace vital."* In "Revelation in the Jewish Tradition" Levinas announces that the return to the Book of Books through midrashic interpretation "marks the reader's participation in the Revelation."[3] How relevant this claim is becomes clear when we examine the importance which Levinas attributes to sacred texts and their interpretation. Yet, Levinas's understanding of texts in their relationship to the community and its ethics is not only grounded in Jewish thought, it also hinges upon a concept of subjectivity that resulted from his analysis of Husserl's phenomenology. Levinas's concept of subjectivity, although opposed to Husserl, is nevertheless the result of a phenomenological analysis. However, Levinas stands traditional phenomenology on its head by letting the notion of the self be derived from the other rather than from itself. He is, thus, giving a twist to phenomenology that turns out to be both ethical and Jewish. Through its constitution by the other, subjectivity is always already given as potentially ethical, i.e., as directed towards the other. In order to understand this conclusion deduced from both Judaism and general ethics, it is necessary to examine Levinas's critique of the modern tradition.[4] It is his goal to ground his conclusions about subjectivity in the Jewish tradition in a way that allows him to transcend but not exclude the Western tradition of philosophy. Many biblical texts have become seminal for theoretical and practical developments in Western philosophy as well. Yet (here the element which is unique to Levinas comes into play) the hermeneutical assumptions about these texts have changed, and with them the import of the texts themselves.

Levinas's theme throughout "Revelation in the Jewish Tradition" is, as we have said, that an exteriority impacts on an interiority. However, literally, exteriorities and interiorities seem to be mutually exclusive. Yet somehow they still do relate to each other through their difference. For Levinas, exteriority and interiority are not mutually exclusive but condition and break up one another at any given moment. They are not just two separate spheres but really one sphere: the inside implies an outside and vice versa. Within this one sphere, however, they are distinguishable.

Although this scheme of one implying its negative opposite sounds much like Hegel, the type of interiority which Levinas discusses, however, is epistemologically different from the position of interiority that Hegel develops in his system. While the interiority of Hegel's system is conceived as a way to abandon radical exteriority, Levinas's suggestion is that radical exteriority is needed for the constitution of interiority. Specifically in Hegel's case, universal reason unfolds in the act of assembling and gathering into itself. Interiority is the interiority of the subject of idealism, the subject, in other words, which (through its own constitution and consequent actions) determines what the world around it looks like. This can be seen in the *Logic* as well as in the *Phenomenology*. Yet, this world is a reflection of the world that is inside the subject, and there is no outside, no exterior. This absence of an exterior world is the most extreme consequence of Hegel's decision to rid his philosophy of the burden of the Kantian thing-in-itself, the only element of exteriority that Kant had permitted. In trying to overcome Cartesian and Kantian dualism, Hegel lets the world be gathered and assembled by (and ultimately collapse into) reason. This is apparent in his early vision of a new eon in which the old ideals of the Greek polis would be realized. Hegel, along with many of his philosophical contemporaries, understood this polis to exemplify the expressive unity which would bind together every aspect of both private and public life. Universal reason must be the basis of all of its aspects including sensibility and public affairs.[5]

Levinas is critical of this system, since it only allows for the rule of the self-same. What this means can be explained in the following way. "It [reason] is a faculty which, despite its 'interiority', is equal to whatever the world confronts it with."[6] Hegel's idea of the polis is formed according to this reason. It is a homogeneous space created by reason. In it, ethics is granted by a frictionless working together of the philosophical, the social, and the religious. Levinas contrasts this idea with his own notion of an *espace vital*, where "space" is constituted by its relationship to a threefold exteriority. The exteriority of the reader, of God, and the exteriority of meaning itself. The relationship between the interiority of the text and this threefold exteriority is constitutive of Levinas's notion of *"espace vital."* It thus implies a notion of heterogeneity that Hegel would have deemed scandalous. Yet, it is precisely here that Levinas locates the ethical. For him this space is given in two different ways: through the reading of Holy Scripture, i.e., through doing midrash, and through understanding subjectivity as something that incorporates the other in the same rather than just being the self-same. Both ways are interrelated and hence condition each other.

Levinas's insists that by finding the possibility of fracturing the self-same he can better understand revelation which otherwise runs up against two kinds of interior totalities that mutually condition one another: the totality of the world and the totality of reason. Hegel's judgment that the stability of the world is an effect caused and upheld by reason blocks the possibility of the fracturing of the self-same and prevents an adequate understanding of what Levinas calls the impact of an exterior or an other.

Though it was actually Hegel who conjured up the absolute system in which being and reason are the same, Levinas charges Kant with initiating this move. Kant, according to Levinas, paved the way for Hegel by making time and space into intuitions, i.e., coequal conditions of perception and reason. Kant's concept of the unity of apperception created the epistemological grounding for the belief that any kind of understanding or perceiving can also be treated as an assembling or conjuncture. Perceiving in Kant's theory entails that somehow the space which is occupied by the perceiver is united with the space of the perceived, i.e., the time and space in which the thing resides is the time and space of our interior intuition. What appears to be exterior is already inside an intuition if it is to be perceived at all, and is thus not really exterior in itself. In contrast, Levinas insists, exteriority must be conceived such that it does not fall into the hegemony of the knower. This can only be done through an examination of language. As such this exteriority is beyond Kant's time and space.

> Ne comporte-t-il pas d'autres significations? Trace d'un départ, figure d'un irrécupérable passé, égalité d'une multiplicité, homogène devant la justice . . . Elles ne se laissent pas interpréter a partir de dévoilement. Et, sans doute, avant elles, l'ouverture de l'espace signifie-t-elle le *dehors* où rien ne couvre rien, la *non-protection*, l'envers du repli, le *sans-domicile*, le *non-monde*, la non-habitation, l'étalement sans sécurité.

Does it not involve other significations? The trace of a departure, the figure of an irrecuperable past, the equality of a multiplicity, homogeneous before justice . . . They cannot be interpreted on the basis of disclosure. And no doubt before them the openness of space signifies the outside where nothing covers anything, non-protection, the reverse of a retreat, homelessness, non-world, non-habitation, layout without security.[7]

Levinas is searching for a space which should, in Kantian terms, be a non-space. It is a space: beyond regular space that is beyond any kind of regular space. It does not come along with perception and is not merely an assembling into the always self-same reason. For Levinas those spaces-beyond, but within, can only be understood and grasped as signifieds (i.e., as repre-sented by signs). They cannot be based on the possibility of their actual disclosure. From within language they signify privation, i.e., an absolute lack.

Subjectivity must be grasped along the same lines. It is the otherness of this privation that gives Levinas reason to raise their phenomenological significance for a new approach to sub-jectivity. Understood linguistically, i.e. through the language in which it is expressed, subjectivity can no longer be under-stood as the always self-same, indestructible ego-unit which it was for Hegel, Kant and later Husserl. The privation signified through language is indicative also of a primordial fracturing of the subject. The subject is hollowed out by an internal lack and thus ready to be filled by the other. This hollowness translates into the language of desire, search, and inquiry all of which imply and perpetuate and absence. They are linguistic modes that resemble intentional acts; yet they are intending an absent and infinitely removed noema, while signifying the internal hollowness of the subject. We are asked to gather our experi-ences of non-space and to understand them as pointing beyond themselves. Like the terms desiring, searching and inquiring all nonspatial experiences are significant because of the exter-nal absence and the internal privation they indicate.

Levinas's treatment of Heidegger shows that the privation

or hollowness of the subject is also connected to the quest for an other. According to Levinas, Heidegger's explanation of the Hermeneutic Circle showed how all beings are somehow related to Being. The question 'What is?' wants to know *what* is! The question itself already is a manifestation of Being which presupposes a relation to Being. As such the 'What is?' question should point to the most common and intelligible characteristic shared by all science and human life, viz. their relationship to Being. Levinas's point is that, though Heidegger is correct about this playing together of Being and beings, he seems oblivious to how exactly this relationship comes to be known. The very existence of the *question* 'What is?' partially resists Heidegger's understanding, since it puts into question the intelligibility of something which should not have to be put into question any longer.

> Et cependant, cette intelligibilité se fait question. Que l'intelligibilité se fasse question — étonne. Voila un problème, préliminaire à la question *qui* ? *et quoi* ? Pourquoi il y a question dans l'exhibition?

> And yet, this intelligibility is questionable. That intelligibility would become questionable is something surprising. Here is a problem, preliminary to the questions 'who? and what'? *Why is there a question in exhibition?* (my italics)[8]

Levinas's interpretation of this peculiar fact, the questionability of intelligibility, is that the 'who?' that is asking the question indicates through it her addressing of an other, beyond the realm of being. How else should there be a question? Temporarily — for as long as the question lasts — that other/otherness is invoked by it. The moment of answering becomes the point where the elipsis of the self-same will be perfected. Only in answering the question is the Hermeneutic Circle again closed. I.e., Levinas sees in the hermeneutic circle, *"Dasein's"* quest for Being, a possibility which, he claims, eluded Heidegger: the possibility of an other. It is this temporary fracturing of the Hermeneutical Circle which, in Levinas's mind, amounts to a temporary fracturing of being.

The center of Levinas's argument is the phenomenological structure of subjectivity. His phenomenology, intent on demonstrating the hollowness of the subject, is both linguistic and anti-ontologistic in character. Linguistically, it is the real subjection of the subject as, for example, in the French expression *"me voici"* which lets Levinas show this hollowness. In it the subject only is as accused, i.e., it is as at the mercy of the other. It is in a state of transcendental passivity, receiving the accusation and hence always responsible. In fact, freedom — the choice between accepting the responsibility or not accepting it — is only possible within the postaccusative phase. Anti-ontologistically, Levinas shows that "la subjectivité n'est pas une modalité de l'essence" ("subjectivity is not a modality of essence").[9] "The problem of transcendence and of God and the problem of subjectivity irreducible to essence, irreducible to essential immanence, go together."[10] Levinas argues against both Kant and Hegel who align the subject with what is knowable in ways that make it seem impossible for the subject to conceive of just those spaces-beyond to which Levinas wants to point as charged with the potential for an ethics. God's transcendence seems to stand paradigmatically for the irreconcilable difference between subjectivity and essence. I.e., the subject is both accused and transcendent. With this notion of accused, yet transcendent subjectivity Levinas makes room for a subject that is positively nonessential. It receives this nonessentiality from the other.

In order to illuminate this notion of transcendence further, Levinas chooses to focus on the fracturing of time, since its stretch between the subject and the other is what first makes known *that* there is an other, i.e., it creates the very possibility for ethics. It is the possibility for an ethics "before," (i.e., an ethics that continually will have to go find this rupture between subject and other in order to locate sociality at the only place it can be found) that is *before*, i.e., prior to, subjectivity. Hence, it is thus only for lack of a better term that the subject is still called "subject" here. The term designates that entity which through inquiry addresses the other, and thus perpetually reveals its fractured nature. Levinas can say that the subject is not really the Kantian subject, but rather the other-in-the-same. The subject is constituted as being directed toward an other. The space between subject and other is "filled" with a potential for responsibility.

We are now in a better position to understand Levinas's critique of reason as a critique of subjectivity. It is the subject's stifling universalism that totalizes the world without giving space to the possibility of the other. Reason as it is commonly understood represents either the subject and everything which it can assemble into its understanding, or the function of (i.e., the "logic behind") the whole world. It is a blanket covering and explaining of everything. It is the foil upon which the world is interpreted and which, as such, excludes otherness. Reason stands for the system created by the subject which assembles the usually temporally dispersed parts of a structure. In Husserl's phenomenology the subject is reduced to the retaining and protaining (retention and protention are the two ways in which the subject understands itself as located between the past and the future) entity that forms the world into a coherent whole. However, coherence is a problematic issue, because it seeks to eliminate the spaces between things and thoughts from which recognition for the other, (and hence responsibility) should proliferate. Thus coherence turns into oneness,[11] a totality, that cannot recognize the other.[12] Levinas is not trying to embrace a new kind of dualism; rather, he is trying to break up the false (and in his eyes fatal) unity of reason introduced through Kant and perfected by Hegel. Its breaking up will not be a regress to Cartesian dualism which failed to demonstrate successfully the existence of the world. Instead, Levinas wants to show the structure that enables the subject to *perceive the world around it as different from itself*. Through the hollowness of the subject it is precisely the materiality of the other which signifies from underneath the world displayed to me by reason. Levinas is trying to explain that phenomenological idealism (knowing the world

through a decoding of our consciousness of the world) is secondary to a more original moment in which the world appears to
me as material and not as a datum of my consciousness. This
materiality precedes reason, yet is irretrievable, since even my
description of it is bound to a *conscious* examination of *consciousness*. All reflective processes are bound by consciousness in this
way. It is the confrontation with the other's materiality, her face,
which first initiates reason. Thus the "cogito, ergo sum" turns
into "cogito — enim semper accusatus ab altero — ergo sum."

This epistemological and phenomenological critique of subjectivity is closely connected to the importance that Levinas gives
to reading Scripture. Our relationship to the text can be framed
by the *"me voici."* The text accuses us and we are truly its subjects. Clearly, it is the subject's hollowness which entails its
propensity for the other and first enables it to read Scripture
as a holy text given by the Other, i.e. by God. The revelation of
the text lies in its materiality and in its spatio-temporal dimension. The text is the material face of God which we are called
to obey. Willingness to interpret is obedience. The interpreter
is not the agent but the passive recipient of God's revelation.
The interpreter thus turns into a prophet whose calling and
message signify the rupturing of the world of reason. Levinas
suggests that obeying God is the first step towards an understanding of the other as our neighbor. Obeying God, who is
revealed in and through the interpretative flow that emanates
from Scripture, will entail the same kind of flow within the
human community. We have a text that is already fissured and
as such allows for interpretation. God reveals himself in those
texts. Furthermore, we have a world bound to and by reason, a
totality thus which needs to be ruptured. Obedience to this God
can effect this rupture.

We are now in a better position concerning the understanding of subjectivity which precedes Levinas's understanding of
sacred texts. I would suggest that Levinas considers the study
of sacred texts on three different levels, all of which support his

claim that the meaning of revelation is first and foremost ethical. To follow God means to love one's neighbor as the other; we are accountable to and responsible for this other through an anarchic decree; but the origin of this decree is both irretrievable and eternally/always constitutive of humanness. The sequence of these levels is by no means arbitrary. It reveals the function of the text as mediating an encounter between its readers and God. Wedged between a reader (whose subjectivity must be described as other-in-the-same) and a God (whose otherness is ruptured by boredom and loneliness) is a text (the salient feature of which is the-ambiguous-in-the-nonambiguous). The one characteristic that all three levels have in common is a certain fracturedness. The levels are 1. The subject and the text, 2. the text, 3. the text and God.

The Subject and the Text

Levinas's valuation of the text is based on a critique of language as intentional. He substitutes for it the language of responsibility. This language consists in the continual unsaying of the text by virtue of interpretation. Just a moment ago we had described interpretation and reading as an act of obedience to God, i.e., the question of reading is one not only between subject and text and subject and language, but also between subject and God. We will return to the issue of subject and God presently, but direct our attention for the moment to the language of the text whose interpreters and readers we are supposed to be. Levinas seems to presuppose a theory of language that sees the origination of languages in the attempt of the fractured subject to rebuild what is missing in its subjectivity. "The call to exegesis,"[13] as Levinas calls it, is a call from within the fractured subject itself. It expresses the desire of the fractured ego to achieve completion through interpreting the text. In order to understand the call of the subject to exegesis we have to look at the text first as language and second as Torah.

Levinas's notion of language is an attempt to emphasize the linguistic quality of the world and the act of knowing it, on the one hand, as well as their interaction on the other. He rejects a correspondence theory of truth as well as the notion that language is intentional (analogously to Husserl's intentional consciousness). He further rejects the "kerygmatic" character of phenomenological language which knows only what it has named. For it knowledge is impossible. The words themselves are the things. For phenomenology "thus, language can be interpreted as the manifestation of truth, as the way being takes to show itself. Logos as speech is entirely one with logos as rationality."[14] Things and objects, in other words, cannot really appear to us. Being and truth are possible only within the linguistic ideality of intentionality.[15]

The problem, then, with a phenomenological linguistics is that its idealism undermines any argument to sustain a sense of a reality which exists in and by itself. There can be no outside for it. Everything becomes a within. Existence becomes an attribute conferred upon things through knowledge. Husserl's philosophy was promising in many ways. An approach that was concerned with phenomena, i.e., with existing things as they showed themselves, seemed like a viable solution to the reality defying character of idealism. Jean Hyppolite[16] quotes Levinas and others as saying how refreshing and invigorating the slogan "Back to the things" was which phenomenology had introduced.[17] But phenomenology retreated instead, through a series of "Meditations" and "Introductions," to the question of how the things *can be perceived*. Its question had become what the structures of the subject are that allow it to perceive phenomena the way they show themselves. The answer, intentionality, leaves no room for a showing and lets perceiving rule instead. Husserl's own deviation from the phenomenological project seems to validate idealism.

But for Levinas phenomenology does not end here. Understood correctly, it can mutate from phenomenological epistemology into phenomenological ethics where intentionality becomes proximity. Despite Levinas's phenomenological heritage, the question how things show themselves is somewhat secondary to the question he has *about* this question: How can the ego recognize the other in her otherness rather than what I have subjectively come to conjecture *as* otherness.

Levinas's project is an attempt to do "original phenomenology." He announces the showing of a kind of materiality that implies transcendence and calls for responsibility. Showing itself, however, entails the preposition "to." Showing implies the utter passivity of the perceiving subject *to* which the face shows itself. The nominatively (i.e., naming) perceiving subject turns into the passive audience towards which the face is turned in accusative demonstration. Beyond intentionality and the realm of ideality, there is a realm of materiality that signifies proximity. Our relationship to that beyond demonstrates responsibility. Before intentionality, before conceptualization and recognition, ideality has been ruptured. A moment of materiality precedes — a moment never forgotten but always suppressed. This moment bears all the aspects of the responsibility which I have for the other; it is the only time of real contact *before* knowing.

Levinas is epistemologically honest enough to admit to the evanescence of such a moment. It cannot persist, since once it becomes known and reaches consciousness, it turns into intentionality and leaves the subject to its own sphere. However, below active consciousness remains passive obsession. The subject remains surrounded by the proximity of the other. Language (and now we have come full circle with this exposition) is the obsession of the I "beset"[18] by the other.

Levinas assumes that prior (logically and temporally) to every particular language a sign is passed on from one to the other. This sign is the sign of obsession of being "beset" with others who, while always the nearest (proximus), remain farthest away (i.e. are absent). Obsession itself is regarded as a "communication without phrases or words."[19] It is silent, opposed to the noisy proclaiming (lat. clamor) of intentionality. It is language, although it lacks everything one would normally associate with language. The language of obsession functions without marks or signs, without a voice or a text. It is a language without a medium. Most of all it lacks the propositional and informational character of the particular languages we know, and yet there is a piece of information that is passed on by it. It is immediate and its piece of information is the "very fact of saying."[20]

The difficulty with this thought is that the very fact of saying must be comprehended as devoid of any representational features. It is evanescent and stands for nothing. This language (viz. the sign of obsession which Levinas also calls the first word) precedes all particular languages which already presuppose communication. The first word is communication itself which as such remains silent and nonthematizable. What is heard, listened to, seen and read are the signs and marks which, based on the event of communication captured in the saying, issue forth from it as the said. Now a new stage sets in — the stage of the said where thoughts and emotions including my relationship with the other, are represented through a set of concepts logically organized, which themselves are represented through marks and gaps that also are logically organized. In short, the said is what we have come to know as languages and texts.

What happened to the saying? It would be misleading to assume that it was transformed into the said, since that would mean the ultimate loss of the saying for human beings, which would in turn entail the impossibility of Levinas's attempt to recover the ethical. The event of communication, the saying, dwells underneath the said. It is always there, presupposed by the said. It is the saying that enables the said to generate the configuration of themes, concepts and meanings that we call a text. However, since the saying cannot be thematized without losing its character of immediacy, it remains a nothing to conceptual understanding, which, unfortunately, is the only kind of understanding we can contribute to this questioning.

Why then do human beings speak at all? If the saying which really is the ethical relationship, nonreciprocal as it is, is always only obliterated by the event of speech, thought and writing, why do humans not just remain silent? What is the reason for consciousness to set in and generate concepts, issues, themes and texts with which we identify the world? Why are human beings determined by a consciousness which is productive in such unfortunate and alienating ways? In short the answer is because, although every act of speaking turns the saying into the said, speaking indicates a level of ethical maturity and a relationship with the other that is preferable to the more aesthetic notion of the saying.

Levinas gives a clearer response to these questions than he does to the problems that arise from consciousness. However, in order to make visible his move from language to text (from phenomenology to the Torah) it is necessary to look more closely at the origins of human speech and texts. The question is why are humans forced to retain the order of the said along with an irretrievable saying? Levinas's remarks about art criticism in his essay *Reality and its Shadow* have implications also for his theory of speech. "Not content with being absorbed in aesthetic enjoyment the public feels an irresistible need to speak."[21] This description of art criticism as a mode of resistance to the persuasiveness of the aesthetic, the sensual, is interesting precisely because Levinas generally prioritizes the sensual over the conceptual. Yet, being absorbed in aesthetic enjoyment (or, one might conjecture, being obsessed with and held hostage by it), somehow turns into a source of discontentment, intolerable for humans. There is an irresistible need to speak, a force stronger than the pleasure derived from aesthetic (that is, merely sensual) enjoyment which drives one to thematize what this aesthesis (the act of aesthetic perception) is all about.

We can see in this example of the aesthetic the difference between a more floating along with the other and the development of responsibility for the other. Once we speak the aesthetic dimension of sheer enjoyment ceases to exist and we experience the otherness of the work of art in its most heightened and emphasized form. What is sensed, whether it is the face of the other or the work of art, is least subject to internalization. It stands in front of us as squarely, objectively and other as can be. I, as the entity which is experiencing this otherness, am perpetually confronted with this otherness (which is other than myself) with my own deprivation and thus I will attempt to draw this other into the sphere of my own.

However, at the same time, the irresistible need to speak is a relentless effort to overcome the gap between myself and the other. It is a force that cannot but reduce what is other to what is self. The sensual and material qualities of otherness are glossed over by conceptual and ideal qualities produced by the subject. The former will eventually fall into oblivion and the latter will become what I take to be reality.

Speaking is symptomatic of this attempt to use conceptual enjoyment to internalize the other. The expression of one's love towards someone else in a statement of affection (e.g., "I love you") indicates both ethical maturity as well as the wish to control and overcome the other. My speaking is my attempt to redeem myself from aesthetic enjoyment and from the tension which the otherness of the loved has imposed on me. But the result is counter-productive. The other cannot be captured in this way. "Language cannot take in the other."[22] In fact, the problem becomes more intense. The words I said, those letters I wrote, are now themselves entities separate from me. More, rather than less, have they become inaccessible to my need to internalize the external.

The intersection which is reached here is crucial to an understanding of Levinas's concern with texts, especially those of the Torah. Textuality, the production of texts, is an attempt to overcome otherness, but, at the same time, it manifests my own alienation from the other. The production of texts is a variation of my need to speak. It is irresistible, because it can never be satisfied. Necessarily, a saying produces or entails a said. This said will cover over the saying and make it invisible and inaudible at any point. What remains is the said in all its different ramifications as written text. Examples of such remainders are any kinds of institutions and laws. Even physical structures, like buildings as well as entire cities, are materialized outbursts of saying and thinking. The relationship between the saying and the said is that of a dialectics without synthesis. The said, which is the amalgamated saying, attempts to gather the other into the realm of the self-same, and in its failure to do so, reveals the invariable otherness of the person I am facing. This continuous failure produces the realization that the discourse produced is really my discourse.

Levinas does not view this move from saying to said as an unfortunate event. He gives his reasons for this judgment in a 1982 interview with E. Wyschogrod.[23] Though for him the "ethical moment is the saying," the said is both needed and unavoidable. While the saying contains the plurality which makes possible "many more relationships of love," it is the said that "unifies the one who speaks. It is that in which multiplicity is reflected in a meaning and in this sense the said is important." Furthermore, Levinas insists that the order of institutions, which itself is a reflection of the said, is indispensable for the existence of civil society: "One could not be a Jew and speak otherwise." In short, Levinas recognizes that a certain sociopolitical structure, and even the possibility of a structure itself is grounded in the possibility of a said, i.e., the at least temporary freezing of the liquidity of the saying.[24]

The Text

The second level is of understanding sacred texts on the level of the text itself.[25] The texts of scripture are entities with an internal revelatory dynamic. Certain peculiar features of the Hebrew language, which in turn entail certain interpretative strategies, also belong to this level. An understanding of the text as the ambiguous-in-the-nonambiguous describes it as a body of signs and marks which, under a certain visible surface structure of meaning, hides a surplus of meaning which can only be brought to light through continuous interpretation.

As mentioned in the beginning of this study, reading (specifically, the reading of the Torah) must be understood as providing the Jewish people with more than just new ideas and concepts. Levinas claims that the process of reading and interpreting has para-material consequences. It opens up a space which takes over all the characteristics of an actual living space, such as a house, a town, or state. Reading creates an *espace vital*. One-dimensional thinking can substitute for three-dimensional space. Somehow, everything the Jews have and can claim to be their own rests in this para-material revelation of the text. "Their nostalgia for the land is nourished by texts, and owes nothing to any organic attachment to a particular piece of soil. Clearly this kind of presence to the world makes the paradox of transcendence less anomalous."[26] Somehow, in contrast with other Western nations, the Jews have come to understand themselves and the world primarily through their "relation with the book. The depths of self are not possible without the book."[27] I will first look at Levinas's understanding of the book, i.e., the Torah, and then at his assessment of the term "the Jews" as readers of the book.

Levinas's position on the book, i.e., on the issue of the text, is not so different from that of traditional Jewish thought. His question is how the texts of the Torah can generate ongoing revelatory interpretation. His answer has as much to do with philology as with hermeneutics. The philological aspect can be understood through a closer examination of the function of the Hebrew language in the Torah. Hebrew, other than the so-called functional or linear languages, can be characterized as a language that proliferates an infinite supply of new and different meanings from the words actually heard or written (in Hebrew the words coexist, and do not fall into immediate hierarchies).[28]

An exegetical practice that already assumes the outcome of the act of interpretation as intended and somehow limited to the number and positions of certain letters basically deprives itself of exegesis as "unfurling the wings of the Holy Spirit to share all the horizons which the Spirit can embrace."[29] Hence, Jewish exegesis has always paid special attention to those parts of the text that did not submit themselves to the immediate understanding of the reader. Ambiguities, underlying meanings, puns, etc. (in one word the nonimmediate), have been at the center of rabbinical interest. As it shows itself in the scriptures, revelation is a mystery in intensity, yet never simply enigmatic in character. The mystery which Levinas is pointing to here is the mystery of a text with gaps and fissures, which opens up, leaves out words, a text that puns, uses anagrams and acrostics, etc. All of this redirects the attention of the exegete away from the surface of the text towards another, even greater mystery — God.

It would seem that Levinas's concept of the text provides absolutely no guidelines for its own interpretation. It is an hermeneutically impossible situation in which the reader must somehow dip into the abyss of meanings of just one word or passage in order to understand revelation. But Levinas thinks differently. The texts with which we are dealing must generate the word of revelation. No matter what is said, asked, thought or assumed about them it must be considered part of that same revelation, i.e. as something that emanates from the events at Sinai. Revelation must be understood as a process of continuing exegesis. "These words and others are all words of the living God."[30] This talmudic principle reveals the structure of revelation. Under these hermeneutical circumstances interpretative truth must be understood as the exegetical result of a multiplicity of readers engaged in the project of understanding the Torah. A unifying dogma in the sense of a creed does not exist. The only limitation that Levinas is willing to place on free textual interpretation is that imposed by tradition. A hermeneutics of subjectivity, as is implied by a multiplicity of readers, allows no fanaticism into the reading process. There is a responsibility towards what Levinas calls "harmonics."[31] Reading must fit with certain verses and the interpretations of these readings must cohere with the whole of tradition. The distinctions between written and oral Torah include that between halakha and aggadah. For Levinas, reading the aggadah is the necessary counterpart to the framework that the halakha provides for explaining and exemplifying the meanings of the law. Both, in Levinas's view, are of equal importance.

Levinas's understanding of the text reflects very distinctly a Jewish sense of the Torah and its interpretations. The Torah is God's word and "contains innumerable meanings." Exegesis must proceed as an *inquiry* into the different possibilities of meaning.[32] Levinas himself invokes the term Midrash and translates it as "exposition, or research, or interrogation."[33] His interpretation of the exegetical function of midrash is reflected in the studies of other Jewish scholars such as Boyarin, Stern, and Kugel.[34]

Reading this text, however, is not at all without difficulties and ambiguities for the Jews. Levinas identifies two hermeneutical modes which in his view parallel — theologically and philosophically — two large groups within Judaism.[35] One is the group of the Orthodox Jews, the other is the group of the Modern Jews who — Levinas thinks — is the majority.[36] The former's commitment to the text is characterized by a marked interest in the "literal sense of the word." They understand revelation to be a "communication between Heaven and Earth" which is supposed to inform human beings of "the highest virtues and most mysterious secrets of God's proximity."[37] Levinas understands this to be a hermeneutical choice made in response to the crisis of religion in general brought about by Modernity. The literal tradition emphasizes — against Modernity — the value and import of tradition and history as the "fresh water" needed to survive the desert of a-religiosity.

But there is another audience that has done away with the sacred text simply because it fails to understand how revelation as an event of exteriority can possibly impact an interiority (viz. affect their lives). They rely on reason alone to explain the world. However, Levinas's contention is that reason alone will not be sufficient to deal with the ethical problems which humankind is facing. For the crisis of religion, the unreasonable — and therefore unbelievable — event of the Revelation, to them, coincides with a more universal and encompassing crisis of the "destiny of the West."[38] The economy of reason (i.e. reason in the various ways it relates thinking and acting, philosophy and science, etc.) has never been able to tackle successfully the problem of death or that of an ever-increasing technology that eventually may make human beings dispensable all together. Understanding through revelation is inaccessible for modern Jews. They need a new sense of how reason and revelation's exteriority need not be mutually exclusive.

The latter group is the audience to whom Levinas addresses the distinction between the said and the saying, i.e., the distinction between a text and its revelatory content. The message is that there is indeed a beyond to the letters. The literal sense does not exhaust the revelation; in fact, it obscures it. Furthermore, revelation needs precisely the modern attitude of doubt or suspicion (i.e., of postmodern hermeneutics) to show itself. Midrashic inquiry into the text is necessary. Revelation itself must be supplemented. Human beings are not simple listeners to the divine message; they indeed participate in revelation as "the only 'terrain' where exteriority can appear."[39] Revelation calls upon what is unique, albeit fractured, within the human. As a process of continuing hermeneutics, it provides humans with enjoyment and pleasure while simultaneously it depends on humans as God's "irruption in Being which stimulates giving."[40] Humans are both the interior and exterior in the concept of revelation. Levinas claims that revelation in the Jewish tradition is something which has never ceased. Jews still experience and engage in it.[41] For the Jew, revelation is the promise given to those who in some way devote themselves to studying the sacred texts. Since, in Levinas's reading, Scripture is infinitely proliferate (i.e. it produces new meanings unendingly) he can claim that every new meaning found by the students of Scripture is an encounter with revelation. Hence, continual interpretation guarantees continual revelation.

Text and God

The third level of understanding sacred scriptures considers the question of the mutual relationship between God and the texts of Scripture, and, simultaneously, establishes the differences between sacred and profane literature. Levinas's basic assumption is that the Bible "is a said that is inspired,"[42] thus invoking the classical interpretation of the Bible in liberal Judaism. Like any other text, the Bible is a text that is part of the order of the said. The texts of Scripture are written in particular languages; they are based on conceptual understanding; their content can be known. In other words, they are accessible to the ideality of phenomenology which, as language, proclaims the existence of something as something. Yet, this text of the order of the said, Levinas tells us, is inspired. Being inspired could be taken to mean two different things. One would be the traditional Christian and also non-Christian concept of inspiration which imagines it to be an act of verbal communication in the process of which God instills into the particular human being a message that he/she should deliver to the world. Inspiration, understood this way, would be no different from any type of common communication; it would be reduced to a simple talking to, which, by the way, includes the possibility of not listening on the part of the prophet, and hence could result in her or him not doing the job at all. Neither are ever the case. Inspiration never fails.

The second possibility for an understanding of inspiration is, if not more Jewish, at least more Levinasian. The texts are inspired. Analogous to his notion of the in-finite which signifies the divine *in* the finite, the meaning of in-spire could be the presence of the divine in the texts. Hence the "in" is less meant to signify a giving than it is to mark God's dwelling in the finite.[43] Something lives and moves in the texts which surpasses their mere textuality, their givenness as a system of signs. This something is revelation. Texts are not themselves revelation; rather, they are "disparate traces of the Revelation [that can be found] in scripture."[44] The Revelation is a saying (dire);[45] it consists of words and forms a system of signs to be interpreted. But it is not the system itself which constitutes revelation. Its measure is not God, but what people hear in God's living word.[46] Revelation is the transcendence of the inspired profane.[47] The term "inspiration" designates not only an act of God, but also a condition of the text as well as the human community. Inspiration, breathing into, presupposes the existence of a void

which can be filled by this breath. Levinas refers to this in
Autrement qu'etre ou au-dela de l'essence where he writes: "que
le sujet puisse etre poumon, au fon de sa substance — signifie
une subjectivité qui souffre et s'offre avant de prendre pied dans
l'etre — passivité, tout entière un *supporter*" ("That the subject
could be a lung at the bottom of its substance . . . signifies a subjectivity that suffers and offers itself before taking a foothold in
being. It is passivity, wholly a supporting.")[48]

Why does God's living word come to the world in such difficult and complex ways? Why doesn't God just reveal God-self?
The difficulty with revelation is that, from an epistemological
point of view, it really ought not to happen. Revelation is God's
point of view. An exteriority simply cannot reveal itself inside
an interiority without either first negating that interiority completely or losing its exterior qualities. However, if God negated
the world, then nothing would be left for God to reveal God-self
to. If, on the other hand, God lost those exterior qualities, then
revelation would lose its significance. Moses must not see God
directly, because either it will kill him or he will not see anything different.[49] Instead God chooses to descend into the finite.
The finite is thus fractured; it is not just finite anymore; it reveals a transcendence which is effected by the divine descent.
At the same time, however, God's own fracturedness is revealed
as well. Although Levinas does not refer to it this way, it seems
to me that his speculation, that God decided to descend because
he was bored,[50] cannot be interpreted otherwise. Where there is
boredom there is a desire, viz., a fracturedness that seeks for
completion and fulfillment.[51] For Levinas, God is an authority
without force. "In the last analysis, he can not do anything at
all. He is not a force but an authority."[52]

MIDRASHIC ETHICS

Despite the established relationship between subject and text
and God and text Levinas does not want to understand this

analogy as a symmetry. It is truly an asymmetrical relationship characterized by obedience. Ethics is predicated on this obedience to interpret. This ethics is mediated by the relationship between three radically different, but strangely united, determinants-subject, text and God. Two different vectors come together in the text: The midrashic (i.e., inquisitive) attitude of the subject, and the apodeictic (i.e., demanding) attitude of God. There is room, space for both in the text. Although these two seem to be radically different, nevertheless they coincide in their motivation. Both humans' irresistible need to speak and the boredom of God direct our attention to a fracturedness that both sides share and attempt to eliminate through the text.

Can the text achieve this filling of the fracture? Is this completion a symmetrical event for both humans and God? What is the difference between a demanding and an inquiring attitude? The text does constitute a bridge between humans and God. However, both tread that bridge with different gravity and for different reasons. The text is a said. It is an immobile, amalgamated reality of signs and marks, ordered according to a certain rationale. It is repeatable. The text is an institution, but as such it is fractured. Visible gaps and lacunas between letters, sentences and paragraphs, as well as the concomitant ruptures in significance and meaning, render the text fragile on the one hand but strong on the other. The text is like a vacuum which attracts irresistibly, through its brokeness, a perennial filling, an interpretation. This text is inspired. It contains God's living word. It bears revelation. Yet, it is a strange kind of revelation, one that does not impose itself; one that cannot come about by itself, but needs to be triggered; one that needs a site. In their irresistible need to speak, humans experience an "inquiétude de l'homme par l'Infini de Dieu" ("worry induced in [them] by God's infinity.")[53] Speaking is caused by that Other — God — who is infinitely removed from me and simultaneously in-finitely near (proximity). That Other is an object of my desire, but as such it is infinitely removed. It is an object I will never be able to objectify.

However, if my relationship with the Other were constituted by my desire alone, the Other would soon be made into the same. The other would become my slave, my victim, abused by my imposed will. Yet, as we have seen, in all cases the other is not the object of my desire, but rather, is its subject. And as such the other is in control of me. A demand for obedience is uttered towards me. This commandment issues incessantly from a text that is inspired by a moral God. "It is as an ethical kerygma that the Bible is Revelation," says Levinas. However, this ethical kerygma, its proclamation, cannot come from the text alone. The text is a said that by itself cannot generate such a kerygma. It is the movement of reading and interpretation; it is the doing of midrash that gives life to the saying contained in the text. This occurs in the "ethical model of the Bible, the transcendence of understanding."[54]

The text has two different functions for Levinas. One lies in its demand for obedience. The other is constituted by the model character which the Bible has for an ethics in which the one is substituted for the other. With respect to the first, according to Levinas, obedience not only results from the textual studies in which the Jews engage; it is a precondition for the reading itself. Interpretation is an act of obedience. As such it presupposes God's revelation. Hence, interpretation perpetually anticipates revelation.

Despite this notion of interpretation as obedience Levinas is careful not to portray the law of Torah as the yoke which it has come to signify in traditional Pauline/Christian theology. The law provides a frame, a scaffold, which serves to unite the Jews as a people. Common ritual practice, as prescribed by the law, is the element shared by all Jews. It is the weekly readings from the Torah, the wearing of the kippah, or the communal recitation of the "shema" that give the Jews their identity. The Jewish people are united by their common practice even, Levinas claims, when that practice has ceased.[55] The decisions in the halakha about ritual practice are not eternal apodeictic statements given by God. The discussions in the talmuds that produced those decrees are as much part of the law as the decrees themselves. This judgment enables Levinas to say that the mizvot are distinct from any doctrinal unity. It is here that Levinas notes the importance of aggadic discourse over against the halakha.[56]

The prescriptive lessons of ritual practice are only part of what is involved in obedience to God. The study of practice also is a theoretical issue of equal value. Levinas recognizes those who continually interpret the text. They, as much as anybody else who is actually involved in practicing the law, through their study alone, come in contact with the divine as well. Obedience to God includes those who read in obedience. Obedience to the Most High, Levinas says,[57] consists in the impossibility of running away. Every single individual is enticed to respond individually to the Other. The Most High singles out and distributes responsibilities. No one is able to substitute for what I have to do. Freedom is a freedom where no one should attempt to do, what I should do. No one else can do it. Only I am able to refuse the responsibility imposed on me by this divine obligation. The possibility of refusal marks my freedom. It is in this sense that to obey God is to be free ("Obéir au Plus-Haut, c'est être libre").[58]

It is this kind of obedience that allows Levinas to show how the exteriority of the Revelation may have access to the interiority of human beings and their world. It is the "irreducible 'intrigue' of obedience [which] must be taken as a starting point."[59] "Intrigue," could mean a weaving in together, a secret love affair or a secret plan or coup. Obedience in this sense is a derivative product. "It derives, rather, from the love of one's neighbor."[60] Obedience in this way opens up the interiority of the world to the exteriority of revelation. This exteriority is uncontainable; it could never be held successfully within interiority and still be recognized as exteriority. Yet, through obedience a relationship is established which allows for an interchange between the subject and the other.

It is clear how Levinas can tie together the function of the individual as scribe (to complete the works of revelation) with the individual as a fractured (and therefore searching) subject into the one phrase of obedience to God. God, the ultimate other for whom the subject is looking, is partially revealed in the text, and, to the extent that God is revealed, the subject finds modes of self-completion. At the same time this freedom to act in these modes is a given by a revelation which allows for interpretation. This freedom encourages the unique to find in the text what is unique to itself. In other words, revelation is fully particular. However, it is also universal, because it comes to all in its respectively unique shape.

With respect to the second function of the text, the Bible as a model for ethics, one must remember that the text engenders an activity of inquiry and search by the community of interpreters. This search stands paradigmatically for the relationship with the other (the neighbor), since it — like my relationship with the other — demands a submission (here to the text) that does not leave room for a self-same subject anymore. The relation with the text is also an obsession. The interpreter is hostage to the text, and, as such, can now become the site of the text's revelation. The responsibility to the text's revelation expressed through midrashic study is conceived analogously to the responsibility for the other. A midrashic ethics is an ethics that constantly seeks and questions the said, because it "knows" that beyond that said an other is saying. Midrashic ethics requires an ear for the inaudible voice of the other. It requires constant vigilance over a text which hides, underneath a fatal surface totality, the marginalized other, forever. The text of the Torah resembles the text of the world. Institutions, laws, buildings are an expression of the letters of the said. They are indispensable. However, in and between them dwells the infinite, the other. There is a transcendence which worries human beings and inspires them to embark on a restless search. It is a transcendence to which they submit, which directs them, rather than is directed by them.

HUMANS AS THE IRRUPTION IN BEING

It might be possible now to understand how Levinas's concept of the text as *"espace vital"* is predicated upon a thorough critique of the Western notion of subjectivity. Levinas's phenomenology of the subject results in a characterization of the subject as hollow, as accused, as nonessential, and as confronted with various exteriorities to which it submits rather than controlling them. Interpretation is an act of obedience. In it we obey the command to interact with an other. This other can be the other person next to me, it can be just the otherness of the text, or it can be God. Interpretation, in this sense, is a confirmation of otherness. As such confirmation of otherness reading and interpretation and interpretation become prerequisite of the ethics of responsibility that Levinas has in mind.

For Levinas, humans have a unique position in the web of reason. They are not only susceptible to it; they also constitute an interruption of Being. Reason cannot express adequately *"l'irruption de l'homme dans l'Être"* ("the irruption of man within Being.")[61] Revelation enters through that interruption and directs our attention to our neighbor, the other, whose hostage I am, to whom I am accountable in never-ending responsibility. Yet, for Levinas, all three levels, through their relatedness to the text, model ethical transcendence. Midrashic study confirms the transcendence of the text, the subject and God. As such midrash models ethics in a threefold way. Midrashic study understands the text's demand to love one's other while it treats the text as the world which always tries to hide the other. If one accepts the parallels that Levinas himself draws between the said and institutions and totality, then one can see the parallels between the saying, the other, and infinity. The texts of scripture embody them both. The latter, to be more precise, is what is always already disembodied by the text.

We have seen in this first chapter that Levinas's theory of revelation is based on an understanding of the texts of scripture which contain relentless potential for revelation as the unique working together between the finite human and the infinite divine realm. Both together, within the text, form a space that, according to Levinas, is the primordial space for ethics, the *espace vital*. In order for humans to be able to understand otherness and its connection with this *espace vital*, and, hence, to be able to take responsibility for the other, they must read and thus interpret. However, there reading is already an act of obedience to a command from an absolute Other who precedes the text as well as inhabits it. How do we, how can we "relate" to this Other? Somehow, it must be discernible in such a way that it becomes possible for human beings to act responsibly and ethically. However, discernibility of the Absolute must never turn into a "knowing" of the Absolute. Discernibility must avoid all contamination of the Absolute. This problem is phrased most succinctly in the philosophy of Hermann Cohen, whose understanding of the relation between the world and God as a correlation resonates in the trans-essential philosophy of Levinas. This correlation presents itself as the emergence of a space which is the space for the infinite task of ethical action.

Two

The Absolute

Cohen, Rosenzweig, Levinas:
Infinite Ethics

We have used the *name* of God several times in the last chapter. And although we have, in a phenomenological way, established how that God relates to both the text and humanity, we have said little if anything about what this name signifies. In Levinas's approach to devising a Jewish ethics around the concept of *"espace vital"* the status of God is framed by an intense monotheism. This means that for Levinas God is both the only God and the God that dwells in absolute difference. Out of this monotheistic conception grow the epistemological principles that inform our understanding of God and this conception consequently also is at the basis of Levinas's Jewish ethics. In what follows I will trace Levinas's monotheism back to Hermann Cohen and Franz Rosenzweig. I will demonstrate the function that monotheism has in their systems and the return to Levinas to specify his conception of God and ethics.

As someone who is concerned with ethics, Levinas attempts to establish a set of metaphysical[1] criteria universally applicable to all human beings. In order for an ethics to be feasible it is necessary to show its *universal applicability*, i.e., that humans are constituted alike. In addition, one must be able to assume that, given that shared constitution, humans will also have the same cognitive access to the *metaphysical grounding*[2] of such an ethics. In the absence of such a set of conditions ethics becomes impossible and the term turns into an oxymoron, since the term itself already presupposes a kind of generalizability — viz. that of human action as ethical — which is, of course, based on the belief that such universals do indeed exist.[3] Levinas's predominant interest is, in other words, not to find a practical ethics, i.e., a system of rules and regulations that could serve humanity as a guideline to lead a just life. Rather, his interest lies in the theologico-epistemological aspect of ethics. He asks what the founding epistemological principle is that first makes possible the conception of the ethical. This founding principle is God.

God as Infinite

Levinas's approach to this founding principle is Cartesian. He seeks to locate God, and consequently ethics, in our sensitivity for the infinite.[4] In his "Third Meditation" ("Of God, That He Exists")[5] Descartes says about the idea of the infinite in its relation to God that "I see clearly that there is more reality in an infinite substance than in a finite substance, and thus that the whole notion of the infinite is, in a sense, anterior to me to the notion of the finite, that the idea of God is anterior, that is to say, to the idea of myself."[6] Levinas remarks that the idea of negativity and that of infinity are connected.

> La naissance latente de la négation réside non pas dans la subjectivité, mais dans l'idée de l'Infini. Ou, si l'on veut, dans la subjectivité en tant qu'idée de l'Infini. C'est en ce sens qu'idée de l'infini, comme le veut Descartes, est une "véritable idée" et non pas seulement ce que je conçois 'par la négation de ce qui est fini.

> The latent birth of negation occurs not in subjectivity, but in the idea of the Infinite. Or, if one prefers, it is in subjectivity *qua* idea of the Infinite. It is in this sense that the idea of the infinite, as Descartes affirms, is a "genuine idea" and not merely what I conceive by the negation of what is finite.[7]

All this serves to prove that Levinas's conception of the infinite hinges fundamentally on paradigms borrowed from modern philosophy. The idea of the infinite, of course, then, later reoccurs in Kant's philosophy as the thing in itself, the categorical imperative, and the sublime. In very similar ways they break up the continuity of the subject and confront it with a "cogitation . . . comme signifiant le non-contenu par excellence" ("cogitatio [that] signifies the non-contained par excellence").[8]

Furthermore, it is not only Descartes but also Hegel whose thought has significantly influenced Levinas's concept of the infinite. Levinas's infinite is an attempt to avoid the pitfall of Hegel's description of a bad infinity. This infinity is one that knows no outside.

> Something becomes an Other, but this Other is itself a something, therefore it likewise becomes an Other, and soon *ad infinitum*. This infinity is the *specious* or negative infinity, insofar as it is nothing but the suppression of the finite which, however, is reborn again, and is, consequently, never completely suppressed.[9]

Levinas's infinite, on the other hand, is one that is self-contained, yet present in the finite where it disrupts the finite continuity over and over again. We will return to these two philosophers repeatedly.

Levinas's methodological problem is that for him ethics can only begin where ontology is transcended (i.e., the discussion of the infinite is not an ontology). It is for this reason that Levinas, and many other postmodern philosophers with him, have started to use a type of paradoxical language whose function it is to express the need for a grounding while simultaneously continuously transcending that grounding. Thus, for Levinas, the infinite is constitutive of humanness, and, to a certain extent, it is knowable. Yet, at the same time, it is also absolutely transcendent and not knowable. Through a kind of recognition of the infinite (the problematic inherent in using the term "recognition" will be discussed below) human beings are endowed with a desire that ultimately is translated into a reaching out for the other person. Although Levinas never says so explicitly, it seems that he wants to universalize this process of finding the infinite and the ensuing desire into a principal human characteristic called "the ethical."

Levinas chooses as the context for the discussion of this problem an essay entitled "God and Philosophy" ("Dieu et la Philosophie"). He argues that for me to talk about God philosophically requires an understanding of the infinite which in turn requires an understanding of ethics as it is given to me through the presence of the other person. The question of God (i.e., how God can be made explicit in philosophical discourse) presupposes an answer to the question of the ethical. The problematic, however, that is connected with both (and I will return to this repeatedly) is that of a latent substantive connection between God and the world, possibly of pantheism. If God manifests God-self in human beings by virtue of the infinite, then the divine sphere and worldly sphere must somehow be related. Yet, if that is the case, how does one understand the Jewish doctrine of monotheism as it is, for example, used and corroborated in Maimonides and Cohen? Isn't knowing God a way of compromising monotheism by making that which is absolutely distinct into something that can be known?[10]

Levinas turns to Hermann Cohen and Franz Rosenzweig[11] to answer these questions. I would like to show that Levinas must, in many ways, be seen as a Cohenian. His philosophy, implicitly, is a negative response to Rosenzweig's synthesis of Cohen and Hegel. Through it, Levinas develops a theory that in its scope and purpose is quite similar to Cohen's method of correlation. This method, as we will see, rather than claiming the ultimate inaccessibility of God and the question of the ethical, leaves Levinas's thought open to a positive answer to the question of God, as well as a positive answer to the question of the epistemological possibility of ethics.

THE MODERN JEWISH TRADITION

The notion of the infinite is important to modern Jewish thought. Cohen, Rosenzweig, and Levinas, although all three seem to have slightly different views about the function of the infinite, are examples of this tradition. Some of the theological questions that characterize this tradition are: 1. Can the infinite, as a characteristic of God, be recognized? 2. Is it the motivating factor for ethical action in the finite world? 3. (This is a question that is implied by the first): Must an epistemological theory always precede the conceptualization of ethics? In the case of Cohen and Levinas we are confronted with two systems of thought which require much epistemological groundwork before we can understand how an ethics can evolve from it. Both claim that it is the possibility of a certain correlation between the infinite and the finite that makes ethics possible. We will have to look at how this correlation becomes a constitutive factor in a theory of ethics.

The problematic issue, in all three cases, is that once Jewish monotheism is accepted in its full scope (as for instance exemplified in Maimonides and Cohen), an absolute difference between the finite and the infinite (i.e., the world and God) must be assumed. This absolute difference would then also make it impossible for any human being to recognize God, i.e., they would be barred from accessing God epistemologically. However, the absoluteness of this judgment must somehow be mitigated in order to explain the possibility of revelation and the ethical actions which often result from revelation. Cohen's method of correlation provides a solution. This method is used both to explain the difference between God and world and to maintain a relationship between the two (e.g., in creation). As we will see below, the concept of correlation also serves as the key concept in Cohen's understanding of ethics.

Levinas's concerns, I will argue, are similar to those of Cohen in that both attempt to show that the ethical is grounded in, and already shared by, every human being. While Cohen expresses that through the concept of "holiness" ("*Heiligkeit*"), Levinas employs the concept of the one for the other ("*l'un pour l'autre*"). Ethics becomes an infinite movement towards God as the infinite goal, without, however, movement and telos ever becoming congruous (i.e. without ontologizing God). This means that, while God becomes the limit of an infinite movement, God is not part of that movement itself. In Cohen's words: "[The] unification ("*Vereiningung*") is in no way a connection ("*Verbindung*") of the kind objects may have."[12] This translates into Judaism as a clear statement in favor of monotheism and against pantheism.

I will examine these two philosophers through the following five questions: (1) Can it be claimed that both Cohen and Levinas have developed similar concepts emphasizing the unification ("*Vereinigung*") of God and Human being rather than the connection ("*Verbindung*")? (2) Is Levinas interested in the possibility of recognizing God? (3) Cohen asserts that the Holy Spirit as the Spirit of ethical action also becomes the means for the recognition of the Holy.[13] Can this perspective highlight Levinas's attempts to work out the non-difference between the Holy and the ethical? (4) Is it legitimate to identify Levinas's concept of the subject as openness (he uses the image of a lung to explain the character of this openness) with Cohen's concept of correlation? (5) What exactly is it that makes humans want their spirit to develop towards holiness?[14]

The position of Franz Rosenzweig, between Cohen and Levinas, is more difficult to explain. Rosenzweig's account of monotheism is ambiguous since his claim is, especially in part three of the *Stern*, that somehow human beings have a share in the absolutely divine. He thus compromises the absolute difference between God and world that both Cohen and Levinas want to affirm. Consequently, Rosenzweig's affirmation that ethics deals with an infinite development or task remains half-hearted. Although in Part I, Book I of the *Stern*, Rosenzweig posits a radical difference between the three ideal elements God, Man, and World, in Part III, Book III, he claims that human beings already participate in God's eternal realm through what he calls "my eternal portion" ("mein ewiger Anteil"). Here the questions to be addressed to Rosenzweig's thought are the following: (1) Is he able to uphold monotheism (i.e., the difference between God and the world; and, more specifically, is he able to maintain the difference between God and the Jews)? (2) Does he understand the relationship between the human being and God to be an infinite movement? (3) Does he fall into the trap of ontologizing God?

Hermann Cohen

The concept of creation in Cohen's *Religion of Reason* is probably the key to understanding his method of correlation. For Cohen, the problem of creation is that of the interface of being and becoming. His aim is to maintain God's uniqueness (i.e., God as being), and, at the same time, to assert God's presence in the world through creation (i.e., God as the cause of becoming).[15] How can being, which, by definition,[16] is unchangeable and eternal, cause becoming? Cohen has to show (1) that becoming is part of the concept of being and (2) that nevertheless being and becoming are not identical.

With respect to (1) Cohen establishes that one can understand the relationship between being and becoming through privative discourse about God which is superior to simple negative statements. With respect to (2) he shows the separateness of being and becoming by referring to one of God's attributes, viz. infinity, which itself is a privation. Negating this attribute, non-infinity, produces the finite (i.e. the objects of the world) as separate from God. Thus, it is the negation of privative statements about God that make possible an assessment of God's relation with the world and explain the logical mechanics of creation.

Relation with God as "Unendliche Aufgabe"

For example, in his *Religion*, Cohen says the following:

> Und dieser Hinblick auf Gott kann nichts anderes zu bedeuten haben als den Hinblick auf die zwar unendliche, nichtsdestoweniger aber sich verwirklichende Lösung der unendlichen Aufgabe. Die Lösung ist unendlich, denn sie ist nur ein Moment in der unendlichen Aufgabe; sie bedeutet aber, als dieses Moment, wiederum das unendliche Gelingen, den unendlichen Erfolg. Gott kann keine Aufgabe stellen, die nur eine Sisyphusarbeit wäre. Die Selbstheiligung muß zu dem unendlichen Abschluß kommen in der **Vergebung** der Sünde durch Gott.

> This looking toward God can mean nothing other than looking towards the solution of the infinite task, a solution which, though it is infinite, nonetheless actualizes itself. The solution is infinite, for it is only a moment in the infinite task; but the solution at this moment signifies infinite success, the infinite result. God can assign no task that would be a labor of Sisyphus. Self-sanctification must arrive at its infinite conclusion in the *forgiveness* of sin by God.[17]

The term "unendlich" ("infinite")[18] here designates two different things. One is an aim, a point of resolution (*"Lösung"*) of the process, and the other is a task (*"Aufgabe"*) or process itself. The concept of "Unendlichkeit" is central to Cohen's understanding of the relationship between humans and God. Whereas he uses it to describe God much like Parmenides described being,[19] Cohen also employs it to clarify the *relationship* between the finite and the infinite (i.e. the human and the divine realms). This relationship is an infinite approaching. Cohen thinks that the main function of holiness is the development (*"Entwicklung"*) of the spirit of knowledge into the spirit of the will and action.[20] This development is infinite. It is a potential infinity in the Kantian sense. This means that the goal of the progression (viz. a *completed* spirit of action) will not be reached. Such completion would necessarily paralyze this spirit. Instead, Cohen believes that the state of nonfulfillment has to be maintained to assure the continual human striving for an ethical community. Though it will never reach its goal fully, the question itself — of how this relationship can take place — will be resolved in this process. Cohen's insight is that the infinity (*"Unendlichkeit"*), as the correlative nexus between God and humans preserves an element of flux which is crucial to ethics. Ethics is only understood appropriately as an *"unendliche Aufgabe"*[21] directed towards the infinite itself — God. To try to conceive of this *"Aufgabe"* as possibly coming to an end, (viz. that the finite and the infinite have become one and that humans and God are finally united) would be an impossible, and doubly heretical, thought. It is doubly heretical because it either assumes that humans have made themselves infinite, and now are like God, or have gathered God into the realm of the finite. Both options are equally absurd for Cohen.

Negation and Privation: God as the Origin of All Activity

Cohen's choice of the term *"unendlich"* is motivated by a certain logical property which distinguishes this term from the formulations "not limited" or "not finite." This distinction is that between a privative and a negative judgment. Negative judgments are statements which imply positive ones. However, privative judgments, as we will see below, maintain a level of relative negation which, upon further negation, turns positive. Cohen uses the term "inactive" (*"träge"*) as an example of an original privation which, upon negation, turns into a positive statement. God is non-inactive. The difference between negating a negation and negating a privation is that the former is the negation of a finite judgment, the latter however negates an infinite judgment. Had we negated the sentence "God is passive" the negation "God is not passive" would have implied nothing but the fact of God's activity. In negating the privation (i.e., an infinite judgment) however, the resulting sentence, "God is not inert," reveals God as the origin of all activity. It can thus be deduced that the resulting positivity must be rooted in the concept of God. *"Gott ist der Ursprung der Aktivität"*[22] ("God is the origin of activity"). In this way Cohen shows, solely through logical deductions, the unity of being and becoming.

Whereas a negation always takes the form of a finite judgment, a privation always takes that of an infinite judgment. For Cohen the concept of infinity is nothing but a logical terminus. It functions in his philosophy as an index for a certain kind of negativity that is different from a traditional negation which is derived from its opposite — the affirmation (*"Position"*). Infinity is what distinguishes a privation from a common negation. A privation by itself, however, remains, qua infinite fullness, an empty concept.[23] With the exception of the one thing it does not designate, it designates everything and, hence, is not useful as an attribute of God as well. Only negated privations can describe the nature of God adequately. A negative theology, one that attempts to talk about God by saying what God is not, would always implicate the prior use of an affirmation of God, the negation's opposite, which is logically impossible. Another example might further clarify this. To say that an object is non-red is different from qualifying it as not red. The former leaves open an infinity of other color possibilities. The latter does not leave open those possibilities, but instead creates an opposition which eventually erases the original quality in question, redness, hinting instead towards another color that can be attributed to the object . Hence, to say that something is infinite rather than not finite leaves open the possibility of an infinity of finite things along with the infinite object. God's infinity, in other words, implies a realm of finite things which is itself infinite. It is the implication of finiteness given through the concept of God as infinite which enables Cohen to understand the act of creation as an infinite act located in the concept of God without drawing God into the realm of the finite. The negation of God's infinity renders visible the infinite world of finite things. This world remains absolutely separated from the infinite; yet its creation comes from within the infinite itself. Hence, the infinity of the realm of the finite serves as the explanatory background for the infinity of the ethical task, a task that aims at God but never reaches its end. Since finite things proliferate from God infinitely, the ethical task, the spirit of action which is located in this finite realm, will never come to a rest.

To be sure, Cohen is not claiming that the infinite can actually be thought or conceived. He is however saying that, formulated as a privative concept, in-finity — that which lacks finitude — can be derived logically *within* the framework of human reason. In addition to this improvement of how to understand God, the concept of infinity leaves open the possibility of a finite realm which a negative judgment would have obliterated. Infinity is nowhere to be found *in* the realm of the finite. It is not immanent to this realm but absolutely exterior to it. The non-finite or infinite is, in Cohen's words, a relative nothing.[24] It is the result of a thought process which tries to understand the origin of the somethings which surround us, i.e., the origin of existence. Since existence cannot be explained from existence, but also not as derived from an absolute nothing, Cohen posits this relative or privative nothing as a gateway through which thinking has to pass in order to make sense of existence. In this constellation, he asserts, the unity of nothing (infinite non-something) with being is obvious and necessary. Being could not be explained without this peculiar nothing.[25] Yet this nothing is not a concept correlative to being, but a conceptual "swingboard" ("*Schwungbrett*")[26] to aide one in understanding the genesis of being.

Anti-Materialism: The Holy Spirit and the Correlative Relation

At first sight it seems that Cohen has succeeded in showing how thinking can cope with the question of God. Without compromising God's uniqueness he can show that thinking can arrive at an understanding of God that does not only explain God but, in addition, sheds light on the relationship between God and world. By taking advantage of the quality of God's infinity, Cohen avoids the dilemma of either having to make a positive statement about God (which would automatically come down to

always saying nothing but what God is not) or of resigning to a
type of negative theology which, masked as ignorance of God,
would logically always presupposes the positive (i.e., knowledge
of God). Yet, privative judgments, and a forteriori the concept of
infinity, allow a discourse about God that does not objectify God.
It is only in and for thinking that a relative nothing like infinity
can serve as an adequate description of God. God's uniqueness,
viewed from this perspective, has not been disrupted; it is only
on an intellectual perspective through which one has come to
understand God. Still, God has the same absolute distance from
the world as before.

Nevertheless, it is difficult to understand why *thinking* should
provide us with an understanding of a God that can be separated from the rest of reality. Even to think about God seems
like an act that is bound to dissolve the absolute difference en-
tailed by God's uniqueness. Thinking cannot be separated from
the world, the sphere of somethings. Thinking itself, in a
Berkeleyan sense, is the production of somethings. Hence, thinking God implicitly suggests that God can be turned into a something. This would not be a problem as long as one maintains
that that exactly is the reason why it is impossible to conceptualize God. It does, however, become problematic, if one attempts
to retain the possibility of understanding God by positing thinking as a sphere that admits no logical contradictions. In other
words, given the premise of God's uniqueness in the radicality
Cohen suggests, thinking God compromises God's uniqueness/
otherness.

Cohen thought that this problem could be avoided by rigorously defining the purely conceptual, abstract character of the
relationship between humans and God. The term "correlation"
expresses this connection.

> Die Vermittlung [zwischen Gott und Menschen] darf aber nur
> begrifflich als Korrelation gedacht werden. Sobald sie nicht in
> der Strenge der begrifflichen Abstraktion gehalten, sobald sie als
> eine gleichsam materielle Verbindung von Kräften, die alsdann
> zu Personen werden, vorgestellt wird, nimmt die Verbindung den
> Charakter einer Gemeinschaft an.

The mediation [between God and humans], however, can be thought of as correlation only conceptually. As soon as it is not confined to a strict conceptual abstraction, as soon as it is imagined as a material connection of powers, which afterwards become persons, the connection assumes the form of a community.[27]

In other words, the notion of a conceptual understanding of God functions for Cohen based on the radical rejection of any material elements in this connection. In separating the realm of concepts from the realm of matter Cohen therefore reveals *his* Cartesianism. That is to say that everything that assumes the notion of a material communion between God and humans must be ruled out rigorously. Instead, Cohen defines the conceptual relationship between God and humanity as spiritual.

The Holy Spirit is a conceptual abstraction constituted by the correlative equation of divine and human participation. The Holy Spirit is not a separate entity that mediates the two. It is the relational stratum within which both God and humans are dedicated to holiness. Within this stratum holiness (i.e. ethical action) can become their task. Yet both sides remain absolutely separate in it. The Holy Spirit is an attribute of the relation which only develops in the correlation of God and humans.[28]

Based on his reading of the Talmud,[29] Cohen interprets the Holy Spirit to be what is affected by virtue. Moral activity leads up to the Holy Spirit as a human characteristic.[30] Thus, for Cohen, the recognition of the moral and the recognition of God are indifferent to each other. The correlative relation between God and humans consists in the human desire to recognize God, a desire which can only be fulfilled by way of moral activity. For Cohen ethics serves as the correlative element between the finite and the infinite. In this context however, ethics becomes that same "unendliche Aufgabe" mentioned above. It cannot function as a means to establish an *identity* between God and humans. However, in the process of this "unendliche Aufgabe," the Holy Spirit becomes an attribute of those humans who engage in moral action; who strive towards the ideal holiness which God represents by God. It does not engender that type of action.

Correlative Relation and Moral Action

This last claim has absolute import in Cohen's philosophy. If the Holy Spirit were something that incites moral action, then (1) a third element would have come into existence, between God and humans, which from a Jewish perspective would be absurd; and (2) the absolute difference between God and humans would collapse, since in that case a connection between the infinite and the finite sphere would be established. The Holy Spirit is nothing that could have existence independent of God and humans. It can develop only between them as a spirit of mutual holiness that arises from human moral action.

What, however, is it that triggers the move to moral action within humans and the human community? So far, Cohen's attempt to show how the Holy Spirit correlates but does not unite the two elements has been successful. However, it seems as if there needs to be a connection prior to that of the gradually established correlative link. This connection would first determine both the aim and direction of human activity. Why do human beings follow the call to holiness? How can they hear this call? Something must be there already which makes them receptive for that kind of call. Cohen's writing remains utterly obscure when it comes to answering these questions. Monotheism, he claims, is inhabited by a "obscure drive" ("*dunkler Drang*") to follow the "trace of ethics" ("*Spur der Ethik*"). Prior to any moral activity, and the subsequent development of a Holy Spirit, there is a trace of ethics (an image of holiness) which monotheism is driven to follow. Hidden in this move of "self-sanctification" ("*Selbstheiligung*") lies the path to the individual. As Holy Spirit one becomes an individual.[31]

Cohen's vagueness about this problem of the origin of ethical action is a function of the complexities that result from the connection between an exterior (divine sphere) and an interior (worldly sphere). He himself made God's uniqueness, which, as I have said, designates not only God's oneness but also God's separateness from the world, one of the prime issues of his book. And yet, in this passage he is forced to give in to the power and logic of the origin. He is forced to respond to the question, Whence did this come? Somehow, through monotheism, the individual is endowed with an image of ethics. It is really just a trace, and the drive to follow it is dark and hard to discover. Cohen himself affirms that the human striving for ethics is modeled on the telos of God's "Heiligkeit" which entails that, prior to moral action, God somehow entered the sphere of the finite in order to give humans the "trace" they need to follow. Yet, despite this entry into the finite, ethics without that infinite space between human beings and God would be an oxymoron. Had God entered the finite and now inhabited it in a pantheistic sense, viz. as part of everything, then ethics (i.e. voluntary obedience to the demand of sanctification) could never take place. In a world where one is forced to concede epistemologically that "*Deus sive Natura*"[32] the idea of ethical freedom becomes absurd.

It will be worth while keeping in mind the different perspectives which this passage from the chapter on the Holy Spirit provides. Cohen's conception of ethics is close to that of Levinas. Their conceptions of God, the infinite, the trace, the individual and the drive towards ethics resemble each other. Levinas's infinite — the infinite in the finite — has the resonance of Cohen's obscure drive that inhabits monotheism. Levinasian expressions like "being drawn to," "accused by," "held hostage by," "being obsessed by" and other metaphors that express an imperative responsibility for an other (sensed prior to all consciousness) could very well be interpreted as that strange drive about which Cohen speaks. And, as we will see in the next chapter, Cohen's interpretation also coincides with Levinas on the question of the individual. The individual, the subject, is an effect of ethical responsibility. It is only after I have been identified as the one responsible that I — as the individual — am free to decide whether to follow the call or not.

Franz Rosenzweig

In contrast to Cohen, Franz Rosenzweig's treatment of sanctification ("*Heiligung*") focuses less on the ethical aspect which we

could observe in Cohen as it does on epistemological considerations, viz. the question of truth (*"Wahrheit"*). This aspect of
Rosenzweig's thought is a direct outcome of his opposition to
the systematic approach to truth of Hegel's philosophy. Rosenzweig claims that truth could not be captured as a system. He
has the initial insight that the search for truth, and the system
on which such search is predicated, run contrary to a concern
for ethics. However, in rejecting Hegel, Rosenzweig develops his
own system, again in search of truth.

Sanctification

Sanctification is the process that drives everything that is not
yet sacred (*"heilig"*) towards sanctity (*"Heiligkeit"*). The terminus of this process is absolute truth. What this means is that
truth, absolute truth, can only appear where the possibility of
representation, one for the other, has ceased. Representation
would already signify an internal fissure of the world, between
its objects and truth itself, between signifier and signified, and
thus open up the possibility of non-truth.

> Wo dem einen Namen keine anderen Namen mehr sich entge-
> genwerfen, wo der eine Name all-ein ist und alles geschaffene
> ihn und nur ihn kennt und bekennt, da ist die Tat der Heiligung
> zur Ruhe gekommen. Denn Heiliges gilt nur solange es noch
> Unheiliges gibt. Wo alles heilig ist, da ist Heiliges selbst nicht
> mehr heilig, da ist es einfach da. Solch einfaches Dasein des
> Höchsten, solch ungekränkte allherrschende und alleinherr-
> schende Wirklichkeit jenseits aller Not und Wonne der Ver-
> wirklichung, das ist die Wahrheit. Denn Wahrheit wird nicht,
> wie die Meister der Schule meinen, am Irrtum erkannt; Wahrheit
> bezeugt sich selber, sie ist eins mit allem Wirklichen, sie scheidet
> nicht in ihm.

> There where no other names any longer confront the one name,
> where the one name is al(l)-one and all that is created knows and
> acknowledges him and him alone, there the act of sanctification
> has come to rest. For sanctity is meaningful only where there is
> still profanity. Where everything is sacred, there the Holy itself
> is no longer sacred, there it is simply there. This simple exist-
> ence of the highest, such unimpaired reality, omnipotent and

solely potent, beyond any need for or joy in realization, this is truth. For truth is not to be recognized through error, as the masters of the school think. Truth attests itself; it is one with everything real; it does not part in it.[33]

It is interesting to observe how in this passage Rosenzweig has already moved away from the thought of Cohen. While the latter emphasized infinite movement as the vehicle for ethics (*"unendliche Aufgabe"*), the former conceives of the possibility of an absolute rest, a standstill of this movement where the *"Aufgabe"* will have been achieved. In spite of this change, one might still want to read Rosenzweig's concept of rest as one of the Cohenian limits which the infinite task is approaching but never reaches. In this case, the passage preserves a strong messianic tone without collapsing the difference between God and humans.

The telos of sanctification, as Rosenzweig himself makes clear in this passage, is truth. The condition of complete and total sanctification is necessarily self-effacing, because of its lack of anything non-holy. The Sacred can no longer be identified as such because it has become an all-encompassing reality. All is sacred, hence nothing is sacred. In Rosenzweig's language this state is called a *"Wirklichkeit jenseits aller Not und Wonne der Verwirklichung"* ("reality... beyond all need and joy of realization"). Sanctity has become a fully real (*"wirklich"*) reality (*"Wirklichkeit"*), and, consequently, is no longer in need of sanctification as a means to accomplish reality. Sanctification belongs to the old order where truth and reality were still separate from each other. It has now become obsolete and unnecessary. Hence, reality in this sense has moved beyond the necessity of the sanctifying act or deed. There simply does not remain a gap between is and ought, and this condition only can be called truth. Truth is what is indivisible, not what is different from error. *"Wahrheit und Wirklichkeit"* (truth and reality) are one and the same. For Rosenzweig, oneness must be the end-point of the movement, since it repeats congruously the absolute oneness of God. God's own command, that he is one, becomes the guiding limit for a reality which approaches truth asymptotically. Once reality can be called one from the standpoint of truth the goal is achieved.

The Dual Understanding of Truth

One can sense in the above passage a desire on Rosenzweig's part to come to terms with the problem of Kantian dualism. The term *"Wirklichkeit"* designates for Rosenzweig the ideal limit of cognition towards which the world moves. He thus insists on the difference between the object as we can know it and the noumenal quality of *"Wirklichkeit,"* the is and the ought, the concept and the thing in-itself, which sets in motion a process towards its own erasure. It is this difference which in the face of God's oneness turns into what has to be overcome. Reality can only be called true once this difference is erased. Truth is not the condition of an epistemologically clever dualism; truth is absolute monism. However, this is dangerously close to pantheism which Rosenzweig, as much as Cohen, wants to avoid. Truth, as far as it is the predicate of God, although one with reality, remains above reality. To say God is truth does not mean that God and truth are the same. Rather, God is more than truth.[34] Truth and reality do indeed continue in this last phase where the Sacred becomes unidentifiable. Yet God always remains more; truth is only one of God's predicates.

In Cohen the term *"Heiligung"* was understood to express the infinite process/task towards the infinite goal. Rosenzweig seems to offer a similar option. Yet, there are some important differences worth mentioning. First, Rosenzweig invokes an ultimate oneness that in the end is the mark of the reality that has come to coincide with truth. Second, Rosenzweig's explanation of the human ability to conceive of the ultimate goal towards which sanctification should proceed differs from Cohen's explanation. Cohen, it might be remembered, took recourse to the traces of a dark drive which motivated humans to seek fulfillment of the ethical in order to reach the infinite goal. It was at this point that we started to question the radical distinction between God and humans which he established at the outset of his book. In contrast, Rosenzweig stipulates a difference between *"Leben"* (life) and *"Schauen"* (seeing, envisioning, gazing).[35] The latter is where truth can become a part of human knowing, not as experienced however, but merely as "geschaut" (envisioned). Let us look at the whole passage:

> Im Leben also bleibt der Mensch Mensch; und wenn er auch Gottes Stimme vernehmen, Gott erleben kann, so erlebt er deshalb mitnichten etwa auch das, was Gott erlebt. Im Schauen aber schaut er, eben weil er hier aus dem flüssigen Element des Erlebens ans Ufer tritt, unmittelbar was Gott erlebt. Er schaut es in Gott. Gott selbst erlebt es. Das ist ein großer Unterschied. Für ihn ist es immer nur Wahrheit. Aber für Gott ist es mehr als Wahrheit. Für Gott ist es Erlebnis.

> Thus, in life a human being remains a human being; and even if he can hear God's voice, even if he can experience God, he still doesn't experience what God himself experiences. In the process of envisioning, however, he envisions immediately what God experiences; precisely because he steps out of the liquid element of experiences onto the shore. He envisions it in God. But God himself experiences it. That is a big difference. For him it is always only truth. But for God it is more than truth. For God it is experience.[36]

For Rosenzweig, then, the difference between human truth and divine truth does not lie in the type of truth as it does in the way it is experienced. Whereas God can actually experience (*"erleben"*) truth, human beings have to exit the stream of fluid experience in order to be able to at least envision (*"schauen"*) truth from a solid standpoint. Yet, this envisioning is inferior to the way God knows truth because God can actually experience it. It is thus the suspension of *"Erleben"* that gives humans truth. Rosenzweig is aware of the agency which all human beings have in deciding if they want truth or not. Truth is appropriated by way of an existential acknowledgment of its existence for the here and now of my life. When I say "truly" (*"wahrlich"*) I am, through an affirmation of the truth of what is my part here and now, participating in the "'whole' truth" (*"'ganze' Wahrheit"*). That it is only a part and not the whole and complete truth as

God experiences it, is irrelevant for Rosenzweig since "truth must be verified (*"bewährt"*) . . . precisely in the manner in which it is generally denied, that is, by leaving aside the 'whole' truth and by yet recognizing the portion (*"Anteil"*) that one holds as the eternal truth."[37] It is through recognizing "my eternal portion" (*"mein ewiger Anteil"*) that I am confirmed as participating in and towards truth. It is thus in the rupture of "Schauen," not ethical action, that humans can become aware of their eternal portion of truth.

Provisional Summary of Cohen and Rosenzweig

It can be inferred from this general description of Rosenzweig's concept of truth in its relationship to God and humans that, like Cohen, Rosenzweig is aware of the problem of pantheism, and, consequently, eager to avoid a theology which claims the oneness and sameness of the world and God. One could even argue that hidden behind Rosenzweig's terminology of "whole truth" and the "my eternal portion" lies the same distinction between the finite and the infinite which Cohen sought to emphasize. God and world are radically distinct from each other. Yet, in this radical alienness one must be able to find a common ground which allows for revelation to find its way into the human community and for redemption to envision the direction into which it should proceed. Hence, here, as in Cohen's case, we find the paradox of human participation in something in which, by definition, humans cannot participate. Rosenzweig's concept of *"Mein ewiger Anteil"* should be anathema, since (1) the word *"ewig"* (eternal) explodes the notion of *"mein"* (mine), i.e., a personal and thus non-eternal notion. Furthermore, (2) if the eternal does indeed show up as *"Teil"* in what is not eternal, then the notion of God as the one and totally other becomes problematic. In addition to these problems, (3), Rosenzweig's notion of *"mein ewiger Anteil"* generates a rather static understanding of how truth can be envisioned (*"geschaut"*): an eternal portion is one which we have always had, and, in order to recognize it, we have to step out of the stream of experience. This is quite different from Cohen's *"unendliche Aufgabe."* As such it is detrimental to formulating a concept of *"Heiligung"* as a *process* within which ethics then would become the key catalyst for redemption.

Cohen's grasp of these problems seems much firmer and more decidedly on the side of ethics as well as on the side of God's uniqueness than Rosenzweig's. The notion of *"unendliche Aufgabe"* does two things at the same time: 1. It establishes a connection between the human and the divine realm, and as we have seen earlier, it even locates the existence of this divine realm within the human sphere. It is the trace of ethics which triggers what Cohen calls the *"unendliche Aufgabe."* 2. The connection through *"Heiligung"* remains task (*"Aufgabe"*) and cannot be claimed as an already appropriated *"ewiger Anteil"* that has always already constituted my life.

EMMANUEL LEVINAS

A century later, Levinas's is still struggling with the same question. The problem remains because Levinas accepts the following three claims implied by Rosenzweig and Cohen: If (1) we understand that monotheism means that there is an infinite space between God and human beings, and if (2) we understand that such a space is necessary for any genuine ethics, because it is the space of volition between the ethical agent and the ethical telos, if (3) we understand that ethics is inspired by and directed towards an infinite goal, viz. God, then the question which we had already asked about Cohen and Rosenzweig is implicitly repeated: From where do humans get their ethical motivation if not from their ethical telos? If, however, that telos is God, and thus an *infinite* goal, how can such an infinite goal show itself within the sphere of the finite, i.e., the world? Would that not put into question the monotheistic concept of God? Can we preserve the infinite despite cognition?

God and Philosophy

Levinas's answer to the last question is "yes." Although traditional philosophy has had a history of destroying transcendence[38] through ontologizing it, i.e., identifying thought with being, Levinas believes that *"Dieu ne peut être énoncé dans un discours raisonable qui ne serait ni ontologie, ni foi, . . ."* ("God can be expressed in a rational discourse which would be neither ontology nor faith").[39]

There are precisely two possible solutions to this problem. (1) One can opt to use the term "being" just with reference to God. Nothing else but God would have being. The world would be a place of lack and want and God would represent Parmenides' being. This is Cohen's conceptual choice. (2) One could also decide that God is something wholly otherwise than being. In that picture the whole world would belong to the order of being. Whatever we say, feel, observe, etc. would be vested with the essential, i.e., the copula "is;" God, here, must thus be absolutely different from being. The latter is Levinas's conceptual choice.

> Le rationalisme philosophique se refuse à accueillir la transcendance du Dieu d'Abraham, d'Isaac et de Jacob parmi les concepts dans lesquels il n'y aurait pas de pensée.
>
> The transcendence of the God of Abraham, Isaac, and Jacob [cannot be accepted] among the concepts without which there would be no thought.[40]

Traditional philosophy, Levinas charges, works in the following way: Only those concepts and ideas can be considered meaningful that are intelligible. However, the criterion of the intelligibility of a concept, whether it is real or not, is existence. In other words only those concepts that refer to something which exists are meaningful and a meaningful concept must be found within the framework of existence, i.e., the framework of being. This identification of meaning and existence is problematic for Levinas and, as we will see, also for Jewish thought in general, because it implies that the concept of God can only be meaningful if God partakes in being, like all the other things which we consider meaningful. That however would dissolve the difference between God and humans, and would lead to either a pantheistic universe or — which amounts to the same — an absolute monism of God alone. In either case the infinite space for ethics would be lost. Only this space, however, can grant sanctification as an ethical mode, chosen voluntarily.

The Infinite as Privation of the Finite

It is the existence of such an infinite space for ethics whose existence Levinas would like to assert when he says that human beings are endowed with a desire for the Good. And it is precisely the idea of the infinite which allows us to recognize such a desire *without*[41] ontologizing it. Infinity is not just a negation of the finite. It is not simply the completely other to our everyday human experience of finiteness. It can not be just that, because, as such, it could not be recognized. In such a constellation even a positing of an infinite through negation of the finite is logically and semantically false. The infinite would at once become just another part of the finite and lose its salient characteristics of infinity. In other words, an infinite, completely other to the finite, cannot be conceived unless one is ready to make major logical sacrifices.[42] Levinas, thus, has to ask how is it that we can play with the idea of the infinite at all?[43] How can it be — or become — part of our thinking and not be reduced to the finite? How can it enter a realm of sameness (i.e., a realm where everything is seen through the same mediating consciousness) without becoming part of that sameness? In Levinas's terminology: How can the infinite be kept dis-interested, i.e., outside the realm of being, uninvested in being?

> [Il est] comme si la négation incluse dans l'Infini à l'égard du fini, ne signifiait pas une négation quelconque ressortissant du formalisme du jugement négative, mais précisément *l'idée de l'Infini*, c'est-à-dire l'Infini en moi . . . comme si . . . le in de l'Infini signifiait à la fois le *non* et le *dans*.
>
> . . . it is as though the negation of the finite included in Infinity did not signify any sort of negation resulting from the formal

> structure of negative judgment, but rather signified the *idea of
> the Infinite*, that is, the Infinite in me . . . it is . . . as though the
> *in* of the Infinite were to signify both the *non* and the *within*.[44]

Although Levinas does not employ Cohen's terminology he is
getting at something very similar to the latter's negation/priva-
tion distinction. The *in*, Levinas asserts, does not erase the finite; it does not function like a *not* but instead points to that
which is non-finite. The infinite leaves the finite intact. From
within the finite comes recognition of its own privative difference. It is the infinite which first makes possible thought and
the finite. Or better, it is the "non-comprehension"[45] of the infinite which puts thought in its place. Only in identifying what it
can no longer understand can thought become itself, i.e. finite.[46]
Yet there remains a space between the finite and the infinite
and, at this stage in the development of thought, a peculiar tension begins to rise between the finite and the infinite. The finite
is now reaching out for the transcendence of the infinite: It *desires* it.[47]

Desiring the Infinite

It is difficult to determine what really happens in this step towards the desiring of the infinite. And it is even more difficult to
understand how Levinas arrives at the conclusion that the finite
desires the infinite. A "before" to this phase of desire can obviously not be *thought*, and yet it has to be posited to understand
the fact of thought's desire for the infinite. Again, the questions
that would have to be asked here touch on those of the perfection or imperfection of the divine. Is it at all possible to equate
the divine and Levinas's infinite? Was there a divine desire which
made the infinite reach out for the yet inert finite in order to
blow the spirit of life into it? Do we have a reversal of tensions
and desires which now puts humans in the position of reaching
back towards the infinite — the divine? There still seems to be
an important difference. The unknown infinite divine was actually able to "get in touch" with inert thought. Thought, however, now that it is activated can only desire the infinite but not

reach it.[48] "This amounts to a cogitatio not comprehending the cogitatum that affects it utterly . . . the infinite signifies precisely prior to its manifestation."[49]

There is little room for Levinas to navigate. On the one hand, he does not want to fall back into claiming the existence of an absolute difference between God and humans, but, on the other hand, the difference should also not collapse into one. Infinity's most salient trait, transcendence, is unthinkable in relational terms which would limit its transcendence immediately. A relationship presupposes some kind of co-presence that would destroy infinity at once. What remains is desire. What remains is — in Greek (viz., Western philosophical) terms — the unfulfilled, the vacuum, the abyss, that, in other words, which calls for filling, fulfilling, bridging, etc. yet can never actually be satisfied in that desire. What remains in Jewish terms is something very similar to the concept of 'Ruach Ha Kodesh', the Holy Spirit. In fact, the more we realize the impossibility of the filling or bridging, the more intense the desire becomes. Levinas calls this factum the hollowing out by desire.

Desiring the Infinite as God

Based on Levinas's Cartesianism we understand that the idea of God is present to us by way of the infinite. Moreover, we desire this infinite, and we strive to coincide with it. Since our desire, then, is a desire for God, and since for Levinas God is good, our desire is a desire for the Good.

Levinas's concern now is with the epistemological fine line which he is trying to walk between a normal relationship which means co-presence (and thus indifference) and the absolute difference between desire and transcendence.[50] In order for desire not to end up as a simple, profane relationship, that which it is aiming for must be totally separate. Such a thing is designated in the holy. Yet, even the holy has something to which we humans want to be attached, something that is thus likely to be drawn into the realm of interest and self-sameness. Therefore, to enhance the separateness of his concept of the Holy, Levinas asserts that it becomes manifest in the least desirable thing of all: the other. Yet, only through an ordering from the desirable can my gaze be directed towards what is nondesirable. In other words: My concern for the other comes from something that is other than me, viz. the holy. The holy, as which Levinas showed it in his phenomenology of the infinite, makes itself felt as hollowness in thought, and thus can affect the change towards the other.

Desire for the good as desire for the other[51] prevents desire from narcissistically desiring itself — the Good — too much. Therefore it is forcefully reversed towards what it desires the least, viz. the other.[52] The Good thus becomes a third element which "compels me to goodness."[53] More than before, the remoteness of the Good in the third person expresses the unbridgeable void between it and the desire which desires it. Thus, Levinas can say: "To be good is a deficit, waste and foolishness in a being; it is excellence and elevation beyond being. Ethics is not a moment of being; it is otherwise and better than being, the very possibility of the beyond."[54] To be good means recognizing the existence of a lack or hollowness (the lack of desiring the other) within oneself. This lack is un-improvable.

CONCLUSION

All three philosophers have, as we have seen, let certain epistemological considerations precede their questions and assertions about ethics. Ethics, and a forteriori Jewish ethics, cannot be understood without such a preliminary analysis of the epistemological factors that determine the human condition. Since all three assert an ethics which is contingent upon a direction towards the holy, all three have to ask how, simultaneously, that holy something can be known. But knowledge, and here I think Levinas makes the strongest claim, cannot function as a means to know God. His concern is that, once we know God in a traditional sense, the difference between God and any other thing end God's holiness. Levinas, thus, avoids any Rosenzweigian notion of a coinciding with absolute holiness and absolute truth.

For both will render superfluous any ethical action. Rather than understanding human existence as already being endowed with that *"ewiger Anteil"* which, read in an ontological way, would suggest that holiness is achieved, Levinas, like Cohen, understands the holy as an asymptotic goal which is approached infinitely through ethical action. Moreover, if we came to know the holy as something in us, not much space would be available for a freedom that *chooses* holiness as its goal. In that case holiness would be already achieved. It would be an ontological datum of what it means to be human, and no one would have to strive towards it any longer.

Cohen and Rosenzweig (although less convincingly), as well as Levinas, agree that somehow the goal of holiness and sanctification must be available to human beings without running the risk of being understood as such an ontological datum. There is in all three thinkers an effort to describe a relationship between the divine and the human sphere which does not immediately consume the space between them. In that case human freedom would be preserved and not fall into an order of necessity.

Independence

However, I would like to suggest that the key-parallel between Cohen, Rosenzweig, and Levinas is their insistence on an *independence* between God and humans. The term "independence," explained in Cohenian terms, means that independence is the privative derivative of the term "dependence." Independence is not non-dependence. Dependence as a mode of relation between the two spheres is *not* erased by the term "independence." Instead the term goes beyond dependence and hence can express the dependence of the two spheres as well as the infinite realm beyond it that provides the type of freedom which is indispensable for any ethics. Here lies the answer to one of the questions I asked in the beginning. Levinas does indeed suggest that a recognition of the holy is synonymous with that of the ethical. However, the two realms are not collapsed into each other, but purposefully kept separate.

If it is true that independence is the correct way to describe the relational mode between divine and human sphere, then the next question will again be epistemological. How do we know this? Rosenzweig, as is already clear from the above examination, moves farthest away from the monotheism that attempts to save God's uniqueness. In his judgment, human beings have something holy already, viz. their eternal portion, that lets them recognize the divine sphere. The problem with his account is that it turns holiness into something that we already possess. That, however, makes ethics (as a means to attain such holiness) dispensable. Rosenzweig is ontologizing the relationship between the divine and the human sphere and ethics is on its way to being dismissed. His answer to the question, how do we know, is by exiting the stream of experience and envisioning (*"schauen"*) the ultimate goal.

While both Cohen and Levinas seem much more careful in their approach, they too indicate this same tendency. Cohen's solution to the epistemological question is that of the dark drive that urges us to follow the trace of ethics. This, in other words, is something that belongs to human beings in their constitutedness. Although with hesitation, Cohen is thinking ontologically as well. Levinas, on the other hand, reverses the order. Before we know the divine sphere, we come to know the other. Before any thinking about the relationship between humans and God comes the recognition of the face of the other. Ethics, at least initially, precedes the epistemological question. In retrospect, however, the same question also applies to him. Only this time it has to be asked in conjunction with facing the other: How do we know the other? How can I save the other from becoming me in the very act of knowing her/him?

Knowing the Other

I would like to say initially that Levinas does not really provide a solution to the problem. Knowing something, recognizing it, understanding it and the many other modes of relating to a something, all presuppose a knowing which — once we know it — again presupposes another knowing and so forth (Hegel's bad infinity). Levinas is quite aware of this and formulates "every thesis is convertible into a doxic thesis, a positing or recognition of entities, a welcoming of presence. Disclosure remains the event of spatiality and the mission of a subject."[55] What this means is that the origin of such knowledge will remain hidden. It cannot be disclosed. That is what Levinas means when he refers to an irretrievable or irrecuperable past. But Levinas's goal is not to show from where knowledge, especially knowledge of the other, originated. His concern is to show how in knowing the other, we are indeed engaged in a type of knowing that is different from any knowing conditioned by a hermeneutical circle. In knowing the other, Levinas claims, we encounter alterity. I will devote the last part of this chapter to illuminating more of what he means by that.

The source for understanding for what Levinas means by encountering the other is Cohen's concept of the Holy Spirit. Cohen's use of the term is twofold: (1) It is a stratum of correlation within which both God and humans work towards holiness. (2) It is a step, already an elevation to which human moral activity can lead. In the latter sense Cohen distinguishes between a normal spirit through which moral action is converted into the Holy Spirit. The two usages are not mutually exclusive. The spirit as the stratum between God and human beings is turned into Holy Spirit at the very moment that humans engage in moral action. What does this presence of spirit mean to which Cohen is referring? Why can spirit already be a stratum for both humans and God?

It seems to me that Levinas is indirectly answering these questions. Although his train of thought is motivated by a very different consideration. Is it possible, he asks, to go beyond essence and to leave the space that, as Kant explained, accompanies every representation? In the course of his argument Levinas discovers privative significations of space which, while signifying a non-space, also "signify the end or the hither side of the dark designs of inwardness."[56] He assumes that with the discovery of the privation of space he also discovered a realm which is not as spatially limited anymore as Kant suggested. He concludes that such a non-space can be called nothing but "freedom." Again, a privative derivative does not dissolve the relation between the privative expression and the term of which it is a privation. Between non-space and space remains a connection that Levinas chooses to represent by the metaphor of "breath." In the case of freedom, for example, Levinas stipulates, that it is this absolute freedom, given through non-space, that *animates* freedom in regular space.

In the Latin language the word "animus" means mind, spirit, soul, or just simply breath. The relation between space and non-space as animus, "spirit," is similara to Cohen's "stratum" relation. For Levinas *I* am exposed to the other in the same way *lungs* are exposed to breath.

> ... la respiration est transcendence en guise de dé-claustration; elle ne révèlle tout sens sans que dans la relation avec autrui, dans la proxinité du prochain, qui est reponsabilité pour lui, substitution à lui. Ce pneumatisme ne pas le ne-pas-etre, il est desintéressement: tiers exclu de l'essence, de l'etre et du ne-pas-etre.
>
> Breathing is transcendence in the form of opening up. It reveals all its meaning only in the relationship with the other, in the proximity with the neighbor, which is responsibility for him, substitution for him. This pneumatism is not non-being; it is disinterestedness, excluded middle of essence, besides being and non being.[57]

I think it is quite obvious how Levinas repeats Cohen's distinction between a uniting and a connecting by substituting the lung/breathing metaphor. We can see how carefully he constructs the analogy between this metaphor and the relationship to the other in order to avoid any real connection between the two sides. But aside from rendering thinkable the meaning of one's relationship with the other, one cannot avoid reading this also as a metaphor for the relationship with God. The taking in of the air of the other, in-spiration, is, simultaneously, metaphor for the only way the term "God inspired" can be understood *without* compromising monotheism. God inspired cannot mean that one is inspired *by* God. It rather has to be understood as an inspiration that, though coming from the *other*, once inhaled, signifies a moving closer to *God*, without ever being a reaching.

Recognizing God

We are now prepared to ask once more: Is Levinas interested in a recognition of (i.e., an epistemological access to) God? In other words, who is God in his philosophical discourse? Levinas's notion of God is marked by a peculiar inside-outside relationship. Although God is the uncontainable par excellence (i.e., outside the inside), God is, at the same time inside the inside. "The Idea of God is in me, but God already breaking up the consciousness which aims at ideas, and unlike any content."[58] Levinas quotes Descartes in his "Third Meditation" as saying "in some way I have in me the notion of the infinite earlier than the finite — to wit, the notion of God before that of myself."[59] Yet, at the same time he says that "the transcendence of God cannot be stated or conceived in terms of being, the element of philosophy, behind which philosophy sees only night."[60] In another context, Levinas brings up God by saying that "ethics is an optics of the divine. Henceforth, no relation with God is direct or immediate. The Divine can be only manifested through my neighbor."[61]

I think it is clear from these quotations that epistemological access to God is one of the pillars of Levinas's ethical theory. For both Levinas and Cohen, God serves as a limit for the movement of ethics. That in itself would be paradoxical, for who would want ethics to be limited? Yet, the peculiar necessity of this limit lies in its infinite inaccessibility. Ethics can never take in God, and God can never take in ethics. It would, hence, be wrong to apply teleological meaning to God. Ethics is based on a freedom that could not bear being drawn by a telos. Yet, that freedom is a difficult freedom. Difficult because it is juxtaposed between the realms of the human and the divine. No matter what one decides to do with that freedom both realms will be affected by it.

Perhaps it is misleading to talk about a recognition of God. Levinas repeatedly tries to emphasize the ineptness of cognition in this matter. Cognition has the disadvantage of an utter subjectness. It reinforces the monadic walls around the subject that do not allow for the possibility of receiving the other. Recognition carries with it a similar meaning that is reinforced by the fact that it indicates a repetition, as if this cognition had taken place once already. The German *"Erkennen,"* as well as the French *"reconnaissance,"* express much more accurately how to understand this relationship to God. Both languages distinguish between two different kinds of knowing. One would be expressed by the English word "to know" (in German *"wissen"* and in French *"savoir"*). Phrased in this way, knowing means sure knowledge, implying the clarity and transparency of the object. The other meaning of knowing, however, supplies a much more diffused concept of what it means to know something. Both *"kennen"* and *"connaître"* express a certain vagueness regarding the transparency of the object while at the same time expressing familiarity with it. The English word "recognition" would never be translated as *knowing* again, but always with that slightly more vague notion of *"erkennen"* or *"reconnaître."*

Yet, what weighs even more in this argument is the fact that the German word for "epistemology" is *"Erkenntnistheorie"* and the French is *"théorie de la connaissance."* Thus the question of Levinas's interest in a kind of epistemological access to God must be looked at from the stand point of precisely that vague, somewhat intangible, knowledge. God cannot be known, but God can be *"erkannt"* or *"connu."* In addition to these philological considerations, it might be helpful to recall that Cohen's project in *Religion* is precisely to show how "the spirituality of monotheism demands a share in reason (*"Vernunft"*), a share in knowledge (*"Erkenntnis"*), especially if monotheism is also to create ethics."[62] Cohen also recognizes that *"Erkenntnis"* is a gift from God.

The first of God's favors (*"Gnade Gottes"*) is the endowment of knowledge (*"Erkenntnis"*), and there can be no other kind of favor (*"Gnade"*) but that which is dependent on knowledge (*"Erkenntnis"*). Thus knowledge plainly becomes the fundamental condition (*"Grundbedingung"*) of religion, of reverence for God.[63]

Cohen thus repeats Descartes' move by assuming that knowledge is something that is put in us by an entity greater than ourselves.[64] Levinas utilizes this concept of an idea being put into us and — after first putting it in question — concludes that

La mise en nous d'une idée inenglobable, renverse cette présence à soi qu'est la conscience, forçant ainsi le barrage et le controle, déjouant l'obligation d'agréer ou d'adopter tout ce qui entre du dehors.

the putting into us of an unincludable idea overturns that presence to self which consciousness is, forcing its way through the barrier and checkpoint, eluding the obligation to accept or adopt all that enters from the outside.[65]

Like Cohen, Levinas asserts that the idea of God is put into us by God and serves as a condition without which ethics could not develop.

This notion of an idea being put into us is not only reminiscent of Descartes but also carries with it the signs that usually adhere to the calling of a prophet. In the next chapter I will attempt to show how prophetic calling is a relevant concept for Levinas. By illuminating the connection between his philosophy and his frequent mentioning of the prophet Ezekiel we will see that Ezekiel is a good example for someone obsessed with the responsibility for the other. Ezekiel thus stands paradigmatically for the subject in its relation to the other. Ezekiel is the subject that struggles with God, the Other, over the task of becoming a prophet. As subject he attempts to resist and God who indeed appears helpless over against Ezekiel's will-power. But the idea of the infinite (i.e., not the idea of God but that of the neighbor), literally put into Ezekiel, eventually forces Ezekiel to subject and to commit himself to prophecy.

THREE

Agency

Ezekiel: Fragmented Subjectivity

In summing up the results of the preceding chapter we come to see the following: In Levinas's thinking divine fragmentation of the finite subject — first visible as my desire for the holy — translates into an altruistic fragmentation, a being hollowed out, of the finite subject — visible as my desire for the other to command me as neighbor. The finite and infinite are woven in with each other, and form a unique structure of agency and obedience vis-à-vis the other. Recognizing God not just as an external force, but as the infinite in ourselves, results in obeying God's command to love our neighbor. Only a radical monotheism that emphasizes both God's absolute difference as well as the apodeictic nature of God's commandment can have this effect of agency and obedience. Hence theology always translates into ethics. In this chapter we will look at the case of the prophet Ezekiel in order to better refine this agency/obedience structure. The study of Ezekiel will show that Levinas's ethics, despite his rather openminded approach to the interpretation of the Bible, is predicated on a notion of absolute power that rests with God. It will further show, however, that God's power only reaches as far as the actual commandment goes. Everything beyond that is up to the agency of the individual.

THE LANGUAGE OF CONSTITUTION

Although the question of the human constitution will concern us increasingly in this and the following chapters, it is with much caution that we have to approach it. The language of constitution is almost inevitably ontological. And it is precisely that kind of language which Levinas seeks to transcend in favor of a language that, although descriptive, continually delineates the ontological realm *without* becoming dependent on that realm. To be sure, Levinas's project is not to abandon ontological discourse altogether. The language of being, i.e., the language of the said, has its function as a stabilizing factor in the world. Yet, as such a stabilizing factor it also already entails its own problematic. If being really encompasses everything, then, once stabilized, the world becomes a nonmoving entity in which change is impossible. Given the fact that change does indeed occur, one could critique this view as simply false. But that alone is insufficient for an understanding of Levinas's project. Beyond the mere ontological weaknesses that such a theory of an all-encompassing being might have, Levinas seeks to show its extreme untenability from the ethical viewpoint. In other words, merely critiquing Descartes, Kant, Hegel, and Heidegger for their failure to describe the difference between being and becoming is an enterprise that remains fundamentally tied to the quest for a plausible ontological theory. Levinas's point is that a theory of being is not just philosophically unsound, it is ethically unjustifiable. The epistemological corollaries of ontology (its boundedness to a theory of the subject and its consequent inability to even begin to understand alterity) require a theory of being otherwise; it requires something that stands outside of the realm of being, that can penetrate and disrupt it, and thereby preclude the total solidity of being. With that in mind, we can say that Levinas is not trying to convince us that there are no grounds for ethics. Rather, his goal is to show that, in ethics, grounds, because of their logocentric nature, are counterproductive and apt to make us forget the other rather than letting her talk to us. We have to see how exactly Levinas enables us to embark on that kind of an ethical discourse.

The logic of the finite and the infinite developed in the previous chapter raises fundamental questions about the status of agency, when it is applied to a theory of human beings. It also puts into question the possibility and significance of divine agency. Do the concepts of the finite and the infinite impede each other, or are they mutually enabling? How dependent or independent on each other are these two aspects? Can the finite resist the infinite and refuse its command? Can the infinite refuse the finite? Can I deny my altruistic fragmentation, i.e., my ethical nature? How far can that denial be carried? For Levinas, the answer to these questions is hardly in doubt. Agency in the sense of a subject acting on an object is problematic, if one is to take seriously the kind of altruistic fragmentation of the self that I described above. "We can never be clear of our debts to the other. It is an infinite responsibility, a responsibility which does not suit my wishes: the responsibility of a hostage."[1] What could the responsibility of a hostage possibly be? I would like to give a preliminary explanation by means of a temporal sequence, even though Levinas has his own reservations about the doings of time.

Submission and Proximity

Our fundamental state-of-"being" is that of a hostage. Prior to everything else we are captured and forced into the kind of passivity that only the concept of the hostage can express. Yet, at this point we have not yet started to be human, i.e. responsible subjects. That can only happen through a second step in which we either accept or reject the responsibility that we are endowed with. Thus, initially (and here I mean "primordially"), agency, in Levinas's account of ethics, turns into a paradox. The meaning of our ethical nature can only be explained through images of absolute passivity. Only when tied down and held captive, when, in other words, the flux of power between me and the other is absolutely nonreciprocal (i.e., when the other has only

power over me, but I do not have power over the other) is the
ethical situation established. If I as subject acted vis-a-vis the
other, I would, by the simple fact of this action, already have
obstructed that nonreciprocal nature.

In putting it this way, however, Levinas goes far beyond a
state of "altruistic fragmentation" or of "being hollowed out by a
desire for the Good."[2] Both images retain an ever so vague notion of subjectivity. Yet, the more we move into an understanding of ethics as nonreciprocal, the more we lose the subject which,
along with its agency, turns into a zero-point (i.e., a nothing).
From Levinas's point of view, this move is necessary, since any
notion of agency over against the other would invoke a dialectic
relationship similar to Hegel's master/slave dialectic. Although
he takes up the point of absolute submission in that dialectic
and transforms it into the anarchical and relentless inauguration of an ethics of responsibility for the other, Levinas asserts
that this relationship through responsibility is precisely nonreciprocal rather than dialectical (like it is in Hegel). It is the
legacy of Hegel that, in Levinas's view, has distorted the concept of a relationship with the other into a struggle for mutual
recognition. For Hegel the goal of such a struggle is a self-consciousness which can only be attained through a struggle with
another consciousness.[3]

For Levinas, ethics originates in the eternally perpetuated
moment of my submission to the other. This moment leaves me
vulnerable, exposed, naked and torn up: It signifies as "l'un-
pénétré-par-l'autre" ("one-penetrated-by-the-other").[4] The effects
of such a one-sided, nonreciprocal relationship are devastating
for Hegel, but also for the modern understanding of subjectivity. First of all, there is no return to the ego, i.e. , to the subject
as the locus and center of knowledge and, therefore, of power.
Our ethical agency is manifested negatively as powerlessness.
Second, not only is there no return to the subject, but there
really is no subject at all. The beginning is sheer ". . . susception.
Passivité antérieure à toute receptivité. Transcendante" (". . .
susceptiveness. It is a passivity prior to all receptivity [since

even receptivity maintains an ever so slight notion of subjectiv-
ity], it is transcendence").[5] Third, ethics can no longer be approached from the angle of What-we-think-is-good-for-you, but,
instead, becomes a matter of what the other commands me to
do. The subject has to await with open ears what the other thinks
is good for her. Fourth, ethics becomes dependent on a moment
of sensibility, rather than cognition, and thus reveals as expedi-
ent Kant's notion of a (subjective) good will, as well as Husserl's
attempt to explain how we understand the world by laying open
the structures of consciousness:

> La sensibilité est exposition à l'autre . . . mais l'en deça du libre
> et du non-libre qu'est l'anarchie du Bien . . . En deçè du point
> zéro qui marque l'absence de protection et de couverture, la
> sensibilité est affection par le non-phénomène, une mise en cause
> par l'altérité de l'autre, avant l'intervention de la cause, avant
> l'apparoir de l'autre;

> Sensibility is exposedness to the other . . . It is the hither side of
> the free and the non-free, the anarchy of the Good . . . On the
> hither side of the zero point which marks the absence of protec-
> tion and cover, sensibility is being affected by a non-phenom-
> enon, a being put in question by the alterity of the other, before
> the intervention of a cause, before the appearing of the other.[6]

Levinas is saying, that, if such a nonreciprocal relationship
can really take place, then, at least momentarily, we will contact the other in her direct material givenness[7] rather than
through the veil of cognition. Levinas is claiming nothing less
than that the ethical encounter will lift the spell of a world that
only reveals signifiers and never signifieds. When the other commands me, nothing remains between her and me. I in turn become her signifier, one for the other.

In the previous chapter we encountered the good as the goal
of our desire for the infinite. Now the language of desire has
been replaced by that of submission. The good speaks to us
through the alterity of the other. In doing so it radically

> Elle dépouille le Moi de sa superbe et de son impérialisme
> dominateur de moi. Le sujet est l'accusatif sans trouver recours

> dans l'être, expulsé de l'être, hors de l'être, . . . sans fonde-
> ment, . . . réduit à soi, . . . sans condition.

> strips the ego of its pride and the dominating imperialism char-
> acteristic of it. The subject is the accusative, without recourse in
> being, expelled from being, outside of being, without a founda-
> tion, reduced to itself, and thus without condition.[8]

Levinas is making room for the possibility of a subject dia-
chronically juxtaposed between self and other in such a way
that the self becomes a null-site or nothing whose existence can
only be inferred through an understanding of the other as the
non-self, i.e. the privation of self.[9] Levinas calls this relationship "proximity," which is the result of his working through
Husserl's concept of intentionality. Whereas intentionality expresses the cognitive vicinity of the subject to an object through
a process of thematizing (knowing something as something),
proximity[10] precisely names the closeness of a powerless "subject" to a commanding other.

> Il ne suffit donc pas de dire la proximité comme rapport entre
> deux termes et, comme assuré, en tant que rapport, de la simul-
> taneité de ces termes. Il faut insister sur la rupture de cette
> synchronie, de cet ensemble — par la différence du Meme et de
> l'Autre dans la non-indifférence de l'obsession excercée par l'Autre
> sur le Meme.

> It is then not enough to speak of proximity as a relationship be-
> tween two terms, and as a relationship assured by the simulta-
> neity of these terms. It is necessary to emphasize the break-up of
> this synchrony, of this whole, by the difference between the same
> and the other in the non-indifference of the obsession exercised
> by the other over the same.[11]

It is impossible for us to escape the command of the good which
Levinas later equates with God. We *are* obsessed by it.[12]

THE PROPHET EZEKIEL IN THE WRITINGS OF LEVINAS

Contrary to the textual evidence I have provided so far to suggest that Levinas is indeed going in the direction of a zero-point

nonreciprocal ethics, I would like to show how, nevertheless, Levinas establishes a kind of human agency that deals directly with the relationship between God and humans. This human agency is counterposed to the images of fragmentation and hollowing out (all involve a dialectic relationship) that pervade his writing and thus furnish the backdrop for a social world upon which a nonreciprocal ethics first becomes possible. My point of entry for this enterprise is the prophet Ezekiel.

The Explicit Use of Ezekiel in Levinas

Levinas gives us scattered evidence that he is aware of this biblical figure and his relevance for his own project. In the essay "Revelation in the Jewish Tradition," he uses the pericope in chapter three of the book Ezekiel, where the prophet is forced by God to eat the scroll, to explain the almost physical relationship between the people of Israel and their Book.[13] Similarly, in the essay "God and Philosophy" Levinas describes the experience of the infinite being put in one as an experience of being "dumbfounded," and thus unable to speak about it.[14] Clearly, we have here a reference to the events in Ez. 3:26–27. Two more references can be found at the outset of his book *Autrement qu'etre ou au-dela de l'essence* where he introduces the text by quoting Ez. 3:20, 9:4–6, a commentary on Ezekiel by Rashi and two quotes from Pascal's *Pensées*.[15] In general, however, it must be admitted that Levinas himself, despite his mentioning of Ezekiel, never gives a full explanation of the prophet's significance for his philosophy. I will therefore have to take recourse to other sources and apply them to Levinas's philosophy in order to show the connections between his thought and the thought proposed in the book of Ezekiel.

The Implicit Use of Ezekiel in Levinas

This, however, is not easily explained. On the one hand, it seems as if he would like to limit it to exactly that type of nonreciprocal ethics which we have looked at before. This would explain his emphasis on the responsibilities of the watchman towards the House of Israel as cited in *Autrement*. On the other hand, the progression of the book of Ezekiel itself suggests another more reciprocally oriented approach that takes into consideration the possibility of agency on the part of the prophet.

Ezekiel is not just God's mouthpiece, like many other prophets, although one might glean from the text that God would like it that way. The textual reality is that God struggles to convince the priest Ezekiel to become a prophet. Ezekiel resists the pressure of the idea and chooses to remain silent through the course of the first two and a half chapters. God confronts him with awesome visions. The sight of the "chariot" is only one of many things with which he tries to impress the priest and persuade him into opening his mouth so that God can speak through him. Ezekiel is aware that the slightest reaction to God's attempts would destroy his defense. He is, hence, not willing even to utter a sign of awe or terror. In the end, of course, God wins. But the circumstances of that victory are thought-provoking: rather than voiding Ezekiel's prior resistance, it instead emphasizes his own deliberate action.

Agency: Resisting God

The significance of the figure of Ezekiel for Levinas's thought can be demonstrated on three levels. First, we have to look at agency and at Ezekiel and God vying for control over each other. Contrary to everything I have said about the role of the subject in Levinas's thought so far, the prophet is able to maintain a sphere of agency over against God's most powerful attempts to convert him into a prophet. Ezekiel's silence, although at first sight born out of his helplessness and awe vis-a-vis the things that God lets him see, becomes as André Neher[16] observes an increasingly aggressive, i.e. active, silence. His refractoriness to God's attempts at conversion, however, is bought at a very high cost. Ezekiel loses agency concerning his spatial whereabouts as well as concerning his freedom of thought. The one moment of agency that is left to him is that of resistance against

God. Every bit of energy goes into the effort to remain silent, since once he opens his mouth, and even if it is just to moan or sigh, he will have opened his mouth for God to speak through him. Ezekiel is able to fend off the command of the holy, which Levinas posits as the focal point of human desire in his essay "God and Philosophy."[17] One might remember that it was the human desire for the infinite that became a vehicle for God installing the command to love our neighbor. My desire for the holy was converted into a desire for the other. God can command us, precisely because we are, through our desire, susceptible to the holy. In the first two chapters of the book of Ezekiel it is that susceptibility about which God is fighting with the priest. The command of the holy fails vis-a-vis Ezekiel's determination.[18]

We also have to look at these events from the perspective of God's efforts to convince Ezekiel. These first couple of chapter's illustrate what Levinas means when he says that God's "authority is often without force[, that] he is extremely powerful [but] in the last analysis he cannot do anything at all. He is not a force but an authority."[19] Indeed, God seems to be absolutely powerless over against Ezekiel's willfulness. And if one wanted to read the term "authority" literally, one could say that God really singles himself out and becomes "άὐθος" (alone). The solution to our difficulty is that we have here another moment of the Cohenian distinction between "*Verbindung*" (connection) and "*Vereinigung*" (unification). The fact that the two spheres of the divine and the human are not connected accounts for the impossibility of any theurgic efforts on the human side as well as any "anthropourgic" ones on the part of God. In other words, as God cannot be coerced ritually or magically, so humans cannot be coerced in that manner either. In the person of Ezekiel, God comes face to face with the fact that human beings were created as beings who possess their own free will and thus can even resist God, if they decide to do so. Ezekiel, thus, reaffirms a tradition of refractoriness that goes back through Job, the prophets, Moses, and Abraham to Cain and Adam. With the possible exception of Job, Ezekiel is the most unmoved by God's attempts to exert vertical force on him. That God has to struggle with Ezekiel, that he has virtually no effect on him, highlights Ezekiel's agency over against the overwhelming power of God. Ezekiel can hear and see the visions and there is no doubt that he receives the messages God sends to him. However, Ezekiel declines to respond and remains silent. No matter how much Ezekiel is actually susceptible to God's power, as is evident from the impact that the visions do have on him, he remains refractory to God's efforts to penetrate him.

Eating the Scroll: The In-Finite

Second, Ezekiel can be read in terms of his relationship with the text. With respect to this issue we have to turn to the events in Ez. 3:1–3. Although God is unable to make him speak, God can open the prophet's mouth and feed him the words which he is supposed to prophesy to the people of Israel. We can observe here the importance that the text has as a medium between human beings and God. "Feed and be satisfied." With those words God shoves the scroll down Ezekiel's throat. Since God cannot penetrate the human sphere and become part of their finiteness, something else has to substitute for God. This substitute is given as a text, viz. as scripture. However, it would not be enough for Ezekiel just to read what is written on the scroll. Instead the words given by the infinite have to be integrated and incorporated into the finite as representative of the infinite. The finite has to consume the infinite in order for the infinite to be co-present with it. Thus, the book of Ezekiel allows us to further refine the notion of the infinite in the finite. That infinite can show itself (in the particular case of Ezekiel) as the text, i.e., as scripture, in the finite rather than God in the finite.[20]

It seems to me that this move towards an understanding of the relationship between the text and human beings as consumptive must be read not literally, but as an attempt towards establishing a new conception of the ontological constitution of human beings. It retains the notion of uniqueness for God *and for human beings* (neither God consumes humans nor do they consume God) while at the same time substituting scripture as a vehicle for a dialogue between them. Revelation, therefore, becomes effective as textual revelation. God can only reveal Godself through the letters, i.e., through the signs of the text. Prayer is possible only as interpretation. Humans can only reach out for the divine by a sustained effort toward understanding scripture. Maybe this is also where the name of the prophet has its proper place. The name "Ezekiel" is translated by many as "being strengthened by God." With respect to the food that the prophet receives from God, such a translation seems to be adequate. But the name could also be translated as "fettered by God." The fetter, in this case, is the inevitability of our moral responsibility for the other, which is given to us through our createdness as finite beings into whom the finite has been integrated. Here it is reaffirmed through the actual eating of Scripture (i.e. the totality of God's word).[21]

Ezekiel's Responsibility

There is a fourth aspect to the Book of Ezekiel that provides us with the hermeneutic framework for the interpretation described in the previous paragraph. In the end God succeeds; Ezekiel succumbs to God's will and prophesies to the house of Israel. This rather surprising conclusion of chapter three cannot be accredited to God's relentless efforts to impress Ezekiel with his power. We have seen above that God maneuvers himself into a rather difficult position by trying to persuade the priest with an exhibition of power. However, now, in 3:12–27 God moves the priest from his isolation into the vicinity of other human beings and installs him as their watchman (צֹפֶה) stipulating the following:

> Situation A. God sentences the wicked to death, and the watchman does not issue a warning. The wicked will die because of iniquity, and the prophet will be held responsible for their death.
>
> Situation B. God sentences the wicked to death and the watchman does issue a warning. The unrepentant wicked will die because of iniquity, but the watchman's life will be spared.

Situation C. Righteous persons who backslide and who are not warned by the watchman die when God puts a stumbling block before them, and God holds the watchman responsible for this loss of life.

Situation D. When righteous persons who are about to backslide are warned by the watchman, they do not backslide and both they and the watchman save their lives.[22]

The significance of this moment lies in the fact that God here diverts Ezekiel's attention away from God towards his fellow human beings, and by so doing prioritizes Ezekiel's horizontal relationship with other human beings over against the vertical relationship with God which had proved to be nonviable. This strategic move on the part of God makes Ezekiel accept his lot and prophesy for God. It is the moment of responsibility for the other which makes the prophet vulnerable and hence penetrable to God's command. Now, the text that God fed him before can actually begin to generate meanings, which will then be proclaimed to the Israelites as God's word. Moreover, in an additional move, God adopts Ezekiel's refractoriness and silence. God decides that God's mouth-piece Ezekiel will be dumbfounded, i.e., remain silent, as long as God wants him to, in order to communicate to Israel God's unwillingness to deal with them. Yet, motivated by the above responsibility, Ezekiel will not withdraw from the community. Instead he presents his silence as prophetic silence, i.e. as God's anger, to his fellow human beings.

The Significance of Ezekiel as a Type

It should be clear by now that Levinas's scattered references to the prophet Ezekiel are in all likelihood not just coincidental. He can use the prophet 1. as a model for a monadic subjectivity which, through absolute silence, can avoid contact with God, and simultaneously also isolates itself from the world; 2. as an example of the unique relationship between God and humans which cannot be established vertically but only horizontally;

3. as a model for the differential functioning of Scripture as the communicative medium between humans and God; and 4. as a paradigm for the notion of responsibility which, in Ezekiel's case, is to be stronger than all willfully self-imposed silence.

The prophet Ezekiel can serve as a case-point that Levinas's project is to show that ethics is possible only through a fragmentation of the subject which holds open the desire for the social. We have preliminarily called this type of fragmentation "altruistic," thus indicating its direction towards the other. Furthermore, we can now see that this altruistic fragmentation precedes everything else involved in the relationship with God. The subject has sufficient agency to ignore or blind out everything but the social imperative, and the only power available to God is to hint at that imperative in order to get the subject to follow the command to prophesy. We might venture to say that even God's revelation, scripture itself, would not matter, did it not fall on the rather fruitful grounds of that altruistic fragmentation of the subject.

The book of Ezekiel does not leave us in doubt about God's marginal and, somehow powerless, position. Neither does Levinas. Let us recall that "God is not a force, but an authority." God has authorship, and hence He was able to create human beings (like, for example, the prophet himself). But inscribed in that authoritative authorship are two things: the possible denial of God's word and absolute responsibility for the other. If that smacks of Deism, as if God had created us free and now let us go to do our own thing, then let us also recall that, for Levinas, God is the one who hints to the social imperative and thereby awakens our understanding of our social responsibility. Just as we had seen in the previous chapter that a relationship with God can only be established as a relationship with the other, so we can now see that, for God too, the way to establish a relationship with human beings is through the other. The framework for the vertical relationship to take place is given horizontally. It becomes a condition sine qua non.

THE PROPHET EZEKIEL IN THE THOUGHT OF COHEN

The prophet Ezekiel is not only an important paradigm for Levinas but also appears frequently in Hermann Cohen's writings. I would like to look at his interpretation of Ezekiel to see if there are any connections with Levinas's reading of the text.

Individuality Constituted by the Other

For Cohen, Ezekiel stands paradigmatically as the prophet who shed light on the relevance of the individual as well as the God of the individual. In Ezekiel's prophesy, for the first time, individual sin, if not atoned for rightly, is no longer something whose ramifications might be felt by following generations. Sin now becomes the decisive passage-way towards becoming an individual. Linked to this process of individuation is a second moment of increasing altruistic awareness. Through understanding my own sin and consequent suffering I can now also understand the suffering of the other compassionately.

> Jecheskel hat den Gott des Einzelmenschen der Religion überliefert. Und jetzt kann die Frage von Du und Ich von neuem anheben. Wenn es zunächst gefährlich schien für die Sittlichkeit, daß das Du unter das Zeichen der Sünde träte, so ist das echte Spiegelbild für die Sünde, so ist der Spiegel, als das Mittel der Selbsterkenntnis, jetzt gefunden. An mir selbst soll ich die Sünde studieren, und an der Sünde soll ich mich selbst erkennen lernen. Ob andere sündigen, das hat mich weniger zu interessieren, als daß ich nur einsehen lerne wie ich selbst in meinem innersten Wesen mit der Sünde behaftet bin. Und anstatt aller Sentimentalität mit meinem Leiden soll ich vielmehr empfindsam werden für meine sittliche Gebrechlichkeit.

> Ezekiel transmitted to religion the God of the individual man. Now the question of the Thou and the I can be raised anew. If it at first sight appeared dangerous to morality that the Thou be under the sign of the sin, then the real image of sin, the mirror as a means of self-knowledge, has now been formed. In myself I have to study sin, and through sin I must learn to know myself.

> Whether other men sin has to be of less interest to me than that I learn to realize how I myself, in my innermost being, am afflicted by sin, and instead of all sentimentality about my suffering, I should rather become sensitive to my moral frailty.[23]

Again the question of subjectivity, or individuality, is central in this passage, as it was before in our discussion of the prophet himself. Cohen recognizes that the problem of social responsibility cannot be solved by just emphasizing the importance of the phenomenon of the other over against the self. Yet, he simultaneously understands that connected to the process of understanding myself as a sinful individual is an understanding of the other, the "you." Sin in Cohen's judgment is understood by the prophets to be the imbalance between "poor and rich [as] the greatest danger to the equilibrium of the state."[24] Thus, in my recognition of my sinfulness I come face to face not only with the other but also with my responsibility for the suffering of the other. Her suffering, in turn, makes me suffer. As a result, the fact of my suffering indicates the successful individuation of me as subject. This is what Cohen describes as becoming sensitive to one's *own*[25] moral frailty which is a becoming sensitive to the nonreciprocal character of my relationship with the other. It is thus that Cohen can assert that "the self-knowledge (*"Selbsterkenntnis"*) of sin is indeed a transitional point for the engendering of the I, but it is not the conclusion."[26] The conclusion, for Cohen, is given through "the atonement, which depends on liberation from the consciousness of guilt."[27] That, however, can only be granted through the support of the community which represents the state and the law.[28] It is "this social reality [that] becomes the stepping stone for the true individual, who is purified in the I."[29]

Cohen makes an important distinction relevant to our discussion of Levinas. At first sight it might seem that the method he introduces is based on a reciprocal relationship between the self and the other. However, it is important to understand the difference between I/other and I/Thou that Cohen develops. The I is the result of a process of individuation that starts with the perception of one's own suffering and concludes with the notion of one's own sinfulness expressed in that suffering. This sinfulness is described negatively as my lack of responsibility for the others around me. These others, however, are not yet "thous." There thouness can only occur to me after my sin has become clear to me. Only then will I be able to understand others' sin compassionately and thus transform them into thous for me. In other words, for Cohen, too, the relationship with the other evolves as nonreciprocal. It is characterized by a gradient, here described through the metaphor of sin, that puts me into the other's debt. The gradient makes me slide towards the other and face her in her inalienable difference from myself.

This discovery might be gleaned from Levinas's texts as well. The rise of subjectivity is a postethical event, if one takes the ethical event to be the encounter with the face of the other and thus the encounter with one's responsibility for the other. The genesis of subjectivity takes place in deciding for or against that responsibility. "I am responsible even for the Other's responsibility."[30] That the other is suffering too, that she too is sinful and has a responsibility to others including me, can only become part of my awareness *after* I have already understood my own responsibility for the other. What Levinas is saying is that only the type of humble self-recognition (i.e. individuation through sinfulness) that Cohen describes can bring me to a point where I can see the other without waiting for her to make the first step towards picking up her responsibility. "I am responsible for the Other without waiting for reciprocity, were I to die for it. Reciprocity is [the other's] affair."[31] In other words, Cohen's progression to the "thou" — the recognition of the other's subjectivity — is conditioned by the preceding full recognition of my own responsibility (through understanding my sinfulness as moral frailty, i.e. as my nonreciprocal relationship with the other) and subjectivity in humility, since only from there is it possible to conceive of an ethics that does not expect the other to make the first step, but instead demands that of the I. Levinas repeats this move and integrates it into his own thinking, without, however, using the more Christian category of one's individual sin on which Cohen relies.[32]

FROM FRAGMENTATION TO THE I/THOU

It seems to me that this juxtaposition of Cohen's thought and the tradition of Ezekiel with the thought of Levinas clarifies some of the difficulties involved in his notion of subjectivity. For Levinas subjectivity is not given as self-consciousness, as it is for Hegel, or as the form of a unity of apperception, as it is in Kant. Subjectivity is given in potential form as subjective fragmentation, a being directed towards the other and a spontaneous recognition of our responsibility for the other. According to Cohen, only self-recognition can lead the fragmented subject to its relationship with the other and subsequent atonement. We encounter this emphasis on self-recognition again in Levinas when he says that it is *my* task first to act on the responsibility that connects me with the other. We are, in effect, dealing with two kinds of subjectivities. One is the broken subjectivity that has yet to understand its suffering and sinfulness with respect to the other. The second is the subject that has gone through that process and now enters the stage of an I/Thou relationship, where both sides coincide in their mutual recognition and responsibility for each other without expecting the other to make the first move. This might explain better the paradox one frequently encounters in Levinas's texts between a subject that is not yet a subject but is already able to discern the command of the other and thus subject itself to that command and a subject that evolves from such a subjection.

The thematic of this double subjectivity resonates, I think, in the Ezekiel quote at the beginning of *Autrement*. It also puts into question some of what I wrote in the beginning pages of this chapter. The question whether or not subjectivity exists prior to my submission to the other is not yet solved. The idea behind the question of subjectivity is that one has to consider it from different angles and then, in good phenomenological fashion, synthesize what one has seen. From my own angle there can be no question that vigilance for the other (i.e. the task of being a sentry) is my obligation to which I am fully susceptible. Yet, being fully susceptible cannot mean that all I can do is become a sentry. Even if I decide to ignore the command, my susceptibility will not have been erased. The command does not cease to issue forth with my refusing to heed it. From another angle it is clear that vigilance could not function without a certain ability for self-control and circumspection. In other words, subjectivity is also a condition of my obligation to the other. The prophet Ezekiel seems to exhibit both angles paradigmatically. God installs the priest to be a sentry, which requires Ezekiel already to exhibit some degree of subjective awareness and ethical responsibility. Maybe it is his priestly profession that makes him especially eligible for this task. Maybe his initial response to God and his final yielding to God's command indicate that he had already thought through the question of vigilance and responsibility. Clearly, the task of being such a sentry can only be taken seriously if the commitment to the other is heartfelt. And it is therefore without hesitation that — once it is uttered — Ezekiel accepts the command towards susceptiveness to the other.

FRAGMENTATION AND COMPLETION

It seems to me that at this point a deeper discussion of this altruistic fragmentation is necessary. Why is it a fragmentation? If fragmentation occurs, is it possible for the subject to complete itself?[33] And, most importantly, how justified is it to use a theory of fragmentation as the backdrop for an ethics that emphasizes the other over against the self? The latter question is of major significance, because Levinas's critics maintain that a functioning ethics will have to consider the positive aspects of self-hood before it is possible to take care of the other.[34] They maintain that the Levinasian approach doesn't erase, but exacerbates the problems of monarchic hierarchy, and that an ethics that requires self denial to the degree Levinas's ethics does cannot possibly be in the interest of any human being, and hence will not prove to be viable. Clearly, what is at stake here is Levinas's proposition that an ethics, if it should work at all, must be nonreciprocal. It would have to be completely "for-the-other" without me expecting anything in return. The contention against such an ethics is that under such circumstances the other would be free (and almost encouraged) to abuse me, since the self has been reduced to a nothing. The end state of such a vision would be the tyranny of the other. Obviously, the assumption behind such an argument is that one's respect for another person is generated by that person's self-respect. If, in other words, another person, in her attempt to be completely there for me, has given up all her self-interest, then, the argument runs, it would be impossible for me even to recognize that person as a person. Abuse, in that case, would be a necessary consequence.

The problematic inherent in this argument is that, contrary to Levinas's assertion that we have to start out with a situation where there is no subject, this one assumes that the other is the subject which can now act upon all those who have submitted themselves to her. In Levinas's theory, however, the other has no identifiable subjectivity either. Subjectivity can only be ascertained on a secondary level, after the encounter with the other. The possibility of abuse is thus ruled out. When Levinas speaks about the other commanding me, he does not refer to the kind of command effected through, for example, a military hierarchy. The command, given by the other, is nonverbal. It is given through the phenomenological event of the face-to-face-encounter which will be discussed in the next chapter. To put it in rather crude terms: the other cannot help commanding me, she is not in control of the responsibility that she elicits in me. The other is not responsible for my responsibility for her. She is not responsible for my exposedness to her and she is not responsible for the decisive moment that I am in because of her. This moment is the moment of potential subjectivity. It is the moment when I am faced with the task to make a decision about whether I want to accept my responsibility or not. It is therefore my fragmentation, the possibility to perceive the other's command, that functions as a potential for subjectivity that later generates subjectivity.

No matter how God tried to influence Ezekiel, however, it would have been without effect had it not been for a peculiar trait of human existence that Levinas tries to capture in the notion of the face-to-face encounter. This encounter is probably the crucial factor in the germination of ethics, since it awakens in me the responsibility that I have for all human beings, however, each of them in her or his particularity. In the face-to-face relationship Levinas begins to conceptualize the community not just as a community of readers mediately related through a text or as listeners encountering a prophesy. The face-to-face relationship is the *im*mediate encounter between one and the other and therefore the core of the communal itself. In other words, here again we are confronted with a concept that emphasizes radical otherness while simultaneously emphasizing the possibility of a phenomenal knowing of such otherness. In this immediate relation, then, phenomenology turns into an epiphanic phenomenology or a phenomenology of the face.[35]

FOUR

Community
Phenomenology of the Face

In chapter 1, I already discussed the difficulties inherent in the traditional phenomenological approach as practiced by Husserl, and, to some degree, by Heidegger. Despite their initial commitment to a philosophy that goes back to the things themselves, a philosophy that concerns itself with the world as it shows itself, all phenomenologists finally retreated to a phenomenology of the structures of consciousness. Levinas believes that ethics can only succeed if it is able to account for the other in her radical difference from the self; for him, the problematic of traditional phenomenology lies in its failure to ground alterity epistemologically. However, the term "epistemological" has to be applied with care, since it already invokes the problem of knowledge and hence the problem of the subject. Levinas attempts to construct an epistemology in such a way that knowledge neither thematizes,[1] nor gathers nor assembles the aspects of alterity into the sphere of the self-same. The result is that alterity cannot be treated as a fact anymore, since facts are pieces of information that come to be known *by the subject*. It is instead an epistemology that radically displaces the subject and prioritizes the other.[2]

Towards a Community of the Face

However, the grounding of ethics in the hollowness structures of the subject is only a first step. Levinas's approach contains notions about an ethical base-community which needs to be worked out more. The foremost aspect of this communal ethics is the face. In it Levinas captures an aspect of materiality that is crucial for seeing that his philosophy of the other is not just a reversed phenomenological idealism. The face of the other is the real face in front of me. It is open to sense-perception. That is, when I see the other's face I enter an aesthetic relation with her which bears the potential for ethical transcendence. This transcendence results not only in a kind of ethical universalism but in my true responsibility towards my neighbor.

Invoking the neighbor in this material sense is reminiscent of the *Yom Kippur* tradition in the best possible way. The *espace vital* is not only a textual ideal space but a material space where I am responsible to and make peace with my neighbor. The material face of the other is the original site of Ts'dakah.

In order to work out this materiality of the face we will have to take a better look at Levinas's critique of phenomenology. I will contend in this chapter that Levinas sees phenomenology and otherness as two sides of the same coin, they represent the humans primordial constitution as materially ethical. Despite his anti-phenomenological rhetoric, Levinas attempts to devise a type of radical phenomenology that, rather than dealing with the structures of consciousness, investigates the possibilities for experiencing the material phenomenality of the other. Rather than me constituting the other as phenomenon, it is the other, qua phenomenality, who constitutes me as person. Levinas locates the site of such phenomenality in the human face. The face of the other shows itself in the constant double mode of exposure and demand. It is such that it conditions the "I" as responsible for the other. Rather than being a mirror, i.e., rather than functioning within the modality of aggressive self-reflection à la Lacan, through which the subject encountering the face can understand and recognize itself as whole, the face of the other, here, reduces the subject to a nothing, a null-site which only after this event can turn into a real subject and acquire agency.

The kind of phenomenology that Levinas seeks to inaugurate is centered around the word "epiphany." He uses this word to express a concept that counters phenomenology's traditional emphasis on appearance and action. Both "phenomenology" and "epiphany" derive from the same Greek root-word which means either "to let see" or "to show." However, in more original etymology, both words can be traced back to the Greek word for light.[3] The word "epiphany" means to appear suddenly or, more literally, to show against/towards; both meanings should be retained to get an original rendering of the word. Phenomenology can be translated as the science ("λογος") of what shows itself. Thus the word "epiphany" read together with the word "phenomenology" describe Levinas's project as "epi-phenomenology," a phenomenology that emphasizes the direction of the phenomenon's appearance towards the observer as well as the modality of such an appearance as sudden and rupturous. Simultaneously, we have to keep in mind that the terms "epiphenomenon" and "epiphenomenalism" normally designate a "by-product of a basic process which exerts no appreciable influence on the subsequent development of the process."[4] It is, in other words, used traditionally to down-play the significance of something vis-à-vis something else. The use of the term "epiphany" could then also be understood as an ironic use of the word, intent on contesting the marginalizing attention that the face and its ethical transcendence have received in the past.

Before we can actually go deeper into Levinas's analysis of the face and its function for ethics, it is necessary to take a look at the type of phenomenology on which he draws, i.e., Husserlian phenomenology.[5] The problematic inherent in that phenomenology has to do with the possibility of a valid intersubjective constitution.[6] Husserl's question was: How do subjects relate to each other and how can I even know that other subjects exist? He had shown how, through a subjective constitution, the subject can arrive at an understanding of itself as such. Furthermore, through a secondary objective constitution, the subject can understand itself as part of the objects gathered under the term "world." In short, Husserl arrived at a point where the subject could understand itself and the world. Yet he failed to account for those parts of the world which, like that subject itself, are different from all other objects; Husserl could not conclusively show the phenomenological necessity for the existence of other human beings. He ended up *deriving* the theory of intersubjective constitution from both subjective and objective constitution.

Husserl's European Scientific Community

Husserl's acclaimed goal was to seek out standards for the proceedings of scientific research that would end what he called the "crisis of European sciences."[7] That crisis was stimulated by the hermeneutic movement of the late nineteenth and early twentieth centuries when Dilthey and others gained increasing insight into the problematic of normative scientific categories from the standpoint of a subject that is susceptible to time and space. What is at stake for Husserl is the validity of an objective, scientific world which, if it is not congruent for all subjects, would automatically lose its scientific status. In other words, if he could not find a way to explain the existence of other subjects phenomenologically, science and scientists as a community would fall apart, since their standards would lack general significance, because they would be merely subjective. Quentin Lauer explains that "Husserl is obliged to find an intentional category comprising some sort of experience of other's experiences. This one can do somehow, he says, by 'empathy' ('Einfühlung')."[8] Since we, as subjects, understand our own body and soul, and the bodies of others by analogy to our own body, we can, after the constitution of the objective world, attribute our uniquely human qualities to others. Thus empathy, as the uniquely human intentional category, can serve to establish a common concept of the experience of the world. In other words, otherness is recognized by association.[9]

This is the vantage-point from which Levinas launches his critical response of Husserl's phenomenological monadology, viz., the primacy of the "interiority of self-consciousness" inherent in phenomenology. Alterity, i.e. the existence of the other, should not be *derived* from the self-certainty of my own existence, since in that case the other would a) never quite shrug off the possibility of just being a subjective projection and b) ethics could never be a true caring for the other, since the subject suffers from a fundamental ignorance of who the other is. The difficulty that Husserl had to face, and which Levinas faces again, is how a true experience of the other can be possible. It should be an experience that is not derivative of the subject but one that lets the other "appear" in her radical difference from me. Although Levinas expresses his reservations about phenomenology[10] at various points, it seems to me that it would be a great misunderstanding not to see how much he indeed struggles with the problem that has haunted phenomenology since its inception, that is to say, how much Levinas is really thinking from within the boundaries of phenomenology. The following exposition of terms that are central to Levinas's position (but originally derive from Husserl's phenomenology) should prove this point. It will, moreover, illuminate how Levinas's enterprise can be understood as a shift from phenomenology to epiphenomenology in the sense defined above. These central terms are (1) expression,[11] (2) appearance, and (3) representation.

The concept of expression (*"Ausdruck"*) is central to the noetic-noematic structures of the phenomenological experience in Husserl's thought, since it represents the juncture or intersection of the noetic (i.e. the processes of perception) and the noematic (i.e. the structures of consciousness that enable such perception). Expression expresses the perceived as well as the modes of that perception. In *Ideas*[12] Husserl observes three different characteristics pertinent to the notion of expression. One can be called its logical completeness; the other its factual incompleteness, and the third its universally doxic quality.

Every reading and understanding, Husserl observes, coheres with a full and free articulation of the meaning of what is perceived. Understanding understood in this way emphasizes its synthetic quality given as expression. "Through this completion of the acts of meaning (*'Vollzug der Bedeutungsakte'*) in the mode of self-production we win complete distinctness of 'logical' understanding."[13] This logical distinctness includes meaning as vagueness, in which case we comprehend something as distinctly vague. The crucial, but simultaneously diffuse import of this passage lies in the emphasis on "the mode of self-production." Somehow, Husserl asserts, the subject is able to provide meaning in such a way that possible lacunas in the coherence of what is perceived can be avoided. The solicitation of meaning is an act geared not only towards a complete understanding of the meaning of some object, but simultaneously to the subject as building and coining a meaning.

At the same time, logically, a completion of the acts of meaning is achieved. From this perspective Husserl distinguishes between a complete and an incomplete expression. An expression is complete when in all its conceptual details it can cover over the material details of what is expressed; otherwise it is incomplete. However,

> Im Sinne der zum Wesen des Ausdrückens gehörigen Allgemeinheit liegt es, daß nie alle Besonderungen des Ausgedrückten sich im Ausdruck reflektieren können. Die Schicht des Bedeutens ist nicht, und prinzipiell nicht, eine Art Reduplikation der Unterschicht.

> . . . it lies in the meaning of the generality which belongs to the essential nature of the expression function that it would not ever be possible for all the specifications of the expressed to be reflected in the expression. The stratum of the meaning function is not, and in principle is not, a sort of duplication of the lower stratum [i.e. the expressed].[14]

Thus, Husserl acknowledges, that, although expression and expressed coincide in a logical sense, in a factual, material, sense they do not.

> Ganze Dimensionen der Variabilität in der letzteren treten überhaupt nicht in das ausdrückende Bedeuten ein, sie, bzw. ihre Korrelate "drücken sich" ja überhaupt nicht "aus."

> Many directions of variability in the [expressed] do not appear in the meaning whose function it is to express; they and their correlates do not "express themselves" at all.[15]

This latter characteristic of the concept of expression raises the question whether the expression and the expressed might even be more distinct than is the case in the type of partial expression described above. Husserl addresses this question by distinguishing between expressing meaning as specifically and as generally doxic. All expressing coincides "with the doxic element latent itself in all positionality." In other words, all expressing involves at its most general a belief ("δoξα") pertinent to and "part of the essential nature of every objectivity as such."[16] The term "positionality" here refers to the subject of expression, which in every case cannot evade its own particularity as a subject positioned in a certain way, i.e., located in time and space.

The first and the third characteristics of the concept of expression particularly show how much expression hinges on the centrality of the subject, the "I" that expresses something. It is a mode of self-production that in every case proves to be dependent on some kind of doxic structure, i.e., a belief-structure which is centered around the noetic subject. Only the second quality of expression, which describes its possible (and therefore) universal incompleteness, gives us a hint of some kind of uncontainable material aspect of the world. Somehow what we perceive about the world or even better *as*[17] the world is not everything, so Husserl is forced to acknowledge that the world exceeds our epistemological grasp. We are thus witnessing a clear return to Kant's thing-in-itself and its radical unavailability. The concept of expression is not suitable to render completely a duplicate of the world, of which it is nevertheless an expression.

We can, furthermore, broaden our appreciation of Husserl's subject-centered approach by looking at his notion of "appearance." Appearance and perspective, he asserts, go together. In other words, nothing could appear to me unless I am in a certain spatial relationship, a perspective, with that thing.

> Es kann nur anschaulich sein, "erscheinen" in einer gewissen "Orientierung", mit welcher notwendig vorgezeichnet sind systematische Möglichkeiten für immer neue Orientierungen, deren jeder wiederum entspricht eine gewisse "Erscheinungsweise", die wir etwa ausdrücken als Gegebenheit von der und der "Seite", usw.

> It can appear only with a certain "orientation," which necessarily carries with it, sketched out in advance, the system of arrangements which makes fresh orientations possible, each of which again corresponds to a certain "way of appearing," which we perhaps express as a being presented from this or that "aspect," and so forth.[18]

The unity of the object then is dependent on the synthetic unity of the different perspectives under which it appeared. "A spatial thing is no other than an intentional unity."[19]

The third concept on which we have to concentrate is that of representation. For Husserl, every representation is a reproduction of "all the ways of being given, and the differences between these, which we find in the sphere of perception. . . . The phenomena in their entirety . . . are modified in reproduction" (*"reproduktiv modifiziert"*).[20] Husserl asserts that "representations, or, to speak more accurately, free fancies (*"freie Phantasien"*), assume a privileged position over against perceptions, and that even in the phenomenology of perception itself, excepting of course that of the sensory data."[21] Husserl traces this property of phenomenology back to a more general one pertinent to all eidetic sciences. We can see how far Husserl has really retreated into the realm of the subject and transcendental consciousness in explaining the phenomenality of the world. The equation between representations and free fancies is not accidental but must be understood as the consequence of Husserl's inability to come to terms with the Kantian thing-in-itself. This will have important corollaries for Levinas's attempt to develop an epi-phenomenological ethics. If indeed representations and free fancies can be equated, and if, furthermore, they must be privileged over against perceptions, then even the other subject, the person next to me, must disappear into the labyrinth of *my* fancies rather than stand in front of me as the source of my ethical obligation, and ultimately, the source of my freedom.

The above excursion on Husserl can be summarized by reviewing the section in *Ideas* entitled "The Cogito as 'Act.' The Modal Form of Marginal Actuality."[22] The concepts of expression, appearance and representation all hinge on the activity of consciousness within the schema of an intentional act. What that means is that the cogito is the central *agency* from which any object is intended, to which all perceptual information is directed and which, in the end, constructs the interpretations of what is perceived. Thus Husserl can say that "the pregnant meaning of the expression 'cogito,' [is] 'I have consciousness of something,' I perform an *act* of consciousness."[23]

LEVINAS'S CRITIQUE OF TRADITIONAL PHENOMENOLOGY

Levinas's problem with Husserl's analysis lies precisely in the latter's penchant for a philosophy of the cogito, which simultaneously emphasizes agency over against passivity. This philosophy, he claims,

> assimilerait le langage à l'activité, à ce prolongement de la pensée en corporéité, du *je pense* en *je peux* . . . La thèse présentée ici consiste à séparer radicalement langage et activité, expression et travail, malgré tout le coté pratique du langage, dont on ne saurait sous-estimer l'importance.

> assimilates language to activity to that prolongation of thought in corporeity, the I think in the I can . . . The thesis we present here separates radically language and activity, expression and labor, in spite of the practical side of language, whose importance we may not underestimate.[24]

Levinas's criticism of Husserl's philosophy is that the latter did not see the radical distinctness between language and corporeal action. In both cases Husserl would have assumed the centrality of the cogito, with the consequence that he would have denied any understanding of the other as radically different. Rather he would have argued as an empiricist that it is just a function or derivative of the cogito's perceptual grasp. And yet, for Levinas it is precisely the difference that opens up between the other and the cogito that makes possible the proliferation of speech. This difference is opened through language.[25]

> The original function of speech consists not in designating an object in order to communicate with the other in a game with no consequences but in assuming toward someone a responsibility on behalf of someone else. To speak is to engage the interests of men. Responsibility would be the essence of language.[26]

Language alone can establish a difference between the other and me that is absolute in character, that as such can create an aura of inviolability around the other.[27]

> Mais la parole procède de la différence absolue . . . La différence absolue, inconcevable en termes de logique formelle, ne s'instaure que par le langage. Le langage accomplit une relation entre des termes qui rompent l'unité d'un genre. Les termes, les interlocuteurs, s'absolvent de la relation ou demeurent absolus dans la relation. Le langage se définit peut-être comme le pouvoir même de rompre la continuité de l'être ou de l'histoire.
>
> Speech proceeds from absolute difference . . . Absolute difference, inconceivable in terms of formal logic, is established only by language. Language accomplishes a relation between terms that breaks up the unity of a genus. The terms, the interlocuters, absolve themselves from the relation, or remain absolute within the relationship. Language is perhaps to be defined as the very power to break the continuity of being or of history.[28]

The advantage of speech over vision is that in speech I cannot exert any control over the other anymore; I am forced to give myself completely. This also implies the advantage of dialogue over traditional phenomenology. The latter, as shown earlier, derives its thrust by prioritizing light ("φως") as the basis of seeing. It is especially the glance (*"Blick"*) that causes consciousness to understand the world. However, in just looking at someone I remain free to determine that person's being and action according to my own will. Yet, in speech we are somehow forced to let go of that power. "In discourse the divergence that inevitably opens between the other as my theme and the other as my interlocutor, emancipated from the theme that seemed a moment to hold him, forthwith contests the meaning I ascribe to my interlocutor."[29]

The Face: The Empirical in Excess of the Cogito

We already saw in the first and third chapters that what makes possible this relationship between the other and me is a certain desire for the infinite that the other represents. Virtually everything we do and think is a derivative of this "metaphysical desire,"[30] as Levinas calls it in *Totality and Infinity*. It is in the face of the other that this desire originates.[31] Simultaneously, however, the face of the other, its epiphany, is the ethical per se which can halt the drive that is inherent in that desire. The difference of the face (as a phenomenological site) and any other object (seen through the lens of Husserl's phenomenology) is that it cannot be intended, i.e., it is not available to the grasp of my consciousness. The face represents a "'more' that refers to a qualitative difference rather than to a quantitative difference."[32] Instead, the relationship between the face of the other and me is characterized as proximity. Proximity is a kind of material nighness or neighborhood in which the other is both constantly present to me, and yet, conceptually, unavailable.

It is here that Levinas examines the concept of expression that we already encountered in Husserl.

> Mais c'est ainsi que l'épiphanie de l'infinie est expression et discours. L'essence originelle de l'expression et du discours ne réside pas dans l'information qu'ils fournirait sur un monde intérieur et caché. Dans l'expression un être se présente lui-même.

L'être qui se manifeste assiste à sa propre manifestation et par consequent en appelle à moi. . . . L'expression ne s'impose ni comme une représentation vraie, ni comme un acte. L'être offert dans la représentation vraie demeure possibilité d'apparence. Le monde qui m'envahit quand je m'engage en lui ne peut rien contre la "libre pensée" qui suspend cet engagement ou même le refuse intérieurement, capable de vivre caché.

But thus the epiphany of infinity is expression and discourse. The primordial essence of expression and discourse does not reside in the information they would supply concerning an interior and hidden world. In expression a being presents itself; the being that manifests itself attends its manifestation and consequently appeals to me. . . . Expression does not impose itself as true representation or as an action. The being offered in true representation remains a possibility of appearance. The world which invades me when I engage myself in it is powerless against the "free thought" that suspends that engagement or even refuses it interiorily, being capable of living hidden.[33]

We can see in this quote the full thrust of Levinas's reading of Husserl. Expression, rather than being a function of the cogito as appearance, action, representation and interpretation, is turned into the mode of presentation that belongs to the material other. Expression is interpreted as discourse and acquires an epiphanic quality in which it is directed towards me as the sudden and rupturous manifestation of the other's "destitution and nudity."[34] Thus, for Levinas expression comes, and only comes,[35] in the form of the expression of the other, and it is heard by the subject as the other's demand for justice. As such "the being that exposes itself [in expression] does not limit but promotes my freedom, by arousing my goodness."[36]

For Levinas, this kind of expression is bound up with the encounter of the face. The face-to-face relationship is the point where difference is established through language, where it is recognized through speech and discourse, where I realize my ethical obligation towards the other and where my freedom is constituted within the realm of ethical decision-making. Phenomenologically speaking, the face is the only phenomenon that in the true sense of the word can appear to me independent of my perspective or orientation. It appears epiphanicly.[37] It is this ethical moment that precedes and inaugurates language and makes possible all signification. That judgment is of utmost importance for Levinas's thought. The giving of meaning to something can only function as a derivative of this primordial relationship with the other. It is always given through the ethical obligation. Nothing can elude this obligation. Only after the epiphany of the face will the world start to make sense.[38] In this context Levinas can also solve the question of objectivity which Husserl relegated to the noematic structures of the transcendental ego. For Levinas objectivity is impossible without the relationship with the other, since it is only the possibility of detaching an object from my own perceiving and its shifting into the sphere of another that makes objectivity (in the sense of generality and thematicality) possible. In short, my sphere alone would never attain objectivity. Rather, it would remain in subjectivity. "To thematize is to offer the world to the other in speech . . . This objectivity is correlative not of some trait in an isolated object, but of his relation with the other."[39]

The astonishing moment in this kind of objectivity is that Levinas, instead of binding it up with the universal meaning of the object in question, emphasizes its objective status as determined discursively. Only through my communication with the other about the object can objectivity develop. Yet, this kind of objectivity does not eventuate a universal oneness. Rather it is one that consists in the perspectiveness (viz. wealth of aspects) that qualify the social.[40] Again, the connections with Husserl are evident. He, too, had advocated perspectives and orientations as the only possible mode of perceiving any object. However, for him perspectiveness was given as an internal mode of the cogito itself; hence it did not require an other. Levinas's contention is that only the social can give perspectives. They are "the surplus that is produced by the society of infinity."[41]

The Face in the Jewish Tradition

Having established this connection between Levinas's thought and traditional phenomenology in the concept of the face, it is now time to turn to the question of the Jewish sources. Levinas himself makes a very remarkable observation in *Totality and Infinity:*

> Le statut même de l'humain implique la fraternité et l'idée du genre humain . . . La fraternité humaine a ainsi un double aspect, elle implique les individualités dont le statut logique ne se ramène pas au statut de différences ultimes dans un genre; leur singularité consiste à se référer chacune à elle-même (un individu ayant un genre commun avec un autre individu, n'en serait pas assez éloigné). Elle implique d'aure part la communauté du père, comme si la communauté du genre ne rapprochait pas assez . . . le monothéisme signifie cette parenté humaine cette idée de race humaine qui remonte à l'abord d'autrui dans le visage, dans une dimension de hauteur, dans la responsabilité pour soi et pour autrui.

> The very status of the human implies fraternity and the idea of the human race . . . Human fraternity has two aspects: it involves individualities whose logical status is not reducible to the status of ultimate differences in a genus, for their singularity consists in each referring to itself. On the other hand it involves the commonness of father as though the commonness of race would not bring together enough . . . Monotheism signifies this human kinship, this idea of the human race that refers back to the approach of the other in the face, in a dimension of nobility, in responsibility for oneself and for the other.[42]

I pointed out earlier that Levinas discusses Rosenzweig's distinction between the individual and the community in relation to revelation. Levinas seems to repeat the same distinction when he first points to the relationships of individuals with each other and then takes them together as a community to explore their common denominator, viz. their relationship to God. The approach of the other through the face is a biblical theme that (even though Levinas does not want merely to understand it biblically) illuminates much about God in relation to the other and the other in relation to ethics. We will, therefore have to look at those passages that invoke the face-to-face relationship to introduce what Levinas calls the human kinship that monotheism signifies. The first and perhaps most important biblical passage is Ex. 33:11, where Moses is said to meet with God face-to-face ("פנים אל־פנים," Ex. 33,11). The interesting aspect of this passage is a series of parallelisms built into it. All of them are there to give a fuller explanation of the meaning of the expression "פנים אל־פנים." The full first half of verse eleven reads in the following way: "And God spoke to Moses face to face like a man speaks to his friend" ("אל־משה פנים אל־פנים כאשר ידבר איש אל־רצהו" ודבר יהוה"). It suggests that the conversation between God and Moses need not entail both parties facing each other. Rather, it says that the kind of conversation they had was comparable to friends talking to each other. Apparently, the author of this text attempted to show the equality that governed this meeting of Moses and God. There was no sense of superiority or inferiority between the two. Rather it was like a friendly encounter. Much, however, depends on the meaning of the preposition "אל." Rashi translates it as "unto" but he notes that the Targum "renders this: 'And it was spoken *with* [my italics] Moses.'"[43] This is evidence that later commentators as well as the author of the original text were sensitive to the ways in which the expression "פנים אל־פנים" (face to face) could be misunderstood (viz. that there is some kind of balance or equality between Moses and God). Rashi defends the text against that reading by translating "אל" as "unto;" the Targum simply substitutes the impersonal "it" ("מלל" in the Hitpael) for the first parallelism ("יהוה אל־משה") and thus avoids the possibility of reading the respective first parts of the following two parallelisms ("איש פנים") as coordinated with "יהוה."

It becomes evident from the reading of this passage that it serves as a bridge between the first six verses of this chapter and the events described in verses twelve through twenty-three. While, at first, God is angry with the Israelites (he calls them a stiff-necked people), the fact that the conversation with Moses is indeed conducted in a friendly manner indicates that God can still look upon them favorably, so that he appears willing to fulfill their requests. It is precisely at this moment that Moses can make his awesome request (v.13): "הודעני נא את־דרכך" ("Let me know thy ways"). This is an explicit request for God to reveal God-self to Moses, i.e., to show him who God is. Rashi interprets this to mean that Moses is inquiring into the soteriological aspects of God's essence in order to find out what it means to find grace in God's sight. In the course of the conversation it becomes clear how God intends to grant that request. In verse 14 God says: "פני ילכו" (My presence shall be (with you)). God, in other words, offers up God's face ("פני") as a sign for presence in order to gain Moses' trust. This, however, obscures the meaning of the previous passage, for it makes it unclear if and how God and Moses had really met up to this point.

Will Moses now get to see God's face after all? Rashi points out that the Targum again carefully avoids that notion. Rather than translating "פני" as "my face" it renders it as "my *shekinah*." Rather than God's face, Moses will "see" God's presence. Still, Moses is not satisfied. He asks a second time (Rashi says that "Moses saw that it was a time of good-will and that his words were being accepted") for God to reveal God-self (v.18): "נא את־כבדך הראני" ("Show me, I pray Thee, Thy glory").

In an interesting rebuttal[44] God grants Moses' second request, while at the same time steering clear of the impression that Moses (or anyone else) would be able to see God's face. Quite to the contrary, everything Moses will see will happen in front of his face ("פניך צל־פניך;" v.19), but "אל־פני" (my face) cannot be seen by anyone, since no one can see God's face and live. Moses will be wedged away securely between two rocks. There he will watch God passing by, but he will be turned to the other way. Moses never gets to see God's face, even though the preceding verses had affirmed precisely that. As Dt. 34:10 says "there has not been a prophet whom *the Lord* knew face to face" ("אשר ידעו יהוה פנים אל־פנים"). By making "the Lord" the subject of this phrase the impression that Moses ever saw God's face is avoided.

No matter how it happened, this encounter with God has great significance for the relationship between Moses and the Israelites. From now on, Moses can truly stand before them as God's representative, since his face radiates and signifies the divine (Ex. 34: 29–35). Rashi interprets this to mean that Moses' face represents the power of sin.[45] Moses' face becomes somewhat of an Archemedian point of morality for the Israelites. The divine otherness that glows in his face is the imperative to do good and stay away from sin. Whenever Moses went to talk to God, and whenever he came back to report to the Israelites, his face would radiate in that way. Only later, he would put on a veil, until he returned to talk to God. What is that veil that he puts over his face? Could it be perhaps his real face? The presence of God in Moses' face might only have been momentary. In any case, after a while, the only thing the people could still see was Moses' actual face.

Maybe the veil is what obscures the beaming of the infinite in the face of the other? Moses' mediating role between God and the Israelites becomes even clearer in Dt. 5:4 where Moses announces to the Israelites that *they* have encountered God face to face ("פנים בפנים")[46] with him standing between them in order to explain what God said.

The only other two places where the expression "פנים אל־פנים" is used are Gen. 32:31 and Judges 6:22. In the former, it is Jacob who wrestles with God and afterwards claims that he saw God face to face. The whole event serves as an etiology for the place named "פניאל" (the face of God). This might actually be the closest one can get to an actual face to face encounter between a human being and God. In Judges 6:22 Gideon only meets with God's angel ("מלא יהוה") face to face, not with God.

Let us return to Levinas and listen again to what he has to say.

> The word "panim" which means "face" in Hebrew, is not a philosophical term in the Bible. I would say that the conception of the face is a certain way of expressing philosophically what I mean when I speak of the *conatus essendi*, the effort to exist which is

the ontological principle. I didn't find this in a biblical verse. But in my opinion that is the spirit of the Bible, with all its concern for weakness, all the obligation towards the weak. But I didn't find that in a verse. You see my terminology does not come from the Bible. Otherwise it would be the Bible to the very end.[47]

What Levinas states here in a couple of sentences is more radical than it might seem to be at first sight. To him, the centrality of the word "פנים" cannot be derived biblically. This seems to dismiss my textual reading on the previous pages. Yet, despite the dismissal of the concept of "פנים" he does not dismiss the Bible. In fact, the face is of such significance in the Bible that he calls it a *"conatus essendi."* The drive or attempt to be is the ontological principle that is reflected in the Bible. In other words, the only thing that Levinas disputes here is that he received the idea of the "face" from the Bible.

How is the function of the face reflected in the Bible? What is it about Biblical religions that sets them apart from other religions? Levinas's answer is: "Monotheism signifies this human kinship, this idea of the human race that refers back to the approach of the other in the face, in a dimension of nobility, in responsibility for oneself and for the other."[48] I think it is evident that we are getting closer to the significance not only of the Bible as a document in general, but, even more so, to the passages in the Bible that establish monotheism as a fact for the human community.

For readers of Levinas's work the idea of monotheism is not unfamiliar. In the chapter on Cohen, Rosenzweig, and Levinas I indicated some of the implications and consequences of Herman Cohen's neo-Kantian monotheism for Levinas. Here, another dimension of this monotheism emerges. Monotheism is more than something that can be defended conceptually by working with the logic of privations and negations; monotheism becomes known biblically through the encounter between God and Moses in the desert. Moses, in his two requests to see God's glory, expresses what Levinas calls the desire for the holy. Yet, at the same time God stipulates that such an encounter must have

ramifications for Moses' work within the human community.
"Seeing" God's face cannot possibly be what should happen. God
is radically other, so that he cannot be seen. We find expressed
here what Levinas means when he says that the face in its ethical significance cannot really be "seen." Though the ethical significance is predicated upon the materiality of the face, it is
precisely not only someone's mouth, nose and eyes that we perceive when we perceive the face. Rather, it is the obligation, the
silent word, that Moses perceived when God finally "passed by
him." It is that obligation which the Israelites felt when afterwards they looked into Moses' face. In both cases we find preserved in the preposition "אל" ("unto") the position of height
and nobility that Levinas mentions repeatedly. The other always addresses me from such a position. She or he is in command of me; I have to give myself over. It is in this sense that
Levinas can say that the face is an appearance, not a phenomenon. It cannot be seen, grasped or thematized.[49] Like God's
face, the ethical dimension of the face of the other remains transcendent and infinitely removed from my intellectual grasp. Yet,
at the same time, once we understand that it is unavailable in
such a way, the face can radiate a light of responsibility to us
that first allows us to become human with respect to the ethical
choice it entails. Furthermore, while the face represents the
"conatus essendi" (the drive to exist), it also stands for the very
limit of that effort to exist. In the face, Levinas believes, is revealed to us the "Thou shalt not kill."

The veil that Moses draws is actually his new face from behind which radiates the ethical transcendence which he and
every Jew with him received from God at Sinai. It, thus, signifies the moment when the epiphanic moment of the face-to-face
encounter (i.e., the pure ethical obligation) achieves its final form
as the material face of the other. Levinas makes clear that the
face is something that "goes beyond those *plastic forms which
forever try to cover the face like a mask* of their presence to perception. But always the face shows through these forms."[50] It
remains an epiphany whose light can never be seen. In the actual

forms of the face inheres the advent of the ethical. However, the lure of materiality is that once I perceive a face with all its wrinkles, curves, freckles, moles, etc., I am irrevocably caught up in its surface. At that point the face cannot have any other significance for me except that of *"Objektheit"* ("objectness"). It is in that sense identical with all the other inanimate objects which, below their surface, offer nothing more than what I had already discovered on the surface. Hence, the physical view of the face can only be a first (though necessary) step to helping us understand what Levinas "sees" in it. "The dilemma the phenomenologist encounters when investigating the face is the one summed up in the description of the biologist who in his research must kill to dissect."[51] In other words, the quality of the face for Levinas is both physical and *meta* physical. The moment of ethical obligation, in which the face precisely *is not* and vision is suspended, can only show "through" the physical forms. This moment can even occur without an actual face being present. The face is the non-present, metaphysical anchor for my obligation to the other. The face is what I respond to when I am re-sponsible. It is in this latter sense that the face is the inauguration of language.

Levinas as Phenomenologist

The question remains to be answered. Can this type of philosophy still be called phenomenology? We have seen how the face avoids precisely those moments that have so far been constitutive of traditional phenomenology. Expression, appearance, and representation all fall into the sphere of the subject, and thus are inadequate for understanding the other. Now we can even add that vision by itself (seeing, and along with it, light) is not an appropriate metaphor to describe what is going on in Levinas's metaphysics. The face is not ready at hand and does not bear the characteristics of extension in space. The face is phenomenon, epi-phenomenon, and epiphany at the same time. The face is a no-thing. Yet, the process in which the face as material transcends the ideal grasp of its beholder and then moves into ethical obligation has a tremendous effect on its beholder.[52] There develops between the latter and the former a gradient which makes the beholder slide towards the face in such a way that the developing nexus between the two is never a "we" but always a "for the other."

FACE-TO-FACE: THE GROUNDING ASPECT OF COMMUNITY

I already mentioned the inherent problematic of this non-reciprocal view of the ethical relationship.[53] Can such an approach ever lead to a social situation in which all participants are equally recognized as full individuals endowed with the same rights and responsibilities? Since this question will follow us into the second part of this book, I would like to take some time now to analyze the work of Alfred Schütz, a student of Husserl's who did most of his work in the area of phenomenology and sociology.[54]

Husserl's Problems with the Constitution of the Other

We had seen that Husserl's concern was with scientific objectivity. This concern gained in importance because Husserl was never interested in a mere empirical analysis of the world but rather attempted to describe the structures of consciousness as they applied to our understanding the world. For Husserl consciousness is always intentional consciousness; it cannot be defined or made accessible without any content. This understanding of the noetic act as intentional opens up a perspective on consciousness as always already related to an other. Yet, Husserl himself is not so sure of his success, however. "[How can] a theory moving within the limits of the transcendentally reduced ego . . . solve the transcendental problems pertaining to the objective world"? "Do I not become solus ipse; and do I not remain that as long as I carry on a consistent self-explication under the name phenomenology?"[55]

Husserl solves this problem with the concept of "pairing." Roughly speaking, pairing is the process in which I draw conclusions about another person's existence based on my own modes of existence. I recognize another's body because I imagine it as something in whose place my body could be. I understand someone else's mental processes because I know about my own mental processes. Pairing, in other words, means the process in which I hold my own experience of myself up against another experience in order then to determine inductively that that experienced being must be like me. Husserl himself asks the question how one can know that what I experience as the other is not merely another part of myself. His answer to this question is rather strange and worth quoting. The other, he says, is something that we perceive knowing that we will not succeed in perceiving it originally. The other comes in the form of a contradictory epistemological event in which we perceive while simultaneously knowing that what we perceive is not the real thing.

> The character of the existent "other" has its basis in this kind of verifiable accessibility of what is not originally accessible. Whatever can become present, and evidently verified, *originally* — is something *I* am; or else it belongs to me as peculiarly my own. Whatever, by virtue thereof, is experienced in that founded manner which characterizes a primordially unfulfillable experience — an experience that does not give something itself originally but that consistently verifies something indicated — is "other." It is therefore conceivable only as an analogue of something included in my own peculiar ownness.[56]

It should be clear from this passage that Husserl does indeed see the problem of the original constitution of the other but while seeing it realizes that the other is something which we can precisely not understand in her originality. The other is marked or characterized by being a perception of which we know that it is unoriginal. In another attempt to define the relationship between the other and myself Husserl defines the other as that which is there while I perceive myself as that which is here. The other is what I would be, if I were there. The alter ego is precisely appresented as other than mine.

However, throughout this whole passage it was not Husserl's intent to speak about the actual other but rather about the question, if it is possible to have transcendental knowledge of the other without simply buying into some kind of naive positivity. Husserl concludes that this project was successful for he could show how it is transcendentally possible for the meditating ego to explain transcendence by way of self-explication. I know transcendentally that there are things that exist not as consequence of myself but rather as external transcendencies. This knowledge of the outside at which, however, Husserl arrives by way of purely transcendental means, assures in his eyes that phenomenology and the transcendental attitude in particular, is not a solipsism but rather that it can account for the other in a noncontradictory way.

Schütz's Symmetrical Face-to-Face Relationship

For Alfred Schütz the task of establishing a phenomenology of the social world is less one of showing the phenomenological constitution of the other through the structures of the transcendental ego. Instead he uses the philosophical position of Husserl as a foundation based on which he wants to get at the core of his own project, viz. the methodological problems that underlie a description of the social world.

> We must then leave unsolved the notoriously difficult problems which surround the constitution of the "Thou" within the subjectivity of private experience. We are not going to be asking how the "Thou" is constituted in an ego. . . . As important as these questions may be for epistemology and, therefore, for the social sciences, we may safely leave them aside in the present work.[57]

Schütz, rather than submitting himself to an analysis of the constitution of the other uses the term "thou-orientation" to indicate that his theory works under the *assumption* that a certain pre-experiential relationship with the other is already given when we begin to analyze the intersubjective relationship. Yet, in order to describe the structure of the social world, Schütz, nevertheless, needs to work on an assessment of the intersubjective relationship, even though his interest is not so much in how this relationship comes about but in how it shows itself. The phenomenon of intersubjectivity, then, leads him on to a more in-depth analysis of the social world centering on the face-to-face relationship.

Quite generally speaking, the phenomenon of intersubjectivity is, for Schütz, conceptually congruent with that of "growing older together."[58] Intersubjectivity is a phenomenon that grows out of a shared sense of time. This shared sense of time occurs when there is a possibility of immediacy or simultaneity between two agents. The psychophysical unity[59] that takes place can be established between two agents who are both present but it also can be established as a kind of simultaneity, a "quasi-simultaneity," between a person present and another person from the past. In order to understand this shared sense of time one needs to have an understanding of both the other as a physical object (even if it is removed) and of the other as a psychic, i.e., intending phenomenon.

To a certain degree, the other is accessible to my own conscious experience. Indeed, in many cases I can know something about the other that she cannot possibly be aware of at that moment and might not even later be aware of unless I tell her. Furthermore, Schütz observes that there exists a certain simultaneity between me and the other in that I can understand my own stream of consciousness only in retrospect, whereas that of the other is present to me whenever I focus on it. The simultaneity is given as time, as *durée*, which Schütz simply calls "the phenomenon of growing older together."[60] There is, in other words, a clear kind of comprehension of the other which simply surfaces in my being able to understand her intentional acts.

> Still your whole stream of lived experience is not open to me. To be sure, your stream of lived experience is also a continuum, but I can catch sight of only disconnected segments of it. . . . If I could be aware of your whole experience you and I would be the same person. . . . Everything I know about your conscious life is really

> based on my knowledge of my own lived experiences. . . . I always
> fall short of grasping the totality of your lived experience, which
> at this very moment is being transformed into a unique present
> moment for you. . . . In summary it can be said that my own stream
> of lived consciousness is given to me continuously and in all its
> fullness but that yours is given to me in discontinuous segments,
> never in its fullness, and only in 'interpretive perspectives.'[61]

As an observer, then, I am thrown back into the modalities of
self-explication in order to understand the experiences of the
other. Based on this phenomenon of self-explication the actions
and words of the other can now become more transparent for
me. However, Schütz stipulates that only when I actively engage in understanding the other person beyond the merely external signs of their behavior, i.e., if I ask them questions about
their project, their plans, etc., only then am I actually in the
process of accessing "the other person's own meaning-contexts"[62]
and am thus in a position to understand what they are thinking, only in that case can we speak of genuine intersubjectivity.

The thesis of the observability of the experiences of the other
alone, however, is insufficient for Schütz to describe the structures of the social world. In order to do that, we need to look not
only at the relationship that I as the observer have with the
observed, but I need to pay more attention to the fact that the
observed and myself are living together, that we are sharing
the same sphere and that, in that sense, the observer/observed
distinction is secondary to our actual living together. In Schütz's
words:

> . . . in accordance with the general thesis of the other self, I not
> only experience you, but I live with you and grow older with
> you. . . . because I live in the same world as you, I live *in* the acts
> of understanding you. You and your subjective experiences are
> not only "accessible" to me, that is, open to my interpretation,
> but are taken for granted by me together with your existence
> and personal characteristics. . . . while I am directly experiencing
> you and talking with you, the whole complicated sub-structure
> of my own interpretation of you escapes my attention.[63]

Schütz's assumption is that this complicated substructure can only be analyzed and understood properly, if we first seek to understand the relationship between myself and the other within the frame-work of the natural experience of the other, i.e., the experience that just experiences the other as a person without necessarily reflecting on the meanings and intentions of that person.

The complicated substructure that is implied by this relationship should be made visible based on the "general thesis of the other self, in other words, from the simultaneity or quasi-simultaneity of the other self's consciousness with my own."[64] It is this simultaneity which Schütz names the face to face relationship. From it any interaction and any move to understand the experiences of the other are derived. The face-to-face situation is the prephenomenological situation per se for it appears in the natural attitude and reflects on nothing but the social relationship that I have with another person.

What does it mean to be face-to-face with someone else?

> I speak of another person as within reach of my direct experience when he shares with me a community of space and a community of time. Persons thus in reach of each other's direct experience I speak of as being in the "face-to-face" situation.[65]

Schütz's insistence on the shared communities of time and space makes the differences between him and Levinas fairly obvious. We already noticed that both time and space exacerbate the significance of being for our understanding of the other. In other words, the totalizing effect that Levinas attributes to being can only occur precisely because time and space are the bridges across which otherness gets connected to sameness and consequently disappears. Levinas only allows these "face-to-face" situations in which time and space are not shared. The face-to-face in Levinas's sense is really not a face-*to*-face at all. There is only one face, that of the other to which I am drawn.

Relating to the other face-to-face, then, means for Schütz that "[the person] shares a community of time with me when [her] experience is flowing side by side with mine, when I can at any moment look over and grasp her thoughts as they come into being, other words, when we are growing older together. Persons thus in reach of each others' direct experience I speak of as being in the 'face to face' situation."[66] In order to be in such a face to face relationship one has to be "intentionally conscious" of the other person. This type of consciousness is what earlier we had already identified as the Thou-orientation. This orientation implies nothing but the understanding of the other's existence.[67] The thou-orientation can be either reciprocal or non-reciprocal depending on whether or not the person of whom I am aware is also aware of me. If she is then the face to face relationship can be called a "pure we-relationship."[68]

There are a couple of conclusions that can be drawn from this: 1. The thou-orientation is not an ontological datum but an experiential one. Being oriented towards another person is not something that we are as human beings, at least Schütz does not make that claim, but rather that the thou-orientation is itself only possible as part of our living in and being part of the world. Schütz, here, reinforces what he had stated earlier in the book, viz. that he was not going to give us the transcendental analysis of the possibility of experiencing the other in the way that Husserl had done it. 2. The face to face relationship can be had as either a one-sided or a mutual thou-orientation. Only in the latter case, however, can we speak of the this relationship as a "pure we-relationship." This pure we-relationship expresses a simultaneity that presupposes a shared time and space. It is reciprocal and symmetrical and as such gives stability and balance to the social relationship. Both the thou-orientation as well as the we-relationship are pre-predicative in the sense that they have to be present to begin an analysis of the phenomenological structures of the social world. Schütz states later that any reflection on or increase in the awareness of the we-relationship reduces one's involvement in the relationship, "and the less l am I genuinely related to my partner."[69] However, Schütz makes clear that the we-relationship is nothing but a theoretical tool in order to get a better understanding of the face to face relationship. ". . . the concrete experiences that do occur within the we-relationship in real life grasp their object — the We — as something unique and unrepeatable. And they do this in one undivided intentional act."[70] 3. The face to face relationship is a relationship that can only be established within the frame-work of vision. It is the sight that I have of the other person thinking and reflecting that gives to this relationship its unique status. Schütz elaborates on this later in the book where he explains that once I am cut off from directly experiencing the other person, once the other person is out of sight, "I am contemporaneous with it, [but] I am cut off from vital contact with it."[71]

Levinas and Schütz: Some Differences

The primary difference between Levinas and Schütz lies in the latter's understanding of the social situation as constituted by the we-relationship, whereas the former attempts to derive the notion of the social from a radical impossibility to say "we." However, for Levinas a "we" could be given only through the communal worshipping of the one God of monotheism. This is a "we" granted by God rather than being a label that the community has found for itself. This "we," in other words, is a silent acknowledgment of our nonreciprocal relationship with God. As soon as the "we" becomes part of the actual social relationship, Levinas sees it become the principle of egotism and solipsism.

For Schütz such an approach can never lead to a social situation in which all participants are equally recognized as full individuals endowed with the same rights and responsibilities. Though he does not rule out the actual existence of such nonreciprocal areas in the intersubjective sphere, but he clearly thinks that they are not what accounts for the social. He claims that the social world is contingent upon meaning that is intersubjective. A nexus between the members of a certain sphere cannot ever develop unless such nexus is given. Levinas seems to be saying "no" to such a conception, since, inherently, it will always favor the perspective of the subject over that of the other. (Indeed, it cannot do differently.) Familiarity and filiality come from a radical and pre-original strangeness which we see in the face of the other. It is an alienness that is inalienable.

This important difference seems less weighty however, if we take into consideration that Levinas's and Schütz's project are different from each other. It is a complementary difference which allows for a synoptic understanding of the work of these two phenomenologists without playing one out against the other. Schütz is interested in the question of the social world and its origin. He is interested in the difference between the community and its participants in such a social world. Levinas on the other hand, wants to focus on the ethical. Whatever that might turn out to be, it is safe to say here that the ethical is by no means the social world that Schütz describes. Levinas's exploration of the ethical does the necessary groundwork for understanding what first moves humans' desire to relate to each other. That desire is ethical and Levinas calls it "responsibility." It is in the mode of responsibility that the social world that Schütz introduces to us can develop. And it is only because human beings do stand in a relationship that lets them learn about the other before they know about themselves that Schütz can discover the phenomenological laws of the social world.

The difficulty with Levinas is that, especially in his philosophical work, he hardly ever moves beyond the initial description of subject versus other. But elsewhere he states that the social is an important aspect of his philosophy, that indeed it is the collective perspective of all readers of Scripture, the "we" in other words, that lets revelation happen. It might be too much to expect him to posit or find a sphere that can have as much of an adhortative sense as Schütz's "we-sphere." This holds true unless one wants to say that Levinas's "we" is a "we" of the one for the other, a "we" in other words in which shared meaning is always deferred to the other and never manipulated from the perspective of the subject.

It seems to me that Schütz's case is very strong, and that possibly it motivated some of Levinas's thinking (it was first published in 1932). I have already pointed towards the problem of nonreciprocity. Schütz does not rule out the actual existence of such nonreciprocal areas in the intersubjective sphere, but he clearly thinks that they are not what accounts for the social. He claims that the social world is contingent upon meaning that is intersubjective. A nexus between the members of a certain sphere cannot ever develop unless such nexus is given. Levinas seems to disallow such a conception since, inherently, it will always favor the perspective of the subject over that of the other. (Indeed, it cannot do differently.) I think that Levinas is saying that in order to respect each other we first have to understand what it means to be other from our perspective. In quite pragmatic terms the advice is, rather than looking for what is shared, let's look for what is different, so that we will not make the mistake of forgetting each other's separate humanness.

The philosophies of Schütz and Levinas, as well as the events at Sinai, can be classified as the search for a phenomenology of relational life. Still, it is a phenomenology that is burdened by the knowledge of history, Hence it can no longer allow itself the optimism of Hegel's polis. That God and Moses met "פנים אל־פנים" speaks for Schütz. However, that Moses never did get to see God's face speaks for Levinas. Only if we are able to keep the other sacred, without abandoning the possibility and actuality of relationships, can the social project succeed.

FIVE

Transition

Judaism as the Matrix Between
Levinas and Derrida

> That I cannot (quite) do. I cannot (quite) hate myself. That is
> simply destructive, self-destructive. I must love myself (a little).
> Even Levinas admits that, if you can get an interview and ask a
> few pointed questions.
>   The problem with Levinas is that he has made ethics in a holy
> of holies, an inviolable inner sanctum, pure and uncontaminated.
> The problem, as Lyotard says, is that he is too monotheistic, in-
> sufficiently pagan — or Dionysio-heteromorphic.[1]

Although John Caputo overstates the problematic somewhat, it
is not a surprise that, in the wake of his philosophy, philosophy
will ask itself how the one who thinks should relate to herself or
himself. Is the relationship to the other such that one is not
only obsessed with the other but, a fortiori, out to deny oneself?
Does one not have to concede that Levinas's approach, by virtue
of being conceived as a negative reaction to Husserl's phenomenology, falls prey to the same injunction that Levinas puts on
Husserl's philosophy? Is Levinas's philosophy not just as much
a philosophy of solipsism as is Husserl's (although this time it
is the pure and absolute solipsism of the other)? Caputo is irked
by the perfection of the Levinasian approach, it is so clean, so
clear-cut that it almost loses sense of what is supposed to be its
center, viz. the thought of obedience, of an absolute obligation
to the other:

> One is always inside/outside obligation, on its margins. On the
> threshold of foolishness. Almost a perfect fool for the Other. But
> not quite; nothing is perfect. One is a hostage of the Other, but
> one also keeps an army, just as a deterrent.[2]

The presence of the self — if only residually — as well as the
inevitable contamination of the pure and absolutely other are
the themes also of Derrida's philosophy, and in particular of his
writings on Levinas. Ethics is precisely not what is pure but
what is contaminated and imperfect. Ethics is the thought of
the other that fails perennially, yet never gives up. Ethics is the
myth of Sisyphus actualized. But how does this reading of ethics and the epistemology of ethics effect the relationship between
Derrida and Levinas?

I don't know if Levinas and Derrida have a relationship in
the way that one would say two people have a relationship. It is
clear that they know each other. But do they relate? I have written many papers and articles on other people. That does not
mean that there is a relationship between them and myself.
What it does mean is that there seems to be a matrix within
which it is possible to relate to the work and thought of another
human being. This matrix of thought is what I am interested
in; I believe that it is Judaism.

Writing *about* this relationship between Levinas and Derrida
has much in common with writing about the relationship between any two people. Right from the outset we are forced to
make a decision about the perspective we would like to adopt
with respect to the description. The decision here is on what is
between Levinas and Derrida, i.e., the matrix of Judaism. If
there should be an asymmetry between the two thinkers than
it will be one that belongs to the matrix and thus to the dialogue internal to Judaism itself. Rarely will it give equal voice
to both of them. What does it mean "to give equal voice?" The
description will, from the start, bear the same asymmetrical
marks that also inhere in Judaism. Rather than charging the
reader who describes the relationship with having caused the
asymmetry, would it not be more prudent to understand that it

is the very asymmetry of time and space that is inscribed in the relationship between Levinas and Derrida? It would be foolish to conclude that one is more Jewish than the other.[3] The asymmetry, if anything, is pertinent to the matrix. It reflects the very tornness of the matrix through which it holds together.

In other words, although this book is about Levinas and Derrida, the analysis of their thought is only a pre-text to get at the conflict that is inherent in Judaism itself. The question, if Derrida is a Jewish philosopher is rhetorical to the extend that the very question already contains the announcement that he is, in-deed. It is an announcement whose intent it is to ask Judaism a question about the principle that resides at its very core: the principle of monotheism. It is only logical, then, to focus on Derrida rather than on Levinas, for it is Derrida who is asking the questions. Rarely are they questions that relate directly to Levinas. However, Levinas remains in the background of Derrida's writing. This manuscript is structured in such a way that the issues that were addressed from Levinas's Jewish perspective in the first part persist throughout the analysis of Derrida's work in the second part. In other words, Levinas's thought is from the very outset understood as one aspect of the Jewish matrix to which and out of which Derrida responds in this book. These are not responses that adhere to a dialogical format in which through a face-to-face encounter Derrida and Levinas would actually be conversing with each other. Rather, they are responses only in the eye of the reader and thus invoke the readers' responsibility for their juxtaposition with the thought of Levinas. In this case I am the primary reader of their texts and through my reading common themes have emerged to which I make both philosophers respond from within their own work. They are the Jewish themes that I announce, not necessarily the ones that Derrida or Levinas would have formulated in dialogical situation with each other. At no point in this book, therefore will it be possible to say that Derrida is actually *giving* a response to Levinas or vice versa. A conversational exchange of themes and ideas is exactly not what I see between these two philosophers. They remain other to each other in a way that cannot be mediated by any text.

I will then call this connection between Levinas and Derrida a relationship. But I urge myself and the reader of this text to keep in mind that it is a troubled relationship. It is "tormented from within," to use a phrase of Derrida's, by how it exceeds the very idea of relationship. I will use this transition to look at some of the issues that Derrida himself identifies in order to clarify his relationship with Levinas. To that end we will take a look at his essay "At This Very Moment in This Work Here I Am"[4] in which, roughly, he presents his relationship with Levinas as an obligation that, however, does not come from a dialogical relationship with Levinas as his personal other (the one whom Derrida addresses as "you"). Rather, Derrida derives the obligation from a "he" who, at first sight seems to be Levinas (since Derrida refers to him as E.L) but who at second sight turns out to be El, God, the absolute other.

In this text Derrida makes it clear beyond any doubt that he is not interested in presenting his relationship with Levinas in the form of a response that was solicited by Levinas. Levinas himself puts an injunction on that type of response, Derrida observes: "If anyone (He) tells you from the start: 'don't return to me what I give you,' you are at fault even before he finishes talking."[5] So, for Derrida, "the trap is that I then pay homage."[6] The simple act of listening to Levinas's words already is a return of sorts, it is an act of disobedience that violates the injunction set up be Levinas. Furthermore, if we listen and obey the injunction to disobey then the return of the gift becomes more and more complete: "the more you obey him in restituting nothing, the better you will disobey him and become deaf to what he addresses to you."[7]

It seems odd that Levinas is so worried about the return. Obviously, no one would want to have a gift that they gave to somebody else returned to them. But for Levinas the issue of the return goes far beyond what one would consider to be a simple sending back of a gift. For him even the gift which is answered by a counter-gift constitutes a return. The returning of the gift, one could say, symbolizes for Levinas the relentless attempt to gain power over each other. To return the gift is an attempt to reduce the debt to the other and to let the other in turn owe us. It means, as Derrida puts it, that one "will still be caught in the circle of debt and restitution."[8] Precisely this is the circle that Levinas attempts to break. The return of the gift, even, if it takes place only in the form of a simple "thank you" would entail the reduction of the otherness (of the one who gave the gift) to a sphere of sameness. The return would establish the symmetrical relationship between giver and receiver and thus interfere with the height and asymmetrical difference that exists between the other and myself. Accepting the gift without return (not even the return of a "thank-you") would amount to an admission of our utter weakness and dependence on the other. The question then is in how far one is really able to accept a gift, for example that of Levinas, fully. Therefore Derrida announces: "Now what I 'want' to 'do' here is to accept the gift, to affirm and reaffirm it as what I have received. Not from someone who would himself have had the initiative for it, but from someone who would have had the force to receive it and reaffirm it."[9] What does this mean? Every return would imply a symmetrical ontological connection. It would reduce the other as giver to the sphere of the receiver and invalidate the supreme act of sacrifice that came with the gift. But is this ever avoidable? It is clear from the text of Derrida's essay, that, nevertheless, Derrida is returning something to Levinas. If this is really the case then Levinas's whole project would be severely damaged. Derrida would have achieved what he was already aiming at in his earlier essay on Levinas, "Violence and Metaphysics," in which his point had precisely been that Levinas's invocation of the other remains incomplete, for Levinas will have to continue to express this other in the language of the same. This time, however, Derrida focuses on the initiative of giving rather than just on the problem of receiving the gift in order to show that the problematic of debt and restitution rests not alone with the need to receive but also with the need to give. He wants to accept the gift of Levinas's work in a way that refuses to grasp Levinas as the *giving* agent, the one who takes the giving initiative, and instead imagines him to be the one who receives it himself. Every giving would itself almost demand restitution, unless the giving itself was forgotten. The strategy for such an acceptance lies for Derrida in the breaking up of the I/you structure. Any giving that takes place within this structure adheres to the debt/restitution economy. The gift can only be a gift from the other, that is a gift that is not restitution, if the giving "I" can be detached from the you. If that were possible, Derrida's response could no longer be considered a restitution but in turn must be seen as a gift as well.

We can see now that when Derrida begins this essay with the words "He will have obligated," he has already undertaken the necessary philosophical refiguring of the relationship with Levinas. The "he" in this phrase is an other who can neither be identified by addressing him/her as "you" nor by using their proper name. For even such an address would amount to a restitution or return and therefore compromise the otherness of the other. Derrida, instead, chooses to address this other as E.L. thereby leaving it open whether the intended addressee is Emmanuel Levinas or, with his initials as the medium, El the God of the Hebrew Scriptures. Derrida, in other words, understands his own obligation as deriving not necessarily from Levinas but rather from the absolute itself. With this observation, however, we are reentering the argument of Derrida's earlier essay on Levinas, "Violence and Metaphysics." For the question now becomes how one must and can relate to that which is absolutely other from oneself and the world. Derrida's initial response to Levinas in "Violence and Metaphysics" (which is a response to Levinas's *Totality and Infinity*) was very critical. Essentially the critique boils down to an argument from language in which Derrida shows relentlessly that the language that Levinas is using to talk about the other remains the language of logocentrism and sameness unequipped to thematize the other. In "At This Very Moment In This Work Here I Am" Derrida once again turns to Levinas's writing.

> How, then, does he write? . . . How does he manage to inscribe or let the wholly other be inscribed within the language of being, of the present, of essence, of the same, of economy, etc., within its syntax and lexicon, under its law?[10]

These questions, no matter how much they are questions that Derrida is asking of Levinas and his style of writing, are of course also Derrida's own questions. How to write about, to and for the other is also a central question for Derrida's own work which reiterates the absolutely other with as much relentlessness as does the work of Levinas.

Derrida's analysis of Levinas's texts culminates in the repeated assertion that Levinas is a negotiator, calculator and risk-taker. He is constantly aware of the fact that language itself is "unbound and hence open to the wholly other, to its own beyond, in such a way that it is less a matter of exceeding that language than of treating it otherwise with its own possibilities."[11] Levinas is aware of the potential that language has to be open to the absolutely other as well as its other potential to close in on itself and draw the other into a sphere of sameness. Negotiating these two potentials is the strategy that Levinas chooses for his texts.

> Treating it otherwise, in other words to calculate the transaction, negotiate the compromise that would leave the nonnegotiable intact, and to do this in such a way as to make the fault, which consists in inscribing the wholly other within the empire of the same, alter the same enough to absolve itself from itself.[12]

This is the factual response that Derrida considers to be Levinas's response "in deed"[13] or "in actu." It is within his own texts that this negotiation takes place. It is not an act that would precede his writing but it is woven into his writing. It is a response to the other that "approaches writing in enjoining itself to that for-the-other."[14]

But this negotiation implies also the taking of a risk. For "in the same language, the language of the same, one may always ill receive what is thus otherwise said."[15] It is "the risk of obligated negotiation . . . what he himself also calls the inevitable 'concession.'"[16] "The negotiation thematizes what forbids thematization, while during the very trajectory of that transaction it forces language into a contract with the stranger, with what it can only incorporate without assimilating."[17] Language, Derrida does not get tired of emphasizing it, is indispensable for the passage beyond that is indicated by the title of Levinas's second major book *Otherwise than Being or Beyond Essence.* "Logos remains as indispensable as the fold folded onto the gift, just like the tongue of my mouth when I tear bread from it to give it to the other."[18] "E.L. takes calculated risks in this regard, risks as calculated as possible. But how does he calculate? How does the Other calculate in him so as to leave room for the incalculable?"[19]

As it turns out Levinas's strategy is based on a principle that Derrida calls "series" or "seriality." It consists in the rhetorical repetition of certain key phrases that, taken by themselves, are obviously self-contradictory. In a series, however, i.e., when repeated several times, this phrase "does not enclose the Other but on the contrary opens itself up to it from out of irreducible difference."[20]

> But although, between the two 'moments,' there is a chronological, logical, rhetorical, and even an ontological interval — to the extent that the first belongs to ontology while the second escapes it in making it possible — it is nevertheless the *same moment*, written and read in its difference, in its double difference, one belonging to dialectic and the other different from and deferring from the first, infinitely and in advance overflowing it. The second moment has an infinite advance on the first. And yet it is the same.[21]

Derrida claims that trying to understand the way Levinas's texts work involves understanding this method of seriality. We cannot, in other words, look at a single sentence of his work, analyze it, try to understand it, and hope that the otherness beyond being that Levinas wants to evoke will show itself in just a single phrase. We will have to look at the whole text and become part of its beat. This text by itself is nothing but part of the logos again. Alterity is not even dwelling in its margins. Any punctual reading of the text will render only this sameness of the logos and thus replicate a reading unable to sense the alterity towards which Levinas is directing us. The experience of alterity from within a system of signs and spaces that itself is still part of the logos is the result of a rhythm of repetition and a resonance of sameness driven to their very extreme. It is rhythm and resonance running berserk. The experience of alterity is a resonance-catastrophe. This alterity, however, is not just the alterity of Levinas as the other or author of the text. The use of his name would mark a point of exchange and thus reiterate the economy that resists alterity. Rather, the text is returned to an alterity without a name, E.L. This is no longer Emmanuel Levinas, but El, the God who absolutely resists being named. The jealousy with which God guards God's name, is the catastrophic alterity against which we run up in trying to return the text. There is no final name for this text, there is no signature to which it can be returned.

But aside from the possibility of discovering alterity in this serial way in the texts of Levinas, Derrida continues to wrestle with what he calls the possibility of contamination that occurs when we read Levinas's texts. No reading will be able to obey the injunction not to return the gift of the text. Any reading of the text is itself already a return of sorts. It is an understanding and as such a replication of textual logic itself geared towards returning something to the author and thus towards making her/him part of an exchange or economy that can only function based on sameness. "It's a sort of fatality of the Saying. It is to be negotiated. It would be worse without negotiation. Let's accept it: What I am writing at this very moment is faulty."[22]

Levinas's texts, then, are planting the reader between two extreme alternatives of reading. One is the reading that comes up against the alterity of the Other. This alterity is guarded by jealousy and by the desire to keep it apart from the same. The other reading is the reading which returns and thus disrespects the alterity of the other and thus contaminates it. Both readings are inherent in one and the same reading. Any reading of any text will already exhibit the characteristics of this difference between jealousy and alterity on the one hand and ingratitude and contamination on the other. Revelation, the showing of alterity, remains uncertain and fleeting in this differential reading of the text. For Levinas it is a reading that is an "uncertain epiphany, on the verge of evanescence."[23] But it is just this evanescence, "the precariousness of revelation," that shows itself in humanity and thus predestines it to be the site where jealousy and ingratitude meet and struggle with each other.

Given the intricacies of the relationship between a text and its interpreter and, a fortiori, between Derrida as Levinas's interpreter, it seems obvious that a text that aims at talking about both philosophers cannot just simply compare the two. Comparison presupposes a structure of context based on which one can compare. A comparison ultimately says that the parties compared are the same, with various computations and translations to connect them, of course, but they are the same. Therefore, rather than choosing the language of comparison, I would prefer to use the Cohennian model of correlation in order to talk about the relationship between Derrida and Levinas. The assumption is, then, that it would be wrong to think of the genesis of Derrida's thinking as in any way related to the work of Levinas by way of emergence. Derrida's work does not emerge from the texts of Levinas, but one might say, in the way that Hermann Cohen speaks of the relationship of being and becoming, that their respective texts bear the marks of a logical connection. Derrida's work is the negation of the privation of all of Levinas's work. This can be exemplified by looking at the first chapter of each of the two parts of this book. Whereas Levinas speaks about text as sacred scripture (i.e., the privation of all other texts), Derrida deals with all other texts in order to negate it and to show that their translation amounts to nothing but the holy Ur-language. Whereas Levinas speaks about God, i.e, the privation of everything else, Derrida will speak about truth, i.e., the negation of everything else that aims for God. It is in this way that the chapters of the two parts of this book correspond.

In other words, I am reading Derrida and Levinas differentially. The difference between the two is the space, the khora, in which dwells the Holy and which can only be understood when the difference between Derrida and Levinas is not meant to erase one or the other but to be a productive matrix. The productive matrix, the mother that bears fruit, is the unnamable yet presiding presence between and around both their bodies of work. It nurtures their writing, it gives them difference, and it holds them (together) despite all antagonism, criticism, and lack of understanding. Most of all, however, it holds them despite the asymmetrical reading that any reading of the two philosophers in a linear text like this one will produce. It grants a syn*thesis* that no syn*optic* reading will ever be able to produce.

Six

The Text

Pure Presence and the Task of Translation

THE TEXT AND THE MEANING OF PRESENCE

From an epistemological perspective everything can be understood as a sign, i.e., as an indication of the absence or removedness of pure unadulterated meaning. Linguistic and textual practice as the production of signs is what Jacques Derrida calls writing (*écriture*). He uses the concept of writing as a pattern to show that différance, i.e. a differing/deferring movement, is vital not only to language but to the whole world. This is true despite his cautioning remarks at the beginning of *Of Grammatology*, where he refers to the "problem of language," the "devaluation of the word 'language,'" the "inflation of the sign 'language,'" but he also makes clear that this is a problem that can no longer be contained within the framework of linguistics only, for it has "invaded, *as such*, the global horizons of the most diverse researches and the most heterogeneous discourses, diverse and heterogeneous in their intention, method, and ideology."[1] He asserts that the epoch that we are living in "must finally determine as language the totality of its problematic horizon."[2] It is this epoch, then, that enables the deconstructive strategy.

151

Within the horizon of this epoch it is the ambiguity that inheres in the sign that makes for the most fertile soil for
deconstruction. The distance between the signifier and the signified, between what is meant and what is actually said is the
crucial hinge on which depends much of Derrida's thrust. The
strategy consists in a radical questioning of the opposition itself between signifier and signified. It is an arbitrary opposition
because our access to one part of it, the signified, is severely
limited. The signified is already an ideal limit that can be represented in various ways without, however, ever being truly
presented. It is in the notion of "presentation" that Derrida's
work achieves some significant, albeit negative, contiguity with
the work of Edmund Husserl.

His critique of Husserl is twofold. First, Husserl neglected to
pay sustained attention to the function and significance of language in the workings of phenomenology. Second, closely connected to the first, is that the problem of language is connected
to the problem of time (as Heidegger discovered already). It is
the very temporality of language that does not allow for what
Husserl considered to be the prime goal of his philosophical
enterprise, viz. the working out of a pure transcendental presence from which our grasp of the world would become understandable in its epistemological foundations. Language, and
consequently also our linguistic grasp of the world, is the negation of any form of pure transcendental presence in Husserl's
sense. By its very nature language is temporal, it is motion and
flux. Presence can never be obtained from it without the violence
of conception that grinds the flux to a halt. But Derrida's contention reaches further than that. Even if we understand the process of violent conception, the result itself will not be presence.

The point of presence itself is an impossibility unless one
begins to understand it from the perspective of that which makes
it possible, viz. the coordinates of an ideal arche and telos coinciding (but never coming to rest) momentarily in the point that
we call the present. Language and meaning come to be mutually exclusive as long as one insists on the necessity of presence

for the conception of meaning. Yet, Derrida does not seek the total dissociation of meaning and language. Rather it is his goal to dissolve the prejudice of an immediacy that supposedly exists between a word and its meaning. The mediacy that he instead alleges is indicative of the structuralist sign/signifier distinction and makes room for meaning as spread out and multiple throughout time. In short, the rejection of the point of pure presence allows for semantic multiplicity and thus must be seen as a move toward the recovery or formation of a space that eventually will also be of ethical significance.[3]

Texts, for Derrida, don't produce an *espace vital*, they themselves are this space. By virtue of being unified in this notion of a single space, Derrida often refers to the world as text rather than as texts. It would lead too far to recapitulate fully Derrida's notion of the text, and the world as text, in this chapter. However, it needs to be emphasized that it is a remarkable characteristic of Derrida's approach to emphasize the analogous structures that inhere in both language as text and the world as text. Since our access to the world is always given linguistically, every object that one can encounter in the world is a linguistic object (i.e., an object mediated by language) and functions just like a sign in a given text. That is, it stands in for something else, viz. the real object, whose absence it marks but cannot recover. Everything that Derrida says of the text is a fortiori true of the world as well. Language mirrors and represents our relationship to the world. That is, everything that we encounter as ambiguous in language is (because of our linguistic access to the world) also ambiguous in the world. The world is no more or less transparent or consistent than is the language we use to access it. It is in this way that we have to understand that textual practice is the key to a worldly practice.[4]

This now also opens up a new possibility for a look at an understanding of the point. The differential character of the textual point of meaning is, simultaneously the differential character of the objects that we access in the world. The semantic difference that is opened up in this way signifies space in the sense that we saw Levinas described as *"espace vital."* Linguistic access to the world makes for epistemological incoherence and ambiguity but it also creates the space that the world needs to be the world in the first place.

HUSSERL'S INFINITE TASK

In Derrida's reading of Husserl we confront the issues that Husserl was so careful to exclude. Where Husserl wanted pure presence, Derrida reads the impossibility of such presence; where Husserl introduces the opposing concepts of expression and indication, Derrida reads both concepts as logical extremes of a process that oscillates infinitely between them without ever coinciding with either one completely. Derrida learned negatively from Husserl. His reading of Husserl — like that of Plato, Rousseau, Lévi-Strauss, and others — is a deconstructive reading, whose intention it is to reveal the inner tornness and disruptedness of a superficially smooth and coherent text. Yet at the same time it also reintegrates Husserl's thought into a larger framework of philosophical explorations, viz. that of neo-Kantianism. It can thus be shown that Husserl's work stands in connection with some of the elements in Cohen's philosophy of correlation, that, in fact, against its own intent, it repeats some of the same patterns deriving from the correlational tension between pure unadulterated meaning and the relentless withdrawal of the cognizing subject.

In 1991 Derrida published an essay[5] that, affirms not only the relationship between Kant's, Cohen's, Rosenzweig's and Derrida's thought but also includes Husserl in this genealogy. Derrida sees in Cohen one of the first philosophers after Plato who understands the platonic concept of the idea as "hypothesis." The implications of this are that

> what we have here, then, under the name of hypothesis, is indeed a determination of the idea as an opening to the infinite, an infinite task for "philosophy as a rigorous science" (this had

already been for years the title of a famous essay by Husserl) or else, Idea in the Kantian sense, an expression which was to guide Husserl too in diagnosing the crisis of European sciences and in defining the infinite task, but also in several other contexts, the most "teleologist" of his discourses.[6]

This is the case, Derrida asserts, although

it is often forgotten when one is interested in Husserl and Heidegger, that this neo-Kantian sequence has largely determined the context *in* which, that is to say also *against* which, Husserl's phenomenology, later the phenomenological ontology of the early Heidegger (who, besides, succeeded Cohen in his Marburg chair — and this also marks an institutional context in the strictest sense), in a way arose: against neo-Kantianism and in another relation to Kant.[7]

The context out of which phenomenology arises is that of the Marburg neo-Kantian concept of the infinite task. It is one of the key terms in Hermann Cohen's terminology pertaining to the correlational method. We encountered this concept for the first time in the second chapter on Levinas and, there, came to understand it as a qualifying synonym for Cohen's efforts to devise an ethical epistemology. The question which he sought to answer was, how can human beings and God be infinitely different from each other, while it is humanity's effort to come closer to God by obeying God's command? Does this not imply some type of relationship between God and humanity? Cohen's answer to this problem became the method of correlation. Between the origin of creation and its ultimate reconciliation with God stretches the realm of the worldly which can only be brought closer to God through a process of ethical transformation. This process, however, is understood by Cohen as an asymptotic approaching of the ideal, God. He thus conceives of it as the infinite movement of human action that will never reach its goal, i.e., become congruous with the ideal. Reconciliation with God has turned into an infinite task.

Derrida is attracted to the concept of "task" and the peculiar tension which it incorporates between an origin and a telos, i.e.,

a past and a future. The giving of the task relates to a past
original event, whereas its fulfillment relates to the future; a
task can only exist within this range; and along with its character of incompleteness it will also already exhibit the signs of its
fulfillment. A task is an event (one could almost say "a space")
that spans from past to future across the present, without the
point of the present ever becoming palpable within it.

Husserl, of course, was looking for a moment of epistemological fulfillment, a moment of unchallenged univocity of meaning
(a moment without task). Yet, what he described best is precisely the unending movement towards meaning and the concomitant task of the philosopher to strive for it.[8] His analysis of
internal time-consciousness, that resulted in his understanding of time as retention and protention in which the present
turns into the nodal point of the intersection of the former two,
is in part a repetition of Cohen's correlational method as well as
a foreshadowing of Derrida's concept of the task. The only, albeit crucial, difference is that Husserl was convinced that he
had indeed secured a way toward understanding the meaning
of the living present. Derrida denies that on three accounts: (1)
Although retention involves a relationship with the past, that
which is past can never be adequately secured; (2) similarly,
although protention involves the future, the actual future event
is infinitely removed; (3) the fact that the present can only be
described via the retention/protention couple is indicative of the
impossibility of obtaining a *pure* living present. The present
remains derivative of its past and future other and can thus
never be pure. In the essay "'Genesis and Structure' and Phenomenology"[9] Derrida points to the irreconcilable difference that
occurs between Husserl's goal to describe the *structures* of the
transcendental ego on the one hand and his insight that the ego
is a genealogical entity that is simultaneously productive, i.e.,
historically constituted.[10] Yet, Derrida observes, the geneticism
inherent in the insight into the transcendental ego's temporal
productivity is neglected every time that phenomenology attempts to gain a self-understanding of a "'science-of-facts.'"[11] It

is, in other words, Husserl's attraction to the hard-core sciences, especially to the ideal of exactness in mathematics, that makes him ignore his own genealogical findings and pay little attention to details of epistemology. He instead attempts to emphasize the factuality of ideality in the form of the living present.

Nevertheless Husserl and Cohen coincide in their usage of the notion of the "task," or "infinite task," wherein a productive dualism is seen as one in which we recognize the ultimate incongruousness or nonreciprocity of its two constituents. Furthermore, it must be a dualism that is understood as a dynamic relationship between those two constituents where one side is consistently drawing closer to the other. In Cohen's case it is the world that approaches God in this way; in Husserl's case it is consciousness approaching the pure living present.

With respect to that dualism, it can easily be seen that Derrida's work in the critique of phenomenology is based on two major aspects. On the one hand, he continually points Husserl to the ineluctably transcendent elements of phenomenology that the latter had sought to exclude. The notion of the pure present is undermined by the temporal constitution of the world which prohibits the pin-*pointing* of presence and instead differentiates it. The result, of course, is that both telos and origin are seen as transcendent, i.e., as infinitely removed. On the other hand, Derrida radicalizes Husserl's concept of "task" — which here amounts to nothing but an epistemological exercise — by confronting it with the notion of transcendence that is inherent in it.

In the following I will discuss parts of Derrida's most important essay on Husserl with special attention to those points where Derrida sees Husserl's theory falter. I will then move on to a discussion of Benjamin's "Die Aufgabe des Übersetzers"[12] which Derrida undertakes in his essay "Des Tours de Babel." Here one can find an actual application of how exactly Derrida wants the concept of the task to be understood, especially over against Husserl. His interpretation of the "The Task of the Translator" ("Die Aufgabe des Übersetzers") is an attempt to come to terms with the implications that the linguistic confusion of the world at Babel has had for the question of meaning, truth, and understanding. The significance of the story of Babel for Derrida is that it locates the problem of meaning between a linguistic understanding of the issues of negative theology, exile, and universal truth. For all three it is precisely the divergence of letter and meaning, i.e., between signifier and signified (that is, the impossibility of saying the signified itself), that brings up the concept of task as the reconciling movement between linguistic expression and signified. We will see how Derrida's understanding of the world as text, i.e., a web of signifiers in relationship to an anarchic origin and an asymptotic telos, also translates the merely semiotic relationship between signifier and signified into that between is and ought.

Derrida's Reading of Husserl: The Possibility of Pure Metaphysics

Before we can discuss those implications further we now have to turn to Derrida's reading of Husserl.[13] To a large extent, this reading turns upon the status of Husserl's work as metaphysical. Derrida points out that Husserl was "ceaselessly criticizing metaphysical speculation, [and] in fact had his eye on only the perversion or the degeneracy of what he continued to believe in and wished to restore as authentic metaphysics or *philosophia proté*."[14] Husserl's life-project (viz. to establish a transcendental eidetic science), Derrida observes, moves from the transcendental to the teleological. It "moves towards a metaphysics of history in which the solid structure of a *Telos* would permit him [Husserl] to reappropriate, . . . [it] seemed to accommodate itself less and less to phenomenological apriorism and to transcendental idealism."[15] In other words, according to Derrida, it is not metaphysics itself that is excluded from phenomenological inquiry but, for Husserl, "phenomenology's purely intuitive, concrete, and also apodictic mode of demonstration excludes all 'metaphysical adventure,' all speculative excesses."[16]

For Husserl, metaphysical adventurousness consisted in the tendency to either historicize or psychologize the possibility of pure presence. A straight metaphysical approach to the problem of meaning, the way Husserl envisioned it, could only be one that was intent on carving out the eternal structures of ideal presence rather than emphasizing the temporalizing, genetic structures that inhere in any given object as well. His concern with the metaphysics of his time was that it had exhibited a "blindness to the authentic mode of *Ideality*, to that which *is*, to what may be indefinitely *repeated* in the *identity* of its *presence*, because of the very fact that it *does not exist*."[17] The denial of the possibility of presence that is inherent in the temporalization or psychologization of an object is that with which Husserl takes issue. He contends that there is moment (*Augenblick*; lit.: blink of an eye) in which we first conceive the meaning (*Bedeutung*) of something. This initial moment becomes the form of the act of understanding. Understanding, in other words, cannot take place without this form. The presence as moment "has always been and will always, forever, be the form in which, we can say apodictically, the infinite diversity of contents is produced."[18]

This concept of pure momentary presence as the starting-point for the discourse of phenomenology and discourse in general is an oxymoron in Derrida's thinking. Without pushing the Husserlian project to the side completely, he is intent on opening up precisely the "adventurous" type of metaphysics that Husserl tried to exclude from phenomenological discourse.[19] Such a metaphysics would precisely underline the temporal-psychological character of conception and, ultimately, make the idea of a phenomenological point or moment of presence in Husserl's sense impossible. He hesitates to accept Husserl's judgment for, superficially viewed, purely linguistic reasons, which, however, turn out to be epistemological contentions of considerable weight. It is phenomenology's language itself that gives away the bias toward the past that is irreducibly woven into the language of the present. Derrida notices that, no matter how Husserl phrases it, the form of the ideal presence cannot

be said or thought without a "modification of presentation."[20]
Husserl himself introduces the terminology that accentuates
this problem. The mode in which the object or the alter ego comes
to the fore of the inquiring subject is either given through "representation" ("*Vergegenwärtigung*") in the case of the object, or
through "ap-presentation" ("*Appräsentation*") in the case of the
alter ego. The two prefixes, in each case, express a doubling
that takes place at the moment the object is made present. Thus
the presented object is never by itself, but can only be presented
by way of a recourse to a preceding notion of its own previous
existence. Presentation is a doubling.

In Derrida's evaluation it is this modification that directs our
glance towards an irreducible element of twofold otherness that
is constitutive of presence and presentation. One consists in the
fact that the object needs to be related to its own past in order
to be represented, the other is that in order to assure the objectivity of the representation the existence of the object also needs
to be verified by another subject. Both emphasize the temporal
aspects of representation. In other words, the moment of representation can only render a picture of the object in question
that is irreducibly past. It is, Derrida points out, a re-presentation. Simultaneously, if what we have grasped as the representation of such an object should indeed achieve the status of
objectivity, a transition to intersubjectivity becomes necessary,
"for intersubjectivity is the condition for objectivity."[21] In other
words, the veracity of our investigating glance, its truthfulness
and adequateness, are dependent on an other with whose understanding we would have to compare or parallel ours.

It is for those reasons that Derrida can insist that the Husserlian project seems to be

> tourmentée sinon contestée de l'intérieur par ses propres descrip-
> tions du mouvement de la temporalisation et de la constitution
> de l'intersubjectivité. Au plus profond de ce qui lie ensemble ces
> deux moments décisifs de la description, une non-présence
> irréductible se voit reconnaître une valeur constituante, et avec
> elle une non-vie ou une non-présence ou non-appartenance à soi
> du présent vivant, une indéracinable non-originalité.

tormented, if not contested from within . . . by . . . the movement of temporalization and the [necessary] constitution of inter-subjectivity. At the heart of what ties together these two decisive moments of description we recognize an irreducible non-presence as having a constituting value, and with it a nonlife, a nonpresence or nonself-belonging of the living present, an ineradicable non-primordiality.[22]

Phenomenology and Language

Husserl's evasion, according to Derrida, consists in the fact that the former neglected the task of analyzing the *language* of phenomenology. Had he done so he would have understood that the language of presence that he sought for was indeed nothing more than "the security of presence in the metaphorical form of ideality [which is] set forth again upon [the] irreducible void"[23] of nonprimordiality. In other words, it is Derrida's contention that phenomenology's methodological need for language suggests a temporal structure that conflicts with Husserl's own attempts to avoid an adventurous type of metaphysics, i.e., one that prioritizes genesis over structure.

Derrida claims that one of the reasons why Husserl was able to ignore the obvious impossibility of avoiding such temporalization was his unwillingness to deal with the impact that the use of language has for the phenomenological project itself. If Husserl had understood the deeper significance that language has for the establishing of meaning, he might have understood as well that only an adventurous metaphysics, i.e., one that does not deny its own temporal structures, could serve as an adequate description of the world. But based on his disdain for such metaphysics, Husserl's attitude toward the problem of language remained ambiguous and caught between three equally misleading ways of understanding the function of language: 1) by understanding it as the bridge between the worldly and the transcendental, 2) by seeing in it merely the logical form of phenomenological description, and 3) by equating language's phonetic quality with the possibility of pure presence.

1. On the one hand, he did understand that it may serve as a
bridge between the worldly and the purely transcendental, i.e.,
between what exists and what is ideal. In every instance that
language is used, it simultaneously points towards that about
which it speaks as well as towards that which this something
really is. Derrida quotes Husserl as saying that there is a parallelism of the two realms ("the purely mental . . . and pure transcendental life").[24] Both Derrida and Husserl agree that this
parallelism entails (and makes possible) freedom, because only
through the difference between the two realms (which first enables the infinite proliferation of language) can variation occur.
Language in Husserl's view is, in other words, indicative of the
distance that exists between the object as thing-in-itself and
the object in its linguistic shape. Yet, if this distinction really
does exist, Derrida observes, then one cannot help but sustain
the impression that the transcendental ego acts "as absolute
spectator of its own psychic self."[25] However, he points out that
for Husserl this difference is ultimately arbitrary and not viable.

> Mais on doit à l'opposé, si l'on est attentif au renouvellement
> husserlien de la notion de 'transcendental', se garder de prêter
> quelque réalité à cette distance, de substantialiser cette incon-
> sistence ou d'en faire, fût-ce par simpler analogia, quelque chose
> ou quelque moment du monde. Ce serait geler la lumière en sa
> source. Si le langage n'échappe jamais à lanalogie, si même il est
> analogie de part en part, il doit, parvenu a ce point, à cette étape,
> assumer librement sa propre destruction et lancer les métaphores
> contre les métaphores;

> But, on the other hand, we must, if we are to be attentive to
> Husserl's renewal of the notion of "transcendental," refrain from
> attributing any reality to this distance, substantializing this non-
> consistency or making it be, even merely analogically, some thing
> or some moment of the world. This would be to extinguish the
> light at its source. If language never escapes analogy, if it is anal-
> ogy through and through, it ought having arrived at this point,
> at this stage, freely to assume its own destruction and cast meta-
> phor against metaphor.[26]

It is a difference that amounts to precisely nothing. Hence,
Husserl insists that it is nothing that distinguishes the two

realms and that, therefore, the spectator-role that Derrida assigns to the transcendental ego is nonpermissible.

2. Husserl was well-aware of the problematic inherent in the sign and had taken precautions to fend off any attack that, based on the question of language, might be launched against phenomenology. For him, the essence of language is not given in its signifying but in its logical function. This means that, rather than looking at language as a system of signs and spaces which stand in certain grammatical, but in particular, also rhetorical relationships to each other, he instead favors looking at language from the viewpoint of logic, i.e., he emphasizes the *"Bedeutung"* ("meaning") that it is employed to convey. By understanding language with the "logical as its telos or norm,"[27] Husserl can avoid the pitfalls that derive from the nonprimordiality inherent in signs. The task now is to show that *"Bedeutung"* is, in the first place, an immediate phenomenon, that, though secondarily tied to language as expression, first occurs purely in transcendental consciousness. Language, thus, is reduced to nothing but meaning's vehicle. It serves as a substrate without any independent significance.

Derrida insists that it is only because of this battle between signification and ideality that occurs within language itself that the two realms first become recognizable. "Language preserves the difference that preserves language."[28] Husserl will have to concede (and this is Derrida's initial strategic step towards undermining Husserl's position) that language be considered as the medium between self-consciousness and objects (in particular self-consciousness' most important object: the self). "Since self-consciousness appears only in its relationship to an object, whose presence it can keep and repeat, it is never perfectly foreign or anterior to the possibility of language"[29] and thus to the possibility of temporalization.

3. Although Husserl would probably concede the role of language in this matter, he would also insist that this language must be understood in a way that enables the phenomenologist to avoid the loss of presence as it would inevitably occur if one were to look at language as a system of signs. The only way for

Husserl to achieve that is to go along with the rest of the Western tradition and to prioritize language in its relationship to the phonic element that inheres in it in spoken language and through the use of phonetic spelling. Since the voice (see *Of Grammatology*) has traditionally been understood as the "medium of immediacy," i.e., as the coincidence of meaning and presence, it can fulfill two purposes for Husserl. As expression it will convey meaning. Yet the process of conveying will be immediate and thus preserve self-presence.

Derrida comes down heavily upon this claim. His arguments, for instance in *Of Grammatology*, are famous. "All signifiers and first and foremost the written signifier, are derivative to what would wed the voice indissolubly to the mind or to the thought of the signified sense, indeed to the thing itself."[30] As with letters the voice is nothing but a system of signs that is as much the result of a differential production as are letters and written language in general. The imagined immediacy conveyed by the sound of the voice is deceptive, since it hides the sign-character, and therefore the deferral, that even attaches to this type of language.

Language and the Idea in the Kantian Sense

The significance of Husserl's treatment of the problem of language does not only become clear through the determinations that it makes about the language of phenomenology itself, but also through the impact that it has on the general aim of a pure, transcendental self-presence. Despite his attempts to define language in a way that is conducive to the phenomenological project, Derrida observes that Husserl is forced to do more in order to insure the possibility of pure presence. "Every time this element of presence becomes threatened, Husserl will awaken it, recall it, and bring it back to itself in the form of a telos — that is an idea in the Kantian sense."[31] In other words, every time Husserl is unable to affirm the existence of pure presence he will turn this necessity into a ideal philosophical goal. Thus he vacillates between affirming its actual existence and affirming its teleological necessity. Yet, it is this Idea in the Kantian sense that, in Derrida's reading of Husserl, first opens up "the possibility of something indefinite, the infinity of a stipulated progression or the infinity of permissible repetitions."[32] Only in this juxtaposition of presence — between retention and the Idea in the Kantian sense — can such a repetition affirm sameness. Virtually the same description of Husserl's project can be found in "'Genesis and Structure' and Phenomenology" where he writes:

> Ce que Huserl veut souligner par cette comparaison entre science exacte et science morphologique, ce que nous devons retenir ici, c'est la principielle, l'essentielle, la structurelle impossibilité de clore une phénoménologie structurale. C'est l'ouverture infinie du vécu, signifiée en plusieurs moments de l'analyse husserlienne par la référence à une *Idée au sens kantien*, irruption de l'infinie auprès de la conscience, qui permet d'en unifierle flux temporel comme elle unifie l'objet et le monde, par anticipation et malgré un irréductible inachèvement. C'est l'étrange *présence* de cette Idée qui permet aussi tout passage à la limite et la production de toute exactitude.

> What Husserl seeks to underline by means of this comparison between an exact [structural] and a morphological [genetic] science, and what we must retain here, is the principled, essential, and structural impossibility of closing a structural phenomenology. It is the infinite opening what is experienced, which is designated at several moments of Husserlian analysis by reference to an *Idea in the Kantian sense*, that is the irruption of the infinite into consciousness, which permits the unification of the temporal flux of consciousness just as it unifies the object and the world by anticipation, and despite an irreducible incompleteness.[33]

and simultaneously:

> La présence à la conscience phénoménologique du *Telos* ou *Vorhaben*, anticipation théorétique infinie, est indiquée chaque fois que Husserl parle de l'*Idée au sens kantien*.

> The presence of *telos* or *Vorhaben* — the infinite theoretical anticipation which simultaneously is given as an infinite practical task — for phenomenological consciousness is indicated every time that Husserl speaks of the *Idea in the Kantian sense*.[34]

Derrida asserts that *"within* consciousness, in general there is an agency which *does not really* belong to it."[35] This "within" reflects on the twofold problem with which Husserl is confronted: On the one hand, it points towards an internal alienation that takes place within the point of pure presence, and on the other it again thematizes the inevitable temporalization that is a corollary of this alienation. For Husserl the "within" gives direction to the phenomenological analysis, yet, at the same time, it reiterates the threat of degenerate metaphysics, one that will end up as transcendental psychology rather than transcendental philosophy.[36]

Hence, it becomes clear that pure self-presence, as envisioned by Husserl, is rejected by Derrida as an epistemological impossibility. Rather, presence is always constituted as impure, i.e., as undermined and subverted by something that is not itself. Presence thus becomes secondary to the alterity that constitutes it. Meaning is available through retention (an image from the past) or protention (an image from the future; the idea in the Kantian sense in the most extreme case). Presence however, the sheer now, turns out to be but a metaphor for the temporal and spatial distension of the object. The voice can only "simulate the conservation of presence," but ultimately it cannot succeed in uniting the difference between the world and the transcendental. As such, as voice which is heard in the world, it only reaffirms the difference between the two.

Husserl, who knows about the problematic inherent in his use of language and the idea in the Kantian sense, therefore, retreats to what he calls the "phenomenological voice" which is heard in the complete absence of the world. But for Derrida this approach to the possibility of pure presence and therefore to that of meaning amounts to saying that meaning is conceived solipsistically, i.e., nonderivatively. It furthermore would be an attempt to say that there is a possibility for a language without signs, i.e., a language of immediacy. Against this he holds that meaning as soliloquy is an impossibility and that the formation of meaning can never be understood as pure presentation

(*Gegenwärtigung*) but instead must be seen as re-presentation (*Vergegenwärtigung*).

Meaning as a Leap away from Itself

The force of Derrida's argument against the possibility of such a phenomenological voice lies precisely in the fact that meaning cannot be obtained as a unitary event, as Husserl would like to have shown. It instead has to be inferred through a differential process that simultaneously employs the modes of what has been and what will be. This, in turn, entails a moving away from an understanding of meaning as a punctual phenomenon towards an understanding that recognizes meaning's temporal distendedness. Against Husserl, Derrida holds up the fact that meaning is only possible because a difference has already occurred. This difference is the difference between the signified and the signifier, the arche and its multiple expressions as language.

Meaning is precisely tied to an "*Ursprung*," i.e., an original leap away from the thing itself into the realm of meaning. Without this "*Ur-sprung*" meaning could never occur. This is also to say that the "Ur" or "Arche" must be infinitely removed from the realm of meaning in order for meaning to stabilize itself in its temporal distendedness between future and past. Otherwise meaning would collapse back into the silence of its origin.

In other words, at the origin of meaning stands a difference, a primordial difference, which causes meanings to issue forth from it in an attempt to express what was there before the primordial difference occurred. Thus expression will thus always run up against the boundaries of the "primordial non-self-presence."[37] "Thus understood, what is supplementary is in reality *différance*, the operation of differing which at one and the same time both fissures and retards presence, submitting it simultaneously to primordial division and delay."[38] Derrida thus observes that, given this differential structure, any for-itself structure really only is an in-the-place-of structure, i.e., is representative of something else more anterior than itself. "And contrary to what phenomenology — which is always a phenomenology of perception — has tried to make us believe, contrary to what our desire cannot fail to be tempted into believing, the thing itself always escapes."[39]

This escape, however, is of archic as well as teleological nature. Origin and telos likewise are infinitely deferred and removed from the attempts of expression to attain meaning. The telos is replaced by the idea in the Kantian sense while the origin is supplemented by a primordial difference. Both function as regulatives vis-à-vis the realm of philosophical reason that distends between them.

Husserl is vacillating between origin and telos. When the former becomes inaccessible, he will assure his phenomenological inquiry through the affirmation of a telos as an idea in the Kantian sense. Thus we end up with a differential model and an emphasis on the infinite opening of phenomenology toward something that it will never be able to include.

Unfolding of Space: The Trace of Presence

To summarize, we can say that the thrust of Derrida's argument hinges on his understanding of language as rhetoric rather than form.[40] In particular, it is the fact that language is unthinkable without the sign that helps Derrida launch his argument against Husserl. The character of the sign is such that, whatever it signifies, whatever it stands for, it will never be absolutely congruous with its signified. The word "presence" stands for something; so do the words "now," "*jetzt*," "*maintenant*," etc. They all, supposedly, designate a moment, a short interval of time that will have disappeared immediately. Yet, the saying of such a word already implies a lag of time. The moment of the word's actual utterance is not the moment that the word itself was meant to indicate. We can thus repeat the word "now" infinitely always lagging behind the moment which it is trying to capture. Simultaneously this moment escapes into the past and into the future. While the moment that we attempted to say originally disappears into the past, new moments waiting to be said emanate from the direction of the future. There seems to be a cross-over between the future and the past. Perhaps that is what we commonly call the present. However, this present is eternally restless and unavailable to our intellectual grasp.[41]

Precisely this moment is the target of Husserl's philosophy. He knows about the effect of the past and the future on the present. He is aware of the slippages in meaning that occur exactly because time does not stand still but passes by in a continuous flow. But somehow, he thinks, it must be possible to find an Archemedian point of meaning that is independent of such changes. Only if we can find such a point can we also explain the meaningful structure called "world" to which we all claim we belong, and which we all understand similarly, with certain differences to be sure. For Husserl this point is the "living present, the self-presence of transcendental life."[42] It is the living present which is turned into the "source-point" of temporality, which "can ensure the purity and ideality, that is, openness for the infinite repeatability of the same." It is Husserl's insight in the infinite and eternal persistence of the present and all that is derived from it, that forces him to insist on the presence as the proliferating substratum of meaning. Derrida puts it very forcefully:

> C'est donc le rapport à *ma mort* (à ma disparition en général) qui se cache dans cette détermination de l'être comme présence, idéalité, possibilité absolue de répétition. La possibilité de signe est ce rapport à la mort. La détermination et l'effacement du signe dans la métaphysique est la dissimulation de ce rapport à la mort qui produisait pourtant la signification.

> The relation with the presence of the present as the ultimate form of being and of ideality is the move by which I transgress empirical existence, factuality, contingency, worldliness, etc. — first of all *my own* empirical existence, factuality, contingency, worldliness, etc. To think of presence as the universal form of transcendental life is to open myself to the knowledge that in my absence beyond my empirical existence, before my birth and after my death, *the present is*.[43]

Targeting the present as the center of philosophy's search for meaning has, in short, the redeeming effect of suspending one's own death and of creating the space for life. Husserl's phenomenology

> [est une] philosophie de la vie, non seulement parce qu'en son centre la mort ne se voit reconnaître qu'une signification empirique et extrinsèque d'accident mondain, mais parce que la source du sens en général est toujours déterminée comme l'acte d'un *vivre*, comme l'acte d'être vivant, comme *Lebendigkeit*.

> is a philosophy of life, not only because at its center death is recognized as but an empirical and extrinsic signification, a worldly accident, but because the source of sense in general is always determined as the act of *living*, as the act of living being, as *Lebendigkeit*.[44]

Thus Derrida's question, put in another form, is if death is really overcome through the phenomenological method. The answer is negative precisely because even the language of the living present remains language and therefore is based on a signified/signifier structure which inherently implies delay and the deferral of the present. Even the use of spoken instead of written language does not solve the problem of deferred presence. The illusion of immediate presence evoked by the sound of one's own voice can only hide insufficiently that even the sounds of my spoken language, the phonemes, are nothing but signs and thus have the same supplementary character as any other sign.

Derrida's answer to this philosophy of presence, however, would be misunderstood, if one wanted to construe it to mean the complete sell-out of archic and/or teleological structures. The impossibility of an actual pure presence does not erase the possibility of a potential presence. This potential presence of an origin or a telos, i.e., this attempt to head back towards the originally signified, is given by way of the trace and the deconstruction of the transcendental signified. The desire for such a signified is expressed in Husserl's philosophy as well as in all of modernity's philosophical writings. Obviously, it is exactly this point that makes Husserl's project susceptible to Derrida's critique. The indefinite metaphoricity of Husserl's descriptions, i.e., the act of substituting signs (words) for the ideality of presence, questions phenomenology from within and brackets precisely the pure presence which Husserl sought to elicit. With reference to Peirce and Nietzsche, Derrida asserts that "the self-identity of the signified conceals unceasingly and is always on the move. . . . From the moment that there is meaning there are nothing but signs. *We think only in signs.*"[45] What is left of the signified is a trace. The trace is Derrida's answer to an ontology that attempts to seek meaning in the assertion of the ideality of the present. The trace is what expresses "relationship to the illeity as to the alterity of a past that never was and can never be lived in the originary or modified form of presence."[46]

We can thus see that Derrida's contention with the Husserlian project, and most every other philosophy developed in the Western hemisphere, is the misleading assertion of a *point* of present that accompanies them all, which they can, however, never verify. Instead, the search for the present and its obvious nonfeasibleness translate into a violence that attempts to procure the present that cannot be held down. The written inscription of the spoken word turns out to be a vain attempt to stop the present from moving on. Yet what remains is not the present but just the inscription which, in order to be made present again, will have to be infinitely repeated. Even the oral expression of a word takes on the same violent structure, since it is nothing but the assertion of a present that can never be obtained.

Despite this assessment of the direction and scope of the Western tradition, it can be said that Derrida's introduction of the trace as the epistemological potential for a pure space of presence recasts this tradition in a framework of search, task, and hope rather than in one of ultimate abandon. He does not reject metaphysics, in particular not the adventurous type and instead demonstrates that the latter is, in fact, the only one that can make sense from a perspective that seeks to understand the world from the perspective of temporality. Deconstruction rejects Husserl's rejection of an adventurous metaphysics and instead affirms it as the only metaphysics possible.

This moment in the analysis of language, the moment of the recognition of the infinity of the system of signs, the recognition of the trace rather than the signified, etc., and the recognition of the task that is involved in attaining truth through language, this moment is the moment of ethics. It is the moment of Babelian ethics in Derrida's understanding, i.e., an ethics that knows itself given as the task to minimize the difference between signified and signifier, that understands language as the expression of the infinite distance between the signifier and the transcendent signified, but that also is constantly informed by the ever distant signified.

The Ethics of Babel

In order to understand what this signified is and how precisely it signifies, we will now have to turn to another important essay by Derrida that tackles expressly the question of language from within the framework of the story of Babel (Gen. 11: 1–9). The advantage of discussing this essay at this point lies in the fact that it exemplifies the way in which Derrida attempts to weld together his critical insights into Husserl's work in order to construct a new adventurous metaphysics. The two insights are that no philosophy can possibly escape the temporal structure of its own language and that the deferral of the point of the present will lead to the referral toward an infinitely removed, asymptotic ideal.

"Des Tours de Babel",[47] published in 1985, is essentially a treatise on the issue of translation and deals in its main part with Walter Benjamin's *"Die Aufgabe des Übersetzers."*[48] Derrida understands Babel as the archetypal attempt to built a universal kingdom with a universal language spoken in it, humanity is forced into a double-bind in which on the one hand it is forced to give up its claims to universality, that is unimpeded communication across all of humanity, and in which it is, on the other hand, forced to engage in translation every time something is said by someone. Babel, for Derrida stands for:

> l'inadéquation d'une langue à l'autre, d'un lieu de l'encyclopédie à l'autre, du langage à lui-même et au sens, il dit aussi la nécessité de la figuration, du mythes, des tropes, des tours, de la traduction inadéquate pour suppléer à ce que la multiplicité nous interdit. En ce sens, il serait le mythe de l'origine du mythe, la métaphore de la métaphore, le récit du récit, la traduction de la traduction.

> the inadequation of one tongue to another, of one place in the encyclopedia to another, of language to itself and to meaning, an so forth, it also tells of the need for figuration, for myth, for tropes, for twists and turns, for translation inadequate to compensate for that which multiplicity denies us. In this sense it would be the myth of the origin of the myth, the metaphor of metaphor, the narrative of narrative, the translation of translation, and so on.[49]

Babel is more than just another one of those stories from the book of Genesis. It is the story where the origin of the linguistic condition of humanity is revealed to us. Babel etiologizes what humanity has been all about: having different languages we simultaneously recognize the need to bridge the differences through translation, however, that translation is always impossible. There remains, however, the radical inadequation of one language to another, the necessity of figurations, myths, and tropes to say and express what cannot be said directly.

How did this come about? Babel is a description of how humanity wanted to make itself a name in order to become powerful and to avoid dispersion throughout the world. They were, in other words, interested in universal power and a genealogy that would secure them as one people. One sole language, symbolized through the one tower that would reach the sky with its top, was supposed to guarantee their persistence. "יהוה," seeing what happened on earth, decided to frustrate their efforts and to turn around what they aspire for. As a consequence the people did not longer understand each other and were dispersed around the world.

The story does not give the reader much information as to why exactly God is displeased with the people. Is it the one name they are looking for, or is it the totality that they are trying to reach as one people? Derrida asks the crucial question when he says: *"Ne peut-on alors parler d'une jalousie de Dieu?"* (Can one not speak of a jealousy of God?) In his reading it is God's anger, his *"ressentiment,"* that makes him impose his name against that of the people. *"Sur quoi il clame son nom: Bavel, Confusion."* In the traditional reading of this particular passage *"son nom"* is usually related to the city. The translation would thus run "he claims its name: Babel, Confusion." Yet, the French translation that Derrida derives his interpretation from also allows for a second reading that translates the expression "son nom" as "his name." Thus, God is proclaiming his name over the city. And again that name would be Babel, Confusion.

This *"croissance,"* this crossing of meanings, is of so much significance for Derrida, because it indicates the above-mentioned "double-bind" under which the people are put in this story. With reference to Voltaire's *Dictionnaire philosophique*,[50] Derrida points out that "Babel" can either mean "confusion" (but then it would not be clear if the confusion of the architects who built the city was meant or if it was used in reference to the people's language) or "Babel" could also mean "God the father" because as Voltaire writes: *"Je ne sais pas pourquoi il est dit dans la Genèse que Babel signifie confusion; car 'ba' signifie 'père' dans les langues orientales, et 'Bel' signifie 'Dieu'"* ("I do not know why it is said in *Genesis* that Babel signifies confusion, for *Ba* signifies father in the Oriental tongues, and *Bel* signifies God).[51] The question is, in other words, if God imposed confusion or if God imposed God's name on the people. And if God did the latter why was the result confusion? Derrida interprets: *"Et on ne peut plus s'entendre quand il n'y a que du nom propre, et on ne peut plus s'entendre quand il n'y a plus de nom propre"* ("And understanding is no longer possible when there are only proper names, and understanding is no longer possible when there are no proper names").[52] By imposing the one name, the name of the father, God imposed the proper name as such in light of which all other proper names had to fade away. There was nothing but and nothing more than the one proper name. Confusion resulted, since now the people were no longer able to understand each other. The proper name was proper only to one: God. And the people had to understand that reaching out for their own proper name, as they had done in attempting to finish the tower, was always also a reaching out for the proper name of God, which was precisely what they were not allowed to do. However, now that they were condemned to translation, every act of translation by itself turned into a search for the proper name, i.e., that common denominator that would make a translation possible. Derrida concludes that *"Dieu déconstruit. Lui-même."* ("God deconstructs. Himself.") God deconstructs himself and thus makes it impossible to refer to God except by way of infinite rapprochement. Every translation, every word is an attempt to reach for the proper, the one, a totality. But this predicament cannot be dismissed as something worthless. Human beings are forced to speak and interpret, because, since Babel, they lost their unity and thus their communal understanding.

Husserl and Babel

We now have to move back to Husserl and investigate what the effect is that universal translation, i.e., the inevitability of translation for any act of human communication, has on Husserl's phenomenological project.

The main characteristic of Husserl's philosophy is his search for an unadulterated present, a living present, a moment (*"Augenblick"*) in which meaning is grasped free of all temporal constitution. We had already preliminarily pointed to the problematic of such a position when it starts to investigate its own linguistic basis. The mere saying of such a present will already delay it in such a way that its attainment will be forever barred.

There still remains a connection, to be sure, with the original, that which was to be said, but we can almost sense how the moment disappears while we are still busy grasping it verbally. Thus, this connection is simultaneously what renders evident the lag, the deferral, that has elapsed.

Translation is, in Derrida's view, only a special case of this general observation. The goal of a translation is, obviously, the retrieval of the meaning that a certain text had in the original language. It is the rendering transparent of a document for an audience that otherwise would not have access to that document. But what a translation also invokes while rendering meaning in this very special and technical way is an unbridgeable distance between the original and the translated text. It would be impossible to equate the two documents, implying that one was exactly like the other. Instead the relationship between the original and the translation will be comprehended as one in which the absence of the original is felt continuously. The product of translation is not the original; it is not its mirror-image; it is not even close to the original. It is, in many respects, another original, created, however, with another text in the back of the mind of the translator. However, this relationship with a past original is not the only characteristic of translations. Derrida claims also that "in a mode that is solely anticipatory, annunciatory, almost prophetic, translation renders present an affinity that is never present in the presentation."[53] Although we had mainly talked about the original as a past, an event, text, etc. that was awaiting its reproduction in the new transparency of a translation, Derrida instead now invokes the future. Translations also function in the anticipatory mode. In and through them is announced an affinity, a drawnness, or belonging together that somehow would not become transparent without the translation.

Benjamin and Babel

That which is announced, and which we had already looked for in the original, is meaning, or better, truth. Truth is precisely not reached through or at the moment of presentation. It is only sensed as an affinity, as an announcement. Derrida follows Benjamin when he says that

> Cela n'est pas sans rapport avec la vérité. Elle est apparement au-delà de toute *Übertragung* et de toute *Übersetzung* possibles. Elle n'est pas la correspondance représentative entre l'originale et la traduction, ni même adéquation première entre l'original et quelque objet ou signification hors de lui. La vérité serait plutôt le *langage pur* en lequel le snes et la lettre ne se dissocient plus.

> truth is apparently beyond every *Übertragung* and every possible *Übersetzung*. It is not the representational correspondence between the original and the translation, nor even the primary adequation between the original and some object or signification exterior to it. Truth would be rather the *pure language* in which the meaning and the letters no longer dissociate.[54]

In other words, what Derrida is saying here through the text of Benjamin is that, similar to the non-self-presence that stands in the way of Husserl's goal of *"Vergegenwärtigung,"* similar to the Kantian idea that always replaces that goal when it becomes clear that it cannot be reached, a translation also stands for meaning, the truth, as a whole. It is an aspect of the movement, the infinite completion of a task infinitely removed. "But the sign of that growth is 'present' (*gegenwärtig*) only in the 'knowledge of that distance,' in the "Entfernung," *the remoteness* that relates us to it."[55] It is for this reason that Benjamin can talk about the task of the translator. When one engages in the business of translation one is immediately caught between an inaccessible original and an infinitely removed ideal or telos. The task is to contribute to the rendering of meaning by translating the text that is given. The crossing of languages as it occurs in and through the process of translation "assures the growth of languages."[56, 57]

What is the reference point of such progress or growth (Benjamin)? Benjamin speaks of a task, and it is mandatory for us to find out towards what point exactly that task is going. Derrida's reading is instructive because it reiterates his reading of Husserl's playing with the idea in the Kantian sense. Where the latter substitutes this idea teleologically, i.e., whenever the living present cannot be obtained, Benjamin refers to God or "a thought of God" ("Auf ein Gedenken Gottes").[58] The guarantor of translatability is, for Benjamin, God. "Benjamin named God at this point . . . guaranteeing the correspondence between the languages engaged in translation."[59]

But there is more at stake in Derrida's reading of the story of Babel. "God also appealed to translation, not only between the tongues that had suddenly become multiple and confused, but first *of his name* . . . he is also a petitioner for translation."[60] We can see how in this reading the emphasis on God is shifted from that of a mere reference point to that of the all-embracing task itself. The latter interpretation clarifies that God's announcing God-self as "God the father" did nothing but create confusion. No one understood this name correctly. The confusion of languages that entails the announcing of the name is really a confusion about God's name whose comprehensibility now is to be retrieved through translation.

> Car Babel est intraduisible. Dieu pleure sur son nom. Son texte est le plus sacré, le plus poétique, le plus originaire puisqu'il crée un nom et se le donne, il n'en reste pas moins indigent en sa force et en sa richesse même, il pleure après un traducteur.

> For Babel is untranslatable. God weeps over his name. His text is the most sacred, the most poetic, the most originary, since he creates a name and gives it to himself, but he is left no less destitute in his force and even in his wealth; he pleads for a translator.[61]

For Benjamin, as we have pointed out already, the notion of growth is essential in this connection. The need/petition for translation entails a growth of language, since every translation contributes to breadth in meaning and understanding of the text. This growth goes towards "a kingdom which is at once 'promised and denied where the languages will be reconciled and fulfilled'" ("*den vorbestimmten, versagten Versöhnungs- und Erfüllungsbereich der Sprachen*"). It is a holy growth ("*heiliges Wachstum*") which, however, never succeeds. "There is something

untouchable, and in this sense the reconciliation is only promised."[62] A promise is the announcing of something to come. It
draws me towards something, it entices me into it. Here it is
reconciliation that is promised. A translation that can promise
such reconciliation, or even just evoke the desire for such reconciliation, "is a rare and notable event."[63]

This promise also constitutes the task for the translator. The
task is to get to the sacred text intended in and through the
holy growth of languages. It "marks the limit, the pure even if
inaccessible model, of pure transferability, the ideal starting
point from which one could think, evaluate, measure the essential, that is to say poetic, translation."[64] "The sacred surrenders
itself to translation which devotes itself to the sacred."[65] We
had already seen how the act of translation establishes archic
and teleological connectedness. It is of much significance for
Derrida that in translating we respond to something/someone
else (a text or speaker).[66] Generally a translation would not so
much be seen as responding to an original but as an attempt to
represent that original symmetrically in another language. The
juxtaposition of translation and response gives life but also separateness to the text since it impedes absolute congruousness
between it and its translation. In a way, a response is always
impossible. The otherness or radical absence of the speaker or
text in an epistemological sense makes a translation or response
futile. If an order of translation should be possible at all, a translation or response must be able to refer to a third that represents the original as well as the translation. In the previous
section we had already seen that, based on the story of Babel,
this third can be the name of God, i.e., being. Translation requires such a third, yet, in the Hebrew context, it prohibits it at
the same time, since the reference to God goes exactly against
the command not to use God's name. With respect to translation, hence, humanity finds itself in a double-bind structure. It
is both forced to and prohibited from translating.[67]

It is obvious that Derrida's reading of Benjamin leads us right
back to Husserl's idea in the Kantian sense as well as to Cohen's

concept of God as the correlational limit for the asymptotic function of human ethical action. The similarities between Derrida's thinking and that of Benjamin and Husserl go back to a common root which might lie in the 19th century, with Hermann Cohen's system of Jewish neo-Kantianism. We have not yet undertaken to show how exactly Derrida's thrust also goes towards the ethical. That is, we have not yet sufficiently proven the connection that goes from Cohen through Levinas to Derrida. This connection should show that, as for Cohen so also for Levinas and Derrida, the relationship with an absolute, or the idea in the Kantian sense, or God always translates into ethics. Right at the end of "Des Tours de Babel" Derrida writes about the epistemology of translation (and we might say now the epistemology of human existence in general) that "this situation, though being one of pure limit, does not exclude — quite the contrary — gradations, virtuality, interval and in-between, the infinite labor to rejoin that which is nevertheless past, already given, even here, between the lines, already signed."[68] The attempt to rejoin with something that is already past yet not yet present either is the continual theme of the condition in which humanity finds itself. Translation, literally translated, means not only to substitute the words from language for the words of another language. Translation means "*übersetzen*," to cross over the "Red Sea," or into the promised land. For Derrida, translation includes the crossing over into the realm of truth, the absolute, towards which we always translate.

The realm of truth is one to which we can only relate apocalyptically. Truth is the event that stands at the end of an infinite process of translation. Infinite because every attempt to grasp truth is a simultaneous failure and success to understand it. "Apocalypse" in Derrida's reading does not mean catastrophe but deferred truth. It is the tension that develops between now and a promise that comes to us from the future. That tension is the apocalytpic condition in which humanity finds itself both as the unveiling of truth as well as the exiling from it.

SEVEN

The Absolute

Apocalypse: Epistemological Exile vis-à-vis Truth

APOCALYPSE AND ABSOLUTE

The essay "D'un ton apocalyptique adopté naguère en philosophie" (Of a Recently Adopted Apocalyptic Tone in Philosophy) published in 1983 belongs to a set of papers first read at a conference apropos the work of Derrida.[1] The title of the conference was "Les Fins de l'homme (A Partir du Travail de Jacques Derrida)." It repeated the title of an earlier essay by Derrida in which he analyzes Heidegger's essay "On Humanism." He shows in it how the phenomenological project moves away from a description of the empirical ends of humanity to those that it calls transcendental. "Transcendental phenomenology is in this sense the ultimate achievement of the teleology of reason that traverses humanity."[2] The consequence is that transcendental thinking is contingent upon "mortality, of a relation to finitude as the origin of ideality . . . The name of man . . . has meaning only in this eschato-teleological situation."[3] The theme of the conference that the latter essay was first presented at was "Philosophy and Anthropology."

We can see from this short sequence of Derrida's work that there has been an inherent thematic continuity with respect to the question of how one can understand humanity's relationship with its own end. We have seen, in fact, that in his earlier work Derrida first moves to show that such an end indeed exists and that it is an informative factor in Husserl's phenomenology whose self-understanding derived precisely from the rejection of such ends in the form of infinite tasks in favor of the affirmation of an immediate and pure present. But not only Husserl, also Heidegger, was caught in a similar situation. His description of Being was bound, as Derrida points out, to a certain proximity of the being of Dasein to itself. Yet this proximity could not be expressed other than by recourse to a certain phenomenological metaphor that was intricately connected to the equation of light and truth.

Derrida's analysis both thematizes the topic of the end of humanity through its reading of Husserl and Heidegger, but it furthermore questions the "security"[4] that this kind of thinking still exhibits with respect to the relationship between humanity, its own being, and its end. The various descriptions of the end of humanity have only added to the "equivocality"[5] that exists with respect to "the play of telos and death."[6] It is this equivocality that causes "the violent relationship of the West to its other"[7] and simultaneously enables deconstruction to develop a strategy against this violence that uses "against the edifice the instruments or stones available in the house."[8]

> In the reading of this play, one may take the following sequence in all its senses: the end of man is the thinking of Being, man is the end of the thinking of Being, the end of man is the end of the thinking of Being. Man, since always, is his proper end, that is, the end of his proper. Being, since always, is its proper end, that is, the end of its proper.[9]

How should humanity position itself with respect to the thinking of the/its end? Is the tone of this last paragraph necessary or is it a deliberate obfuscation of a rather simple idea? Why is it that Derrida seems to think that the end of humanity, i.e., its purpose, may coincide with humanity's end, i.e., its death?

Whence comes the apocalyptic notion that seems to be going through Derrida's writings like a red thread?

Derrida himself had suggested that discourse, i.e. language and reason were nothing but the result of an invisible, unconceptualizable, inaudible, etc., non-concept by the name of "différance." The originality of this non-concept lay in the fact that it was supposed to bracket the significance of archeological and teleological thought for philosophical concepts and instead viewed thinking, speaking, rational discourse, irrational discourse, in short life, as proceeding in a badly infinite manner, viz. by adding signifier to signifier without either coming closer to a telos or being able to trace itself back to a single common origin.

Already in this description we can notice the conceptual breadth of Derrida's apocalyptic tone. On the one hand he seems to be suggesting that the end of philosophy in all its institutional forms is at hand. But on the other hand, the word "apocalyptic" seems to invoke just the opposite, viz. the infinite task of a philosophical discourse that will never find an end. We find ourselves in a double-bind trying to avert the claim of the death of philosophy on the one hand, yet also discontent with the notion that philosophy might never end, i.e., that it might never succeed. The fear of infinite rest, implicit in the notion of death, is just as strong as the fear of infinite motion. Derrida is introducing both notions into the discourse of philosophy, causing the "*Sisyphoi*" of traditional philosophy to think about the possibility of being forced to roll the boulder of philosophy up the hill for the last time, forever.[10]

To be sure, Derrida could have chosen a different tone. We know from the preceding chapter how he views the linguistic constitutedness of the world. Language is an infinite reservoir for more world to be created through speaking. Hence the only thing that we can do with a reasonable hope of success is analyze the ways in which language works. Upon what is it built? Where does it originate? The answer, or at least part of the answer, is that language works as a system of signs organized in a highly arbitrary fashion. One sign seems to be building on another. All of them are in either indirect or direct contact with each other, but all of them as a whole seem to be without boundaries. Even internally, i.e., within the synchronic and topical unity of the text, the introduction of another sign will not cause a rupture or a situation of non-signification, but instead, this sign will immediately be integrated into the context of meaning. Thus, Derrida is saying, like Kant, that our epistemological grasp of a thing (as the origin of signification) will never be more than the representations that our perception gives us of those things. Yet, the possibilities of such representations are unlimited.

We saw in the last chapter, however, that Derrida has cast this observation about the function of language in a frame that emphasizes signification not just as an infinite process but as an infinite task. This is an important difference, since with the introduction of the task comes the awareness of some kind of telos that directs it. Why, then does Derrida formulate these issues in the apocalyptic style that he is known for? Why not use Kantian language in order to talk about the incongruence of the thing in itself and its concept, why not use Husserl or Cohen to talk about the infinite path that leads to true exteriority? One reason, of course, is that it would be misinterpreting Kant's *Critique of Pure Reason* to read it as the programmatic forerunner of recent postmodernism. Kant did foresee the rise of postmodernism, albeit negatively, and was concerned with defending reason against it. He believed in the agency of the subject, its power to synthesize, analyze, analogize, to pass ethical judgment and to understand true art. The light of reason that illuminated the world and made it coherent was coming from the subject. It was given to us as reason and has been shining forth since then to illuminate our analytical activities within the world (i.e. the subject shed light on what it wanted to understand). What we see, know, and understand, according to Kant, we do so because we give it light. This insight, however, did not seduce Kant into thinking that everything was subjectively relative. Instead he assumed that, as subjects, we are all constituted in the same way. Thus, coherence and objectivity are guaranteed (even though this objectivity is an objectivity of subjects, not of objects) and the world still makes sense, even intersubjectively. Therefore, Kant would not have agreed with Derrida after all. There is truth and it can be attained through an adequate analytic of human consciousness.

Another reason for Derrida's adoption of the apocalyptic tone despite Kant is that philosophy (at least in Europe) never officially questioned the status and function of absolutes and thus never came to terms with the problem of non-meaning and illusory truth claims. Both Jamesian or Deweyan pragmatism were ridiculed in Europe for their unwillingness to submit to absolutes (they were either called superficial or — with allusions to Nietzsche — renegade) and the Continent proceeded to produce a philosophy that was built on the assumption that absolutes do exist, even though they might not be available as other existing things are. The reasons for such a development are various and this is not the place to investigate them. Suffice it to say that the edifice of Western culture as a whole is vitally dependent on the belief in absolutes and consequently begins to tremble the moment those absolutes start to disappear.

Derrida is *not* arguing against the social and intellectual necessity of absolutes. That is one of the claims that I want to venture in the course of this chapter. Instead his aim seems to be to lay open a certain intra-absolute necessity that will reveal the combined absolute/nonabsolute structure that both the things that we call absolute and the things that we call nonabsolute carry within themselves. Absolutes do change because of that inherent structure. Deleuze and Guattari show very effectively how such changes can be understood.[11] Yet, that does not mean that we can dispense with them altogether. From the point of view of thinking, absolutes are indispensable. There is at least a need for a certain methodical absolute through which the rational and the irrational, the ethical and the nonethical, can be arranged in a certain way that makes them palatable.

Yet the problem is that absolutes are by nature not palatable. An absolute talked about has already become a dis-solute open for interpretation and hence open for opinions.

It is here that Derrida's contribution to philosophy begins. The death of philosophy is meant to point towards the dissolute nature of a discourse whose self-understanding has so far been shaped by what it attempts to talk about: truth, i.e. the absolute. As such, as philosophy confusing itself with absolute truth, philosophy is dead and has always been dead. Yet, as a discipline that seeks truth and has made truth its absolute, it still functions and it will not stop functioning until it has coincided with its telos (absolute truth). The latter of course also signifies its dilemma. The fact that its telos is an absolute makes it clear from the outset that philosophy will not succeed. Thus, we are faced with some rather strange questions that investigate the performance of philosophy as a way of human thinking. The questions are: 1.1 Is it sensible to pursue a project (the project of truth), if it is evident that that project will never succeed? 1.2 Can philosophy aim at something less than truth, that will, however, be more successful? 2.1 Does it make a difference whether philosophy thinks it will know truth eventually or whether it thinks it will not know it? 2.2 What can be the advantages of a discourse that knows itself to be failing perennially?

Within the framework of Derrida's essay about the apocalyptic tone, questions have to be added that concern the relationship with Levinas which, in this piece, is only implicit, but strongly implicit. Under this heading belongs the question of a particularly Jewish sphere in which Derrida begins to think about the question of the apocalypse, maybe inspired by Levinas, but also critical of Levinas's project, especially concerning the function and position of the other.

Apocalypse in Translation

It is only towards the end of his essay "Of an Apocalyptic Tone Recently Adopted in Philosophy" that Derrida explains why he chose to speak/write on this topic. His reflection comes from an etymological perspective which — as we have seen in the previous chapter — can simultaneously be archic and teleological. We have to keep in mind that as such (as an enterprise of a thoroughly archic nature) the viability of analyses based on etymological findings is, from the standpoint of deconstruction, questionable. Although such analyses are usually geared towards bringing out hidden, lost, or forgotten meanings of a certain word or idiom, one cannot overlook that the methodology of etymology is highly synchronic, i.e., it assembles into the present the diachrony of meanings of a certain term, and thus does epistemic violence to that term. In other words, etymological analysis is based on a functioning theory of the concept which is, however, exactly what has become questionable in Derrida's work. It seems to me that this might be the source of a possible misunderstanding of Derrida's intentions and the scope of deconstruction in general. We will see that the goal cannot be to claim the impossibility, inviability, or incredibility of conceptual discourse at large. That would be a fairly self-defeating and ridiculous exercise. The task that deconstruction has set for itself is to shake up the false security of pure meaning, i.e., of an allegedly nonambiguous world in which thought and action can be measured against an unchanging and unadulterated truth. The task of deconstruction is, in other words, to preserve the moment of ambiguity that so much of philosophy and thinking in general is wanting.

It is of utmost significance in this connection to emphasize that, despite lingering possibilities of synchronism, Derrida's reading does not reject the relationship between terms, texts, and the world with their respective origins and teloi. Rather the defense of diachronism against synchronism turns on how this relationship is described and understood. Such a description is more than just a neutral accounting for certain facts. It is rather a description that is concerned with the maintenance of the apocalyptic structures that inhere the world and thus must be seen as a strategic description. The etymology of the term "ἀποκαλυπτω" is an example of such a strategy. It hollows out the colloquial catastrophic notion that the world has assumed in our language and instead substitutes a field of meanings that demonstrate the term's archeological and teleological connections.

Derrida states that "Ἀποκαλυπτω" is the translation that the authors of the LXX (Septuagint) chose for the Hebrew "נלה." "נלה" has two main meanings around which fields of submeanings have developed. One is that of "unveiling" and the other one is that of "abandoning" and "going into exile." It is in the former sense that the LXX uses the word "ἀποκαλυπτω." Right from the beginning of his essay it is clear that Derrida avoids understanding the term "apocalypse" in its colloquial sense of "catastrophe" and instead seems to substitute for it the more mystical notion of unveiling from the LXX. This mystical notion opens up the possibility of an interpretation that moves him quite close to Levinas's philosophy of the other as well as that of Benjamin's holy growth of language.

Central for this connection is not the Greek but the Hebrew term "נלה." Derrida himself only refers to its significance as disclosure or unveiling. Yet through his translation of the term "ἀποκαλὑπτω" into "נלה" he has tapped a whole set of other meanings that also belong to this term. Translating, of course, stands for more than just a literal activity. In the previous chapter we saw that it is adequately understood as a human condition. The fact that it is already hampered so severely shows the limits and restrictions that exist for that condition. The term "נלה" which, in Jewish culture, aside from simply being a word with a certain meaning attached to it, also can function as a categorial term designating that translatory condition as an epistemological one. This will become clearer if we look more closely at the different meanings that this term has in the Hebrew language. Aside from the notion of "unveiling" and "to lay bare" in the Kal and the Hiphil tenses, the term "נלה" can have the meaning of "emigrating," "being deported" or "going into exile." Before we can appreciate the significance of this translation for the project that Derrida pursues in the essay on the apocalyptic tone, it is necessary to consider a little more what the meaning of exile ("נלות") is in the Jewish tradition.

Apocalypse as Exile

For many Jews exile has to be understood as part of God's command to spread the message of monotheism. Exile so understood is nothing but a global mission which requires the Jewish people to go into the world and live, but not mix, with gentiles and pagans. In most cases this meaning of "נלות" was secondary to another one, however, which took exile to be a divine punishment for the sinful ways in which Israel had lived. It would then be seen as the direct response by God to the ways in which the people of Israel had conducted themselves. Given these two general meanings of "נלות" the question is whether the Jews are asked to wait out the time of exile until God either decides that they have been punished enough or that their mission is achieved, or if they can seek to end their exilic existence by looking for another and new way of living as a united people (Zionism). We can thus summarize that in both cases "נלות" had to do with the relationship between God and Israelites and, on a secondary level, with the pagan world. Yet, this is not enough to understand the centrality of the term for Derrida (and for Levinas for that matter). In order to achieve that we will have to consider the meaning of "נלות" for those who had to endure it.

What does it mean to be in exile? In all cases being in exile points towards a situation of removal or distance from what once used to be familiar. One is away from one's home-land, possibly also away from one's own family. In almost every case exile involves at least a partial, surrender of one's own language in favor of the language that is spoken by the majority of the people into whose land one has been brought. This would indicate that exile also implies being under the control and rule of another people. Consequently, one has to live under constant surveillance and observation. One might have to endure poverty and exploitation, and in more general terms one would have to live under the increasing dominance of the ruling country's customs and habits while one's own traditions would fall into oblivion.

"נלות" then, is an experience of utter alienation, of being determined by others, of losing one's home, land and habitat, in short: of losing oneself. What the exilic thematic suggests, aside from the historical fact of a people's exile, is that being in exile involves an involuntary abandoning of, or going away from, one's self in order to adopt the customs and habits of another people who now are to determine much of what the exiled people used to decide for themselves. Being in exile invokes the theme of being held hostage by someone. The exilic situation emphasizes how the other (the other customs, language, government) becomes the center of the one who is in exile. Simultaneously, the exiled will posit their return to the self as yet another other which is to come in an unforeseeable future. Thus, their self now appears as distended between the two limits, one is the other that controls them and one the other for which they are longing. Stabilized by the equal tension between non-self and controlling other and non-self and longed for other, selfhood and self-determination have been replaced.

Arnold Eisen[12] points out how the exilic moment in the history of the Jewish people has turned from a mere historic fact (like the exile in Egypt or the exile after the destruction of the second temple) into a "tradition of reflection unbroken since Genesis [which] has not lost its hold even today, when part of the Jewish people has returned to its promised land." For the Jews, Eisen claims, exile has had too strong an impact to be forgotten. It now conditions and evokes a "desire to exorcise the terrors of dispersion by giving them a name." The exilic condition has come to name two main situations which, as Eisen points out, are both already part of the account of Creation in the book of Genesis and both reveal a progressive shattering of an original unity. The first one is the exile in which Adam and Eve find themselves after they have eaten from the tree of knowledge. This initiation into knowledge is of much significance because, while providing new insight into the things that surround the two proto-humans, it simultaneously lets an infinite distance elapse between them and those things. They have moved into an epistemological situation where they understand the world conceptually, i.e. through signifiers. The signifieds will now be infinitely removed. This situation also has an effect on the relationship between humans and God. God cannot be known anymore or, with reference to the above, God can *only* be known. Here we have an account of what will be the relation between God and humans from now on. Humans are removed from God and the Garden and instead have to struggle with the obstacles that the world will set against them. Still, as human beings, they are united.

The second exile is announced after Cain has killed his brother Abel. Eisen remarks that here an escalation of the first exile is introduced. Not only will Cain have to struggle like his parents, but also taken away is his unity with the human community so that he will be unable to count on the recognition and protection of other human beings. Anyone could kill him. He has become a true outcast whom only God can protect. The impossibility of this situation is obvious. Cain (who now stands representatively for humanity) is epistemologically removed from God and the world while at the same time ethically removed from his community and hence is thrown back into a relationship with God which he will never understand, yet has to strive for, if he wants to live.

Eisen ends up defining exile as "the awareness of being somewhere else than where God is and humanity should be."[13] In other words exile has turned into a question of theology and ethics or of theological ethics. Exile has become a hermeneutic condition without which Jewish thinking cannot be understood adequately.

Apocalypse as an Epistemological Condition

Along the lines of Derrida's attempt to define "נלה," i.e., unveiling as the origin of the apocalyptic condition, I would like to push the exilic problematic even further. Can it also be understood as an epistemological condition? Is it possible to say that knowing, i.e., the process of thematizing and assembling things into my consciousness, is an attempt to overcome one's own inner (and outer) exile?

The exile-thematic is not foreign to Derrida, although the present essay does not deal with it specifically. In an essay on Edmond Jabès,[14] however, Derrida spells out his reading of the meaning of exile for the Jews. "The necessity of commentary, like poetic necessity, is the very form of exiled speech,"[15] and one can thus infer that for Derrida the very bed-rock of Jewish thought, its infinite proliferation and interpretation of commentary-literature, is precisely what marks it as a tradition that has been, and still is, exiled. The very existence of a commentary literature is the sign for the Jews' distance from the fulfillment of the promise, i.e., from the truth. This, of course, presupposes that somehow the content of the promise, truth, is known *already*, that it can be conceptualized. Derrida confirms this notion. This "already" "precisely signifies the original exile from the kingdom of Being, signifies exile as the conceptualization of Being and signifies that Being never is, never shows *itself*, is never *present*, is never *now*, outside difference (in all the senses today required by this word)."[16] Exile, he says with reference to Jabès' work, must be understood as the difference between speech and writing. Whereas speech indicates immediacy, i.e., the immediate presence of speaker and listener to each other, writing presupposes the absence of both, speaker (writer) and listener (reader) to each other. Both find themselves marked through a separation from each other. Derrida quotes Jabès saying "The garden is speech, the desert writing. In each grain of sand a sign surprises." And a little later Derrida himself comments: "The Judaic experience as reflection, as separation of life and thought, signifies the crossing of the book as an infinite anchoritism placed between two immediacies and two self-identifications."[17] Writing is indeed a process of exiling oneself. In writing one is forced to withdraw, to give up the written, to leave and let the reader interpret the text. Yet, at the same time exile is deferred in my writing, since through it I can give myself a name.[18]

Obviously, exile and literality have become synonymous in Derrida's reading. When we have to write we enjoy the freedom of nonimmediacy, i.e., of being removed from the object of our writing, yet, simultaneously, we are enslaved to an eternal rupture between ourselves, our writing and what we are writing about. This, Derrida claims, is especially true for the Jews. Their existence is described as that of the people of the book. But this statement, aside from understanding the Jews as a people concerned with interpretation and exegesis of Scripture, also becomes a verdict. For

> quand un Juif . . . proclame le Lieu, il . . . ne déclare . . . pas la guerre. Car nous rappelant depuis l'outre-mémoire, ce Lieu, cette terre sont toujours Là-Bas. Le Lieu n'est ce pas l'Ici empirique et national d'un territoire. . . . La liberté ne s'accorde à la Terre non-païenne que si elle en est séparée par le Désert de la Promesse.

> when a Jew . . . proclaims a site, he is not declaring war. For this site, this land, calling to us from beyond memory, is always elsewhere. The site is not the empirical and national Here of a territory . . . Freedom is granted to the nonpagan Land only if it is separated from freedom by the Desert of the Promise.[19]

The separation also is a separation from God. Since the garden, i.e., speech, was lost, the immediate relationship with God was lost as well. The distance that has developed between God and humans "is respected only within the sands of a book."[20] It is speech's exile[21] which makes commentary and poetry necessary. The nomadic and exiled Jew erects a "fragile tent of words"[22] in the desert of infinite meanings. Yet, the exile remains. Derrida observes that "Jewish consciousness is indeed the unhappy consciousness"[23] of Hegel's Phenomenology.

Apocalypse as Exile and Desire

We are now in a position to ask if, along the lines of Eisen's definition, this unhappy Jewish consciousness is not a desire to be where God is and where humanity should be? Epistemologically, then, exile would describe precisely that nonreciprocal situation, metaphorically described as desire, between self and other, to which Levinas has been pointing relentlessly. It is one's desire for the Holy that is redirected by the Holy towards what is least desirable, viz. the other person next to one's neighbor. To be in exile means to feel and live according to one's infinite desire for the infinite good which translates into one's giving oneself over into the service of the other person. But to be in exile also means to accept one's own disposition as selfless self, distended between controlling and longed for other. It means to understand the reality of oneself as subject to be that of a point, i.e. a mathematical nothing. Yet, for Levinas my desire for the other person is triggered through God's command. It is a command that redefines the meaning of the word "holy" by saying that holiness consists precisely in our effort to take up the proximity between our neighbor and ourselves ethically. In marked difference from Derrida, Levinas, who does not really espouse the notion of "exile" the way Derrida does, confronts us with the un-ambiguous clarity of our neighbor's proximity. Proximity is a call for immediate action and servitude, not for epistemological search or commentary. However, Derrida's description of the relationship with truth and Levinas's description of the relationship with the other have in common the characteristic of desire. "Exile" as well as "serving" express the desire to get closer to the object, i.e., to get closer to truth or the other.

Yet, this desire for the other must be motivated through something and it is the other meaning of the Hebrew term "נלה" that will furnish the clue to that question. "נלה" also means "to unveil" and "to disclose." As such it is always related to something that is veiled and closed, thus marked by a fundamental difference of radical unknownness. That other and unknown thing

can hence arouse curiosity and desire for more knowledge about
it. In the Kal construction the verb can a) indicate the laying
bare of someone's ear for the sake of a revelation; it can b) be
read as a warning to do things in a certain way; it can c) concern the revelation of a secret, and it can d), as a past participle,
indicate the general accessibility of a document. Niphal and Piel
both point more towards the physical connotations of the word.
The Niphal indicates the reflexive meaning as to unveil or un-
dress oneself. But it can also mean the showing of God or of the
revealed. The Piel connotes the passive meaning as being unveiled or being undressed or the opening of someone's eyes.

The connections between the two main meanings of the verb
are difficult to recognize. "To unveil" and "to emigrate" do not
seem to have much in common at first sight. It seems, however,
that both meanings indicate a certain coming out of oneself, a
decentering. Something that formerly was a whole inviolable
unit (i.e., a secret, or a nation) which becomes dispersed and
spread out. Is not the spreading of a secret, its unveiling, simply a way of sending that secret into exile? And is not sending a
nation, a whole people once united, into exile an act of unveiling, an act of shaming them before the eye of another? Dispersion
as control seems an important aspect of this understanding,
since control increases with the increasing spreading of either
the people or the secret.

Rather than understanding the two meanings as meaning
the same, one could also attempt an understanding that derives one from the other. The exilic moment constitutes, as we
have seen above, a situation of alienation and otherness. Between self and foreign ruler, language, customs, etc. A tension
develops that can only diminish if one starts to unveil or un-
mask the other and gradually make it familiar with, that is
integrate it into, the sameness of the self. In that case one would
be able to say that my will to know, my will to uncover or unveil
is affixed to the exilic condition which first removes me from,
and, consequently, makes me aware of the other. In other words,
"נלות" produces or entails "נלה."

By involving the etymology from "αποκαλυπτω" to "נגלה,"
Derrida reveals his awareness of the fundamental import that
the exilic condition has for the project of thinking and of philosophy, i.e., for the desire of and progression towards truth.
The exilic moment, as a moment of distension of the self, represents what Levinas calls the ethical, viz. our absolute relationship with the other which predates all thinking and acting and
which makes language proliferate. The nonexilic, hence, turns
into an asymptotic limit towards which humanity strives in the
sense Eisen described it for the Jews. Derrida thus affirms that
being in an apocalyptic condition is being in exile from truth in
a paradigmatically Jewish way.

KANT'S DISTINGUISHED TONE

However, this condition is not just characteristic for the Jews
alone. It is treated by Derrida as a universal of the human constitution. He shows this by analyzing two texts that both deal
with the question of the apocalyptic. One is Kant's "Von einem
Neuerdings in der Philosophie Erhobenen Vornehmen Ton"[24] and
the other one is "The Apocalypse of John," the last book of the
Second Testament. The Kant essay is the one after which Derrida
named his own article on the apocalypse. Instead of using the
adjective "*vornehm*" which means as much as distinguished or
noble Derrida uses the term apocalyptic. Kant's main concern
with the noble or distinguished people is their claim that philosophy is either dead or that its death is immediately impend-
ing. Realizing that this claim is in particular directed toward
the kind of philosophy that his own name stands for, Kant begins to develop the differences between his type of thinking and
that of the noble ones in order to show that philosophy is not
dead at all.

Kant is mocking that the distinguished people, rather than
making use of the natural light of reason, seem to prefer talking about truth through vague feelings and assumptions, thereby

mystifying things that are really rather clear. His concern, however, is complex. On the one hand, he says, the people who claim that they have immediate access to the truth through immediate intuition (*"unmittelbare Anschauung"*) seem to have an advantage over those who have to rely on conceptual intuition (*"begriffliche Anschauung"*). Those who possess the former, Kant complains, will despise the latter. Yet, and this is Kant's second concern, it lies in the nature of conceptual intuition — true philosophy — that it requires much work (*"Arbeit"*) before one can truly appreciate its results. However, "everyone deems themselves distinguished (*"vornehm"*) to the degree that they believe they do not have to work" (my translation). Furthermore, he sees a severe confusion of issues at stake in the attempts of the distinguished to talk about truth through recourse to their feelings. It is in fact of great importance to remember that feeling can only be a secondary way of understanding truth, after the principles of understanding have been revealed through the work (*"Arbeit"*) of philosophy. Yet, the adepts of the distinguished tone seem to prefer a presentiment (*"Ahnung"*) of the truth to the truth itself. Such presentiment, however, proves fatal to true philosophy, since it rejects the possibility of reaching truth through concepts, and in fact claims that concepts themselves are subject to the presentimental approach, and thus cannot be known fully anyway.

Everyone who thus claims to be in the possession of truth, who claims to do philosophy, ends up substituting images or metaphors (*"bildliche Ausdrücke"*) for the knowledge of the objective (*"Kenntnis des Objektiven"*). They can do so in the name of practical reason, that is, in the name of the moral law which they think comes to human beings through "analogies" (*"Analogien"*) and "probabilities" (*"Wahrscheinlichkeiten"*). Yet, the secret of that law, Kant responds, can only be made sensible (*"fühlbar"*) after a slow and thorough development of the concepts of understanding and the testing of its foundations. Feeling (*"Gefühl"*) is thus a secondary event which follows the tedious working of human reason.

Kant legitimates his intervention with an allusion to a police of the sciences (*"Polizei der Wissenschaften"*) which, he thinks, could not tolerate the vague use of the word "philosophy" as it had become fashionable. However, he thinks that, in the end, the two parties should bury their antagonism and realize that they are seeking the same thing. The veiled goddess before which both sides supplicate is the moral law (*"moralisches Gesetz"*). Yet, the problem with the mystagogues is that they are teaching this moral law as if it worked through its personification (as Isis[25]), which Kant thinks should only be an aesthetic imagination in the form of an after-thought (*"hinten nach"*) to philosophy's logical type of teaching (*"logische Lehrart"*). Representing the idea of the moral law as personified goes along with the "danger of getting lost in fanatic vision (*"schwärmerische Vision"*) which is the death of all philosophy" (*"der Tod aller Philosophie"*).

Kant speculates that the nobles' claim — the announcement that philosophy had been dead for the last two thousand years — might in particular be a result of the enormous amount of work done by Aristotle. "The Stagirite had conquered so much for science so that he left things of only little significance for his followers to seek out."[26] But against that claim he holds that the death of philosophy is not caused by too much but only by too little work. The death of philosophy is caused by precisely those who claim that the eligibility for a discourse on truth derives itself from the insight that truth is nondiscursive. Truth, in this view, can only be talked about asymptotically, through the ever-present veil of Isis. This is what Kant takes issue with, to see truth as nondiscursive is to preempt reason's claim to clear and undistorted truth and instead substitute for it a kind of pseudo-eschatology that favors presentiment. That, however, in Kant's words, basically allows one "to turn the ghost into whatever one wants: lest it be a seeing which should be avoided."[27]

The mystagogues (i.e., those who have adopted the distinguished tone) go even further, however, in claiming that their way of pre-sensing the truth is the only adequate way of dealing with the metaphysical sublimity of reason. Every empirical aspect, i.e., one that transcends presentiment towards real knowledge, must necessarily weaken the transcendental status of practical reason. This, in their view, amounts to the castration (*"Entmannung"*)[28] of reason. Yet, obviously, it is they, in Kant's eyes, who are conducting reason's castration.

It becomes clear that Kant is after more than just the rejection of "distinguished" philosophy. To him philosophy does not just require a relationship with truth but also the adoption of a certain work-ethic that can get one to truth. He introduces a class-distinction between the nobles and the workers (with him being in the latter group) in order to work out the ethos of doing philosophy itself. This sets the tone also for Derrida, since his work with this essay focuses precisely on the task of philosophy.

THE APOCALYPTIC ASPECT IN KANT'S APPROACH

Let us return to Derrida, then, and see how he moves from the question of the apocalypse, i.e., the question of unveiling, to that of the castration of reason and its beyond. Derrida's assertion, corroborated by the "ἀποκαλύπτω"/"נגלה" etymology is that Kant is really fighting against a discourse in philosophy that somehow has wedged itself between the promise of disclosure and the deferral of this disclosure into a moment of an infinite eschatology. Kant instead, in Derrida's reading, goes the way of a decidedly progressive thinker by opting for a belief in a philosophy that has finally been unveiled. Such a philosophy, and this is the thrust of Kant's argument in Derrida's reading, would be accessible to everyone and not only to those mystagogical "supermen" (*"Kraftmänner"*) who claim to have immediate access through immediate intuition.[29]

Derrida's main observation is that Kant, in rejecting the notion of the apocalyptic, that is the notion of an unveiling of Isis, is attempting to bar the mystagogues from personifying the moral law.

Autrement dit, et voilà un motif tranchant pour la pensée de la loi ou de l'éthique aujourd'hui, Kant appelle à placer la loi au-dessus et au-delà, non pas de la personne, mais de la personnification et du corps, comme de la voix sensible qui parle en nous, la singulière, qui nous parle en privé, la voix qu'on pourrait dire en son langage "pathologique" par opposition à la voix de la raison. La loi au-dessus du corps, de ce corps qui se trouve être ici représenté par une déesse voilée.

Put differently, and this reveals a decisive motif for the way the law or ethics (*"das heutige Denken des Gesetzes oder der Ethik"*) are thought today: Kant makes an appeal to locate the law above and outside of, not the person, but its personification as well as above and outside the body and the sensual voice that speaks in us. The latter is the only one that speaks to us privately. This voice, could be called "pathological" in his language, thus contrasting the voice of reason. The law above the body, above this body, found here to be represented by a veiled goddess.[30]

Based on this quote we can say that Derrida notices two things in Kant's attempt to negotiate a contract between the mystagogues and himself: First, the truth is one that is based on the exclusion of a third, i.e., the exclusion of a personified something for the sake of the impersonal voice of reason; second, Kant really does not abandon eschatological discourse altogether but simply substitutes his own "rational version" for that of the mystagogues. The latter is the firm belief in progress and improvement as well as the possibility of absolute truth as humanity's eschaton. The former is the belief that progress and improvement can only function if personification of that eschaton is avoided, i.e., if it is excluded as a third person. "The truce negotiated between the two parties of a non-castrated logos presupposes a certain exclusion. It presupposes a certain prohibited thing. There is an excluded third and that should suffice for now."[31] The exclusion, thus, concerns only a certain third, viz. the personified one, not any third in general, since such a third is indispensable for the notion of progress and improvement. It is such that Derrida can claim that since that time the occident had created an unbreachable contract between the discourses of the end in which even Kant's philosophy of pure reason participates just as much as that of the mystagogues. This discourse involves both, the necessity of the eschaton as such as well as its nonpersonified nature.

In making Kant admit this much, Derrida has already begun to move him into the general area of an apocalyptic discourse on truth. Here truth becomes an end, not an immediately and purely accessible point in the present. Thus, Derrida, contrary to Kant, holds on to the unavailability of truth as an end and, like Cohen and Levinas, understands this end to be an asymptotic concept. Such a concept serves as a limit function for a process that is itself infinite. This process distends between the limit function of its origin and the limit of its end. Both are ideal and thus unreachable. The task of the philosopher, viz. to find and name truth, is infinite.

That Derrida is attempting to suggest a model reminiscent of Cohen's infinite task can be further corroborated with his understanding of the word "tone." Whereas Kant only uses the word tone (*Ton*) as a synonym for "flair" or "characteristic," Derrida examines the tone as a phenomenon and observes that it has a differential structure. The Latin word "tonos" designates a stretched string or rope. Tone, thus, is the difference that occurs between the two points that the string is stretched between. The pitch, i.e., its meaning, is dependent on the tension of the string. It becomes clear that Derrida is suggesting that an apocalyptic tone is a tone inherent in any discourse. The exilic condition is nothing but the tone of those who want to know truth. Their distance from the point of absolute truth and their simultaneous desire for an unveiling of the truth makes way for a thinking that is generated presentimentally. Truth is the other that is available only through presentiment. It stretches me out across an infinite abyss, thus creating a certain tone that depends on how strongly my desire to unveil stretches me. Those who adopt an apocalyptic tone are doing so to unveil truth. But the notion of an adoption is misleading. Truth is perceived as something that is coming, i.e., something that has its point of origin in the future. Thus, in the process of unveiling truth, we subject ourselves to truth, each in our own unique way, thus establishing a unique tone for each of us. In other words, not only is truth a veiled and indeterminate object, but so is the crowd of people who talk about it. Discourse is thus determined by a doubly indeterminate bind. Its end and its origin are given as infinitely fractured. Derrida can thus ask: "Is not the apocalyptic a transcendental condition of any discourse, even any experience, marking or any trace? And the genre of writings called "apocalyptic" in the strict sense, then, would be only an example, and *exemplary* revelation of this transcendental structure."[32]

APOCALYPSE AND PRÉVENANCE

That the apocalyptic involves an other towards which the curious and inquisitive mind extends, towards which it reaches out with the desire for disclosure is a reading which Derrida does not only glean from Kant but actually consolidates by referring to another text which stands paradigmatically for the concept of the apocalypse. This text is the book of "Revelation" or the "Apocalypse of John."[33] It is characterized in Derrida's reading by two mutually reinforcing motifs, the one of waking and the other of coming.

An apocalyptic discourse is one that demands utter wakefulness. It encourages vigilance for something that is to be revealed soon. This something is hidden well ("eucalyptus"). It is obvious that in this aspect the goals of the enlightenment as well as those of an apocalyptic discourse such as the Apocalypse of John coincide. Both are motivated by the desire for *"Aufklärung"* of a something which — of course — is truth. Derrida observes that "the structure of truth would be apocalyptic and for that reason there is no truth of the apocalypse that would not again be the truth of truth. In other words, the apocalypse is pointing towards an absolute truth. It demands its final unveiling, while simultaneously re-veiling truth with every new attempt to understand it.

The demand to be wakeful, however, is the result of the announcement of a coming, i.e., something that is to come which underlines the eschatological character of the apocalypse. Derrida quotes from the "Apocalypse of John" "Wake! And if you do not wake, I will come over you like a thief. And you will not know at which hour the thief will come over you."[34] For Derrida the word "come" is so significant because it designates something that precedes the event as well as something that antecedes it. Yet, it does not thematize the event itself and thus eludes the possibility of a present. It indicates a place from which the request ("come!") issues forth and this place lies both in the past — before the request — and in the future — after the request.[35]

This economy of *"prévenance"* is a structure centered around the perceiving of an order, or just a voice, coming from a place that is conceptually unavailable, i.e. abs-ent.[36] The term "come" is thus an expression of an other, from which it issues, something that is not thematizable linguistically, towards which, however, it points relentlessly. A text, especially an apocalyptic text, is broken through with the structures of this "come." Even the "grammatical, linguistic or semantic categories" are part of this structure and thus cannot be used to analyze the prevenant structure of a text. The difference that is opened up by the come — the difference between a place past and a future place — is tonal. Derrida thus renders a diachronic interpretation of the apocalyptic event. It transcends the synchronic boundaries which normally give to the event its appearance as a system of infinite presence where every point is available and accessible at the same time. The differential or tonal interpretation leads to a beyond where the past/future binary does not hold anymore. This future is eternally absent and the issuing of the imperative "come" can no longer be understood as an event in the German sense of the word as appropriation (*"Er-eignis"*) and thus be tied to the notion of the present, but precisely as its opposite, i.e., as a disappropriation (*"Ent-eignis"*).

Derrida can now demonstrate how the question of the death of philosophy was always one that prevailed. Or, in more general terms, how the discourse about finality dominated occidental culture. The apocalyptic element is one that is inherent in any text; any text reveals a certain transcendental affinity for an apocalyptically removed truth. He clarifies that by pointing towards the different types of absolute truths that have always informed philosophical discourse. As such, truth was always thought of as the endpoint of a way of deliberation and thinking. Yet, this thinking itself already produced the light to illuminate the path to truth (the light of enlightenment that will finally illuminate every vestige, every niche of what might still be veiled, as much as the light of El that shines forth to illuminate the revelations that John sees in the Apocalypse). In the apocalyptic view, ultimate truth means a unity between subject and world such that these terms can become dispensable. This truth, however, is only desired not actual, since in actuality the subject is removed from the world. It only *knows* the world. Its access to the world is epistemological only. Hence, it is such that the subject is in exile. However, this exilic condition is the motor for a movement towards the unveiling of ultimate truth. In other words, the notion of the apocalypse embraces both the condemnation to exile and the promise to ultimate unity. The apocalyptic tone is thus a tone that seeks clarity beyond a distended empirical world. A certain tone always implies a certain tension, a field of tension between several — at least two — sounds. A certain tone implies a certain tuning, an alteration of a tone requires a certain untuning. Yet, in the end the desire is to overcome the tone towards absolute silence.[37]

Implied in this is a moment of anticipation given in the apocalypse that is especially visible in the Apocalypse of John. The word "come" indicates this. To be able to say "come" implies a place[38] and time that is ahead of my own place and time. The word "come" can only be uttered from what is different from me, absolutely different, what thus can establish a tonal, i.e., differential, relationship with me. Thus, for Derrida the apocalyptic structure of a text, i.e., the world, is grounded in a more original structure of *prévenance*, of coming. Such a structure, however, is bound to radical alterity. It is directed towards an absent other which it can never integrate into itself.

THE HERMENEUTICS OF EXILE IN LEVINAS AND DERRIDA

At the beginning of the first chapter of part I, I had already brought in the notion of "exile" vis-a-vis Levinas's characterization of texts as *"espace vital."* For Levinas as well as for Derrida exile turns out to be an indispensable precondition of (Jewish) existence. Space, living space, a fortiori, can only emerge where exile, i.e., temporal/spatial distance from something promised, is given. However, the difference between the two thinkers regarding the notion of "exile" is as striking. Although the notion of space (between relative and absolute truth, between God and world, between other and myself) is the precondition of Levinas's philosophy, he opts to call this space "proximity" rather than "exile" and thereby gives a stability to those spaces that is lacking entirely in Derrida. The latter, quite to the contrary, by precisely defining this space as exile, also inevitably implies its sublation into a nonexilic, an absolute, moment of truth.

This said, it might be permissible to draw the following conclusion. So far, we have encountered Levinas as the more Jewish, the more Jewish oriented, philosopher of the two. Derrida, on the other hand, mostly for his lack of the kind of Jewish education that Levinas underwent, seemed less interested in the Jewish aspect of his own philosophy as well as in Jewish philosophy in general.

Both claims have to be revised now, however, and we will have to continue to do so. Derrida's treatment of the "apocalyptic" through the notion of "נגלה" as well as his interest in and drawing on Jabès' writings must begin to persuade even a critical reader that there is more than just a chance relationship between the philosopher Derrida and the philosophy of Judaism. Derrida's insistence on the notion of "exile" brings to the fore the promise, i.e., the promise of messianism. More than Levinas's thinking could ever be, Derrida's philosophy is informed by the promise of a messianic stage on which exile, i.e., alienation, will be erased.

This is not to say that Derrida believes in the possibility of such a stage and all the tenets that that would include. But it is to say that his notion of unveiling could not be persuasive without at least positing the theoretical possibility of such a messianic stage.

Keeping this in mind it is important to remember that, in assessing the differences between Levinas and Derrida, little of what we have said about the exilic notion of the word apocalypse, and the text in general, is actually explicated by Derrida himself. Although he explicitly refers to the Hebrew word "נלה," he leaves its whole second meaning, i.e., that of the exile, undisclosed. (The only exception is the article on Jabès mentioned above.) However, it is precisely this meaning that moves him so close to Levinas's thought, since it is here that the notion of the exile, the for-the-other, becomes instrumental for his development of a concept of the ethical. We are therefore forced to ask why Derrida did not include more explicitly the exilic moment into his own text, but instead decided to focus more on the apocalypse as an infinite unveiling of absolute truth infinitely deferred. In other words, everything that Levinas ever talks about — viz. the human condition as ethical, a theory that allows us to understand why ethics is first philosophy, even epistemologically, everything that has this familiar ring of first and origin — Derrida pushes to the side in favor of another more pragmatic question. His question is: given a certain desire for what's unveiled and hidden from us, what are the ramifications of such a notion if applied to texts and maybe to the dynamic of life in general, and how vital might such an unveiled be for the human community?

Levinas shows that philosophy, theology, and all other logoi, including language, are only possible because of a certain structure that binds them to the other person. This he calls "the ethical." It denotes a certain estrangement and alienation from ourselves toward the other which could also be understood in exilic terminology. Exile is indeed a perfect metaphor for what Levinas means by the obsession by the other. Yet, as already indicated earlier, Levinas does not offer a notion of unveiling the way Derrida does. It especially cannot be found for his description of the relationship with the other. Thus, what Derrida calls exile as an epistemological condition must be called proximate boundedness as an ethical condition in Levinas's case.

Derrida, on the other hand, is less interested in finding out about *the* ethical. His interest is with ethics, which brings him to emphasize a totally different aspect of the apocalypse. Whereas Levinas would use the apocalypse to delineate the human condition as ethical, Derrida uses it to show how the desire to unveil and disclose is what makes the apocalyptic moment so valuable and vital to ethics. Only a discourse that shifts and questions in light of a truth that lies in the future and is to come — only a discourse that is critical and unafraid to undermine, only a discourse that understands the apocalyptic privilege as duty — can keep ethics alive and thus dynamically enhance the life of a community.

Levinas elects to create another absolute truth. It is given in the face of the other person. His claim is that in the face of the other we can understand our true calling as human beings, that we will understand our duty to act ethically based on that face. He thus makes way for another hierarchy of thinking and acting based on the metaphysical notion of the face. Derrida, although understanding the importance of truth as a methodical absolute, i.e., a type of fictional telos which is needed for humans to develop their desire for truth and its disclosure, stays away from the question of what that truth really might be. Instead the movement of the question itself is what becomes utterly important.

The Ethical Significance of the Apocalyptic Discourse

I would like to take up again the questions I raised in the beginning.

1.1   Is it sensible to pursue a project (the project of truth), if it is evident that the project will never succeed? Based on Derrida's essay on the apocalypse, his answer to this question must be positive. The quest for truth, according to Derrida, is what assures the proliferation of an ongoing discourse on ethics. Only if truth is at stake, without anyone claiming that they have found it, can a community embark on a course of action that will allow everyone to speak freely and give everything the possibility to grow.

1.2   Can philosophy aim at something less than truth, that will, however, be more successful? It would be difficult to find something less than truth. That something would certainly not be falsehood, since aiming for that would involve a very intimate knowledge of truth itself. The "truth" is, philosophy can never succeed, (but that it can be very successfully.)

Derrida refers to this question by alluding to a quote from Blanchot. The latter had asked whether man was capable of a radical interrogation, finally, if man was ready for literature. The reason why Blanchot and, along with him, Derrida align interrogation and literature is because radical interrogation will always have the same open-ended structure that any literary book has as well. Thus the question really is, will human beings ever be capable of the burden of a radical open-endedness that is exilic in its form. Derrida's response, in realizing the force to conceptualize and to understand, i.e., to reduce the open-endedness of the exile that drives human beings, is that it is "incapable half the time."[39]

2.1   Does it make a difference whether philosophy thinks it will know truth eventually or whether it thinks it will not know it? The tricky thing about this question seems to be that philosophy will have to do both at the same time. It will have to forget its telos while at the same time desiring it all the time. A philosophy that thinks of itself as definitely on its way towards truth will obviously tend to exclude other discourses, e.g., religious or psychological discourses. Rather than thinking of itself as a device towards reaching a certain goal most efficiently, analogous to the logic of capitalism, philosophy must concentrate more on the potential and the possibilities that are inherent in its own thinking.

2.2   What can the advantages of a discourse be that knows itself to be failing perennially? In one word, humility. From the standpoint of ethics it seems utterly important to understand that no single, newly achieved insight, concept, etc., can explain the world comprehensively. Truth understood as unity, as is implied in my reading of Derrida, must be understood as a goal which will get distorted immediately the moment one or several human beings think they found it and attempt to impose it on the rest of the world. A philosophy that knows itself as failing will hopefully exhibit sufficient self-criticism to abstain from totalitarian claims. It might very well be that such unity is much more "achieved" in the process of struggling towards truth which involves all of humanity.

The wish to reduce the lapse between different significations with respect to meaning or an original signified, i.e., the wish to end exile and come back into a state of immediacy, is clearly there. Yet Derrida warns that "to allege that one reduces this lapse through narration, philosophical discourse, or the order of reason or deduction, is to misconstrue language, to misconstrue that language is the rupture with totality itself."[40] In other words, if we reduce the lapse we actually make way for a regress to a totality that only language can break. Like Levinas, Derrida here recognizes the threat that a totalitarian thinking presents to humanity. Like Levinas, he also conceives of language as that which is capable of breaking such totality. Yet, in marked difference from Levinas, Derrida does not reintegrate language into a hierarchy, viz. that of the one for the other, but instead insists that it is language itself which poses the infinite question to totality and thus makes way for ethics.

What kind of language could that be? Did not Levinas show in "God and Philosophy" that no matter how philosophy decides to approach the question of the other it will always end up in a logocentric hierarchical discourse? Is not truth as the goal of the apocalyptic discourse always already coopted by precisely that discourse? How can one talk about the other and truth without falling into that aporetic condition? Or better: how can one not talk? Will not silence be more adequate for the reception of what is ineffable? Is not the denial or negation of any discourse about it the only way to sustain the epistemological alterity of the other, an alterity that would otherwise immediately be integrated into our discourse and become indistinguishable from the other "objects" that discourse describes?

These questions are the questions of negativity. If truth and the other are coopted by discourse, then the goal must be to ward off that kind of discourse and find other ways of speaking — negative ways. But how do I speak? Derrida disapproves of the discourses of negative theologies. In his mind they do not end the cooptation of the other by positive discourse, but reinforce it. The question remains: what can I say? Will I be relegated to saying what this absolute is not? Will all I can do be to say *that* it is not? But Derrida does not favor this simple negational approach. Agency, i.e., being able to act over against the absolute cannot just be its negation. For any negation amounts to being nothing but a finite judgment. Negating the absolute, then, would be to turn it into something finite, Precisely that is what Derrida wants to avoid. Agency over against the absolute must go beyond negation towards a new kind of affirmation of the infinite nature of the absolute.

In the following chapter we will look more closely at the reasons for Derrida's rejection of negative theology. We will follow the philosophical development of negative theology from Maimonides through Cohen and Rosenzweig and then discuss Derrida's reception of it first in his earlier work and then, especially in a fairly recent essay (1987) about the question of negative theology given at a conference in Jerusalem. It will become increasingly clear, I hope, that what Derrida first introduced under the principle name of "différance," along with his rejection of negative theology, is very much informed by the neo-Kantian/Cohennian attempt to understand humanity as stretched out between an origin and a telos, both archically or teleologically unavailable, but both also accounting for a differential, asymptotic movement of humanity towards an infinitely removed goal.

EIGHT

Agency

Differentiality and Negativity

APOCALYPSE AS THE CRITIQUE OF NEGATIVITY

We have many times alluded to that which the apocalypse circumscribes. It is that which is to be unveiled, the event from which we must perforce always perceive ourselves to be in exilic distance. Yet, although that distance is there, and although it is infinite and can never be positively overcome, it remains a stretch, i.e., a tone, produced, as we will see in this chapter, through its attachedness to an infinite origin and an infinite end. A tone is a differential phenomenon and as such it is also an apocalyptic one. The tone is another way to talk about Derrida's most original concept, i.e., différance. This concept is tied to an understanding of God as an infinite goal and infinite origin, not unlike the concept of God as the asymptotic limit in Cohen's philosophy. We will see that Derrida's epistemology of the infinite task is only a stepping-stone for an ethics of the infinite task. The task is conceived within the 'bracket' of an end and an origin, a telos and an arche that is divine; the bracket is God. This, again, is the prevenient structure that out of a deep past announces a remote future. Prévenance is what named the connection between the trace of ethics and redemption. It nourishes the human community so that it can progress towards this telos and come increasingly closer without, however,

212

coinciding with this telos at any time. It remains infinitely removed, and humanity thus remains stretched out towards it infinitely.

Despite these initial similarities between Cohen and Derrida it should not be underestimated that their attitudes towards philosophy, towards the project of rationality, are radically different from each other. There could not be any doubt for Cohen that it was rationally possible to describe the relationship between God and the world and the subsequent move to an understanding of the meaning of ethics. For Derrida on the other hand, even though he employs a model similar to that of Cohen's method of correlation, it is precisely the alleged rationality of the world that is in question. The tonal suspension of the world that, in Cohen's case (as correlation), served to prove the rational progression of the world does the exact opposite in Derrida's case: it disintegrates it; it breaks up and fractures rationality infinitely. The difference between the two philosophers lies in their treatment of presence. For Cohen, the nonpresence of God and the unavailability of the other take on an axiomatic character, whereas Derrida never ceases to treat these issues apocalyptically, i.e., from the perspective of the temporary rationality of nonpresence.

But let us return to the commonalities between Derrida's and Cohen's methodologies. Both recognize that we cannot positively grasp the notion of absolute otherness within the context of ontology; thus, everything we attempt to understand must necessarily move into a sphere of sameness. Our attempts to overcome this predicament, i.e., to leave the cognitive exile we are in and to understand absolute otherness, can be infinitely perpetuated. Yet, we will remain within the realm of the same and thus never transcend the sphere of the bad infinite. Ontologically speaking, the other can never be represented adequately through the language of being. This language always indicates sameness. Yet, it is precisely this notion that Derrida attempts to question with the concept of différance. In his account différance is neither a word nor a concept. It is and it is not. Différance is neither origin nor telos. It is neither active nor passive. It cannot be aligned with similar claims that are made about God through negative theology. Yet, différance is not anti-theological. Derrida's reservations about negative theology do not stem from the fact that it is a theology, but from the obvious failure of *negative* theology to comprehend the absolute difference between God and the world, between Being and that which exists. Is différance not a negative theology? Derrida is asked, after the lecture "Différance," and his answer is: It is and is not!

We will have to find out why Derrida's answer is more than just the witty talk of a French philosopher tired of the continental tradition, yet unable to really break out of it. Derrida purposely lets différance oscillate between a negative and a positive claim and thus creates a situation of restlessness, of a relentless going back and forth between the two without being either one or the other.

NEGATIVE THEOLOGY IN JEWISH THOUGHT

Negative Attribution in the Thought of Maimonides

The problem of negative theology has occupied many philosophers before Derrida. In this chapter I will draw on this tradition from the Jewish perspective in order to show how Derrida's philosophy can easily be understood as its continuation. I will therefore start out with Moses Maimonides' understanding of negative theology, then move on to Cohen and Rosenzweig, and from there move to analyze Derrida's own claims on this question.[1]

Maimonides has frequently been understood as the initiator of the so-called theory of divine negative attributes. Yet, Z. Diesendruck emphasizes[2] that Maimonides could hardly be called that. Many of his precursors already employed the method of negative attribution. Maimonides' attempt was precisely to reject that method as invalid, because, like positive predication, negative predication also involves a "duality in definition . . . of the subject and the predicate." Negative attributes were a "commonplace" at Maimonides' time and he rejects this commonplace for reasons that we will soon understand.

Maimonides' problem with understanding the nature of God is, as Diesendruck, says "the duality in the definition . . . of the subject and the predicate." This can also be formulated in terms of Aristotelian philosophy and, prior to that, through the questions set out in Plato's *Parmenides*. Aristotle establishes in his predicative logic the difference between a substance and its predicates. In a sentence with the structure x is y, x and y are necessarily different from each other (with x being the substance and y being the predicate). If y is attributed to x, then x by itself must necessarily be less than with y included, and x must be divisible, since it is whatever is designated by x and everything that is designated by y. Thus the question is: If God is one, indivisible, eternal, and infinite, but particularly indivisible, then we are confronted with a problem concerning the possibility of speaking about God. Since, grammatically, most sentences consist at least of a subject and a verb, i.e., two separate parts, and since the verb has an attributive position with respect to the subject, the impression arises that, with respect to the subject, the predicate is a different, secondary entity. In this way every sentence must make it seem as if there is a difference between God and the attribute that is given to him through human thinking. For example, to say that God is almighty is from a subject-predicate perspective to say that "almighty" is attributed to God rather than being part of God's essence already. (One could even go further and say that this statement, God is almighty, describes God's participation in the matrix of almightiness.) If these were the case, then one would have to concede that every attribute, in this way, destroys the notion of indivisibility and turns God into a collage of aspects and perspectives.

Maimonides' interest in this question, of course, stems from his reception of the first two commandments of the Decalogue which a) affirm God's oneness and b) insist that humans are not supposed to defile God's name. The problem, then, is if knowing God from our limited and finite linguistically mediated perspective is not already such a defilement. Louis Jacobs states that Maimonides not only rejects such general claims but specifies that true knowledge of God is a knowledge that understands "God's being One by virtue of Oneness, so that no composition whatever is to be found in him and no possibility of division in any way whatever." This, however, can only be the case if God "has in no way and in no mode any essential attribute . . . just as it is impossible that he should be a body, it is also impossible that he should possess an essential attribute." Thus Maimonides rules out all univocal statements with the structure x is y, i.e., all statements that modify or diversify God's essence. The only exception is made for the case where an attribute is not meant to qualify God's nature but rather is meant to describe God's actions. For in that case one can conjecture that that action "if performed by a human being, would be attributed to the goodness of that person's nature."[3]

In chapters 57–59, in book I of the *Guide*,[4] Maimonides explains that seemingly essential attributes are in reality nothing but the translation of an originally privative notion. For example, to say that God is one is not meant to indicate that God could be compared with something that is two or three or multiple in any other way, but it is simply to say that God is the absence or lack of many. That God is not many is what is expressed in the statement "God is One." The positive, seemingly essential attribute of oneness is nothing but a substituted concept for an original privation.

There is, of course, also the group of negative attributes which we have not yet mentioned. Their function is to explain something about what God is not. The problem with them is that, under normal circumstances, they, as well as the positive attributes, describe God's essence, even if in a negative way, and thus particularize it. Maimonides therefore determines that any negative predications of God can only be maintained if they are negations of privations. In other words, only that kind of negation is justified that is directed towards what would otherwise be understood as a lack on God's part.

To summarize what we have found so far: It is impossible in Maimonides' view to say of God that God is strong, since that would predicate God with an added essential attribute and necessarily particularize God's essence. Maimonides' main argument against a positive, i.e. affirmative, theology is that "if one describes Him by means of affirmations, one implies, as we have made clear, that He is associated with that which is not He and implies a deficiency in Him."[5] He instead substitutes the notion that God is not weak. This however, goes beyond the observation from the one/not many example, since here we are not just dealing with a privation but with the negation of a privation. To say that God is not weak is really to say that God is not powerless, i.e., that God is not a privation of power. Maimonides can thus circumvent the problems of positive attribution as well as the inverted ones of simple negative attribution. He ends up with the certain attribution of the attribute of power to God without particularizing God's essence.[6]

Existence as Predication

The crucial difference between Maimonides and a thinker like Derrida lies in their notion of what constitutes a predicate and what does not. For Maimonides everything to the right side of the copula could count as such a predicate. He is not concerned with the copula itself, however, and simply regarded it as the copulatory, i.e. connecting, medium between an essence and its predicate. Its only function is to express existence. God's existence, however, is the only thing that human beings can understand about God immediately. In book I, chapter 58 he asks:

> What then should be the state of our intellects when they aspire to apprehend Him who is without matter and is simple to the utmost degree of simplicity, Him whose existence is necessary, . . . [what should be our state of intellect] we who only understand the fact that He is?[7]

The relation between the substance and the copula is different from that between the substance and an attribute. It is tautological. Existence is not attributed to God (as was omnipotence in the example above). To say that God is, is, therefore, not a case where a duality between subject and predicate is invoked. Therefore, the negation of any other possible predicate (except the copula) were sufficient for Maimonides' purposes in order to leave the nature of God intact. To say "God is" was a tautology at best, but by no means a predicative statement about the nature of God.

For Derrida existence, as expressed in the copula "to be," has a severely predicative nature and is not just tautological. Thus, for him, to say "God is green" is a doubly predicative statement from which one can conclude that a) God is and b) that God is green. The copula entails an additional problematic which Derrida confronts with is his charge that its use implies a mode of thinking that inevitably and inextricably is bound to a thinking that dwells in the present, i.e., a thinking for which otherness is always disguised behind a veil of I-ness, self and sameness; true alterity is unthinkable.

Cohen: Negative Theology as Theology of the Origin

Before I can go on to discuss Derrida's position on the question of negative theology more fully, I would like once again to draw on Cohen and Rosenzweig in order to see how they position themselves vis-a-vis Maimonides' theory. We had already seen that, for Cohen, the crux of the problematic is given as the relationship between God and the world, i.e., the relationship between being and becoming. In the case of the natural sciences he had shown reason to be the fundamental ingredient that illuminates the relationship between being and becoming. To the degree that reason can explicate and clarify the cognitive processes involved in scientific thinking, it also must have its share in the clarification of the relationship between God and world, i.e., as a noncontradictory immanent relationship between God and the world.

Und diese immanente Beziehung des Seins auf das Werden bildet so wenig einen Widerspruch gegen die Einzigkeit des göttlichen Seins, daß diese vielmehr erst durch diese Immanenz ihre Positivität erlangt.

This immanent relation of being to becoming is not in contradiction to the uniqueness of the divine being, which rather acquires its positive content through this immanency.[8]

The problem of this type of cognition, viz. the relationship between immanence and transcendence, is, like in Maimonides, that God's uniqueness must be saved against a cognition that claims to know God fully. Cohen quotes "a Jewish philosopher" as saying: *"Würde ich Dich erkennen, so wäre ich Du."* ("If I were to know Thee, I would be Thee.")[9] Indeed it is Maimonides whom Cohen now refers to extensively in order to point out the failure of negative attribution and the *"ganz andere Wendung"* ("an entirely different turn")[10] which the former gives to the problem.

The failure of negative attribution in the case of God is, in Cohen's view, the result of a simple logical negligence. It is *"ein falsches Beginnen"* ("a false beginning").[11] The attribution of negative attributes can only happen on the basis of the existence of positive attributes. But, Cohen asks, *"hat man denn überhaupt schon positive Bestimmungen?"* ("What, however, could be negated, if there could as yet be no positive determinations?")[12] In other words, if something is negated, that something cannot be the positive determination of what God's being is. Yet, and this is the point at which, for both Maimonides and (with reference to him) Cohen, it is possible to negate deficiencies in God: it is possible to negate what is lacking in God.

We already established the differences between negation and privation in chapt. 2 of part I. Suffice it to say here that a privation is an infinite judgment, its negation must result in an indirect affirmation of the attribute in question, without, however, first positing this attribute. The negation now completely excludes the possibility of the privation in question and thus a "new positivity is founded" which completely uproots the negation.

This new positivity is given not only because we have avoided
a positive predication of God, but also, through the negation
of God's privation, we have arrived at the concept of origin.
Maimonides, Cohen claims, through the negation of privation,
has shown God's *"Genügsamkeit"*[13] (God is sufficient unto God-
self, God does not need anything external to prove or establish
who God is). Only this *"Genügsamkeit"* can explain sufficiently
how it is logically possible that the world is not the result of a
process of emanation from God, but of creation by God. Whereas
emanation thinks the problem of becoming materially and thus
ends up being pantheism, Cohen suggests that *"die Bedingtheit
muß daher logisch so gedacht werden, daß das materielle Hervor-
gehen des Werdens aus dem Sein ausgeschlossen wird"* ("Therefore, one must think of dependence in its logical significance in
such a way that one excludes a material origination of becoming from being").[14]

It becomes clear that Cohen's determination of the immanent relationship between being and becoming, which he still
holds up as the true characterization of the relationship between
God and world, must be modified as the logical immanence between being and becoming that is given through the negation of
privation.

> Nicht dadurch soll das Werden durch das Sein erklärbar werden,
> daß das Werden vorher in dem Sein enthalten war und alsdann
> aus ihm herausgeht — diese Auffassung ergäbe keine rein logische
> Bedingtheit — der Differenz zwischen Sein und Werden wird
> entsprechend gedacht die zwischen Bejahung und Verneinung.
> Die Negation muß von Gott abgewehrt werden: damit wird auch
> das falsche Werden aus dem Sein hinweggenommen. Nun soll
> aber doch das Werden aus dem Sein erklärbar werden. Folglich
> muß das Sein eine Bestimmung in sich aufnehmen, welche es
> zwar von der Negation unterscheidet, welche dennoch aber
> dem Gedanken der Negation in dem Problem des Werdens
> Genüge leistet. So ist der Begriff der Privation entstanden. Und
> so ist er für das Problem der göttlichen Attribute in Verwen-
> dung gekommen.

> Becoming cannot be explained in terms of being if one says that
> becoming was previously contained in being and then proceeded

out of it, for this understanding does not yield a purely logical dependence. The difference between being and becoming is to be thought of as corresponding to the difference between affirmation and negation. Negation has to be warded off from God; through this, becoming, insofar as it is false being, is removed from unique being. Nevertheless, becoming has to be explained by being. Consequently, being must appropriate to itself a designation which indeed distinguishes it from negation, but which answers to the thought of negation as it appears within the problems of becoming. The concept of privation originated from these considerations. And thus it was applied to the problem of the divine attributes.[15]

Thus, according to Cohen, the difference between being and becoming must not be thought as the difference between affirmation and negation. If that were the case, then creation could never be understood but as the negation of God's being. But precisely that is the issue that Cohen wants to resolve here. A negation does epistemological injustice to God since it would explain the process of becoming as one that comes out of the negation of being. That, however, would entail the implication that God's essence is drawn out and spread out into the world and subsequently withdraws as an act of creation. Cohen does not subscribe to this mystical view on creation (and we will have to see later, if this is different for Derrida). As far as Cohen is concerned this view would contradict God's uniqueness. The privation can solve this problem, because it does not have the logical nearness to its object that is present in a negation. God's essence remains untouched.

Rosenzweig: Overcoming Negativity

For Franz Rosenzweig Hermann Cohen's achievements lie in the area of mathematics and thinking and their, newly discovered, reciprocity.

Erst Hermann Cohen ... entdeckte in der Mathematik ein Organon des Denkens, grade weil sie ihre Elemente nicht aus dem leeren Nichts der einen und allgemeinen Null, sondern aus dem bestimmten, jeweils jenem gesuchten Element zugeordneten Nichts des Differentials erzeugt. Das Differential verbindet in sich die Eigenschaften des Nichts und des Etwas; es ist ein Nichts, das auf ein Etwas, sein Etwas hinweist, und zuglseich ein Nichts, das moch im Schoße des Nichts schlummert.

It remained for [Hermann Cohen] to discover in mathematics an organum of reasoning, just because it creates its elements out of the definite Nought of the differential, each time assigned to that required Element, not out of the empty Nought of the one and universal zero. The differential combines in itself the character-istics of the Nought and the Aught. It is a Nought which points to an Aught; at the same time it is an Aught that still slumbers in the lap of the Nought.[16]

The concept of the differential is, in Rosenzweig's view, what makes it possible to overcome negative theology and move on to "a highly positive one." Negative Theology is nothing but the symptom of philosophy's and theology's inability to come to terms with the problem of knowing God. Faced with God's absolute difference, God's absolute separateness from the world, they resign themselves to a weak denial that anything that we know can possibly have anything in common with God. "Thus God could be defined only in complete indefinability."[17]

The problem is methodological. If God is sought as "one con-cept among many," then nothing but the "via negativa" remains to distinguish the concept of God from all the other concepts that form part of our knowledge of the world. In other words, Rosenzweig argues that, from a structuralist viewpoint where the existence of a thing can only be asserted through what that thing is not, a positive concept of God can never be attained. Context alone will not give us an understanding of what God is. "Ignorance" ("*Nichtwissen*") is not enough to avoid atheism and mysticism.[18] Only if it is understood that such ignorance already has an object, and only if it is understood that such ignorance can only be relative, i.e., in relationship to something of which it claims to be ignorant, do we begin to understand the genera-tive potential of the negative. The negative, understood in this way, comes to stand at the beginning of philosophy's and theology's attempts at understanding God. It is nothing that negates God in relationship to the world, but only in relationship to what we know about God. Within the realm of knowledge, i.e., within epistemological confines, our ignorance of God can be taken as the starting point of a process of furthering that knowledge of God.[19] Strictly speaking, Rosenzweig is not at all interested at this point in establishing a link between the concepts of God, man, and world with the actual world. Rather, it is his goal to establish every concept "for itself, dependent on itself alone, in its absolute actuality."[20]

The idea is to begin with the Nought of that which is sought in order to "put it behind us,"[21] as Rosenzweig says. He thus employs the same *"Schwungbrett"* concept that we could already observe in Cohen's *Die Urteile der Denkgesetze.*[22] The Nought can be overcome in two ways: either as an affirmation of everything that is not-Nought, as such, in which case an infinity would be designated; or (in Cohen's case) the Nought itself can be negated with a something from which a finite entity would result. In its first variant this overcoming establishes God as the infinite, though inert, God. God is here complete and impervious infinity. In its second variant an action is designated; every negation of the Nought will again produce a something. Thus here we encounter God as the Creator who, out of an infinity of actions, creates the finite world.

Through a purely logical operation Rosenzweig ends up being able to describe God in a twofold way without having to retreat to the "via negativa" of enlightenment philosophy and theology. God can be affirmed as the infinite itself and God can be affirmed through a negation of God's own Nothing. Mysticism and atheism can be effectively avoided and theology, as an utterly positive, discourse becomes possible.

DERRIDA AND NEGATIVE THEOLOGY

This is precisely the question that concerns Jacques Derrida: "Would a theology be possible?"[23] Contrary to what is claimed against and about him, Derrida is not an atheist. He does not deny the existence of God or a supreme reality. He also does not reject religious discourse entirely, and, in fact, even utilizes such discursive tools himself in order to get to the point he wants to convey to his readers. What this point is, precisely, that it is an emphasis on the impossibility of the point in favor of a differential understanding of the world, has already received some shape and form in the previous chapter, but it will become even clearer now.

We have seen that both Levinas and Cohen in order to speak about the relationship between ethics and God, resort to a language of privations and negated privations. The epistemological advantage of a privation over a negation is its infinite nature. But is this infinite nature indeed appropriate to avoid the essentialism that Derrida is attacking? Can the excess of the infinite, its surplus over against a notion of the finite which manifests itself in the language of being, remain immune to the grip of being? Even though Derrida attempts to convince us that différance cannot be described in terms of negative theology, we have to explore the possibility if, perhaps, différance is an instance of negative, i.e., privative, theology itself.

For Cohen, and presumably also for Levinas, the significance of a privative discourse about God did not only lie in its emphasis on the infinite character of the divine being, but also in its potential for the explanation of creation. The negation of an infinite judgment, i.e., a privation, would entail the proliferation of finite things without ever exhausting or depreciating the infinite. Derrida makes a statement about différance to the same effect. "Différance . . . as the very opening of the space in which ontotheology — philosophy — *produces* ("produit") [my italics] its system and its history, . . . includes ontotheology, inscribing it and exceeding it without return."[24] I am particularly interested in the productivity of différance to which Derrida alludes in this quote. In Cohen's language one could say that Derrida seems to be assuming that différance can, from a certain perspective, be understood as an *"Ursprung."* One, however, that is lost, or absent, or asymptotically removed. More quotes will substantiate this. ". . . Différance is thus no longer simply a concept, but rather the possibility of conceptuality, of a conceptual process and system in general."

> Ce qui s'écrit *différance*, se sera donc le mouvement de jeu qui 'produit', par ce qui n'est pas simplement une activité, ces différences, ces effets de différence. La différance est l' 'origine' non-pleine, non-simple, l'origine structurée et différante des différences. Le nom d' 'origine' ne lui convient donc plus.

> What is written as différance, then, will be the playing movement that 'produces' — by means of something that is not simply an activity — these differences, these effects of difference. *Différance* is the non-full, non-simple, structured and differentiating origin of differences. Thus, the name 'origin' no longer suits it.[25]

In his "Letter to a Japanese Friend"[26] Derrida explains why, or better, in what respect, the term "origin" is no longer suitable for his project. Deconstruction, he says, "is not an analysis in particular because the dismantling of a structure is not a regression towards a *simple element*, toward an *indissoluble origin*." Similarly, during the round-table discussion immediately following his lecture "Différance"[27]: ". . . Différance is not a source, it is not an origin. And that proposition follows at least from this one: there is no simple. One could soon show that the concept of origin never operates without that of simplicity."[28] Finally, in his *Of Grammatology*, Derrida puts the problematic into an appellatory context maintaining that "différance by itself would be more 'originary,' but one would no longer be able to *call* it 'origin' or 'ground'"[29] [my italics].

The quintessence of the above quotations seems to be the following: Derrida rejects the traditional concept of origin because it operates based on the implicit assumption of the possibility of simplicity. Yet, he does not simply discard the whole idea, but instead turns the origin itself into something that is ultimately ineffable. Non-simple, non-full, etc. are all privative terms. They indicate a lack, yet not a negation. They form a peculiar origin that is productive and implicates a concept of genesis or "production of differing/deferring"[30] not unlike that of Maimonides and Cohen. Différance produces everything that we know and subsume under the caption of history and thought. Différance itself never appears in this process, but "différance would also implicate this generative activity. Let us say that différance marks it."[31] A better translation, then, of the type of origin that Derrida still permits is the German word *"Ursprung."* Cohen had already used this word. It designates both the *arche* in the "Ur-" but simultaneously also the insurmountable leap or lapse, the "Sprung," away from the *arche* that has taken place already. That is, the *"Ursprung"* as event puts us into an immediate infinite distance from the origin.

In a meeting immediately following his lecture "Différance" the first questioner, Brice Parain, forces Derrida to elaborate on the issue that this chapter is concerned with as well: negative theology. Let me quote the short interaction that occurred between Derrida and Parain, before I focus more on Derrida's response.

> **Parain**: It [différance] is the source of everything and one cannot know it: it is the God of negative theology and I understand very well . . .
> **Derrida**: It is and it is not . . . It is above all not . . .
> **Parain**: It is and it is not. Thus let us not speak of it.[32]

Parain's decision not to speak of it expresses the realization that Derrida's relativization of negative theology as being and not-being cannot be said without falling back into a system, or an economy, that regards even the status of a negative theology as describing not-being as part of the order of being. Thus, Parain's suggestion not to speak of it further is a recognition of the limits of human discourse in certain areas. And it draws the necessary conclusion: silence.[33] Yet, inspite of Parain's decision to withdraw the question Derrida answers it. His answer is remarkable since it sheds light on a misunderstanding that, I think, can easily be induced, if one is only to read the respective passages in his essay "Différance."[34] There is a double question that is contained in the discussion around negative theology. The first one is: Is Derrida rejecting theology in general? The second one is: Is he just rejecting *negative* theology? It turns out that Derrida's opposition to drawing an analogy between negative theology and différance derives less from the "theology" than it does from what is involved in the process of negating something.

> . . . as I said expressly in my paper, this is not at all the same discourse as negative theology. *Différance* is not, it is not a being and it is not God (if, that is, this name is given to a being, even a supreme being). Also, despite the resemblances I indicated at the beginning of my paper, nothing in such a discourse strikes me as more alien to negative theology. And yet, as often happens, this infinite distance is also an infinitesimal distance. That is why negative theology fascinates me. The reasons for this fascination could be developed from what I said a little while ago, but I think the reasons are obvious. With all that that implies, and it is nothing, negative theology is also an excessive practice of *langue*. . . .[35]

The significance of this quote lies in the fact that Derrida explains that his thinking is not a rejection of theology in general, but of a theology that understands God as a *"being, even a supreme being."* Of course, any theology will have to show how the connection it suggests between logos and God is one that precisely avoids an interpretation of God as being. It is surprising that Derrida considers this a valid theological possibility and makes room for it in his response to Parain. We will have to ask ourselves why he makes this distinction and how it can be carried out without abandoning all theology. It can be said preliminarily, however, that différance's most salient characteristic is that it *is* not, i.e., it is absolutely different from being and beings.[36] Yet, the difficulty is that this difference cannot be achieved by simply negating the connection with being. To say that something is not God is still to say that that something is in a relationship with God, albeit a negative one; thus the economy of being has not been suspended.

Elsewhere Derrida is less assertive about the unusefulness of negative theology and simply resorts to saying that "this [the work of deconstruction and différance] has been called, precipitately, a type of negative theology (this was neither true nor false but I shall not enter into the debate here)."[37] Negative theology, in other words, cannot be unuseful altogether. There are types of negative theology, and one of them might be a more adequate description of what it is that Derrida is intending with the notion of différance.

NEGATIVE THEOLOGY AND SPEAKING ABOUT IT

Everything I have said so far of Derrida's apprehensions about the use of negative theology is gleaned from his earlier texts (esp. "Différance"). What one can certainly sense from those texts is that negative theology is a problematic issue for Derrida. It becomes more than a theological expression: it turns into an epistemological problem that exceeds the question of God, even though it never excludes it. Negative theology, at least up to this point, is not just the agnostic's way of approaching God, but becomes a way of talking in general; it is "an excessive practice of langue." There is, in fact, nothing that does not fall under the same restrictions under which God falls. The moment we really make an attempt to understand an object it begins to slip away from our intellectual grasp rather than becoming more palpable and concrete. In such a situation the object may be approached asymptotically, but it will never be successfully (i.e., fully) described. That's why Derrida can postulate that the apocalyptic is a transcendental condition of all thinking and discourse. Our efforts to understand and grasp objects, including God, will always be confined to a mere unveiling — an endless unveiling as it is, since the folds of the fabric covering the object itself are endless.

There is, of course, a difference between the notion of the apocalyptic being a transcendental condition and the suggestion that every discourse must in the end reconcile itself to negativity. Although Maimonides and Cohen both embraced this principle for the question of how God's uniqueness could be understood in conjunction with God's relationship with the world (esp. with creation), already Rosenzweig, albeit strongly influenced by Cohen, seems to be much more critical of the whole project of negativity. His verdict is that negative theology, negative epistemology, and negative anthropology are a result of a logical misconstruction of thinking. A thinking that begins with the axiom of God's, the world's, and humanity's existence must necessarily fall into the trap of negativity. Only by starting out with their relative nothingness (i.e. their nothingness relative to themselves) can we arrive at their actual positivity. The question that we are left with is how can we speak about God and absolutes in general if the traditional via negativa is barred. Derrida's earlier attempts to deal with this question are eloquent with respect to the impasse that negative theology has reached but it leaves open the question of how to speak.

This question, precisely, is how Derrida takes up the issues again in 1986; albeit this time in a much more outspoken and systematic fashion than ever before. In an essay delivered to a colloquium on "Absence and Negativity" (held in English) organized by the Hebrew University and The Institute for Advanced Studies in Jerusalem, he once again, tackled the question of negative theology. In "How not to Speak: Denials"[38] he again clarifies that the question is not God's existence or nonexistence, but rather if theology is possible,[39] since a pure negative theology is clearly impossible.

The essay is divided into two main sections of which the first mostly deals with the question of how to situate the discourse on negative theology between Plato, Dionysius, Meister Eckhard, and Deconstruction. The second part is divided into three subsections dealing with Plato, Dionysius and Heidegger.

Already in the first paragraph Derrida gives us the main clue for an understanding of the rest of the essay. His project (of speaking about negative theology), he says, has always stood

under the anteriority of an obligation. An obligation which comes
"even before the first word" and "which would be difficult to situate and which, perhaps, will be my theme today."[40] In rough
terms, the problem with negative theology is (as we have seen
earlier) that it proposes not to speak about something, or better,
to speak about that something in negative terms only. Derrida
broaches it from two directions. One, he says, is the fact that
the French word *"dire"* in the context of *"comment ne pas dire"*
can mean both "how not to speak" and also "how to speak in a
certain way and not in another." Thus the title "How not to
Speak" brings up the question of silence as well as that of a
certain eloquence, an eloquence that knows *how* to speak.[41] The
second direction is that of the promise or obligation. His commitment to this lecture had been given in the form of a promise
to speak about negative theology, which itself Derrida interprets
as the first instance of speaking about it. The deferment inherent in the promise, especially in this case as Derrida himself
points out ("Next year in Jerusalem!")[42] is already the beginning of an attempt not to speak about something which requires
precisely that: that one does not speak. Negative theology, much
like the promise to speak about it, "holds to a promise, that of
the other, which I must keep because it commits me to speak
where negativity ought to absolutely rarefy discourse."[43]

> Dès que j'ouvre la bouche, j'ai déjà promis, ou plutôt, plus tôt, la
> promesse a saisi le *je* qui promet de parler à l'autre, de dire
> quelque chose, d'affirmer ou de confirmer la parole — au moins
> ceci, à l'extrême limite: qu'il faudrait se taire, et taire ce qu'on ne
> peut dire.
>
> From the moment I have opened my mouth, I have already prom-
> ised; or rather, and sooner, the promise has seized the *I* which
> promises to speak to the other, to say something at the extreme
> limit to affirm or confirm by speech at least this: that it is neces-
> sary to be silent; and to be silent concerning that about which
> one cannot speak.[44]

Not unlike the tonal relationship that accounts for Derrida's apocalyptic epistemology, the promise also establishes a

connection with something that, however, despite this connection, remains infinitely removed, or totally other. I am purposely choosing the word "connection" here, since in it resonates Cohen's use of the word when he talks about the correlation between God and world. This correlation is not a *"Vereinigung"* (unification), he says, but a *"Verbindung"* (connection). Yet it is a *"Verbindung"* that is different from the kind that one usually finds between objects.[45]

Derrida's point is that when one begins to speak one is already responding to a demand, a word, an appellation anterior to one's own speech. Speaking is always in response to something. Yet, if one was ever to find out what this something really is, one would have to embark on an infinite re-gress in the course of which the only obtainable evidence of the other's demand would be traces of the other, but never the other herself. Still, the promise also generates infinite progress. On the one hand, it is caused by something else, that is now irretrievable, but on the other hand, the question is whether the promise does not exhibit, through its own structure, a similar openness with respect to its fulfillment. Especially in the case of negative theology, where the point is precisely not to speak, the promise to speak about negative theology must undermine and retract itself constantly. In other words, the discourse on negative theology is suspended between its origin and its telos without being able to regress to the former or progress to the latter. It remains tonally, apocalyptically, and in this context also negatively stretched between them, bouncing back and forth between its past and its future.

This state of affairs can be further illuminated by taking a look at another dimension of the discourse of negative theology. Derrida observes that negative theology itself holds a promise, not only the discourse about it. The promise comes in the form of a secret that one has to keep secret, yet, at the same time, divulge as that, viz. as secret. In other words, similar to the demand not to speak, which has to be spoken in order to be heard, negative theology also is forced to speak about its secret which it wants to save from any further discourse. Traditionally, "no mystery is made of the necessity of the secret — to be kept, preserved, shared."[46] Since the secret cannot be known (the only thing that *can* be known is that there is a secret) all discourse that pretends to *know* must be avoided. Hence, Derrida's advice with reference to Levinas: Stay away "from the philosophers or the experts in ontology . . . One is not far from the innuendo that ontology itself is a subtle or perverse idolatry . . ."[47] The idolatry that Derrida refers to is that of knowing God. To know God would mean that we have made God part of the world of objects (which can be known) and thus we have destroyed divine transcendence.

The question that arises from all this is, of course, where, then, is this obscure something, the referent of the secret and negative theology. Can it be situated in anyway or fashion that avoids the trap of ontology while at the same time making it accessible to our understanding? This is the question of the "place" to which Cohen responds with the "trace of ethics."[48] The question is especially interesting in this context because, in answering it, we will encounter an observation made earlier about the patterns of discourse that Derrida chooses for his own writing. In quoting Dionysius on the question of the situatedness of this referent Derrida leads to a point where the former asserts that this referent is neither this nor that, "since it situates itself beyond all affirmative and negative position,"[49] which renders affirmations as well as denials ineffective.

However, this referent even "exceeds privation." The altogether-beyond-character "marks neither a privation, a lack, nor an absence. As for the beyond . . ., it has the double and ambiguous meaning of what is above in a hierarchy, thus both beyond and more."[50] God is beyond being and thus not only a lack of being. This also explains why in "Différance" Derrida not only opposes the kind of discourse that integrates différance into a being/non-being economy, but also rejects a more mystical methodology that attempts to gain access to différance by ascribing to it the characteristics of hiddenness, withdrawnness, or even active withdrawal, he thus opposes an understanding of différance as "dissimulating itself as something, as a mysterious being, in the occult of non-knowledge or in a hole with indeterminable borders."[51] In other words, Derrida rules out the possibility of understanding the very thematic of différance, viz. its shyness and ephemeralness, as comparable to the withdrawal of the holy before worldly existence. Différance, then, one could say, is not *tzimtzum* It is not the shrinking of the divine substance which subsequently makes room for the world to exist. Différance, instead, is the productive backdrop from which proliferate all the oppositions, the truths, the negative theologies, in short everything that relates to being, i.e., everything.[52]

Différance, in one word, "exceeds the order of truth."[53] Yet, if that is the case, the question of how différance can be described becomes inevitable. Certainly, the language of truth has become unuseful. This language is the language of being. It is a language that responds to "what-is" questions.[54] Since knowing takes place in the present tense (note the present participle "knowing"), for an object to be understood and known, it has to be in some kind of relationship with the present. Somehow[55] the known thing will arrange itself into a relationship with the "is" of the what-is question. Even past and future events are related to the present in such a way, viz. as retention and protention, i.e., they become what has *been* "and what will *be*." Yet, on Derrida's analysis, différance "is what makes possible the presentation of the being-present, it [différance, however,] is never presented as such. It is never offered to the present."[56] Différance "is neither a word nor a concept."[57] In other words, although in much of his writing Derrida employs something that resembles the concept of something by the name of "différance," he in fact is not employing that concept.[58] The two things that are commonly associated when asked what it means to know something are suspended in the case of différance. Neither the set of attributes that are assembled into the gathering hierarchy of a concept nor the name and its potential inscription, its physical visibility, are adequate to describe différance.

Différance and the Discourse on Truth

Although what we have adduced so far might look like a complete rejection of any discourse about God (Derrida rejects the traditional discourse on truth that relates truth to existence, i.e., ontology, he furthermore rejects all possibilities of expressing negatively what cannot be said positively about différance) it seems to me that he is not interested in a complete and absolute rejection of the possibility of a discourse on truth. Instead he suggests that the traditional problem of/with truth has been its relationship with the present, i.e., its claim to oneness, its claim to punctual coalescence in the present. Derrida's introduction of différance into the discourse of philosophy is an attempt to clarify that access to truth must be sought through a differential approach which takes into account the processual and dynamic character of truth. In particular, Derrida rules out the two factors that make the punctual reference to truth possible — the existence of a simple origin and the further existence of a telos. In other words, rather than conceiving of truth as a point, like the connection with the present would suggest, it is now to be understood as a dia-gram which takes into account the differing/deferring relationship between truth and its object.

Différance becomes the "new truth," yet in a way that is markedly different from past new truths. Rather than excluding the possibility of deferring and differing change, it is now this change itself that is inscribed into the new truth. It is a diagrammatic truth, i.e., a truth that is "written through" to the end.[59] Truth is suspended as a curve between irretrievable origin and infinitely deferred telos. It is the infinity between zero and one.

The point of the curve is to overcome the point. It was the goal of infinitesimal mathematics and later also of calculus to conceive of such a curve not as a bent line of points but as a continuous whole without interruptions. Mathematically a point is nothing. It does not exist. In other words to say that truth gathers into the point of the present (even if it is by way of retention and protention, as in Husserl and Heidegger) is to say that truth is nothing. Philosophy, theology, history, etc. all would only amount to nothing since their truth values are connected to a nothing. The advantage of understanding truth differentially, i.e. as différance, is that now, between origin and telos, différance opens up the space within which "ontotheology — philosophy — produces its system and its history, inscribing it and exceeding it without return."[60] We will return to this quote and the question of origin and telos below. Suffice it to say for the moment that, on such a curve, it becomes impossible to say that truth is only one of the sections of the curve and not another. If one still wanted to talk about truth at all then it would be mandatory to recognize the whole curve as truth. Yet, since differential curves are infinite (they are also called asymptotic functions) it would not make any sense to refer to the whole curve except metaphorically. Truth is as infinite as the curve as which it can be inscribed.

This understanding of truth does *not* eliminate the aggravation that comes from talking about truth as a punctual phenomenon. Truth still cannot be talked about. But the curve, truth's differentiality, rules out the possibility of saying that something is not truth. "The concept of *play* keeps itself beyond this opposition, announcing, on the eve of philosophy and beyond it, the unity of chance and necessity in calculations without end."[61] With really only a couple of strokes, Derrida has pushed aside one of traditional philosophy's foundational concepts which states that if "a" is the case then "not-a" cannot be the case at the same time. The principle of opposition which had served to rule out some and affirm other concepts and ideas in the pursuit of truth has been put to a rest. Viewed from a differential perspective, truth and non-truth are not opposites but aspects of the same process. However this process remains radically open with respect to both its origin and its telos and can therefore never be understood dialectically. Instead, it has to be understood asymptotically.

The image of the curve itself, however, is misleading. On the one hand, it seems to suggest a movement towards something like an actual goal or telos.[62] On the other hand, it alludes to a kind of continuity that Derrida would always reject. We have to understand that, although the function of infinitesimals is to explain continuity, this can only be done by further and further fracturing the curve into smaller an smaller units which then have to be approximated to each other. The end-result is a curve, or a line from Cohen's perspective, but it remains an accumulation of discontinuous infinitesimal particles from Derrida's viewpoint. The curve is only my image for what he calls a sheaf or curved surface "to mark more appropriately that the assemblage to be proposed has the complex structure of a weaving, an interlacing which permits the different threads and different lines of meaning — or of force — to go off again in different directions, just as it is always ready to tie itself up with others."[63] In other words, if one took a piece of the curve and enlarged it, it would gain not only in width, but also in depth and thus reveal its three-dimensional nature.

Yet, from within the curve this multi-dimensional nature cannot be recognized at all and Derrida is forced to introduce yet another stipulation, viz. that of the "delineation of différance [as] strategic and adventurous."

> Stratégique parce qu'aucune vérité transcendante et présente hors du champ de l'écriture ne peut commander théologiquement la totalité du champ. Aventureux parce que cette stratégie au sens où l'on dit que la stratégie oriente la tactique depuis une visée finale, un *telos* ou le thème d'une domination, d'une maîtrise et d'une réappropriation ultime du mouvement ou du champ. Stratégie finalement sans finalité, on pourrait appeler cela tactique aveugle, errance empirique, si la valeur d'empirisme ne prenait elle-même tout son sens de son opposition à la responsibilité philosophique.

> Strategic because no transcendent truth present outside the field of writing can govern theologically the totality of the field. Adventurous because this strategy is not a simple strategy in the sense that strategy orients tactics according to a final goal, a telos or theme of domination, a mastery and ultimate re-appropriation of the field. Finally, a strategy without finality, what

might be called blind tactics, or empirical wandering if the value of empirical did not itself acquire its entire meaning in its opposition to philosophical responsibility.[64]

The meaning that Derrida here gives to the word "strategic" is opposed to everything one commonly associates with it. Instead of emphasizing the ductive, i.e., leading, notion that the word carries in its various meanings, he instead approaches the word from the perspective of "stratos," the layer, which automatically puts the one who is leading or in charge into the same stratum with the ones that are led. Strategic,[65] here, does precisely not mean the orientation towards a final goal as one might commonly hear it. Juxtaposed with the notion of "adventurous," "strategic" acquires the sense of wandering, of being vagrant, i.e., it is used to indicate a flux whose estuary is as indeterminate as its own flowing. But (we will return to this again) both the notions of "adventurous" and "strategic" also contain what Derrida has just ruled out. Although, when viewed from the inside of the sheaf or field, strategic seems to indicate nothing but immanence, one will have to concede that a field, a sheaf or a stratum is stretched out between things. Similarly, the adventure indicates a coming that again announces a place of coming to or from, something that, in any case, is outside the field or sheaf itself.

Yet, the transcendence or hyperessentiality (the being beyond Being)[66] which this approach suggests has to be resisted. Hyperessentiality would only extend the range of the bad infinity, which cannot break the connection with being, and with every attempt at doing so just reaffirms its attachment to it. We therefore have to turn to one more aspect in Derrida's theory before we can turn to an evaluative summary. Derrida indicates a completely different way of talking about that which is beyond, even beyond being, without any longer belonging to the realm of being itself. It is the word "without" that both Dionysius and Meister Eckhart use to describe the difference between beings and God.

Il n'évite pas seulement l'abstraction liée à tout nom commun et a l'être impliqué dans toute généralité essentielle. Il transmue en affirmation, dans le même mot et dans la même syntaxe, sa négativité purement phénoménale, celle que le langage ordinaire, rivé à la finitude, donne à entendre dans un mot tel que *sans* ou dans d'autres mots analogues. Il déconstruit l'anthropomorphisme grammatical.

It [without] does not only avoid the abstraction tied to every common noun and to the being implied in every essential generality. In the same word and in the same syntax it transmutes into affirmation its purely phenomenal negativity, which ordinary language, riveted to finitude, gives us to understand in a word such as *without*, or in other analogous words. It deconstructs grammatical anthropomorphisms.[67]

The fact that "without" avoids the implication of such an essential generality, then, persuades Derrida to draw the analogy with différance. Much like the circumvented hyperessentiality as well as the avoided negative theology, différance "does not mean anything" can be described only by retreating to the without-formula. The meaning of différance

ce serait "avant" le concept, le nom, le mot, "quelque chose" qui ne serait rien, qui ne relèverait plus de l'être, et de la présence ou de la présence de présent, pas même de l'absence, encore moins de quelque hyperessentialité.

— is "before" the concept, the name, the word, "something" that would be nothing, that no longer arises from Being, from presence or from the presence of the present, nor even from absence, and even less from some hyperessentiality.[68]

Apocalypse and the Ineffable Name of God

I would like to propose the following reflections as possible reasons for Derrida's rejection of a position that attempts to understand negative theology as an analogous principle to the workings of différance. 1. Negative theology runs up against epistemological difficulties which we have discussed above. In short, the claim is that the negation of existence and certain coinciding attributes does not propel one into another realm, beyond existence, but only redefines negatively the relationship with being. 2. Derrida wants to show that différance is an affirming principle. A negative approach can hardly bring out why and how this non-concept can have an affirmative effect. 3. It is not theology that is rejected in Derrida's writing but *negative* theology. Derrida is not interested in making statements about the existence or nonexistence of God. His concern is of much more an epistemological nature. What is wrong about negative theology is not the theology part; it is the attempt to do it negatively. The question of God cannot be solved via negations since they immediately relate God to the economy of being, i.e., they turn God into one among many existents.

> L'infiniment autre, l'infinité de l'Autre n'est pas l'Autre *comme* infinité positive, Dieu ou ressemblance avec Dieu. L'infiniment autre ne serait pas ce qu'il est, autre, s'il était infinité positive et s'il ne gardait en lui la négativité de l'indéfini, de l'απειρον.

> The infinitely other, the infinity of the other, is not the other *as* a positive infinity, as God, or as a resemblance with God. The infinitely Other would not be what it is, other, if it was a positive infinity and if it did not maintain within itself the negativity of the indefinite, of the apeiron.[69]

In this passage, which is meant to be a rejection of Levinas's early attempts at defining alterity as infinity, Derrida lays open what the problems of negative theology are. While otherness, alterity, is always contingent upon the conception of a certain negativity, viz. my own (the other is what I am not), Derrida claims that God must be a *positive*[70] infinity, one thus, whose infinity is *independent*[71] of my own finiteness. "Negative theology was spoken in a speech that knew itself failed and finite, inferior to logos as God's understanding."[72] Its problem is that, against its own intentions, negative theology reinscribes God into history by naming God, even though this naming is achieved by way of an exclusion. By ruling out "every particular determination," i.e. by negating it, God is surreptitiously understood to be the all that is left behind by the negation.[73]

Thus, rather than insinuating a radical atheism, Reb Rida[74] is doing what so many rabbis have done before him — he emphasizes the ineffable character of the name of God. Neither talking nor not talking about God really does justice to the fact that it simply cannot be said.[75] Thus Derrida initiates a radical turning away from divine metaphysics, perhaps based not only on the apparent epistemological problems that discourse on God brings along with it, but also because of the prohibition contained in the second commandment. One should not misuse the name of God. In this context it appears that any usage of the name of God would automatically be a misuse. The name of God cannot be used.

Rather than using God's name, rather than attempting a negative theology, Derrida approaches this question by analyzing the relationship between human beings and "יהוה." The problem that traditional philosophy, and theology as well, had to face is the eternal evasiveness of any concept of God; and Rosenzweig shows[76] that the same is true also for the concepts of the world and human beings. Nothing can be said positively about those entities, so that in the end one is left with only negative assertions about what they are not, rather than what they are. The problem of negative theology is, thus, far more pervasive than the term "theology" might suggest at first sight. Negativity is the stigma and the burden of a discourse that cannot affirm. The suggestion that Derrida seems to make is that, in order to avoid this epistemological dead-end, it is more advisable to look at the relational stratum, the link, the difference which exists between God and humans and which is constitutive, not only of itself, but also of its two end-points.

Derrida thus introduces the term "apocalyptic" into his project. By circumventing all the negative connotations the word has acquired, especially also in connection with his own critics, he makes this term the center of his attention concerning the relationship between God and humans. In quoting André

Chouraqui, Derrida emphasizes that the term "apocalyptic" can mean the following:

> qu'on découvre l'oreille de quelqu'un en soulevant les cheveux ou le voile qui la recouvre pour y chuchoter un secret, une parole aussi cachée que le sexe d'une personne. YHWH peut être l'agent du découvrement. Le bras ou la gloire de YHWH peuvent aussi se découvrir au regard ou à l'oreille de l'homme.

> Someone's ear is discovered in lifting up the hair or the veil that covers it in order to whisper a secret into it, a word as hidden as a person's genitals. "יהוה" can be the agent of this disclosure, this uncovering. The arm or the glory of "יהוה" can also be uncovered to man's gaze or ear.[77]

However, the apocalypse (the act of unveiling) is itself a peculiar phenomenon. It has a differential character, i.e., it exists as something that is stretched out between two points. The apocalypse exists as a tone. The characteristics that we have found already for différance, viz. its differing character which indicates a dissimilarity, as well as its deferring character which designates the passage of time coincident with this dissimilarity, all pertain to what Derrida now, fifteen years later, calls "apocalyptic."

Moreover, we have seen how Derrida calls the play of différance both "adventurous" and "strategic." Both terms had been used to indicate the dialectic between play and system or structure that is incited by différance. But I would like to point out that with the word "adventurous" Derrida was already closer to the notion of 'prévenance' I described in the previous chapter. Advent, the coming to/towards, expresses the vagaries of an itinerary which is, as of yet, unknown. Yet, at the same time the notion of coming itself suggests that there is something towards which one can go or from which something else is coming. This something remains to be unveiled. And if one is to believe Derrida, then this something will never be unveiled but instead will persist to be that infinitely removed asymptote towards which humans strive.

The insight of negative theology was to see that affirmative statements about the nature of God would always be statements that associate with God (i.e., with what is ineffable) something that is effable (i.e., from this world). For example, to say that God is wrathful or almighty, etc. always implicates a worldly, human (and thus finite) notion in connection with what is by nature infinite. Thus negative theology is an attempt to reverse such statements and affirm the ineffability of God's nature by negating every attribute that we could normally give to something we know.

It is for this reason that negative theology becomes nonviable for Derrida. The negation of any of the predicates that Maimonides specified would leave intact the one predicate which seems to exceed them all. And it is precisely this predicate which clouds the absolute alterity that characterizes God. Moreover, even the negation of the copula, i.e., to say that God is not, would be nothing other than saying that God is is-not. Any negation, even the most radical kind, would always reassume the position of positive, i.e., affirmative, being. Maimonides did not consider this a valid criticism. Despite his initial move towards a negative theology he ultimately refuses the conclusion that negative theology is severely handicapped through its necessary reliance on positive statements. In fact, he rejected those who attempted to find something between the categories of existence and nonexistence as people who would think about "things that are merely said; and accordingly they subsist only in words, not in the mind; all the more they have no existence outside of the mind."[78] Yet, he did not seem to understand that the reason why those who were engaged in finding a "mean" between existence and nonexistence did so, because from the standpoint of being, the incapacity of negative theology cannot be shown for the difference between those two categories amounts to nothing. Precisely such a nothing, however, is the "place" for which Derrida is looking. It has to be a place that is absolutely detached from being, yet in a relationship with it that allows for its recognition, albeit veiled, by philosophy. Only then can philosophy embark on the infinite task of knowing it, and only then can it recognize that knowing it has indeed not only epistemological but, a fortiori, ethical consequences.

Aside from the problematic of being, however, I would like to point to another difficulty which contributes to Derrida's resistance to negative theology. Maimonides' system of attributes presupposes an Aristotelian ontology of substance, with the consequence that in general (although not necessarily in the case of God) attributes are conceived as part of the essence of the thing in question (he usually refers to it as "the thing having its definition predicated of [the attribute]" and likewise understands the attribute from the perspective of thingness). Negating things — aside from the copula problems discussed above — does indeed result in the epistemological erasure of those things. This, however, becomes problematic when applied to Derrida's notion of différance. Différance is a term which rather than pointing to an essence, i.e., a stable indivisible entity in the Parmenidian sense, connotes movement and flux. While negative theology is based on the conception of things, différance as a differential expression precisely avoids essences. As a differential term it indicates difference and deferral. Negating such a term would automatically entail the halting and rupturing of its inherent flux and thus result in essentialism.

At the beginning of this chapter, I referred to the problematic of comparing God with, and by means of, secular and anthropomorphic concepts. Maimonides makes clear that such comparison (for example to say that God is One, or that God is strong) can by no means lead to the conclusion that God is such things in comparison to other things which are two or more, or weak or less strong. Maimonides instead emphasizes that those attributes are nothing but the translation of a privation. It is interesting to see that Derrida returns to exactly the same conclusion with his introduction of the term "without." Here again, we have the insight that the only way to overcome essentiality as well as hyperessentiality is to use a language that avoids such "grammatical anthropomorphisms" and instead deconstructs them. The English term "without" is exemplary, in fact, in order to show how such deconstruction might work. "Without" is actually a double command, description, etc. It might be read as Within-outside, or maybe even as withinoutside.[79] Thus, simultaneously the term designates a place as inside and outside and, hence, leaves no other option but to resolve the opposition into neither inside nor outside by focusing on what is between the two.

COHEN AND DERRIDA: ON THE POSSIBILITY OF THEOLOGY

Like Cohen, Derrida is concerned with the attachment between the negation and that which is being negated. Although Derrida's intention should not be described as an attempt to leave God's essence untouched as I did it for Cohen, one can nevertheless claim that Derrida pursues the kind of uniqueness that Cohen talks about when he talks about God. What Derrida is seeking is philosophy's other, yet that other will remain forever ineffable for it. A negation, however, would draw that other into a realm of sameness that it does not belong to, only the "without" can preserve its otherness and thus ward off effectively the temptation of negation.

A last point of comparison between Cohen and Derrida is the latter's mentioning of the infinitesimal. Negative theology must be located at an infinite distance from its own project, Derrida asserts. It has nothing in common with it. However, this infinite distance is also an infinitesimal distance which regards negative theology as a limit with which it will never coincide. Although he never makes mention of Maimonides — and of Cohen only with reference to his essay "Deutschtum und Judentum" — it is easy to see that Derrida's infinitesimal interest in negative theology is shared by his two predecessors and treated by them with equal caution. Yet, whereas for the former two the goal is to describe the possibility of theology in a privatively or negatively defined space, for Derrida it is the question of the possibility of theology itself that is at stake (we started out with that question). He is asking that question despite the discursive limits of a language that cannot but employ the tools and instruments of finiteness and synchronicity and will thus always fail to invoke the other.

The possibility of theology is, however, not only dependent on a theological method. It also demands for a space and a community within which theological discourse can take place. Derrida's contention is that this space, not unlike Levinas's *"espace vital"* opens up through our correlationship with the absolute. Within this space the celebration of messianism as the daily rebellion against what is in favor of what should be becomes the task of deconstruction. The celebrants are a community of individuals who are bound by their insight into the "yes and no" through which anything that is is given, including their own existence as a community.

NINE

Community

Différance as Messianism, Khora, and Minimal Community

DECONSTRUCTION AS DESCRIPTION AND PRESCRIPTION

The purpose of this chapter is to bring together the deconstructive notions of the text, the absolute, and the subject into that of messianism and the khora. We will then move on to an application of this messianic frame to the question of the nature of interpersonal relationships and, again, the latter's relationship to law and justice.

It must be understood from the beginning that deconstruction is a process that takes place within the sphere of the world. The destruction and construction of meaning, the undermining and subverting of certain surface-texts in favor of previously marginalized sub-surface texts is a completely this-worldly phenomenon and, as such, is as close to materialism as it could possibly be. From a Jewish perspective one would have to say that deconstruction is firmly anchored in *ha-Olam hazeh*. A quick look at Derrida's political involvement (texts about Heidegger's and de Man's involvement with the Nazi's, about Nelson Mandela, a united Europe, etc.), as well as his interest in educational matters demonstrates the worldly priority of deconstruction. In this sense deconstruction is a rejection of any metaphysical rationalism.

But "worldly" does not mean positivistic either. Deconstruction can function only because it recognizes the world as a space that is produced by the difference between the actual and the ideal, both of which it takes to be methodological hypotheses, or limit-assumptions. These limit-assumptions have their highest degree of philosophical utility not in their separate pure forms but in differential connection with each other. An understanding that can grasp them as such will be in a position to examine the world as a space between the actual and the rational. The world a such a space is ambiguous. Yet, in an effort to exchange the judgment of ambiguity for the recognition of complexity the deconstructive effort departs with any purist positions in order to understand the world in its multiple and manifold reality. The reality of this departure from rationalism and positivism is guided by its function as a didactic model for ethical action, i.e., as its introduction as an ideal, rather than an actual event.

It is commonly thought that deconstructive thought "opens up" or "creates" a new space or area in which absolutes have lost their significance. Yet, this understanding would do no more than shift the traditional dyadic and binary thinking towards a triadic structure. It cannot, however, illuminate the issue of complexity in an effective way. The mistake inherent in this approach is that it first reifies the binary structure into something from which, secondly, we have to depart, and, thirdly, understands this departure as linearly resulting in the reification of a subsequent stage. Deconstruction, therefore, must not be mistaken for dialectics. A dialectics can only function, if it carefully protects the material purity and temporal discreteness of its thetic, anti-thetic, and synthetic elements. Only if this purity is guarded can linearity become possible. Deconstruction undercuts the tendency to purity on all three levels of the dialectic as well as between ideality and actuality and, hence, causes, so it seems, the collapse of linearity. Yet, deconstruction's self-understanding is, on this level, that of a merely descriptive philosophical methodology. That is to say that deconstruction is not the cause of the impurity but rather just an indicator of an impurity that is always already taking place. Yet, even this descriptive stance has its underlying prescriptive base which can be discovered in the answer to the question "Why does deconstruction describe the world like this?" The answer is that deconstruction does not only detect the relentless tendency toward impurity as described above but simultaneously also senses the countermoves that are intended to preserve purity. It is these countermoves that it considers to be violent and ultimately unethical. In other words, deconstruction targets a certain epistemological prejudice by describing the world in a non-simple, nonlinear, and nondialectical fashion. It is dialectic itself only in so far as one understands its method both as a model for the implementation of a certain kind of thought as well as the actual implementation of such thought. If deconstruction were only descriptive it would be but a natural philosophy or science, describing phenomena without attaching any particular value to them, except the one of existence itself. But deconstruction does not only see the interwovenness of the actual and the rational with respect to the world it also sees it for itself and thus knows itself to choose a path that is both descriptive and prescriptive. Between Hegel's ideal dialectics and Marx's material dialectics on the one hand as well as Darwin's natural dialectic of selection on the other hand, Derrida claims that the world can be grasped neither as a dialectic movement nor through attributing to it the qualifying terms ideal, material, and natural.

Deconstruction's own peculiar entrenchment in the descriptive-prescriptive binary reveals also a commitment to the working out of causes and effects as well as of purposes and ends. Whereas a descriptive approach will ask about the former, a prescriptive one will inquire about the latter. Like any other philosophy, deconstruction has these structures as well. The difference is that it does not stop there but instead engages in a kind of metacritique that scrutinizes its own structures as well. How can this take place? Does it happen simultaneously? If it does not happen simultaneously, then, are we not caught in a new kind of linearity? There is indeed a new kind of linearity that one can observe. Yet, it is not the dialectical kind. It is a step-by-step methodology that focuses on different problems concerning the complexity of the world and its own discourse on that complexity. However, it conceives of this process as an infinite movement or task and does not propose the kind of resolutional quality that inheres in a dialectical system. The energy to do so infinitely is due to an emphasis that Derrida puts on the notion of the messianic as opposed to the notion of the teleological and eschatological. Messianic linearity is the linearity of revolution(s), teleological and eschatological linearity is the linearity of dialectics.

Thus, deconstruction is not an unordered, inchoate, or systemless process. Rather, deconstruction is a concerted effort to bring out and describe the complexity of the world and, hence, of the ethical project as it will show itself to the person who is serious about any kind of ethical implementation. For such a person ethical complexity can easily appear as an overwhelming flood of data, facts, and hypotheses that stand in opposition to each other, that call each other in question and, possibly, even erase each other. Ethics, in other words, can end up in an aporetic situation unable to release itself out of the arrest that the aforementioned complexity has imposed on it. Deconstruction as a messianic discourse on ethics as an infinite task is a compelling argument for the recognition of these structures as fundamentally ethical. We will see that deconstruction does indeed employ various modes of messianic discourses in order to assure the coherence and cohesion of its own project. By doing so it reveals an epistemological framework that allows it the move outside of a mere naturalism to a philosophy that seeks and struggles with the possibility of redemption.

The last three chapters have been an attempt to demonstrate the relationship between the text and the world as text, the absolute, and the subject's differential approach of the absolute. In all three the rejection of arche-teleological thought in favor of différance has been the theme It can be shown, however, that différance on the one hand and arche-teleological thought on

the other are not mutually exclusive. Rather they can be joined
and in this combination form the core of what I would call
Derrida's differential thinking. The combination which I am
talking about is one in which we will look at the interwovenness
of what Hegel calls the good and bad infinities. Knowing the
phenomenological, aletheitic, and theological dimensions of
deconstruction we now must turn to a closer look at how Derrida
treats the issues of time, space, and the social. This happens
paradigmatically within the contexts of messianism and khora.
Through these new contexts we will be able to see how Derrida
arrives at this interwovenness and how it in turn makes for the
possibility of ethical thinking. The point of the following reflections is to investigate how far differential thinking, which is an
epistemological project, can be transformed or, perhaps, can even
transform itself into differential social space. What we have to
show, then, is that in Derrida's work notions of time, space, and
the social converge in such a way that they form a unique social
space that allows for a concept of minimal ethics.

Messianism

Messianism in Cohen and Benjamin

Derrida's understanding of messianism might be best understood on the background of Hermann Cohen's use of the term to
develop an asymptotic social philosophy. We must not forget that
one of the main reasons for Cohen to write the *Religion of Reason* was to demonstrate the superiority of religion to ethics. In
Cohen's mind only religion could recognize the social crisis of
the nineteenth century and provide viable solutions to solve that
crisis. However, the contact between Cohen and Derrida is not
direct but mediated by the philosophy of Walter Benjamin who,
as we had seen already, combines the notion of messianism with
that of translation. It is Benjamin's philosophy which Derrida
uses as a frame to stake out his own claims, yet it is Cohen's
neo-Kantianism that forms the background of Benjamin's work.

One of the thirteen aspects that Hermann Cohen suggests to consider in order to understand "Humanity and the Idea of the Messiah," is the need for a development from the mythological golden age to the messianic future. Whereas the former signifies an ideal situation in which humanity has not yet erred from the commandment of God the latter raises the commandment of God to an ideal status. The messianic future is an age that can be brought about by human action and obedience. Such development makes the difference between the two eons inerasable. Although the creation narrative still seems to allude to the paradise as the golden age, Cohen argues that the sequence of events as it unfolds makes the return to the innocence of this golden age impossible. Innocence is replaced by knowledge (*Erkenntnis*) and, with an eye to the messianic future, makes room for the proliferation of culture. Time, thus, is differential time with respect to ideal creation and ideal redemption. All history turns into a history laced by messianism.

Cohen, furthermore, holds that the issue of time is reiterated in the problem of death. Once it is understood, it produces the question of the continuation of human life (in one way or another) and thus thematizes the question for a future. Cohen's view of the mythological image of death is not only overcome, but is transformed into the genesis of an ethics as an infinite task. Messianism, in its move from the mythological to the religious, is an overcoming of death that effects an expansion of the human understanding beyond the boundaries of the material world towards an infinite moral ideal.

Monotheistic messianism functions, according to Hermann Cohen, within and as a result of the differential relationship that exists between the possibility of the world's downfall (*Weltuntergang*) and its renewal (*Welterneuerung*). Both downfall and renewal are contingent upon God's final judgment and are thus not pre-determined. The move toward either downfall or renewal is not arbitrary but marked by an increasing attention to the ethico-moral quality of God's judgment. This quality of God's judgment enables Cohen to say that within the differential of downfall and renewal human beings develop a sense of necessary purification brought about through the education and guidance by God. The differential allows, in other words, for the conception of a higher ideal, a concept of the good as well as for the development of a concept of history, viz. a history that precisely inscribes humanity's steps on their way to the achievement of the ideal.

Cohen holds that the messianic element signifies to a certain degree the notion of the downfall of the world. The possibility to conceive of such downfall coincides with a certain distance that humanity has from the world. It implies that humans have largely shed their mythic embeddedness in the world and are now able to question "the significance (*Sinn*) and value (*Wert*) of human existence (*Dasein*)." Furthermore, the world is not only understood as a material entity but, more importantly, also as a temporal one. It is seen as eon which includes "especially also human life."[1]

Cohen emphasizes that part of this step towards distance from the world facilitates the objectification of the world, thus allowing for an ethical perspective on good and evil. The notions of good and evil as well as that of time taken together result, according to Cohen, in the conception of punishment as the down-fall of the world but, simultaneously, also include the possibility of a renewal of the world. Common to both speculations is the possibility to conceive of the future of the world with respect to its moral existence and development.

According to J. Zwi Werblowsky messianism is specifically also characterized by a "negative evaluation of the present." This negation of the present, however, went hand in hand with another negation, viz. that of the world to come as the only goal towards which to strive. This world, *ha Olam-hazeh*, had to be saved first. The advent of the messiah could not and should not be hastened (cf. Rosenzweig on the "Schwärmer").[2] In part the messianic structure of Jewish messianism "retained its national, social, and historical basis whatever the universal, cosmic, or inner spiritual meanings accompanying it, are. We can see, in other words, the negation of a present as a "not yet" coinciding with the negation of a future as a "too much, too early." Accordingly, Werblowsky can say that sometimes messianization can go along with a certain demessianization which emphasizes the detachedness of the messianic event from the world as it is at present.

Within Judaism, both concepts, that of the down-fall and that of the renewal of the world, can only make sense if they are taken as being monotheistically juxtaposed. For Cohen, this juxtaposition occurs as the *"Strafgericht Gottes"* (punishing court of God). This punishing presence of God, however, does not only incur punishment but also produces a type of purification which in itself makes room for guidance and education of the world by God.[3]

It is here, that some of the parallels between Cohen and Walter Benjamin become clearer. Benjamin holds that the difference between secular law and divine law is given as the difference of law instituted by human beings and law instituted by God. Whereas the former always reaches back to its mythological origins and thus emphasizes a certain crude mythic violence, the latter is of divine origin and the only violence it knows is, thus, divine. A *"Kritik der Gewalt"* (A Critique of Violence) is, therefore, always a critique of secular versus divine law. In his essay "Zur Kritik der Gewalt"[4] Benjamin determines that the root of all violence is precisely the universalizing character of myth which understands violence to be the tool which according to the law of nature is rightfully used as long as it is for good purposes, e.g., the achievement of power. He opposes this mythic violence to the violence of God whose principle is not power but justice. For Benjamin, therefore, one can say that mythic violence can only increase humanity's need for redemption. Divine, messianic force, on the other hand, is the kind of force that participates in history without just replicating history's progression but by fundamentally reorienting it.

We had seen already that Benjamin, for whom the concept of messianism includes both the weak redemptive messianic power that humanity is endowed with as well as the realm that will follow secular history after humankind will have redeemed itself, believes that the way towards this realm is characterized by the task of translation. Redemption, as the task of the translator, does not just consist in the mere transformation of meaning but really, and asymptotically so, in the accumulation of meaning. The messianic age will have been reached, and redemption will have been achieved once meaning is captured in its fullness and Babel will have been overcome. Benjamin thus furnishes a critique of the concept of mythos that resembles that of Cohen and is picked up by Derrida as well. For Cohen myth is the potential antagonist to all messianic thought because, rather than emphasizing the future, and thus the potential ethical development of humankind toward such a future, it reiterates the idea of a golden age and would thus encourage a regress rather than a development. Benjamin regards messianism as a dynamic that looks back. But this takes place in preparation for the future. Furthermore, Benjamin and Cohen are aware that myth can never establish the quality of a thought that is simultaneously focused on the individual and humankind. Myth would instead favor the concept of a universal humanity and would loose sight of the I/Thou relationship emphasized by messianic religion.

In order to talk about Derrida's relationship to the issue of messianism we need to reconsider the following three areas of his thought, all of which bring into focus the relationship between the question of messianism and the project of deconstruction as Derrida envisions it. The areas are 1. deconstruction as a strategic/adventurous enterprise; 2. deconstruction conceived as negative theology; 3. deconstruction as the apocalypse.

Différance as Strategic and Adventurous

We had seen already that in his article "Différance" Derrida explains the usage of the discourse on différance as both strategic and adventurous. In fact, it is différance itself that turns out to be strategic and adventurous. Différance serves as both infinitely removed origin and infinitely removed telos. It is the suspension that exists between two definite points which, however, are infinitely far away and thus cause différance itself to be infinite. How the two terms "strategic" and "adventurous" complement each other can be seen within the following etymological framework. The strategist is the person who knows speculatively both beginning and end of a certain project. They are hypothetically known and as such firm. Between them the strategist can make assumptions about certain strata. Developments will take place, given the firmness of origin and telos. The strategy, however, experiences a suspension of its own predictability because différance is, at the same time, also an adventurous enterprise. This means that différance undergoes a teleological as well as an archeological suspension both reflected in the word "ad-venturous." The adventurous aspect of différance questions both the foundation and horizon of the deconstructive project and reminds us of the speculative aspect of any strategy. Yet, the ad-venture hides something else. Quite literally the Latin root of the word translates as "to come" (cp. also the French "avenir") It is therefore precisely the adventurous aspect that reminds us of a past having been and a future coming already both announced in the differential suspension of the strategy. The strategic/adventurous terminology appears to give to différance simultaneously the character of a closed and an open system.

Deconstruction as Negative Theology

We had seen that deconstruction resembles Maimonides' and Cohen's concepts of negative theology. It, too, seeks to circumscribe the ineffability of absolutes by way of the negation of privations. Negative theology attempts to express the ineffability of God by negating what God is not. Deconstruction also operates within a space that is defined through a twofold negation. It understands the concepts of origin and telos as privations of an other that can never be captured within the archeological/ teleological framework that is constituted by origin and telos.

As such, as privations, Derrida negates them and hence does not just express a negative side but simultaneously also iterates a positive, affirmative side of an other that would otherwise disappear. In his words, différance will always be expressed as "différance is" and "différance is not." The purpose of such a paradoxical way of putting it lies in the problematic essentialism that even a negation cannot avoid. To say that God is not is still to say that God *is* not, i.e., that God belongs to the order of beings and thus is no different from other objects or persons around us. The second part of the slightly paradoxical expression "is/is not" is not a negation but is the negation of a privation. The negated "is" is not just understood as fullness in Parmenides' sense but already as the lack of something else. Derrida can, thus, lodge significance and meaning right at the invisible dividing line that separates negative from positive essence. This line, however, is nothing and it is into this nothing that différance can now create the somethings that constitute the world. Through the comprehensive usage of privative, negative and affirmative expressions for the concept of différance we come to understand that différance is not only the simultaneously closed and open bracket, as described above but also the productive backdrop for the world as such. The complexity of the world is itself an effect of différance. Or, more precisely, they are effects of the peculiar status of différance's teleological and archeological limits as both existent and nonexistent.

In our discussion of Cohen and Benjamin it has become clear that messianism brings to light the issue of time and history. This is certainly also the case for Derrida. We have to understand that he wants to talk about a time that simultaneously recoils into itself infinitely, because it is without origin or telos yet that also moves toward a telos that is itself infinite. Derrida is attempting to hold together good and bad infinity. He does so by recourse to Benjamin in whose terms the bad infinity is the course towards perfection which humanity can go, if they recognize the extraordinary redemptive function (i.e., the characteristics of the good infinite) that the generation that is presently alive has with respect to the past. This process, however, is in itself infinite and will not come to a final conclusion. Yet, at the same time Benjamin juxtaposes this movement with the day of the messiah. This concept assumes that the process of perfecting has indeed come to a close and that the world is now ready for the messiah. Thus, messianism consists precisely in overcoming the badly infinite world (by way of the good infinite inside of it) in order to make way for the good infinity of messianism. Benjamin, thus, gives power to the present moment while simultaneously suspending that present with respect to the day of the messiah.

For Derrida the "is/is not" structure also entails a negative evaluation of the present that is not only epistemological. It is furnished in two different ways. 1. As a critique of Husserl: Derrida can show that the idea of the present is itself a metaphysical prejudice that can be easily unmasked within Husserl's own methodological framework. 2. As an ethical critique of the political and social crisis that is so symptomatic of the postmodern age: Derrida understands this crisis specifically as a crisis that occurs within the boundaries of education, the center of Western culture. The present is nothing but the reality of a conservative, marginalizing violence that becomes visible, for example in the university, where discourses and disciplines are canonized and catalogued in order to prevent the new sciences to break and cause the collapse of the old.[5]

Différance as Apocalypse

Différance also provides systematicity and stratification. This is in part due to the apocalyptic nature of the differential discourse. Derrida plays on the double meaning, the double-bind that the apocalyptic imposes on us. On the one hand it refers to a process of unveiling, i.e., a process which is destined gradually to shed light on the question of truth. But, on the other hand, the apocalyptic condition signifies simultaneously the endless exile from truth into which we as the searchers for truth are thrust. Every step in the process of unveiling ends up being a reaffirmation of the exile in which we find ourselves and from which we would like to free ourselves, precisely, through unveiling the truth completely. Yet, the transcendental human condition, humanity's apocalyptic situatedness is given as their desire for truth. The apocalypse becomes the hyperbolic expression for truth. Truth itself, however, remains distanced.

The apocalyptic is precisely not meant to mark the event of catastrophe as it does in common English. Apocalyptic is the movement that counters, to a certain degree, that which is eucalyptic, i.e., that which is hidden well. Nevertheless it is correct to say that Derrida's writing is invested with a certain sense of apocalypticity that strongly resembles the catastrophic notion. Derrida holds that the discourse of modern philosophy, i.e., a discourse that has believed in the fundamental nature of the subject and its relationship to the world, is dead or, at least dying. In his essay "The Ends of Man" Derrida says that in Hegel's phenomenological thought "the thinking of the ends of man, therefore, is always already prescribed in metaphysics, in the thinking of the truth of man."[6] Announced in it is "the end of the finitude of man, the unity of the finite and the infinite." "The *relève* or relevance of man is his *telos* or *eschaton*."[7] In this position the end of man has two different significations one is anthropological and the other teleological. Derrida says that "the end of man (as a factual anthropological limit) is announced to thought from the vantage point of the end of man (as a determinate opening or the infinity of a *telos*)."[8] "The name of man has always been inscribed in metaphysics between these two ends. It has meaning only in this eschato-teleological situation."[9] It is our task to determine what Derrida means by this "eschato-teleological situation."

Messianism vs. Eschatology

So far in our observations a certain confusion has prevailed over the difference between what's merely teleological/eschatological and what is a clearly messianic element in Derrida's thought.

One could argue that Derrida's thought, since it does not include notions like Hermann Cohen's *"Strafgericht Gottes,"* is clearly part of the category of the eschatological, i.e., the logos of the last things, but not of messianism. However, we will see that the messianic element in Derrida's thought is given in the discourse on justice. For him justice is both arche and eschaton of a process within which the law is implemented, revised, dismissed, and newly implemented. This process itself is infinite. It is a bad infinity. But through the juxtaposition with justice it obtains a momentum that allows it to point beyond itself, toward a horizon of redemption and absolute justice not yet available. In order to show that Derrida's thought does indeed belong into the messianic category and not only into the teleological or eschatological one, we will, once again, have to look at Hermann Cohen's work.

Cohen holds that in order to understand messianism correctly it is necessary to distinguish it from eschatology. It is only messianism that warrants the infinite development of the human soul. Whereas eschatology can only talk about the last things but does not have any material impact on the world now, messianism "remains within the climate of human existence *(Dasein)*."[10] Messianism, thus, brings to the fore the importance of the development of the individual human soul. But messianism, while paying attention to human existence *(Dasein)*, also brings into focus the development of humanity as a whole. "The dignity of the human being is not only founded in the individual but also in the idea of humankind."[11]

In this complex connection between the individual human being and the idea of humankind. Cohen emphasizes the force of messianism to create a "truly political reality"[12] which will degrade all profane reality of the present *(Gegenwartsrealität)*. Messianism can envision a type of trans-sensuality of the earthly future within the natural development of humankind. In other words, while messianism keeps open the connection with a future realm to come, it simultaneously does not allow for this to happen as the sudden transcendence of the earthly realm but instead fosters human development toward the achievement of the messianic. The messianic is, thus, worked out in the world.

It is this idea of messianism that is also taken up by Walter Benjamin in his essay "Über den Begriff der Geschichte."[13] Based on his insights into historical materialism, Benjamin formulates that part of the development of humankind consists precisely in the weak messianic force that we have been given to redeem the past. In part, the messianic element comes to function especially as that which can effect the temporary stagnation of the present which will allow for the redeeming moment to take place. Benjamin thus resists a notion of pure progress that would ultimately result in nothing but ethical emptiness and suggests instead the conception of a *"Jetztzeit,"* a now-time, which would interpret the concept of the present not as transition but as a time filled with potential for the redemption of the past.

Derrida's position vis-a-vis these different descriptions of messianism must be assessed in a similar way. He has repeatedly confirmed that there is a clear distinction between a messianic and the teleological-eschatologial quality. While the latter two really only contain the notion of deferral, it is the former that actually confronts us with the notion and the possibility of revolution. With respect to the material-political thrust that both Cohen and Benjamin convey to their readers, it seems evident that Derrida is similarly engaged. Deconstruction results from a material world and returns to it in order to change its material progression. It is a force that thrusts humanity back into the world and obliges them to work for truth toward truth. The differential/messianic space of truth that, as we have shown, issues from the simultaneous affirmation of truth and its negation as a privation, confronts us not with truth as a far distant absolute goal but with language as the imperfect representation of truth on the way toward truth.

Within this differential space of truth a new kind of present is established. It is a present that never stays but always changes. It is a present that only "is" with respect to a past and a future that it has clearly not yet reached. And although Derrida would disagree with Benjamin's concept of the halting of the present (i.e., the concept of a *"Jetztzeit"*) as much as he would disagree with the logical possibility of a present in the phenomenological sense, there remains the fundamental question whether the partial unveiling of truth, as it is implied in the apocalyptic view, must not also allow for a presence. Granted, this presence does not last. But Benjamin never says that it should. He speaks, very carefully, of the weak messianic power with which humankind has been endowed. This power, it seems, is the same that Derrida talks about when he conceives of deconstruction as the relentless questioning of humanity's relationship with truth.

Like Cohen and Benjamin, Derrida embraces an anti-mythic attitude that demonstrates not only the ethical weakness of a regress to the golden age but also shows the logical impossibility of such an enterprise. In some of his more recent essays Derrida gives expression to this concern with the future by laying open what I have earlier called the prévenant structure of the apocalypse. From beyond the apocalyptic structures themselves humankind is invested with a voice that invites it to come. It is the "come" that encourages humans to go and embark on the infinite trail of an exiled unveiling of the truth. It is the "come" that announces a good infinity behind the bad infinity that is implicit in the exile/unveiling structure itself. It is, finally, the "come" that suggests deconstruction's investment with messianic thinking and thrusts it back into the material realm of the world in order to redeem it and make it ready for truth.

KHORA

Differential space in Derrida's thought is not only temporal-messianic space but also geometrical space. Geometrical space in this context, however, cannot mean empirical space but only ideal space. It is a space that precedes and succeeds all empirical space, i.e., it forms the differential matrix for the plurality of spaces that we encounter in the world. This space is called "khora." The messianic "come" signifies a past and a future in the mode of the future anterior. It is an interruption and up-rooting of the present and has a revolutionary character that derives precisely from this break with the present as the time of the event. The "come" shifts the focus to a *time* that is both anterior and future, yet never present. The time of the present is, then, what is never present. The intersection or crossing of past and future in the future anterior signals the absence of the present. The messianic, thus, veils presence and shows itself as temporal flux. It "takes place" as a past-future and, by virtue of this peculiar juxtaposition, indicates the problems that coincide with the notion of "taking place."

Yet, to say that the messianic "takes place" already betrays a certain relationship between the temporal and the spatial which we will now have to analyze further.[14] The messianic "come" effects a temporalization of the place. It is the de-determination of the place which, by relating it to the different aspects of temporal flux (and by subsequently discovering the impossibility of this relationship), seems to put a hold on the messianic itself. How can there be revolution without a place? Can messianism ever be revolutionary if it cannot take place? Is there, perhaps, a messianic quality that inheres in the notion of the place that favors the taking place of the revolution? What is it that lies beyond the de-determination of the place? Does the place signify something else, something inaccessible and unavailable? If it is really inaccessible, though, what then is the power of messianism? The messianic timeline, i.e., the redeeming of the past by the future, cannot be meaningful at all, if there is not a present, i.e., a point in which these two aspects of time can meet. Yet, throughout the past chapters we have repeatedly emphasized that deconstruction is most of all a rejection of a scientific type of philosophy that associates truth with the availability of places as points of presence.

Khora as Time and Space

A place can be determined by relating all the dimensions of a given system into a single point. A precondition for such determination is the stability of the given system since its coordinates serve as the cornerstones of the places to be determined. If the dimensions themselves were to be shifting, unstable, or unavailable, places within the system could not be determined. How is a system kept stable? The general answer to this rather vexing question is that the stability of a system depends on the stable unfolding of its various dimensions, and this, in turn, is dependent on the stable unfolding of time.

A di-mension is, as the word indicates, a twofold stretching or unfolding. It is a bi-polar or binary space within which things can be measured in a certain way. The Latin root-word "mens" carries the meaning of spirit, reason, and understanding and also functions as the etymological building-block for the words "mensa" (table, meal, sacrifice) and "mensio" (measuring). The literal translation of the term, thus, carries within itself three of the notions that are most critical for Derrida's project, by integrating in it the question of logocentrism (*mens*), that of time (*mensio*) and that of the divine (*mensa*).

The binary or bipolar character of the dimension is determined by its relationship to a beginning and an end. A dimension is a linear construct. A system is as stable as its dimensions are. Spatial and temporal linearity, however, reinforce each other mutually. It is a linearity that results from a thinking which builds on the availability of beginnings and ends with respect to a certain movement or dynamic. To speak of the beginning and end of a street is to speak of the temporal beginning and end of this street as well. The street would have neither beginning nor end, if it the determination of a temporal beginning and end were impossible.

We had seen in the previous chapter as well as in the chapter on the apocalypse, that for Derrida, the challenge is to show that philosophy has gone awry by subtly assuming the dimensional linearity of all its components, in particular, that of truth. Derrida challenges the stable linearity of dimensions in order to show the world as a multi-dimensional space, i.e., as something that *is not* what we think it *is*. He targets specifically the archic and teleological foundations on which Western thought is built and shows that the relationship to an origin or telos cannot be grasped in its full meaning unless we understand the nonsimplicity of both. This, however, is an attack on linearity itself, since linearity can only make sense as the relationship of two poles (i.e., two ones, or two simples) with each other. That is, the notion of a differential apocalyptic is an attack on our standard notions of time, which is an attack on linearity, which is an attack on the notion of dimensionality, which in turn is an attack on the possibility of systems in general.

Without the notions of time, linearity, dimension, and system we have collapsed the notion of space and, therefore, made it impossible to determine a place. However, since we do determine places all the time in every-day life it is of increasing importance to find out what the meaning could be of the impossibility of the place, i.e., the existence of a non-place. It seems possible that the philosophical base assumption of a fundamental presence, i.e., a fundamental place, is nothing but philosophical rhetoric trying to assure the perpetuation of a certain discourse of presence. It seems furthermore necessary to assume, at this point, that the philosophical notion of presence and the place is built on the prior notion of absence and the non-place.

Khora as Place

Derrida's treatment of the place comes in three different locations. His essay on the apocalyptic tone, an essay on negations and negative theology, and an essay on Plato's concept of the khora. In the first, the place is the purpose of the apocalyptic tone,[15] it is the stage of a *gala*-presentation[16] of the apocalyptic itself.[17] This presentation is preceded and succeeded by the word "come." "Come!" itself cannot be thought within the categorial boundaries of the event. The arrival of that which is to come, unlike any other event, can no longer be tied to an understanding of the place that would simultaneously render comprehensible the event itself. The apocalyptic tone expresses that the place, and thus also the event, can no longer be said.[18] "Come [*Viens*] beyond being — this comes from beyond being and calls beyond being, engaging perhaps in the place where *Ereignis* (no longer can this be translated by event) and *Enteignis* unfold the movement of propriation."[19]

In the deconstruction of time we have seen that both the notion of *prévenance* as well as the notion of propriety are dependent on a certain arche-teleological structure that, however, falters with the insight into the apocalypticity of the human condition. Yet, both are essential for the determination of the place whose de-determination can be seen also as the de-determination of the event. It, thus, impedes the actual coming of the event of truth and makes impossible the "*Eigenheit*" (authenticity/propriety) of the "*Ereignis*." In its stead we find the supplement of prévenance that relentlessly points towards the event of truth without ever reaching it. What then is the experience of truth proper? Where is the place in which one can find oneself congruent with truth?[20] In the future anterior mode the proper place of truth will always have been a secret. Despite this secrecy around truth, however, Derrida talks about a certain topolitology (i.e., a begging or asking for the place) that has always accompanied the discourse on truth. On the one hand, when one has embarked on the search for truth one has to follow a certain prescribed ritual, the secret is both kept secret from the many and divulged among them as secret (i.e., without revealing its content), and, on the other hand, a distinction is made between a holy place and the place where God resides. All the above seem to be organized around truth proper, they seem to allude to or even prepare for an experience of truth itself, but from their own perspective they remain stuck in the realm of an infinite series of attempts to get to truth. They know themselves to be called by truth and, thus, summoned by something whose existence they re-flect yet never represent, they know that the infinite movement that is inherent in the notion of "attempt" never matches the infinity, that is, that which calls. Rest and thus the possibility of the place, can only occur when we forget the asymmetry that exists between the secret and ourselves, i.e., when we forget the secret altogether. As long as we remember and struggle for the place of divine absolute truth, the places and events of profane secular truth will remain in a state of infinite restlessness. How can that be the case?

In order to understand this topolitology Derrida introduces the Platonic concept of 'khora'. The basic principle of this concept is that it stands beyond the logic of noncontradiction, it cannot be conceived by way of binary construction, and thus cannot be conceived at all. Khora is not a regress from the realm of logos to that of mythos,[21] it is rather that which generates this distinction in the first place. Khora is that which gives place and in which things take place. It is a space whose description eludes all spatial metaphors because these would inevitably lead back to an understanding that prioritizes geometrical space and imply a notion of congruence that is alien to khora.

Khora is Derrida's attempt to recast différance in the second of its two aspects: the spatial one (we had already seen how this recasting looks from the temporal perspective). It is an inaccessible space which, however, through the structure of giving and taking place, stands in connection with that which is and results in this relationship as being characterized as a hyperbolism.[22] The difference between khora and that to which it gives place or that takes place within it "is not so alien to Being . . . that the excess itself cannot be described in the terms of what it exceeds."[23] Along the lines of Plato's dialogue *Timaeus*, Derrida speaks of khora as a *triton genos*, i.e., a third species which has a generative function with respect to affirmation and negation.[24] "Third" does not imply a numerical relationship with two others. Derrida explains that "'third species' is here only a *philosophical* way of naming an X that is not included in a group, a family, a triad, or a trinity."[25] Khora precedes all places and despite the generative relationship that it has with them remains separate from them.

Khora itself is a place as well. Yet, it is a place that it is difficult to talk about. It is at the "interior of philosophy" where it anachronizes space and calls forth atemporality.[26] To speak of khora is as important for philosophy as is khora itself for the coming into existence of the world.[27] The import of Khora, it seems, lies precisely in the peculiar temporalization as anachronization that derives from the khoristic structure. That it lies at the interior of philosophy is a reminder that once again the structure that Derrida wants to emphasize here is that of the connection of the good and bad infinity. Khora is an infinite space. Yet, it is not like the infinite space that is occupied by philosophy, it is not an infinity whose origin is induced in the shape of linear progression. It is rather a space whose infinity is given as philosophy's absolutely other. It is the good infinite for it can neither be counted nor accounted for. It cannot ever be captured by the only way that philosophy knows to capture objects: induction. Yet, it is at the interior of philosophy and engenders the inductive process. It is philosophy's object of desire and, therefore, it is not an object at all.

COMMUNITY

Without saying so explicitly, we have already gained insight into the sense of community of human beings in a certain social relationship that is implied in Derrida's texts. For if the apocalyptic is the transcendental condition of humanity with respect to the absolute, and if differentiality is the mode of this condition, if, furthermore, translation is the infinite task of coming to terms with that condition, then we already have an image of the type of community that Derrida has in mind.

The significance of the emergence of the concept of community out of deconstructive methodology for the discourse of modern

Jewish thought lies in the unique position that this term has had in the Jewish tradition. Creation, revelation, and redemption are all predicated upon an understanding of Israel as community. Furthermore, for the concept of the execution of halakhah, i.e., of the interpretation of the law as well as of its application, the community is indispensable. Halakhah is what creates this community and is perpetuated by it. Jewish thinkers from Maimonides through Graetz and Cohen, and on to Rosenzweig and Levinas agree on the importance of the community for Jewish thought. For all of them the community becomes the locale of ethical action. And one could say that it is through an understanding of the sociological structures of the community that one arrives at the recognition of ethics as a primary characteristic of Jewish thinking.[28]

The notions of the "exile," the "infinite task," of the "beyond of negative theology," of the "indispensability of translation" and interpretation and, over and beyond all of them, that of the khora can be characterized as relational; common to all is their participation in a relationship between something ineffable and something effable. This relationship indicates an insurmountable, radical transcendence. Despite the radicality of this transcendence, this relationship still has an effect on the community in its exilic difference and distance from the absolute. The connection between transcendence, ethics, and community is given in the form of a dynamic nonreciprocity that leaves transcendence in its place of ineffability and creates a community in the process of an eternal, infinite striving for that transcendence. As we will see, it is necessary at this point to reiterate Derrida's connection with Cohen and, through Cohen, indirectly also with Maimonidean thinking as we had come to see it earlier. This will enhance our understanding of exactly how a community can be described that is marked by a striving for and towards an asymptotic goal.

Maimonides' 'Imitatio Dei' and a Redefinition of Phenomenology

Maimonides' discontent with the Aristotelian ethical paradigm, i.e., an ethics of the mean, was ultimately based on the relativism and baselessness of such an ethics.[29] Ethical perfection conceived along the lines of such a median ethics can only reflect the social and ethical standards relative to a specified community; but it will not suffice to define ethics universally. The notion of absolute perfection that is implied in raising the status of ethical standards from only immanent significance to transcendence allows Maimonides a conception of a possibly universal ethical community rather than just one of Jews or non-Jews, philosophers or non-philosophers, etc. Such a concept of a universal community, rather than just following intra-societal regulations, will make "imitatio Dei" their prime way of achieving the ethical standard: God.

The peculiarity of the analogy between Derrida and Maimonides is that the former raises the notion of transcendence (and a desire for that transcendence) to that of a transcendental condition (as can be seen in the notion of the apocalyptic), but simultaneously resists the logical second step of defining the focal point of this desire (as can be seen in the notion of the differential). Derrida's thought to some degree reiterates Maimonides' search for absolute transcendence, but he rejects the attempt to do so by means of a "quasi-mathematical" (i.e., rational) method. He would reject in particular the concept of *"imitatio Dei"* itself, as suggested by Maimonides since it presupposes knowledge of God based on which God could be imitated. The possibility of *imitatio Dei* was unproblematic for Maimonides for he never questioned the possibility of knowing God and imitatio could thus take place simply based on the assumption of such knowing. It was precisely knowledge of God that both negatively and positively assured the relationship between human beings and God. For him, it was not the possibility itself of knowing God that was in question but rather the form that such knowing should and could take.

However, *imitatio* understood as the infinite repetition of the task of knowing God allows for an important connection with Derrida's work. Although with his rejection of negative theology Derrida has barred himself from such possibility (i.e., knowledge of God is precisely no longer possible), the uniqueness of his approach lies in the fact that he invokes transcendence despite the impossibility of its negative or positive assessment. This notion of transcendence orients a community which relates to truth as a noncognitive phenomenon. In other words the community relates to truth not by way of negation but by way of privation. Similar to Levinas's notion of a desire that desires more than it could possibly comprehend, so also Derrida's concepts of exile and unveiling in their messianic and khoristic framework illuminate his understanding of a transcendence that can never quite be found. Thus, when I choose the term "phenomenon" for this event of transcendence I have in mind not only Husserl but also Levinas's attempt to devise an epi-phenomenology, i.e., a phenomenology that Levinas redefines through his understanding of the face as the only true "phenomenon." It is precisely the noncognitive, transcendent aspect of the face, that is, its value as a signifier that never stops signifying a beyond, that now marks phenomenology in its true, ethical character. In other words, the term "phenomenon" suggests that for Levinas, but also for Derrida, phenomenology is now characterized not only as a failed project but as an attempt to show how a radical transcendence as an ethical predisposition has become phenomenology's central issue. The term "phenomenon" marks an ontological absence but an ethical presence.

But aside from the conceptual differences that arise when one attempts to align Derrida and Maimonides completely, there also are applicatory differences that pertain to their different conceptions of the type of human community that would receive such transcendence. Contrary to Maimonides, Derrida's understanding of this phenomenology of transcendence undercuts a certain developmental notion that the former apparently believed to exist between ordinary believers and philosophers.

Maimonides believed that the people's median ethics could be overcome progressively through the increasing cognitive energy that was spent on recognizing God's true essence. Once this essence was understood as radical transcendence, positively expressed through God's attributes of action, "imitatio Dei" could begin. In this sense, true ethics was understood as a telos.

Schwarzschild points out that Maimonides overcomes the notion of *"mephursamot,"* which is Jewish-Aristotelian, with his messianology which is Jewish-Platonic. Derrida himself moves closer to the Jewish-Platonic understanding. However, he remains committed to an understanding of orientation that is fundamentally differential. That is, it does not only result from the connection with an ideal future alone but also results from a pre-original relationship with transcendence which precedes the stage of the social and communal articulation and thus puts the community into a position of transcendental-apocalyptic ethicality. In other words, whereas Maimonides' understanding of ethics is based on the possibility of the future realization of true transcendence, Derrida bases his notion of ethics on the acceptance of the reality of a future and an-archic transcendence which first lets "awareness of something" as immanent be a possibility. He therefore shifts into close vicinity to Cohen's notion of the "trace of ethics" and of messianic redemption which led Cohen to believe that ethics is a task always already in response to our createdness.

A Minimal Community Through Différance

From this perspective, Derrida offers us a definition and description of a minimal community for which nonreciprocity, apocalypticity, differentiality, and translation are its most important pillars. It is precisely the an-archic transcendence that exists between the world and its goal that now turns into the paradigmatic structure of social nonreciprocity. The paradigm of epistemological nonreciprocity between truth and the world now reoccurs in the sphere of interpersonal relationships. Only through the nonreciprocal concepts of apocalypticity, differentiality, and translation can we gain an understanding of this transcendence.[30]

The differential approach itself provides nonreciprocity as a future-anterior, khoristic structure. Both origin and telos are infinitely removed from the epistemological grasp of the subject. Yet, the subject remains stretched out towards them in a seemingly futile attempt to understand fully what will never be wholly accessible to it. Precisely this being stretched out, this tonal relationship as Derrida calls it in the essay "Of an Apocalyptic Tone," is what simultaneously carves out the subject, fractures it, and incompletes it to the degree of utter nonexistence. The subject is so totally and absolutely undermined by its other, its origin and telos, that as a subject in-itself it ceases to exist.

Even in the essay "Différance" itself (where Derrida explains the logical priority of différance over against all theology, all systems, and all oppositional thinking) the asymmetrical relationship between those systems of thought and différance itself is not hidden. Clearly, the world as we know it relates to différance, and yet, this relationship is nothing like any other relationship we might know from inside this world, because différance remains absolutely outside and thus eternally evanescent. Yet, différance in-itself does not exist; différance is neither this nor that. The exclusion of the "is" by way of anachronization, i.e., the exclusion of being, is what collapses the possibility of reciprocity and symmetry. Only around an "is," understood as an equal-sign, can reciprocity occur. Without the "is," space loses its linear dimensionality, its contiguity and to some degree its translatability of squares into circles, circles into ellipses, and ellipses into triangles.

The latter, however, is not quite the case for Derrida and certainly not for Levinas. Although they both remain united in their efforts to undermine the thought of being that takes place in the thinking of the ethical, their thought does not head towards chaos or nondimensionality. Nonreciprocity only implies nonlinear dimensionality — it is certainly not nondimensionality altogether. Similarly, the asymmetrical does not deny space in general. Quite to the contrary, we had seen that both the notion of the nonreciprocal and that of the asymmetrical are evoked by a kind of messianic and khoristic space within which the subject finds itself. It is new in the sense that reciprocity and symmetry no longer apply when one attempts to describe it. The nonreciprocal and the asymmetrical describe an infinite space, i.e., an infinite nonlinear dimension in which presence is impossible and which leaves the subject without boundaries towards both its origin and its telos.

Peculiar to this kind of space is that, even though it leaves the subject without boundaries and is, thus, undefinable, it somehow leaves a mark or trace on the subject. The subject will have been aware of its own lack of presence and its being hollowed out by the infinity surrounding it. This is to say that, despite the infinite removedness of truth, the other, and God, they nevertheless show themselves to the subject without, however, ever being epistemologically palpable. This is the function of Levinas's notion of the infinite in the finite as the face of the other or of Derrida's notion of the apocalyptic as a transcendental condition of human thinking, the holy growth of languages, etc. That is, for both thinkers we can apply the notion of a radical phenomenological showing (i.e., a showing of absolute transcendence) that turns out to be constitutive of subjectivity. Without this type of preliminary contact between the finite and the infinite, exile and truth, etc., the asymmetrical space would falter immediately and the world would have to shrink down to nothingness.

Différance and Responsibility

This is a crucial point for both thinkers because it is precisely here that both of them locate their notion of responsibility and, consequently, in Derrida's case, the notion of minimal community. The space that has thus been opened phenomenologically is now interpreted to be of radically ethical significance. Both hold that, when a subject acts (speaks, thinks, feels, etc.), it always already does so in response to an other by whom it was previously effected. My saying just a single word presupposes that it is said to someone, presupposes that it was effected by something and is thus a response to that something. In a very universal sense, both Derrida and Levinas hold that we are in a relationship with the other which is of primordial character and takes place before anything else can possibly happen. Our responsibility is imposed on us before we know it. Subjectivity, which here is radically understood as the act of *living in* responsibility, comes second, after, and always after, the relationship with the other, i.e., the *establishing of* responsibility. This relationship with the other, then, first evokes what it means to be a subject. Without it responsibility would not be the case, it could not take place, and there would, therefore, be no reason for the subject to respond.

Thus, we already have a partial answer to the question of how the concepts of nonreciprocity and the ethical are dependent on each other. Responsibility, as our continuous relationship with the other can only function if the other is "adequately" perceived as other.[31] If otherness is epistemologically taken back into the realm of the subjective, responsibility, in the nonreciprocal sense, discontinues. The only thing left would be an elliptic intra-subjective phenomenon with no ethical significance. It is for this reason that both Derrida and Levinas insist on the radically external alterity of the other over against the subject. Only if it is guaranteed that the subjective really is a function of the relationship with the other will ethics have a chance.

This functional dependence can be taken to the point of theoretically equating the two concepts of nonreciprocity and the ethical. The nonreciprocal is the ethical. It is in this sense that, for Levinas, all philosophy starts with a reflection on the epistemological which, in the end, amounts to ascertaining philosophy's ethical grounds. An epistemology of nonreciprocity is an ethical epistemology. In this sense only, the ethical is absolutely congruent with the epistemological. A primary philosophy is one that meditates the ethical and grasps it as the model for any other relationship on which philosophy will reflect. Philosophy's foundation is the human susceptibility to be effected by the other. Only because of that susceptibility can philosophy reflect on the world as other.

Derrida talks about this asymmetrical, heteronomous space that exists between human beings, and is thus constitutive of humanity, under the heading of "friendship." He emphasizes his understanding of the significance of friendship as a nonreciprocal phenomenon and its import for public, political, and legal discourse.

> Friendship is never a given in the present; it belongs to the experience of waiting, of promise or of commitment. Its discourse is that of prayer and at issue there is that which responsibility opens to the future. But [it] also turns toward the past. It recalls, it makes a sign toward that which must be supposed so as to let oneself be understood, if only in the non-apophantic form of prayer.[32]

In this short quote from the essay "The Politics of Friendship" we encounter again the figure of something that is undefined with respect to its past as well as with respect to its future. Yet, it is this un-definition which simultaneously defines friendship, since Derrida affirms that first and foremost "friendship is never given in the present."[33] In other words, in the terms of Husserlian phenomenology, i.e., as a moment of the living present, the meaning of friendship will never be determined. Instead friendship will only show itself in the mode of a past leading on to a future, circumventing the present. Friendship "signifies first and last this surpassing of the present by the undeniable future anterior which would be the very movement and time of friendship."[34]

The future anterior creates what we have above called a "nonreciprocal space." Although it visibly excludes any connection with the present (the copula is not needed to form this grammatical structure), it nevertheless relates to the present as absence.

The future anterior serves to express that, from the standpoint of a present yet to come (thus, now future), i.e. from a future present, the conclusion or fulfillment of something can/will be understood. Yet, by leaving the temporal stretch that this grammatical tense describes (through the future indexical "will" and the past indexical "have + participle") virtually undefined in its telos and origin, the notion of this future present is undermined and made vague in a way that bars us from determining it as a precise moment or point in time. Thus friendship is tied to an understanding of time that knows of no presence but only of an indeterminable past and future.

Friendship is, for Derrida, only a derivative product of a more general nonreciprocity that is constitutive of my authority as a thinking, speaking, and feeling being. Authority derives from the fact of my responsibility established through the nonreciprocal relationship with the other. It is, then, the other who gives me authority, i.e., responsibility. Derrida observes that no matter whether one says something while assuming authorship of the said or one just repeats something that was said before by someone else, "one has to suppose that I am nonetheless *speaking in my name*. You hold me responsible, *personally responsible*, for the simple fact that I am speaking."[35] That is, here already the meaning of responsibility is implied. Before I ever have said "I" or "yes" to my own utterance, before I can claim it as mine, before I can identify myself as the one responsible, I am already identified as the one responsible for the utterance.

> Before even having taken responsibility for any given affirmation, we are already caught in a kind of asymmetrical and heteronomical curvature of the social space, more precisely, in the relation to the Other prior to any organized *socius*, to any "government," to any "law."[36]

This relationship to the other that charges me as the one responsible before I can take it up myself is the substrate of any friendship as well as of any other social relationship. The communal implication that this structure exerts is that every member of a given community is simultaneously characterized by his/her individual actional ownership or authority while also being aware of the social genesis from which such authority derives (i.e., the fact that authority is always responsibility). Friendship and any other relationship as well are qualified ethically because of their rootedness in a responsibility for, to, and before the other that precedes them. This responsibility is a quality that can be derived from the "asymmetrical, hetero-nomical curvature of the social space."[37] Implied in the notion of friendship is, therefore, the universal of the asymmetrical relationship and its claim for a particular, subjective responsibility.[38]

The intersection here, between the singular and the universal, is crucial since it reinforces the distinction between individual actional authority and its social genesis. The nonreciprocal, responsible relationship to the other makes authoritative what we as human beings in a nonreciprocal, asymmetrical context have already established. It turns into laws. By being announced as such a certain crossing over is emphasized between a private relationship that might exist between an other and myself and the general relationship with any other, or all others, in my social community. Derrida observes that it is the universality of the law that exactly demands that I recognize the singularity and alterity of the other. Thus, public discourse as it is exemplified in a law can only repeat and reinforce what is already given as the heteronomical social space between the other and myself in the first place. Friendship is the one relationship that through its differential structure maintains the heteronomy of the initial relationship with the other. In a friendship the other announces itself as future fulfillment and past origin without ever being integrated into the present. This "respect of the Other," is reflected in public discourse, and here mostly through the law. Although friendship, and a fortiori the relationship with the other, are events that are defined through their singularity, the law actually manifests universally the meaning and scope of such universality.

Law and Justice

The introduction of law into the discourse of friendship is not without difficulties. The universality of legal discourse is simultaneously a violence which inevitably marginalizes and prioritizes that which it is actually supposed to represent and to organize. It is surprising to hear this much confidence expressed in the function of the law as universal discourse, and we will have to turn to another essay by Derrida in order to understand in what way he would like to see the law as a communal concept qualified.

The general distinction that Derrida makes in order to explicate the function of law is that between law and justice.[39] Whereas the latter is an asymptotic concept towards which the community strives, the former is a conglomerate of rules and regulations through which the community seeks to organize and structure itself. The law, as mentioned earlier, cannot but be inscribed violently. "Making law would consist of a *coup de force*, of a performative and therefore interpretative violence that in itself is neither just nor unjust."[40] Law can only be law when it precisely is not legitimated by a meta-structure that gives an explanatory background for the inscription of the law. Law is law only when it is obeyed absolutely. As such, "no justificatory discourse could or should insure the role of meta-language in relation to the performativity of institutive language or to its dominant interpretation."[41] The mystical foundation of authority is nothing but the silence that "is walled up in the violent structure of the founding act."[42] The law, in other words, wants to be taken as absolute, i.e., as its own origin and telos. The moment when its foundation comes to be seem as external to itself, is the moment when its authority begins to disintegrate. Derrida corroborates this claim with an analysis of Walter Benjamin's "Zur Kritik der Gewalt"[43] (which forms the second part of the essay "Force of Law"). Here Benjamin distinguishes between founding and conserving violence in order to show how the law-making state is relentlessly involved in the execution of violent law that can be transcended if not only violence itself is critiqued but the whole state that is its guarantor. Derrida adds to the problem of the founding violence of the law as follows: on the one hand, it is easier to critique such law precisely because it is without foundation and thus indefensible. Yet, on the other hand, this foundationlessness makes such a critique almost impossible since there is no institutional framework that could possibly sustain any kind of critical investigation. "As long as they do not give themselves the theoretical or philosophical means to think this co-implication of violence and law, the usual critique remains naive and ineffectual."[44]

A critique of the law, that is Benjamin's and also Derrida's conclusion, must go beyond a mere critique of the letter of the law. Even if such critique were to point out the immorality of the law, it would still not progress, since the law does not strive to be moral, but solely to be law. What must be critiqued is "the juridical essence of violence . . . and the particular usages that law adopts under protection of [the state's] power."[45] What this juridical essence might be surfaces in Derrida's reflections on the law and justice and also serves as the legitimizing backdrop for the question of the purpose of deconstruction. It is exactly this foundationless violence of the law that makes the law deconstructible. Not only is it built on texts and "transformable textual strata" but its "ultimate foundation is *by definition* unfounded" [my italics].[46] Justice in itself, on the other hand, if such a thing exists, outside or beyond law, is not deconstructible."[47] Deconstruction is possible because of the law's deconstructibility and justice's indeconstructibility. It takes place in the space that separates the one from the other.

But Derrida goes even further. He would like "to show why and how what is now called Deconstruction, while seeming not to 'address' the problem of justice, has nothing but addressed it, if only obliquely, unable to do so directly." Derrida indeed asserts that most of what he has done so far, "discourses on double affirmation, the gift beyond exchange and distribution the undecidable, the incommensurable or the incalculable, or on singularity, difference and heterogeneity are also through and through, at least obliquely discourses on justice."[48] "Deconstruction is justice."[49] It can be seen from this preliminary exposition of the law/ deconstruction/ justice triad that law and justice are never the same.

> le droit est l'élément du calcul, et il est juste qu'il y ait du droit, mais la justice est incalculable, elle exige qu'on calcule avec de l'incalculable; et les expériences aporetiques sont des expériences aussi improbables que nécessaires de la justice, c'est-à-dire des moment où la décision entre le juste et l'injuste n'est jamais assurée par une règle.

> Law is the element of calculation, and it is just that there be law, but justice is incalculable, it requires us to calculate with the incalculable; and aporetic experiences are the experiences, as improbable as they are necessary, of justice, that is to say of moments in which the decision between just and unjust is never assured by a rule.[50]

The problem with law (and here we have one answer to the question that first made us embark on the question of law and justice) is its universality. Justice always concerns singularity; it is about the individual relationship, the friendship, the non-reciprocal relationship with the other, which is different at every moment of its existence. Justice concerns something that simply cannot be universalized. Yet, the law does create a discourse that claims universal applicability (i.e., an order within which all particular situations of friendship can be rendered).

> Comment concilier l'acte de justice qui doit toujours concerner une singularité, des individus, des groupes, des existences irremplaçables, l'autre ou moi comme l'autre, dans une situation unique, avec la règle, la norme, la valeur ou l'impératif de justice qui ont nécessairement une forme générale, même si cette généralité prescrit une application chaque fois singulière?

> How are we to reconcile the act of justice that must always concern singularity, individuals, irreplaceable groups and lives, the other or myself as other, in a unique situation, with rule, norm, value, or the imperative of justice which necessarily have

a general form, even if this generality prescribes a singular application in each case?[51]

Injustice already develops, according to Derrida, where language is no longer universal, where not the same idiom can be shared and, consequently, where people are "judged in an idiom they do not understand very well at all. And however slight or subtle the difference of competence in the mastery of the idiom is here, the violence of an injustice has begun when all the members of a community do not share the same idiom throughout."[52] This, obviously, is a situation that can never be avoided; injustice begins with Babel. The slight difference that Derrida alludes to is one that always haunts any discourse, in particular the discourse on justice.

Thus justice becomes the experience we are never fully able to experience. It is an aporia, as was mentioned earlier, through which everyone has to go who wants to reflect on justice and the law that claims to institute itself in the name of justice. The significance of such a relationship with justice consists in the fact that we must *"rendre la justice"* implies a "responsibility without limits."[53] Rendering justice means never to yield to the claimed universality in law, "constantly to maintain an interrogation of the origin, grounds and limits of our conceptual, theoretical, or normative apparatus surrounding justice."[54] In short, rendering justice means to maintain a deconstructive attitude. And though "any deconstruction of this network of concepts in their given or dominant state may seem like a move toward irresponsibility . . ., on the contrary, deconstruction calls for an increase in responsibility." This attitude "hyperbolically raises the stakes of exacting justice."[55] The word "hyperbolically" here reminds us that we are still within the limits of a neo-Kantian/ Cohenian discourse. Justice in this view is an ideal towards which the human community strives asymptotically, yet, from which it is always simultaneously apocalyptically removed.

This situation is characterized by an almost existential tension. (As far as I know this is the first time that Derrida ever really admitted to and commented on that point). In the exilic, yet hyperbolically striving situation of humanity on its way to justice, the deconstruction of the traditional networks and norms creates a vacuum, an epoché, that generates anxiety. Yet, precisely in and through this anxiety we get to the moment of suspense in which "juridico-political revolutions take place."[56] Deconstruction finds its motivation and drive towards critique precisely in "this always unsatisfied appeal." It gains authenticity, one might be tempted to say, by realizing its own utmost limit as anxiety. "I know nothing more just than what I today call deconstruction."[57]

All would be simple if law and justice could be distinguished this easily. But the reality is that they pose a complexly interwoven structure. This, precisely, is the reason why deconstruction's relentless task is the taking apart and analyzing of this ever-changing relationship. Justice can never exist by itself. As human beings we would not know about justice other than through law. Therefore justice always is a reinterpretation of the law. As that reinterpretation it is simultaneously conservation and destruction, which ends in the relentless reinvention of the law.

Justice takes part in the messianic-khoristic framework described above and, thus, justice is never present. "There is never a moment that we can say *in the present* that a decision *is* just."[58] Law is nothing but the representation of this impossible presence. As such, however, it becomes even more violent. "And it is in this *différance*, in the movement that replaces presence, it is in this *différantielle* representativity that originary violence is consigned to oblivion."[59]

In order to render justice we must further accept the struggle between the decidable and undecidable. In Derrida's view, justice can never be attained but only be sensed as the aporia of an undecidable through which everyone who wants to act in the name of justice will have to go. The result of such a process is a madness that stems from an extreme desire for justice that can, however, never be stilled. We, thus, have again the allusion to the movement without end that was announced already in

Derrida's use of the term "hyperbolical." And once again he picks up on the same theme in his placing of justice not in the future but as an "à-venir," as a "to come." Justice and the differential negation of absolutes — like the apocalyptic situation — are characterized by a structure of prévenance that draws all movement towards an ineffable place. Justice is in no way involved with the production of the present the way the future is in Husserlian or Heideggerian thinking. It rather is something with an advent, whose arrival is beyond the triad of past-present-future, but towards which we are nevertheless directed, (or tonally stretched out, we could say, after our rereading of his "Apocalyptic Tone").

DECONSTRUCTIVE PRACTICE OF HALAKHAH

To draw some preliminary conclusions we have to say that as singular human beings we will always have prioritized our responsibility for the other (or better, the other will have been prioritized for us), no matter if we live it responsibly or not. That is to say, epistemologically human life is actually constituted ethically, for the other. This is a result that is also reached by Levinas. But, Derrida adds, this singularity of my relationship with the other can actually be taken up as a public universal discourse; it can become a rule, an issue, or a topic. In fact, the word "friendship" itself already signifies such a process, because as friendship the heteronomical relationship to the other becomes palpable for thinking and reflection and thus turns into a public issue. As such, however, it simultaneously turns into a violent discourse, one that inscribes itself without founding itself. It is a discursive imposition of the strongest kind. The singularity of friendship suffers from this inscription, it falls into oblivion, and more: it is challenged in its own legitimacy. The singular is a threat to the universal. From it comes the relentless dynamics of subversion. Yet, it is essential for the human community to formulate such a universal structure even if it will be turned over (revolutionized) at every instant of its actual application. That is why Derrida insists that justice can only be done as the reinvention or reinterpretation of the law. Similarly, friendship can only be approached through the relentless formulation of the universal which protects friendship for an instant and then needs to be collapsed in order for friendship to develop. Yet, this moment of development is also already the inception of a new universal formulation. It is Derrida's intention to show that, like friendship, any public discourse continuously goes through the experience of alterity and nonreciprocity; even if it is unnoticed at times. The other, as the other person that I confront as my neighbor, as the singular, nonreplaceable being, becomes transparent even in the obscurity of the law through the transcendentality of my experience of responsibility as it is given in friendship. Derrida refers to this phenomenon as the "minimal community" preceding any other relationship, "a sort of friendship [that] had . . . been sealed before any other contract: a friendship prior to friendships.

Derrida does not merely attempt to locate the problem of the ethical in the social sphere but relocates it as the question of human constitutedness. This is a move that we can also observe in the work of Heidegger who, in his "Brief über den Humanismus," shows how the ethical condition of humanity must be redirected toward the *"Frage nach dem Sein."* Derrida's question is a question for being. But it is a question that wants to use the structures of interrogability themselves in order to avoid the stifling and fascist tendencies to which Heidegger's work is susceptible. This can only succeed if we understand that it is merely a first step to describe the structures of the world by way of the messianic-khoristic framework that Derrida introduces to the discourse of philosophy. It is a second step to say that, in part, this description is followed by the prescription never to cease description. For only if description is maintained as a relentless discourse on its way to truth and justice, only when we see that this kind of discourse does indeed have a deeply solicitous (i.e., uprooting) effect, will we also understand the ethical necessity for it to be maintained.

CONCLUSION

It has become, by now, quite a commonplace to speak about the ethics of deconstruction. Indeed there are whole books that are devoted to exactly that issue.[1] In many of these works one can sense the urge to defend deconstruction and postmodernism. Many declare themselves ethicists, not in the sense that they are driven by the concern to make ethical judgments about the world, but in the sense that they deem it ethical that someone rush to Derrida's, et al., defense.

It is clear to me that from a certain level Derrida is indeed in need of such a defense. The rumors that his philosophy is attempted anarchy, that it has no ethical concern whatsoever, that its only goal is to destroy foundations without building new ones, that it is nothing but philosophical perversion, and much more, all these are rumors against which Derrida needs to defend himself. But we need to leave it up to him to do so. My interest in this book was rather to demonstrate how some of the insights of Derrida's and Levinas's philosophies can lead one to the construction of an argument for something that has gotten out of fashion in postmodern circles, viz. the consideration of absolutes. The argument against such consideration follows a certain pattern: the thought of the absolute leads to absolutism, absolutism leads to totalitarianism which in turn leads to fascism and thus to all kinds of abominable crimes that have been and will be committed against humankind.

One is tempted to say, with a somewhat grandiose gesture,

well then, let's get rid of those absolutes! This gesture has been the naiveté of a generation that thought of absolutes as positivistically given. Ridding oneself of certain forms of government, of certain people, of certain ways of thinking, etc. were all thought of as solutions to what the turn to postmodernism had made unavoidably clear: that our culture bears the marks of oppression and marginalization and that it is up to us to remove those marks.

There is a great enthusiasm that inheres in this attitude. Yet, there is a question that remains on the outset of this whole move and that is the question of success. How successful will the cleansing process, which we have, no doubt, embarked on already, be? What kinds of improvements will we be able to reap from the forces that drive this renewal? Is there a horizon of perfection and of bliss that will grow until we have actually reached it? Is there a promise of a world after, i.e., one in which the injustices that derive from the misguided veneration of the absolute are overcome? Can the sweeping forces that are over-turning so many of our previous assumptions about power, tradition, etc. provide us with rest, once it is over?

Here, I think, another turn needs to be taken within the postmodern field. It comes right from the center of one of its most famed off-spring: deconstruction. On the one hand, the new direction into which we are asked to go is one that reinstates a discourse about the absolute. It is misleading to think that the questioning of absolutes such as truth, God, ethics and others implies an immediate shunning of those absolutes themselves. Yet this questioning reveals to us that absolutes are not what we thought they were. As absolutes in question they turn into differentiated absolutes, absolutes that can become productive. An absolute in question is not one that simply disappears, rather it is one that can now exert the delimiting (i.e., the ab-solutional) effect that inheres in it. This delimitational effect takes place in the world. This is to say that when we question the absolute that formerly had been perceived as a source of oppression, we don't remove the absolute itself but only turn the absolute into a source of freedom.

All depends on how we position the absolute. The course of deconstruction gives an example of how this positioning could take place. If we succeed in understanding the absolute as a phenomenon whose absolute existence is given as its own differentiation, i.e., as the difference between its own infinitely removed origin and telos, then we have created an absolute that, through its own inner (apocalyptic) tension, turns into a point of orientation from which derive new challenges and inspirations for the development of the world.

But this process is infinite. There is a horizon, yet it does not become larger with time. The process that deconstruction describes is one in which differentiated absolutes turn into nondifferentiated ones, which in turn have to be newly differentiated. The horizon itself is an absolute that undergoes differentiation, in order to avoid or cure its own totalitarian tendencies. The messianic force that I think one can detect in the work of Derrida and Levinas does not derive from the promise of a final solution but rather from the insistence that messianism is something revolutionary that takes place as a "daily kind of messianism."[2] The juxtaposition of messianism with the notion of the daily is a crucial juncture for deconstruction since here it demonstrates what, I think, lies at its heart: the connection of good and bad infinites. It is the connection of an infinite promise with an infinite surmise, of infinite rest with infinite activity. The good infinite gives to the bad its infinite spatial and temporal depth, the bad infinite gives to the good infinite what it could not have by itself: life.

The subtext of this book has been from the outset to show that, as a part of their shared Jewish heritage, Derrida's philosophical work is indeed as intricately involved with the question of the absolute as the ethical as is Levinas's work. I have purposely chosen to pay as much attention to the philosophy of Levinas as I have, because it seems to me that only if we understand the thrust of Levinas's Jewish thinking adequately in its scope and purpose will we also be able to assess how Derrida fits into the same framework and maybe even gives it a new shape. That there is a difference has been noted by many. However, most analyses of this relationship end up affirming something like Levinas's commitment to ethics in contrast to Derrida's commitment to philosophical speculation.

It is certainly true, however, that the term "ethical" finds much more mentioning in Levinas's writings than in Derrida's. The function of the whole first part of this book was, in part, to show how Levinas works and builds on explicating the ethical as the epistemological framework that in fact constitutes philosophy. One of the conclusions that we were able to draw in chapter 4 of part I was that, in a radically phenomenological sense, the face, in its absolute otherness, constitutes the only true phenomenon (viz. a phenomenon that is not constituted by the structures of transcendental consciousness, but one that is radically other and in turn first gives structure to something like transcendental consciousness).

It is the crucial point in Levinas's writing that it is the face and not any other object that has this constitutive power. The otherness of the world, the difference between the objects that surround me and myself, can only be grasped because I have experienced difference prior to these observations as the one between the face of the other and myself. It is in this sense that the ethical relationship grounds my grasp of the world, whether it be philosophically or religiously.

Based on this formal first axiom, Levinas describes the consequences of such a relationship. First and foremost there is the question of how such a relationship between the other and myself can be thought. Is not the moment of thinking the other also the moment where one has bluntly broken down the boundaries that protected alterity from any intrusions? Or otherwise said, is Derrida not right when he asks in "Violence and Metaphysics"[3] if the other, in the absoluteness that Levinas wants to assert, can ever be integrated cognitively? Levinas devotes much time and space to answering this question adequately. The answer is thoroughly paradoxical because it involves the simultaneous assertion and denial of something as well as a rhetoric of seriality that evokes the other rather than demonstrates it. The relationship between the other and myself is analogous to that of the infinite and the finite. On the one hand, the two are radically distinct and unrelated, yet, on the other hand, how could we even begin to think about the other or the infinite, if not a trace of what those words signify were somehow located inside our capacity to understand?

Here the thought of Hermann Cohen becomes instrumental. Like Levinas, he understands the relationship with the other as a deferred moment of the relationship with God, the holy, or the good. It is a relationship that is governed, perhaps called into life, by something that Levinas calls "desire," or "metaphysical desire" for the holy. Yet, this desire is averted into an ethical task to love one's neighbor. If we live up to the obligation and responsibility that are implied in this task, then we can decrease the distance between the world and God, without, however, ever reaching a point where God and world would coincide, i.e. where the task was actually fulfilled. The ethical implies an infinite task. Through exploring the relationship between God and the world, Cohen gives us the tools to understand and gain epistemological access to the other. The in-dependence that exists between the two sides is, simultaneously, a correlation. Without this correlation the ethical and the call to responsibility would be unthinkable in the way Levinas describes it. Yet, since the relationship is desirous, since it exists because of a lack, Levinas can refer to the subject as fragmented or hollowed out by the thought of the other. And we should refrain from saying "hollowed out *by the other*," since that would imply a type of agency on the part of the other which the other does not yet have.

In the Jewish tradition this relational model has important consequences also for the understanding of Scripture and Revelation. Scripture has an effect comparable to that of the other. It becomes, phenomenologically speaking, the phenomenon that ruptures, and thus reveals, the isolation of the reading subject. Thus for the Jew, the relationship to the text becomes paradigmatic for the relationship to the neighbor. The irresistible need to interpret the text is analogous to the irresistible need to speak to the other and to say *"me voici,"* since in both cases it is the metaphysical desire for the absolutely other that triggers it. The text elicits the same kind of responsibility that also governs my relationship with the other. This relationship, qua distention between text and self or other and self, turns into a life-giving relationship, one that creates an *"espace vital."* Here I believe we can encounter one of the most radical turns effected by Levinasian epistemology: there is a notion of radically indispensable life-space that comes out of an equally radical commitment and obedience to the other. It is clearly to Levinas's merit, besides developing such an epistemology within the sphere of Western philosophy, that he points simultaneously to its much older place in the Jewish tradition.

All of the above concern the status of subjectivity itself — modernity's favorite child. A subjectivity that is formed and shaped in the way described above exhibits a peculiar kind of passivity, of non-agency vis-à-vis the world and, a fortiori, vis-à-vis the other. This kind of subject is not yet a real subject in the sense of an authority. Rather, it is indeed sub-ject and it responds to the call of the other with the exclamation *"me voici,"* "here I am." It responds as if accused, as if held hostage, as if being obsessed. And that is indeed the case. With respect to the other, and thus with respect to the whole world surrounding us, I am not free but called into a relationship. I have no control over this call itself. However, freedom is not entirely ruled out by Levinas's thought. In fact, it comes in after the initial obsession and now has an even stronger claim on me. For it is now that I know of the inevitability of my relationship with the other that I am free to choose whether I want to live up to that responsibility or not. Ezekiel's freedom consists in the very fact that he can choose whether he wants to obey the call to prophecy or not. He is unfree with respect to being haunted by this call.

Thus, it is in the notion of responsibility that Levinas attempts to mediate the difference between the other and myself, the infinite and the finite, the agent and the passive one, etc. In responsibility a relationship is established that does not forget about its nonreciprocal origin, indeed that cannot forget about it, and therefore is driven to give itself over into the service of the other.

It is clear, I think, from the above, that Levinas's primary concern has been to rethink the epistemological framework of Western philosophy and perhaps Western thinking in general. It is in this sense that I would like to call him a philosopher of the ethical. He is not, and this is the crucial distinction, an ethicist. His philosophy nowhere exhibits the signs of a move towards application — it shows no concern whatsoever for recent social or ethical problems, but it does indeed show more concern than most anybody else has shown up to the present point for what must be the framework of a successful ethics.

Derrida develops quite a similar framework, mostly because his own philosophical interest leads almost naturally to a philosophy that questions the problematic of alterity. (That this happens not only in dialogue with Levinas but also with other Jewish thinkers can be seen, for example, in the difference that develops between the two with respect to Derrida's notion of "exile" and Levinas's notion of "proximity.") Like Levinas, Derrida, furthermore, launches his attack on Western philosophy (and an attack it can still be called) from a standpoint that is radically critical of the twofold problematic inherent in being. He exposes being in its attempted and violent manifestations as well as in its epistemological impossibility. Derrida's critique of the Western concept of God is not a critique that aims at affirming atheism, but rather is one that is infinitely startled by the many futile attempts that have been made to explicate God discursively as origin and telos.

However, the interesting character of Derrida's approach derives from the fact that he does not cast away those concepts. Both origin and telos become important in a new challenging way, viz. as somethings that cannot be attained, but only be approached. The relationship that exists between such unattainable origin and telos creates an infinite matrix of meaning, interpretation and action between them. Différance is just another name for exactly that type of relationship. It is a differential relationship, that like a mathematical differential, produces an infinite function between its asymptotic limit and its origin.

Like Levinas's other, Derrida's origin and telos are differential marks of a thought and life that have a function that cannot just be dismissed as insignificant because it is unattainable. Derrida gathers this significance in the notion of the exile, or apocalypse, that is, the unveiling, ever-distanced relationship that binds me epistemologically to the truth. He thus is able to express the same notion of nonreciprocity which Levinas is trying to express. Yet, he achieves this by way of a model that expresses relentlessness, or restlessness, that stretches out between the origin and the telos. Levinas's model expresses a static nonreciprocity, an epistemological frame one might say with all due caution, but Derrida now puts the picture into the frame. This picture is a collage that exhibits eternal-internal movement, i.e., one that never stays the same. It is a collage which responds to the promise, i.e. the "come," as much as it responds to the past that, albeit irretrievable, makes it possible at any given moment. Between the "re-" of re-presentation, that points to a lost but ever renewed origin, and the "idea in the Kantian sense" that announces the eternal future telos, the present becomes impossible and is substituted by the subjects eternal vacillation between those limits. Only violently can presence attempt its luck at turning from a nothing into a something. Yet, even so, the violent attempt will never attain the present but only become an affirmation of the past.

With the escape of the moment, i.e., the present, into an eternal differential, which constitutes the apocalyptic condition of humanity, Derrida also dismisses the modern notion of subjectivity. "Here and now" are identified as the future anterior "will have been," in which the present is eluded and the subject experiences itself as thoroughly fractured by an other that is origin and telos at the same time. Friendship interpreted in Derrida's terms turns into the differential between what was and what will be, yet it can never assert itself as presence. Friendship is an exilic situation, in need of translation as the vehicle towards ending this exile, and thus mirrors the relation with truth in which every single human being already stands.

In other words, there is a task here too. It is an infinite task that tries to overcome (i.e., translate) the eternally dichotomized situation that exists between signifier and signified. It is the task of the translator. As language expresses simultaneously the impossibility of achieving unity between signifier and signified, so it also expresses the desire to communicate, and thus the reference to a signified which makes translation (and communication as a special case of translation) possible. By taking recourse to Benjamin, Derrida emphasizes the growth of language that takes place through interpretation and translation. Yet, this growth again is directed and aims at a limit, a sacred language, which will have made translation dispensable. But there is also the task of unmasking a reason that will attempt to rush the moment of reconciliation and hastily proclaim that differences have been overcome, that everything is translatable to the degree of translations dispensability. The task is to approach reason as a principle or an absolute, as something that must be rendered in the way it was discussed in the previous chapter. As such it can have effects that can indeed uproot the monotony and self-sameness of a given system. As such it can provide the flow, the ever-renewed overcoming of stasis, that could take hold of a system that does not know itself related to such an absolutely external outside. However, announcing the principle of reason as such, as principle, is already announcing the totalitarian and marginalizing effects that this principle will entail. Hence, at the same time this announcement demands a relentless inquiring into the principle of reason. It demands suspicion towards its motivations and agency. Otherwise we will lose sight of what is marginal to reason and what it itself can never adequately understand. Derrida thus emphasizes vigilance as a never-ending, infinite task.

Philosophy resonates in everything I have said so far about Derrida. Again and again it is the correlational understanding that brings to the fore the type of relationships that modernity has to dismiss under the guise of a critique of pure reason or that it had to integrate as the movement of a spirit coming into itself. The catalytic, i.e. enabling, position of Cohen and Husserl cannot be overemphasized in this context. And no matter what Husserl is said to have thought about Marburg neo-Kantianism, his philosophy certainly reflects a great deal of thought that seems to have come out of or at least paralleled that school.

So far the differences between Levinas and Derrida have only been slight. Whereas the former conceives of epistemology as a result of a relationship between other and self, the latter, while including the formats groundwork, moves on to explore the character itself of such a nonreciprocal relationship. Derrida, as well as Levinas, emphasizes that a radical phenomenology that understands the other as the only true, though inaccessible, phenomenon, results in responsibility. Here too, the ethical is in this sense the epistemological. Epistemology can never be conceived outside the sphere of the ethical. It is intricately related to the radical decentering of the subject which is opened to the world and to the other by the other and thus finds itself filled with a world that it only has access to through the impact of the others otherness. More than Levinas, Derrida moves on into a direction that attempts to understand the ramifications of such an epistemological situation on the social sphere. Here, Derrida points out that authority is, based on one's epistemological/ethical relatedness to the other, a phenomenon that can be said to display a social genesis. The other makes me responsible and thus forces me to be an authority over what I do and say. That I am responsible, that I am an authority, is taken up into legal public discourse and made into the foundation of any Western society.

This in itself, however, is not enough, since it does not determine in what sense otherness and marginalization are congruous and have to be protected. That, it seems to me, is the one flaw in Levinas's system. It does not ever make clear what, in a situation of applied ethics, can be done to protect the marginal and oppressed. It only insists that both sides, oppressor and oppressed, do stand in a relationship of inevitable responsibility for each other.

For Derrida the vigilance described above implies more than that. Superimposed on the discourse of epistemology and alterity we can find in his thinking the discourse of power and marginality. It is not enough to just emphasize the ethical relationship. Once that it is done one has to move on and define how such a relationship can actually turn into a situation of ethical action. And here we can see Derrida at his most radical but also at his most ethical. For the sake of differentiality, the state represented by the government, i.e., the more powerful entity, has an obligation to grant actual freedom and space to those who are marginalized. If a state used its power to suppress such marginal, counter-cultural movements, it would inevitably hinder the differential production and the plurality that are characteristic of a society that lives between irretrievable origin and inaccessible telos. A state has to protect those who potentially might have the goal of undermining it.

Derrida combines this description with a call to practice. The kind of ethics that he envisions is based on a strategy that, just like the origin he describes in "Différance," is non-simple. It is multiple, because it is tonally stretched out between origin and end. It is thus a practice that itself can only be based on the assumption of the possibility of pluralism. In the sense that this pluralism sets an end to the one and uniform reason, philosophy finds itself in a perennial crisis. Yet, philosophy can also support and reinforce such pluralism by letting itself be investigated, by investigating itself the structures of its own thinking and the structure that make possible its own thinking. In this sense philosophy might still be called the queen of sciences, but now it is the queen that constantly dethrones herself, knowing that only that way she will have access to the kind of limited power in a minimal community from which humankind can benefit.

Last but not least, it seems clear that a thinker whose conceptual framework is based as strikingly on some of the more important theoretical assumptions of modern Jewish philosophy as that of Derrida must be considered a Jewish thinker as well. It matters little at this point what he himself announces his heritage to be. Not because it is unimportant, but because as the author of his philosophy Derrida might very well be the least equipped to categorize his own project for us. In comparison with the explicitly Jewish thought of his contemporary Levinas, but also in comparison with Maimonides, Cohen, Rosenzweig, Jabès, Benjamin and others, it becomes clear that Derrida's discourse — about exile, the unpronounceable name of God, unveiling, the infinite in the finite, translation and interpretation, an ethics of responsibility, and a community that exists through differentiality — is never just Jewish by accident. His thought is, one might say, certainly more understatedly Jewish than that of those others just mentioned. Derrida has come a long way from his first essays on Husserl to his latest pieces on negative theology, the apocalypse, and on Cohen and Rosenzweig. It has taken him much time (almost a life-time) to come to terms with the fact of his own inscribedness in this tradition. But it might very well be the case that his work is nothing but an autobiographical effort, written along the lines of his own life. From that perspective then it can be understood almost intuitively why Derrida reminds us: *"En ce moment même dans cet ouvrage me voici."*

NOTES

Notes to Introduction

1. Jürgen Habermas picks up on this in his essay on Derrida "Uberbietung der temporalisierten Ursprungsphilosophie: Derrida's Kritik am Phonozentrimus," *Der Philosophische Diskurs der Moderne: Zwölf Vorlesungen*, pp. 191–218. Habermas identifies Derrida as a philosopher whose emphasis on writing is analogous to the rabbinic emphasis on writing rather than scripture. "Offensichtlich ist Derrida im Anschluß an Levinas, von jenem jüdischen Traditionsverständnis inspiriert, das sich weiter als das christliche von der Idee des Buches entfernt hat und darum gerade der Idee der Schrifgelehrsamkeit strenger verpflichtet bleibt" (195). Derrida, according to Habermas, embodies a return to the messianism of Jewish mysticism as an attempt to overcome the political-moral insensibility and aesthetic tastelessness of neo-paganism (197). Habermas observes in this context that Derrida's work maintains a relatedness to a God who is understood as transcending the world fully (216–17). In all this, Habermas senses, ultimately, an unacknowledged return to a discourse on God. The deconstructive critique of ontotheology is not a critique that hinges on the critique of theology itself but rather on the critique of what Habermas calls "eine unverbindlich gewordene Ontotheologie" (an ontotheology that has become abstract). Unfortunately, although Habermas's approach bears all the right marks, and he does indeed understand Derrida's and Levinas's projects to a large extent, one simultaneously senses the disdain that he harbors for precisely such a mystical/theological approach. He cannot but diagnose that deconstruction increases the rubble on top of the foundations, of exactly those foundations which it wants to recover (216). Michael J. MacDonald, "JewGreek and GreekJew," *Philosophy Today*, shares Habermas's rejection of the mystical as a genuine philosophical discourse but attempts to show that Derrida's and Levinas's conceptions of the trace

are linguistically based rather than mystically motivated. He unfortunately thus misses the whole theological renewal that derives from the emphasis on the ethical absolute present in Derrida and Levinas.

2. For much of the motivation for the following reflections on autobiography and marginality I am indebted and thankful to my friend and colleague Thomas T. Downey whose insight into the connection between the life of a philosopher and his/her concomitant thinking has made a strong impression on me.

3. One of the interesting side-aspects of this tendency is that it is true for both departments that supported deconstructive theory (mostly English and Comp. Lit. departments) and those departments that opposed it as naive and unphilosophical (mostly Philosophy and Religion departments).

4. Tom Downey pointed out the peculiar double-meaning of description in this sentence.

5. Richard Kearney, "Jacques Derrida: Deconstruction and the Other," *Dialogues with Contemporary Thinkers: The Phenomenological Heritage*, pp. 105–127, (henceforth referred to as "Kearney"), wrongly thinks that the year was 1931. But Peter Engelmann, "Jacques Derrida," *Philosophien*, p. 70, (henceforth referred to as "Engelmann") and Imre Salusinszky, "Jacques Derrida," *Criticism in Society: Interviews with Jacques Derrida, Northrop Frye, Hal Bloom, Geoffrey Hartman, Frank Kermode, Edward Said, Barbara Johnson, Frank Lentricchia, J. Hillis Miller*, pp. 11–24, (henceforth referred to as "Salusinszky") as well as Christopher Norris, *Derrida*, (henceforth referred to as "Norris") all know the correct date, i.e., 1930, rather than 1931.

6. Interview with Jacques Derrida, *Nouvel Observateur*, "Philosophie: Derrida L'Insoumi," pp. 71–83; ("henceforth referred to as "Nouvel Observateur").

7. *Nouvel Observateur*, p. 74. This quote also appears in Norris', *Derrida*, p. 11. However, Norris seems to take this as evidence that Derrida's Jewishness had no impact whatsoever on his subsequent writing. This, however, is an unfortunate interpretation, since one only has to continue reading the interview to find overwhelming evidence for the way Derrida was affected by his Jewish background. It is difficult to understand why Norris cuts the rest of the interview. It is, in any way, an unfortunate elision.

8. *Nouvel Observateur*, p. 74.

9. *Nouvel Observateur*, p. 75.

10. *Nouvel Observateur*, p. 75.

11. *Nouvel Observateur*, p. 75.

12. Engelmann.

13. Engelmann, pp. 54–55.

14. Ibid.

15. Kearney, pp. 107–108.

16. Ibid.

17. *Nouvel Observateur*, p. 75.

18. Ibid.

19. Jacques Derrida, "Ponctuations: le temps de la thèse," *Du droit à la philosophie*; "Time of a Thesis: Punctuations," ed. by Alan Montifiore, *Philosophy in France Today*, pp. 34–51; henceforth referred to as "Time, pp. French/English").

20. Time, p. 441/36.

21. Time, p. 443/38.

22. Time, p. 448/42.

23. Time, p. 450/44.

24. Ibid.

25. Derrida has published widely on topics concerning education, the university and related school systems.

26. Time, p. 456/48.

27. Time, p. 458/49.

28. All biographical material on Levinas is taken from the following three sources:

    1. Kearney, pp. 47–49.

    2. Stephan Strasser, *Jenseits von Sein und Zeit: Eine Einfuhrung in Emmanuel Levinas's Philosophie*.

    3. Robert M. Seltzer, *Jewish People, Jewish Thought: The Jewish Experience in History*.

29. Seltzer, pp. 483–84.

30. The Hebrew introduction to *Otherwise Than Being or Beyond Essence* (p. iv) reads in the following way: "In memory of the soul of my father my teacher, R. Yechiel bar Abraham Halevi, my mother my teacher, Deborah bat R. Mosheh, my brother Dov bar Yechiel Halevi, and Aminadav bar Hechiel Halevi, my uncle R. Shmuel bar Gershon Halevi, and my aunt Malkah bat R. Chayim."

31. Kearney, p. 51.

32. Ibid.

33. Kearney, p. 119.

34. A summary of this attitude can be found in John D. Caputo's recent book *Against Ethics: Contributions to a Poetics of Obligation with Constant Reference to Deconstruction*. Caputo uses Hegel's and Kierkegaard's interpretation of the Biblical story of the sacrifice of Isaac to show that Hegel thought of Judaism and the Jews as constantly having to give up what they love (Isaac) as being forced and willing to go into exile and be removed from their native soil, in short, as a people which flaunted the alienation and estrangement from that which they desired most.

35. On the question of the relationship between Hegel and Judaism cp. Robert Gibbs, *Correlations in Rosenzweig and Levinas*. Gibbs' book sets out with a reflection on the thought of Hegel who deemed himself the end of philosophy and the power of Jewish thought to reorient philosophy, i.e., to reopen it and to give to it an ethical dimension which it had lost through the reduction of the other into ultimate identity in Hegel's thought. For a close reading of Gibb's text and the postion that Rosenzweig takes vis-à-vis Hegel cp., my "Hegel in the Thought of Rosenzweig," *Postmodern Jewish Network*. Also, Steven S. Schwarzschild, "Alienation — Judaism as the Philosophical Issue Between Hegel and Kant," unpublished manuscript. Rather than putting into question Hegel's anti-Jewish attitude, which is not in doubt, it is mandatory that we take a look at how subsequent Jewish philosophy has dealt with the Hegel-question. For example, despite Gibbs's affirmations to the contrary, it is evident that Rosenzweig, inspite of himself wrote a work of Jewish philosophy that, in many of its aspects bears a fascinating resemblance to the work of Hegel. Schwarzschild rightly identifies Judaism as the issue *between* Hegel and Kant. But this "between" is also crucial evidence for the fact that Judaism is not wholly against Hegel. The "between" indeed paves the way for the postmodern "in-between" which I think informs the methodology and ethics of deconstruction. In this sense it can be said that Schwarzschild himself had begun to cross over into the postmodern realm (cp. my "Postmodernism in the Thought of Steven S. Schwarzschild," paper delivered at the AJS in 1994). This Jewish tendency towards Hegel despite Kant can be observed also in the work of Hermann Cohen (cp. my essay "The Concept of History in Hermann Cohen's *Religion of Reason out of the Sources of Judaism*.")

36. Violence and Metaphysics, *Writing and Difference*, pp. 79–154.

37. Gibbs, *op. cit.*, is one of the few readers of Levinas who does not choose to reject Derrida as Levinas's unserious critic but reads Derrida's challenge to Levinas in "Violence and Metaphysics" "Jewgreek is greekjew. Extremes meet" as a challenge to both philosophy (i.e., the thought of Hegel) and Judaism to begin a new era of thought that understands the simultaneity of a "universality that is not totalizing and an obedience that is neither knowing nor naive" (p. 174).

38. Richard Cohen's book *Elevations: The Height of The Good in Rosenzweig and Levinas* is an example of such a dismissive reading. Cohen does not misunderstand Derrida, however. His reading of him as someone who can "live with both Hegel *and* Levinas" that is as someone who does not want to decide between either Athens or Jerusalem is quite accurate. The problem is that he takes this notion of "hypocrisy" (p. 319) i.e., of falling short of deciding and (while seeking shelter behind Levinas) asserts that Levinas would call this irresponsibility

(p. 315) or immorality (p. 318). In addition, Cohen aligns Derrida with Heidegger's Nazi-past, by claiming that Derrida's philosophy implies that "moral strength" in philosophy "can rely on no more than the good of bad fortune of a thinker's personality, itself something of a cult, rather than insisting upon the unity of life and thought, for goodness" (p. 320).

39. Despite some similarities in the approach I would still distinguish my description of that of the philosphy of the limit described by Drucilla Cornell, *The Philosophy of the Limit*. Cornell suggests that the term deconstruction is itself an inadequte representation of the scope of the Derridean project. The latter, she claims, has a "special kind of quasi-transcendental analysis" (p. ix) in mind which cannot really be captured by the term deconstruction. Renaming deconstruction into the philosophy of the limit has the advantage of 1. upholding the tradition as an important part of the Derridean analysis, especially with respect to the concept of the system, and 2. philosophy of the limit refers to the material limit that idealism reaches and fails to transcend when it comes to the description of reality (p. 1). Furthermore, Cornell holds that the idea of the limit rather than that of deconstruction will be able to safeguard the other as that which is absolutely other to any philosophical system, including that of deconstruction itself. This will in the end serve to enhance the ethical project that deconstruction is all about (p. 2). While I agree with Cornell on the importance of the limit in Derrida's philosophy, I do think that her wanting to replace the term deconstruction with the term of her choice indicates a certain uncertainty with respect to the effect of those limits, what she calls very acurately a "deconstructive intervention"(p. 9). This might be a problem that derives from the fact that it seems that she conceives of the limit more as something that has to do with the future than with the past. She talks about the preservation of a certain kind of utopianism in Derrida's philosophy (p. 8), but she never really explicates the relevance of her insight into the limit with respect to the archeological questions that deconstruction raises as well. This, however, strikes me as an important oversight, for it is precisely the course of the deconstructive intervention to undermine and then asymptotically reestablish the double limit that exists with respect to any object whether it be of material or immaterial nature. The effect that this intervention has on the object is "de-construction" or "Ab-bau," i.e., a paradoxical building and tearing down of structures. This begs the question of the logical connection that exists between the limits and the world. My suggestion is that it consists in what Cohen calls the method of correlation, i.e., the negation of the privation of the absolute. Without this double limiting and without further analysis of how the limits actually connect with the world, an analysis of the ethics of deconstruction must remain without force.

Notes to Chapter One

1. Emmanuel Levinas, "La Révélation Dans La Tradition Juive," *L'Au-Delà Du Verset: Lectures et Discours Talmudique*; "Revelation in the Jewish Tradition," trsl. and ed. by Sean Hand, *The Levinas Reader*, pp. 190–211. Henceforth referred to as "Revelation," p. French/English.

2. Revelation, p. 158/191.

3. Ibid, p. 162/194.

4. The term "modern" is practically synonymous with what Levinas calls "Greek" elsewhere. Robert Gibbs in his paper "'Greek' in the 'Hebrew' writings of Emmanuel Levinas" points out that for Levinas "Greek represents the style of that language, which is universal, conceptual, anti-metaphorical and philosophical." (p. 3)

5. Cp. Charles Taylor, *Hegel*, pp. 3–51.

6. Revelation, p. 160/192.

7. Emmanuel Levinas, *Autrement qu'être ou au delà de l'essence*, p. 226 trsl. by Aphonso Lingis, *Otherwise than Being or Beyond Essence*, p. 179. Page references from hereon as "Autrement, p. French/English."

8. *Autrement*, p. 30/24.

9. Ibid, p. 20/17.

10. Ibid.

11. One might want to say that Levinas's whole project is based on a misunderstanding of Plato's theory of forms as it was critiqued in Plato's *Parmenides*. Parmenides' argument with Socrates is that the latter assumes that a form covers all its material instances like a blanket. Parmenides responds that not every part of the blanket can be with every form. Does all matter then participate in the same form? Possibly Levinas is mistaken in his analysis of Being as creating a totality which eventually envelopes everything. Somehow in this understanding he presupposes a thinking based on Plato's theory of forms. In this dialogue Parmenides points out to Socrates that if one understood a form to be like a blanket covering all material instances which belong to it, then one would have to admit that each instance is covered by a different part of the blanket, and thus that form is divisible. The question is why does Levinas fail to take this fact into account? Would an Aristotelian theory of forms — the one that actually does away with forms as infinite, unchangeable and indivisible — solve Levinas's problem? It would at the least provide the disconnections necessary to open up the gaps and fissures which Levinas needs to think ethics.

12. In an interview with Edith Wyschogrod in 1982 (distributed as hand-out at the *AAR*-meeting in Chicago in 1988), Levinas picks up on the question of oneness which he understands as a Neo-Platonic concept. "For the Neo-Platonists plurality was always a privation of actuality . . . Discourse was always less than the unity of the One."

13. Revelation, p. 160/193.

14. Emmanuel Levinas, "Language and Proximity," trsl. by Alphonso Lingis, p. 109. Henceforth referred to as "Language."

15. Interview with Wyschogrod, Levinas stresses in this interview that his interest in language is not to be understood as a "Kehre" away from phenomenology. Language is instead grounded in phenomena but does not have any revelatory power by itself in the way Heidegger suggests that "Die Sprache spricht."

16. Jean Hyppolite, *Genesis and Structure of Hegel's Phenomenology of Spirit.*

17. Cf. also Jacques Derrida, "'Genesis and Structure' and Phenomenology," *Writing and Difference*, trsl. by Alan Bass, p. 155: "The phenomenologist, on the contrary, is the 'true positivist' who returns to the things themselves, and who is self-effacing before the originality and primordiality of meanings. The process of faithful comprehension or description, and the continuity of explication must dispel the shadow of choice." Steven S. Schwarzschild, *The Pursuit of the Ideal: Jewish Writings of Steven Schwarzschild*, pp. 231f. is rather disconcerted about this move to the things themselves, since in his view it is constituted by "the complaint that Cohen's [thought], and rationalist 'critical' thought in general, was too abstract." Schwarzschild includes Bergson as well as Husserl in the list of people guilty of this charge, without mentioning that the former (through his understanding of the dynamic but infinite grasp of the ineffable through intuition) but even more so the latter (through his conception of philosophy as an infinite task) included concepts into their systems that are reminiscent of the Kantian regulative idea and, if one does not want to call them Cohenian, one has at least to call them neo-Kantian.

18. Language, p. 123.

19. Ibid, p. 120.

20. Ibid, p. 125.

21. Levinas, "Reality and its Shadow," p. 1.

22. Levinas, "The Ego and the Totality," p. 41.

23. Interview with Wyschogrod.

24. I will use this distinction again in the last chapter on Derrida where he makes a similar distinction between law and justice.

25. Previously I mentioned how the status of the text could be called "ambiguous-in-the-non-ambiguous." I suggest this term because it indicates the dual nature of the text with respect to meaning, which resembles the dual nature of subjectivity as other in the same. Furthermore, the term indicates the fractured condition of the text itself. It is this condition which makes the text available for reading and penetrable for interpretation.

26. Revelation, p. 159/192.

27. Interview with Wyschogrod, pp. 10, 11.

28. The point which Levinas makes comes through clearly in Eilberg-Schwartz' study "Who's Kidding Whom." Eilberg-Schwartz explains the differences between Hebrew and other languages by using a model borrowed from chemistry. Whereas most of the functional, linear languages are based on an atomistic model — i.e., we analyze them according to the sequences of their letters — Hebrew follows a molecular model. Within molecules the sequence of atoms can change, bringing about different kinds of chemical elements and compounds. Eilberg-Schwartz suggests that it is exactly this kind of change which a successful interpretation of the Hebrew texts should bring about as well. Any Hebrew word contains a certain number of meanings which is dependent on the number and kind of letters which the word contains. In Eilberg-Schwartz' interpretation, revelation would be an event intended at the creation of the Hebrew language. Moreover, revelation is limited to the amount of possible meanings that can be derived from a particular word or passage. It is by no means infinite and it cannot be associated, he asserts, with the free-play-methodologies of recent poststructural interest in the Hebrew texts. Eilberg-Schwartz does indeed provide a very insightful scheme for the structural and philological aspects of the Hebrew language. Yet, it is obvious that Levinas's interpretation and use of the sacred texts goes beyond that.

29. Revelation, p. 166/197.

30. Ibid, p. 167/198.

31. Ibid, p. 166/197.

32. The word "inquire" is a translation of the Hebrew root "d-r-sh" of which "Midrash" is a derivative form.

33. Revelation, p. 162/194.

34. Daniel Boyarin, *Intertextuality and the Reading of Midrash*, p. 15, interprets midrash to be a product of the heterogeneity of the Bible which in itself entails a heterogeneity of interpretations. The midrashic interpretations either double the heterogenous elements found in the texts or they attempt to fill the gaps between them. In both cases the goal is to obtain an interpretation that preserves the text as a single document in marked contrast to the emphasis of historical critical research on different strata of the so-called source hypothesis. A reading of those texts must necessarily be a strong one, that is equipped to gloss or explain the gaps and fissures of the text. Boyarin suggests that that is done through the conjecturing of intertexts which reflect "the culture in which aggadah [is] produced." Boyarin is not sure whether midrashic discourse must be understood as historiographic in character or whether it is nothing but a reflection of the "interpretive strategies which the Bible itself manifests." However, in at least one case he states unequivocally that "the materials which provide impetus for the gap-filling are found in the intertext in two

ways: first in the intertext provided by the canon itself, the intertext and interpretive interrelations which exist and which can be made to exist between different parts of the canon and second, within the ideological intertextual code of the rabbinic culture" (p. 17). Boyarin's reading of midrash is congruent with that of Stern and Kugel. David Stern, "Midrash," *Contemporary Jewish Thought: Original Essays on Critical Concepts, Movements and Beliefs*, ed. by A.A. Cohen and P. Mendes-Flohr, pp. 621–27. And James Kugel, "Two Introductions to Midrash," *Midrash and Literature*, ed. by G.H. Hartman and S. Budick, pp. 77–105. Stern sees the two main functions of midrash to be (1) representing a certain ideology of a certain rabbinic school, and in (2) solving the lexical and grammatical problems given through the text. Based on these premises Stern and Kugel elaborate on what Levinas calls the lack of a unifying dogma. Midrashic discourse can draw on any part of the Bible to explicate or refute the passage or word in question. In doing so, Kugel states, the midrashic interpreter enters the past while keeping one foot in the present. Midrashic discourse is about building interpretive bridges between past and present.

35. Revelation, p. 160/192.

36. Levinas uses the terms "orthodox" and "modern" in this way in his essay. My own sense is that rather than reflecting on the actual distinctions between certain Jewish groups he just uses them to indicate a certain relationship to the Jewish faith in general.

37. Revelation, p. 160/192.

38. Ibid.

39. Revelation, pp. 162–63/194.

40. Ibid, p. 172/202.

41. This claim is so important because with it Levinas contradicts much of the traditional rabbinic stance on revelation since the beginning of the common era. The traditional read is that revelation ended with the prophets Haggai and Zechariah.

42. Interview with Wyschogrod, p. 15.

43. For this cp. Levinas essay "God and Philosophy," ed. by Sean Hand, *The Levinas Reader*, pp. 166–90 and the second chapter of this dissertation "Infinite Ethics: Cohen, Rosenzweig, Levinas."

44. Revelation, p. 168/199.

45. Ibid, p. 174/204.

46. Ibid, p. 163/195.

47. Levinas thus merges the concepts of two phenomena, revelation and inspiration, which were traditionally kept apart in Jewish Theology and considered different phases of Jewish history. Cp. K. Kohler, *Jewish Theology*, pp. 39–40.

48. *Autrement*, p. 227/180.

49. For this cp. chapter IV of part I of this dissertation where I

discuss the relevance of Levinas's concept of the face in connection with Moses request to see God.

50. Cp. "Interview with Wyschogrod," p. 5.

51. Franz Rosenzweig, *Der Stern der Erlösung*, trsl. by William W. Hallo, *The Star of Redemption*, pp. 36–39 (henceforth referred to as "*Stern*, p. German/English"), seems to imply the same kind of fracturedness when he describes the mythic God who needs to reveal himself in order to end his loneliness.

52. Tamra Wright, Peter Hughes, Alison Ainley, "The Paradox of Morality and Interview with Emmanuel Levinas," *The Provocation of Levinas*, p. 169.

53. Revelation, p. 178/207.

54. Ibid.

55. Levinas's stance on ritual reflects very much that of Franz Rosenzweig. The latter sees in ritual the one force strong enough to unite the Jewish people as a whole independent of where they are in the world and how Jewish they think they themselves are. Cp. Rosenzweig, *Stern*, part III, book I.

56. Judah Goldin, "The Freedom and Restraint of Aggadah," ed. by Geoffrey H. Hartman and Sanford Budick, pp. 57–77, esp. pp. 68–69. In Goldin's view aggadah and halakha have equal value. The "ein somekhin al ha-aggadah" (one may not invoke aggadic sayings as support) seems to have no relevance for him. Goldin claims that the aggadah had virtually no authority when it came to implementation into a real life context.

57. This, actually, is the heart of his whole philosophy.

58. Revelation, p. 172/202.

59. Ibid, p. 176/206.

60. Ibid.

61. Ibid, p. 178/207.

Notes to Chapter Two

1. The term "metaphysical" needs some further explaining I have chosen it since universal applicability cannot be thought other than *above* the physical. I am aware of the risk of such terminology being reappropriated by onto-theology. But it seems to me that knowing that risk is sufficient protection. I am, furthermore, not quite alone with my choice of this term. Bernard Forthomme promises *La métaphysique d'Emmanuel Lévinas* in the subtitle of his book *Une Philosophie de la Transcendance: La métaphysique d'Emmanuel Lévinas*. He believes that "la métaphysique de Lévinas s'élève radicalement contre l'écimage de la pensée contemporaine où domine, sans conteste, la dimension d'horizontalité: chez lui, la déhiscence verticale s'avère pré-originelle

ou pré-archique." (p. 170) He understands this vertical dimension to be given as "le désir métaphysique de l'Autre" (Ibid). Forthomme insists that "chez Lévinas évidemment, la hauteur reçoit un statut métaphysique et celle-ci ne peut en aucun cas être réduite à une expérience de la hauteur comme expérience de la verticale du corps lui-même." (p. 175) Based on these observations about Levinas's concept of the other and the face Forthomme announces a "métaphysique du visage" in Levinas's work which "doit être absolument distinguée d'une réflexion philosophique sur la physionomie ou l'expressivité humaine." (p. 175) In other words, the face turns into a criterion of metaphysical character in a way that emphasizes absolute transcendence or, as Forthomme calls it, "transascendance." On the back of the book Levinas himself comments on Forthomme's efforts: "Ses pages sur le visage — sur la "métaphysique du visage," sur la possibilité de la métaphysique qui ne serait pas une onto-théologie — qui ne serait pas ontologie, mais "au-delà de l'Être" — sont vigoureuses et pénétrantes."

2. Robert Gibbs pointed out to me that the notion of grounding is problematic in Levinas vis-a-vis the latter's attempts to shatter a philosophy that is based on the unity of substance and an understanding of the world as the result of the ontological difference, i.e. as derived from that substance. It seems to me, however, that one cannot ignore the strong grounding implications that inform Levinas's work. Especially his descriptions of the subject in a state of a passivity, more passive than any passivity, indicate the proximity of an arché that can never be made present through questioning, i.e., that is unavailable to any process of objectification. Bernhard Casper seems to be saying the same when in his essay "Denken im Angesicht des Anderen: Zur Einführung in das Denken von Emmanuel Levinas," in *Verantwortung für den Anderen: Zum Werk von Emmanuel Levinas*, p. 26 he asks: "*Aber ist dies ["etre autage pour autrui"] nicht in der tat die Grundsituation des Menschen in der Geschichte? Die Grundsituation, die freilich erst heute ganz offenbar wird? Ist unsere Grundsituation in die sich dann überhaupt erst alles andere einträgt und von der alles andere abhängt, nicht wirklich die, daß jeder von uns von dem anderen Menschen, den wir töten können und doch nicht töten können, ausgegangen ist?*" And a little later (pp. 30–31) he acknowledges "*daß [wir] mit aller geistigen Archäologie, mit allem Graben nach Gründen, der primordialen Situation des Uns-in-der-Verantwortung-Findens nicht auf den Grund kommen [können]. Vielmehr finden wir uns als Menschen in der Verantwortung für den Anderen immer schon vor.*" Casper is introducing here the crucial distinction between a grounding and an epistemologically accessible grounding. Levinas, in Casper's reading, denies the possibility of the latter but certainly subscribes to the former. Still, Gibbs's contention is necessary, since it marks the difficult path that

Levinas is trying to find between a thinking of substance that would just reinforce hierarchy and a thinking of non-substance that does maintain responsibility.

3. An interesting side-aspect of this issue is the question if Levinas's rejection of totality also means a rejection of theory. On that question confer Wayne Floyd Jr., "To Welcome the Other: Totality and Theory in Levinas and Adorno," and Alphonso Lingis, "The Origin of Infinity," *Research in Phenomenology*, pp. 27–45. Both authors hold that Levinas is seeking to give a new face to theory in the sense of a methodology that does not totalize, i.e. understand the world as grounded in Being. Floyd argues that one cannot just substitute ethics for epistemology and instead suggests to reinvestigate the possibilities of a theory along the lines of Adorno's Critical Theory, i.e., a theory that will continually question and undermine itself, in order to avoid the amalgamation effect which inheres in traditional theory.

4. For a closer analysis of the question of the origin of the infinite confer Alphonso Lingis, "The Origin of Infinity." Lingis shows that there is a difference between "openess in being" and its being "thematized with the idea of infinity." Thematized infinity virtually destroys openness and replaces it with a concept of pretentious epistemological access. Lingis emphasizes that it is precisely that kind of access that we do not have. He instead suggests that Husserl's concept of the horizon stands for the openness into which all finite thinking eventually loses itself, into which it disappears. Lingis understands this horizon as an eternal future from which the present issues forth. There is thus a parallel to Levinas's thinking here in the fact that the present is not something self-given, as for instance in Husserl, but given by an other. However, Levinas's other is located in the past not in the future. Furthermore, Lingis emphasizes that in his model the present is possible through an "Es gibt" inherent in the future. He thus chooses to focus on a term first coined by Heidegger and explicitly rejected by Levinas. It must remain unanswered if Levinas might agree to a formulation of the "es gibt" that centers around the giving of the present by the other instead of expressing the inevitability of Being.

5. René Descartes, *Discourse on Method: An Other Writings*, trsl. and introduced by Arthur Wollaston, pp. 117–34.

6. Descartes, *Discourse*, p. 127.

7. Emmanuel Levinas, "God and Philosophy," trsl. by Richard A. Cohen and Alphonso Lingis, *The Levinas Reader*, "Dieu et la philosophie," (henceforth referred to as "God, p. French/English"), p. 106/187, note 5.

8. God, p. 105/173.

9. Hegel, so quoted in Emmanuel Levinas, "Ideology and Idealism," *Modern Jewish Ethics: Theory and Practice*, ed. by Marvin Fox, p. 129.

10. Obviously, not every Jewish philosopher or theologian understands monotheism in this radical way. I am, in particular, refering to Cohen, when I say monotheism, since it is Cohen with whom Levinas is in dialogue. However, monotheism has always been a question or problem within the realm of Jewish philosophy and it seems to me that it is in that sense that Cohen, Rosenzweig and Levinas are treating it. On the question of monotheism in Jewish Philosophy cf. Norbert Samuelson, "The Concept of Worship in Judaism," paper given at the *Academy for Jewish Philosophy.* Samuelson shows that the form of monotheism that one can find in modern Jewish philosophy mainly derives from the thought of Moses Maimonides. It is, however, not necessarily representative of the concept of the deity in classical Jewish philosophy. Samuelson writes: "While Maimonides' philosophical/theological judgements had an authority among subsequent generations of rabbinic thinkers equalled by no other rabbi, his radical version of negative theology was the single most *unrepresentative* [my italics] expression of how classical Jewish philosophers interpreted biblical statements about God" (p. 4). However, for the lineage of Jewish philosophy that goes back to Maimonides (and Cohen, Rosenzweig, and Levinas belong to that lineage) the main paradigm for the relationship between humans and God was given as knowledge. Thus we can see that among Jewish Aristotelians prevailed a primacy of epistemology that also became formative in the area of modern Jewish philosophy. The difference between the two areas consists in the fact that whereas classical Judaism mainly sought to explain the relationship epistemologically, modern Judaism added the criterion of the ethical to it. In both cases it is God's infinity that prevents humans from actually reaching God through either epistemology or ethics. In a conversation Edith Wyschogrod objected to the connection between Levinas and Maimonides, saying that "Maimonides' Aristotelianism would be far more removed from Levinas" and that the latter has more of a Kantian agenda. This remark is crucial since it reflects an ambiguity in Maimonides' thinking. On the one hand, Maimonides believes, in response to Jewish and Islamic mysticism, that only philosophy can guide human beings in truly understanding God. On the other hand, he is also the one who is acutely aware of the limits of reason that confront human beings if they try to understand God. It is the latter aspect, I believe, that makes it possible to emphasize the Kantian agenda in both Levinas and, retrospectively, also in Maimonides. His and probably also Levinas's point is that reason is not sufficient, and that something else will have to happen for me to understand the other, and God.

11. Two relatively short essays that deal with the relationship between Levinas and Rosenzweig and Levinas and Cohen are Wayne Floyd, paper given at the *AAR,* and Edith Wyschogrod, "The Moral

Self: Emmanuel Levinas and Hermann Cohen," *Daat: a Journal of Philosophy*, pp. 35–58. Wyschogrod argues that Levinas is "in significant conversation with Cohen's thinking" (p. 36) although in some cases he and Levinas also show significant differences. The latter, according to Wyschogrod, can be seen most clearly, if one examines Cohen's ontology as well as his view on totality. Both concepts are, as is well known, critical for Levinas, since he charges them with bearing most of the violence of the philosophical tradition of the West. Wyschogrod notes that for Cohen it is precisely the inequities between different human beings, their social differences, that have to disappear in order for there to be a just society. Levinas, although certainly critical of socio-economic differences, would maintain that, in an epistemological sense, differences, viz. the difference between the other and me, are of tremendous import. This leads on to the second point. For Cohen the question is how one can gain an authentic self, an 'I'. For Levinas, on the other hand, the question is how I can truly perceive the other. In other words, what is an interim stage on my way to an authentic self, in Cohen, is the final (and beginning stage) in Levinas. The ethical, for Levinas, is nothing that can be developed, but is something that precedes everything that appears (p. 53). Wyschogrod ends her essay by focusing on the concept of the infinite in Cohen and Levinas. She states that it is the infinite that provides both Cohen's and Levinas's philosophies with "the open-endedness of the moral realm which gives the self its meaning" (p. 58). The claim that involves the logic of the infinite will be further developed in this chapter.

12. Hermann Cohen, *Die Religion der Vernunft aus den Quellen des Judentums*, trsl. by Simon Kaplan, *Religion of Reason Out of the Sources of Judaism*. (Henceforth referred to as "*Religion*, p. German/English") p. 122/105. "Die Vereinigung ist keinerlei sachliche Verbindung." This is, in any case, a very obscure way of putting it. The choice of the term "Vereinigung" to shed light on the character of the correlative connection is, at best, half-hearted. "Vereinigung," more than any other word, esp. more than the word "Verbindung," expresses exactly the oneness ("Ver-ein-igung") of the two correlatve terms. Cohen thus, by choosing this term, plunges right into the affirmation of an "All," i.e., a unitary togetherness between world and God that seems odd given his utter precaution with the concept of the unique God at the outset of the *Religion*. The term "Verbindung," on the other hand, expresses a binding ("Ver-bind-ung;" "Band" (Germ.): string, rope) of two separate ends. It thus would indicate, if Cohen means what he first stipulates so cautiosuly about the unique God, the type of relationship between world and God so much more appropriately.

13. God, p. 124/107.

14. *Religion*, p. 119/102; Cohen initially interprets the act of self-sanctification on the part of humans to be a defense against the power of sin. We will see later that he is less certain about this origin than it might seem to be the case in this passage.

15. Cohen develops this method as a critical response to any pantheistic concept of God and world.

16. Cohen assumes the Parmenidean conception of being as eternal, infinite and unchangeable. He equates God with Parmenides' being and becoming with the world.

17. *Religion*, pp. 241–42/207.

18. For the following discussion cf. Hermann Cohen, *Logik der Reinen Erkenntnis*, "Die Urteile der Denkgesetze," henceforth referred to as "Urteile," pp. 79–120.

19. Cohen argues that proclaiming God's oneness will not suffice to characterize God. Though this term would sufficiently separate God from the polytheistic notion of a multiplicity of Gods, it fails to account for the fact that polytheism also has a penchant for God's representing nature. The Jewish God, Cohen argues, cannot be brought into touch with nature in that fashion. God has being in the sense layed out by Parmenides, i.e., that nothing else has being; he characterizes Being as eternal, unchangeable and infinite ("unendlich"). God and nature cannot mix or blend in with each other, yet, and that is the crucial point in Cohen, somehow the world is supposed to show the fullness of God. Hence the question is, how can the infinite show itself in the finite?

20. *Religion*, p. 116/100. The literal translation of the term "Entwicklung" would really be "unwinding" or "unwraping." This sense also is retained in the English term "development" if we remember that its Latin root-word, "velo," actually means "to wrap." The prefix "de-" thus expresses the negation of "to wrap." The importance of the term "Entwicklung" comes less from its wraping derivative than it comes from the translation that uses the word "unwinding." In this sense "Entwicklung" is very close to the Hegelian unfolding, suggesting a type of change that does not change the essence of what is changing.

21. I am using the German "unendliche Aufgabe" instead of the English "infinite task" because the former does not only express the infinite and processual elements of this relationship but also the initial passivity on part of the humans expressed in the word "Aufgabe." "Aufgabe," literally translated, means "on-giving." "Aufgabe" suggests that something is given on to me by an other. It thus suggests a nonreciprocal (passive-active) relationship which is crucial for the concept that Cohen tries to employ. Alphonso Lingis points out that also for Husserl "subjectivity becomes authentic, becomes authentically itself, attains the highest sort of life possible for it, in opening upon an

infinite time, time of *infinite tasks* [my italics] ("The Origin of Infinity," p. 42). This shows that at least potentially there is a Jewish-Neo-Kantian lineage that goes from Cohen through Husserl to Levinas. This would explain much of Levinas's "Cohenianisms" and, simultaneously take into consideration that Levinas never studied Cohen extensively.

22. *Religion*, p. 73/64.

23. Z. Diesendruck, "Maimonides' Theory of the Negation of Privation," *PAAJR*, p. 142: "[If privations only were employed to describe the nature of God] . . . the concept would be free of corporeality, plurality and all the rest of the anthropomorphistic elements but it would also be empty of all that which gives meaning to it altogether.

24. Urteile, p. 92.

25. Cp. Urteile, p. 93: "Das Nichtsein ist nicht etwa ein Korrelativbegriff zum Sein; sondern das relative Nichts bezeichnet nur das Schwungbrett, mit dem der Sprung kraft der Kontinuität ausgeführt werden soll."

26. Urteile. This translation is odd because in English as well as in German we only know of "Sprungbrett" ("springboard"). That Cohen uses "Schwung" rather than "Sprung" indicates his emphasis on the logical *energy* that derives form the relative nothing. The word "Schwung" in German has the connotations of élan, flexibility, elasticity, activity. One needs "Schwung" to do a "Sprung."

27. *Religion*, pp. 116–17/100.

28. Ibid, p. 125/108.

29. *Avoda Zarah*, 20.

30. *Religion*, p. 126/108.

31. Ibid, p. 124/107.

32. That is the reason why in Spinoza's works it is the multitude who is really free, for it is their ignorance of God's omnipresence (as posited by Spinoza) that gives them choice.

33. Franz Rosenzweig, *Stern*, pp. 426–27/(my translation).

34. In other words, the mathematical definition of transitivity (a = b and b = c then a = c) is not valid in this case. Rather, Rosenzweig formulates the relationship as a = b and c = b.

35. Hallo translates "Schauen" as "perception." This is insightful, since it emphasizes the epistemological quality of the word. Yet it is also limiting, since it takes away the more visual qualities that the word "Schauen" can have.

36. *Stern*, p. 439/(my translation).

37. Ibid.

38. God, p. 95/168.

39. Ibid, p. 96/169.

40. Ibid, p. 96/168.

41. The term "without" will play a more important role in some of the following chapters on Derrida. Suffice it here to say that "without" is a unique term equipped to express the peculiar notion of an inside that neither is nor is not the outside and an outside that neither is nor is not the inside. In Levinas's case the same term serves to express the equally peculiar relationship between the finite and the infinite.

42. This is precisely Derrida's criticism of Levinas in "Violence and Metaphysics," trsl. by Alan Bass, *Writing and Difference*, pp. 79–154. Unfortunately most people have not had the patience to read slowly through that essay and consequently criticize Derrida, unfairly, for reinventing a kind of dialectic that would leave nothing but play between the good and the bad, i.e. reinforce a frivolous relativism. But Derrida's critique of Levinas stands, I believe. It is the simple observation that Levinas's terminology of allegedly absolute concepts (the other, war, peace, etc.) is, in this absolute form, in-comprehensible. Only if one understands them in their privative value, i.e. infinite as the non-finite, other as the non-same, etc. will it be possible for the intricate relationship that these concepts have with their opposites to come to light. The question of a real absolute is left untouched because it could not be said.

43. Levinas is only doing what Kierkegaard did in the *Philosophical Fragments*, trsl. by David F. Swenson, when he speaks of the passion of thinking: What is that unknown which gives no rest to thinking and lets it get heated up in trying to grasp it? Like Kierkegaard, Levinas also equates this unknown with the divine.

44. God, pp. 105–6/174.

45. Ibid, p. 109/176.

46. This also explains Levinas's use of the term "passivity" or the even more emphatic "more passive than all passivity." Until thought is infected with the idea of the infinite through recognition of its own finiteness, it remains inactive, passive. Only after this contagious event can thought become active and reach out for the infinite.

47. Note how this whole description of the infinite "dipping" into thought to effect the recognition of the latter's finiteness has a clear likeness to God's handling of the inert materials in the creation story. Levinas is repeating the creation story in philosophical terms.

48. Possibly, Levinas intended a deliberate parallel to Cohen's and Rosenzweig's idea of describing the relationship between God and Humans by way of an asymptotic function.

49. God, p. 109/176.

50. With this question, however, Levinas seems to be beating a dead horse, since a solution is not possible. The existence of this middle ground — or whether he will fall off the rope or not — can not be proved or shown. The question is merely rhetorical since Levinas will, of course,

assert the existence of such a middle-ground on which his whole project is based. For the sake of this project I will here follow his assumptions about such a middle ground.

51. God, p. 113/178.

52. Again Levinas works with Husserlian terminology. The noesis/noema structure becomes that of desire and the desirable. The change which Levinas suggests is that from the outside the object of desire can be moved. In Husserl's noesis this step has to be taken by the ego itself. What Levinas works out, in other words, is that the desire/desirability structure is part of the noesis/noema structure. In fact one can say that the latter always determines the functioning and direction of the former. Only a being, entity, etc. which is external to this structure will be able to break it. From the inside such a move must be impossible, since it would always again run up against the priority of its own desires.

53. God, p. 114/179.

54. Ibid.

55. Levinas, *Autrement*, p. 226/179.

56. Ibid, p. 226/180.

57. Ibid, pp. 228–29/181.

58. God, p. 105/174.

59. Ibid, p. 106/174.

60. Ibid, p. 125/185.

61. E. Levinas, *Difficile Liberté*. "Jewish Thought Today," *Difficult Freedom*, trsl. by Sean Hand, p. 159. (Henceforth referred to as "Difficile.")

62. Religion, p. 105/91.

63. Ibid.

64. Cp. René Descartes, "Meditations," in *Discourse*, pp. 101ff.

65. God, p. 107/175.

Notes to Chapter Three

1. Revelation, p. 206.

2. God, p. 177.

3. Only over against such another consciousness is it possible for me to stake my life absolutely while simultaneously the other will *think* that she has actually succeeded in taking my life. When the other deems herself victorious, then I will know that I have staked my life and thus exist. Her desire to supersede (what I have given deliberately) will eventually give me recognition of myself. At the brink of my own death I gain self-recognition through the other's assumed victory, which will, in turn, strengthen me to supersede her.

4. *Autrement*, p. 64/49.

5. Ibid, p. 157/122.

6. Ibid, p. 95/75.

7. It is a significant turn away from Cohen to emphasize precisely the material givenness of the other rather than my relationship with her/him by way of the spirit. Materiality for Levinas signifies the transcendence of reason and the ideal. Furthermore, as such, as the material that has overcome the ideal, it signifies true ethical transcendence.

8. *Autrement*, p. 140/110.

9. Levinas, in other words, employs implicitly the concept of the asymptote that we already encountered in Cohen. In it the other becomes the upper limit of the function and the self its origin. The graph of the function itself is subjectivity.

10. The English "proximity" is the translation of the French "prochain" which literally translated means "neighbor" or "the next." Bob Gibbs pointed out to me that the theme of proximity is, of course, also expressed in the idea of God's nearness "קֹרֵב" as it can be found for example in Ps. 69:19 and Ez. 44:16.

11. *Autrement*, p. 107/85.

12. The reason why it is important to italicize the word "are" in the preceding sentence is the unusual passive usage of the word "obsess." This word derives from the Latin "obses" = hostage and "obsessio" = siege. The passive mode of both underlines the notion of the subject's absolute passivity over against the other I mentioned earlier.

13. Revelation, p. 199.

14. God, p. 175.

15. *Autrement*, dedication.

16. André Neher, *The Exile of the Word* (henceforth referred to as "*The Exile*.") Much of my analysis in this chapter is indebted to Neher's very thorough and original reading of Ezekiel's silence which can be found on pp. 18–22, 152–69, 198–209.

17. Neher, "*The Exile*," Introduction.

18. Cp., *The Exile*, chapter 1, pp. 27–29.

19. Tamra Wright, Peter Hughes, Alison Ainley, "The Paradox of Morality: An Interview with Emmanuel Levinas," p. 169.

20. Cp. chapter 1 of the first part of this dissertation.

21. The root word "חזק" can assume four different meanings depending on the modus and tense that it is in. In the Kal it can mean "tightly bound," but also "to overwhelm" (cf. Is. 28:22, 1Sam. 7:50, Ez. 3:14, etc.). In the Piel it can mean "to confirm" but also "to improve." In the Hiphel it assumes the meaning of "to strengthen." And in the Hithpael it means "to gather one's strength."

22. Ralph W. Klein, *Ezekiel: The Prophet and His Message*, p. 29.

23. Hermann Cohen, *Religion*, p. 25/22.

24. Ibid, p. 26/23.

25. My italics.

26. *Religion*, p. 233/199.

27. Ibid.

28. Ibid.

29. Ibid, p. 233/200.

30. Emmanuel Levinas, *Ethics and Infinity: Conversations with Philippe Nemo*, translated by Richard Cohen, p. 99.

31. Levinas, *Ethics and Infinity*, p. 98.

32. It remains open though, how exactly Levinas pictures an evolving community from this type of ethics. Cohen, as can be seen from the quotes, is concerned with the viability of a community in which the imbalances between the rich and the poor will be erased for good. Levinas never makes such a statement, which is unfortunate. However, one might try to understand his philosophy as a pre-communal effort in search for the answer to the question what is it that makes communities begin to evolve. That is, Levinas can be understood correctly only, if one surmises that he is attempting to delineate the conditions of communal togetherness which he finds in the pre-original desire for the holy and the good.

33. I would like to acknowledge here that the term "fragmentation" is my own interpretation of what Levinas proposes. He, himself, uses a terminology that emphasizes the same sociological constitutedness within a different metaphoric context. His has a more three-dimensional character as he talks about hollows, the hollowing out of desire, caves, etc. Mine emphasizes the two-dimensional aspect. I continue to use the term "fragmentation," because it seems to me that Levinas, although he is trying to overcome Hegel, is highly dependent on him. By using the concept of desire to describe the relationship between the individual and the Good (God), he makes a two-dimensional understanding of that relationship almost unavoidable. The clue is, it seems to me, that both the three-dimensional as well as the two-dimensional images are insufficient by themselves and need to be juxtaposed with each other. Levinas tries to do exactly that. The infinite, for example, is outside of me and my desire for it makes me linearly and two-dimensionally bound to it. But simultaneously the infinite is also in me. It creates a hollow within me which can only be understood three-dimensionally.

34. Conversation with Gibson Winter (Spring '91) about Alfred Schütz and the latter's possible influence on Levinas's thought.

35. Throughout the writing of this first part of my dissertation I have felt it necessary to write more on the connection between Jacques Lacan and Levinas. I am not aware of any biographical encounters between the two. However, it seems evident to me that the two thinkers share more than just their nationality and hence (from the

American view-point) their liking for the obscure. Although Lacan was not Jewish, his thinking seems to have been pertinent to Levinas's for the simple reason that Lacan had thought through Hegel's master/slave heuristic and started to apply his interpretation of it to the study of psychoanalysis. His thought is characterized by a determined turn against the old Freudian model that still prevails in psychoanalysis. This model is informed by a reading of Hegel that emphasizes the existence of "Selbstbewußtsein" as the locus of the existence of knowledge. "Selbstbewußtsein" becomes the center for the recognition and ordering of the world. The more incomplete "Selbstbewußtsein" the more incomplete and haphazard are our attempts to master the world. Accordingly, this model requires the therapeut to help the patient find the lost parts of her self and help her implement them back into her general self in order to release her as a psychologically completed human being. At stake is, in other words, the completion of "Selbstbewußtsein" without which a normal relationship with the rest of the world becomes impossible. Lacan's contribution to this discussion lies in the effort he makes to hold open exactly that characteristic which Freud tried to close: the fragmented "Selbstbewußtsein." In reflecting on the mirror-stage, Lacan formulates that they led "me to recognize in the spatial captation manifested in the mirror-stage, even before the social dialectic, the effect in man of an organic insufficiency in his natural reality... I am therefore led to regard the function of the mirror-stage as a particular stage of the function of the image, which is to establish a relation between the organism and its reality — or, as they say, between the Innenwelt and the Umwelt." (Jacques Lacan, *Écrits: A Selection*, trsl. by Alan Sheridan, p. 4)." For Lacan it was a mistake to believe that healing the patient in psychoanalysis must include the completion of her fragmented Selbstbewußtsein. To the contrary, he observes, that it is precisely that fragmentation, or insufficiency that forces the patient to establish relationships with her outside world. Thus, for Lacan fragmentation is a fundamental coordinate of the development of the social. However, one has to understand that the social is nothing but a function of the subject's desire towards self-completion. What drives the subject is the relentless need to fill the gap of its own fragmentation. Lacan, therefore, rules out the possibility of any kind of altruism altogether. Instead he diagnoses a fundamental aggressivity inherent to those activities that we would traditionally call altruistic. The "philanthropist, the idealist, the pedagogue and even the reformer" (*Écrits*, p. 7) all have nothing else in mind than the goal of self-completion. It is here, obviously, that Levinas and Lacan go separate ways. In fact, one might speculate that it is precisely this notion of a lack of altruism and its substitute, blatant aggressivity, that led Levinas to reformulate the Hegelian master/slave heuristic altogether.

For him, as described earlier, the desire for the other, which Lacan explains as the need for self-completion, turns into the desire for the Good. This desire finds itself directed towards the other, but not in an attempt to devour the other and make her part of my self, but really in an attempt to give myself to the other fully. Only indirectly, viz. when I will have realized my responsibility and am forced to accept or reject it, can I become a subject. Levinas's allusion to the mirror-stage is the face-to-face encounter. Yet, this encounter does not fuel my aggressivity. Rather, it leaves me passive and open to the command which inevitably issues from the other. Rather than letting desire function as a means to a finite end, viz. the completion of the self, Levinas understands desire to be created by the infinite. It thus becomes an infinite desire for an infinite goal that can never find fulfillment. For Levinas and Lacan alike, the social is a function of a lack which the "subject" experiences as desire. However, whereas for the former this lack is infinite and interpreted to designate the ethical itself, the latter sees the lack directed towards a finite end (fulfilled consciousness) and interprets it as aggressivity. It would be worthwhile to further investigate the relationship between the two thinkers. Especially on the grounds that Lacan, too, indicates that he understands the process of such self-completion asymptotically, i.e. as infinite. If that is indeed the case, it would remain to explain why such a fundamental disagreement could occur between Lacan's and Levinas's perspectives. A perfect example for the Freudian tradition of psychology that tries to read fragmentations as psychotic and abnormal is a little off-shoot in the Ezekiel discussion that developed in the '50s. I refer to Edwin C. Broome's article "Ezekiel's Abnormal Personality," *JBL* 65, 1965, pp. 277–92. Broome states that the "feeling of something unusual has persisted" in the analysis of the Book of Ezekiel. He refers to the revelatory events at the beginning of the book as "seizures" of "catatonic variety [thus indicating] a fundamental psychic disturbance . . . a form of schizophrenia, which is true psychosis" (p. 279). The descriptions of Ezekiel being overwhelmed and feeling like fetters were being put on him are possible evidence that the Israelites attempted to confine him because he had become dangerous or simply hallucinatory. "In either event he was psychotic" (p. 280). Furthermore, Ezekiel exhibits, in Broome's analysis the same "grandiose attitude [and] grandiose narcissism" that most psychics display in order to emphasize their subsequent demise as victims of their environment (p. 283). Also, with reference to the Merkabah, everyone who is familiar with this type of disorder knows that persons who have them love inventing machines that represent the system of influences by which they feel pressured (pp. 285–86). Ezekiel is thus an inherent masochist. In fact, it is a special form of female masochism since the images of pricks, briars and scorpions in the beginning of the book all betray the illusion of penetration. And of course the scroll . . . Who would not think that the eating of the scroll must be some phallic imagery (p. 288)? He is, furthermore, attempting a return to the pre-natal (p. 285). The sharp sword in chapter 5 can only indicate the secret castration wish that Ezekiel was harboring. One can see from this example that people have gone to great lengths in order to characterize fragmentations like the ones Ezekiel exhibits as somehow deficient and thus in need of treatment. Whatever the truth is with respect to Ezekiel, we have to entertain the possibility that the priest was simply upset by the obligation he felt and consequently he had to struggle with it in various ways before he could finally yield to it.

Notes to Chapter Four

1. The etymology of the word "theme" might clarify what Levinas means. "Theme" derives from the Greek verb "τίθημι," and the Greek root word "θε-." The verb form generally means "to order" or "to put in a certain position." As a noun the words "η θεμις" means just "the holy order" and in most cases "the holy order instituted by God." It is just this sense of an ordering coming about through the subject that thematizes that Levinas criticizes and attempts to circumvent through an epiphanic phenomenology (more about that later in this chapter).

2. It would be justified to categorize Levinas as a post-enlightenment philosopher whose goal it is to break through the tradition of Spinoza, Leibniz and Hegel that emphasized an absolute consciousness constitutive of the world. Levinas instead reiterates the Kantian problem of a thing-in-itself, "something out there," that cannot be captured and that instead captures the subject. Yet, different from Kant, Levinas attempts to capture exactly that thing-in-itself as the other, instead of relegating it to the realm that pure reason cannot broach. Kant himself, of course, realized the importance of the thing-in-itself as an asymptotic (regulative) concept for reason itself and treats of it quite extensively under the guise of the theory of the sublime in the *Critique of Judgment*, trsl. by J.H. Bernard.

3. The Greek words are "φαινομαι" and "φως."

4. *Dictionary of Philosophy*, edited by Dagobert d. Runes, New York: Philosophical Library, 1960.

5. On the relationship between Levinas work and that of Husserl's and Heidegger, see Adrian Peperzak, "Phenomenology — Ontology — Metaphysics: Levinas' Perspective on Husserl and Heidegger," *Man and World* 16: 113–127. Peperzak shows how Levinas moves from an earlier, very critical analysis of Husserl's work to a much more appreciative reading, particularly vis-à-vis Heidegger. Whereas at first Levinas critiques Husserl for his concept of intentionality as the presence

of consciousness to the object and thus the primacy of theory, he later gives more emphasis to Husserl's concept of the horizon, which seems to indicate a certain nonobjectifiable part of any "Sachverhalt" (theory). In the end, however, the problem with Husserl remains the omniscient and omnipotent position of the transcendental ego which is co-present to being and whose relationship to being can only be defined through knowledge. Although Levinas takes a stand along with Heidegger against Husserl in these first essays, he later also opposes Heidegger precisely because the latter, although opposing Husserl, did not manage to avoid Husserl's emphasis on knowledge. For Heidegger it resurfaces as "Seinsverständnis."

6. A very complex and insightful study about the question of intersubjective relationships was written by Marco M. Olivetti, "Philosophische Fragen an das Werk von Emmanuel Levinas," *Verantwortung für den Anderen un die Frage nach Gott: Zum Werk von Emmanuel Levinas*, pp. 42–70. Olivetti observes that most of the modern attempts in philosophy to think through the problems of the intersubjective (Fichte, Husserl, Heidegger) are based on Kant's formulation of the unity of transcendental apperception. Since this notion suggests the unity of subject and object, an intersubjective relationship cannot be thought otherwise than as one that is postulated by the subject. Such a relationship, however, minimizes the significance of the other in his/her alterity. Olivetti, thus, understands Levinas as a philosopher who is trying to transcend the condition of the unity of transcendental apperception.

7. Edmund Husserl, *The Crisis of European Sciences and Transcendental Phenomenology: An Introduction to Phenomenological Philosophy*.

8. Quentin Lauer, *Phenomenology: Its Genesis and Prospect*, p. 152. The term "empathy," of course, has had major importance since Kant, in order to assure the possibility of universal standards for the recognition of art, introduced it into his aesthetic theory in the *Critique of Judgment*. It later became a most important term for the romantic movement and its attempt to ground humanity in some type of universally shared characteristic (cp. Charles Taylor, *Hegel*).

9. Edmund Husserl, *Cartesian Meditations*, trsl. by Dorion Cairns, pp. 112–13. A good discussion of this problematic can also be found in Hans Georg Gadamer, *Truth and Method*, pp. 221–22. "The other person is first apprehended as an object of perception, which then, through empathy, becomes a 'Thou.' In Husserl this concept of empathy has no doubt a purely transcendental meaning, but is still oriented to the interiority of self-consciousness and fails to achieve the orientation towards the functional circle of life, which goes far beyond consciousness, to which, however, it claims to return."

10. See for example Emmanuel Levinas, *Ethics and Infinity: Conversations with Philippe Nemo*, translated by Richard A. Cohen, p. 85.

11. My friend and colleague Uwe Ritter reminded me of the long history of the concept of expression. During the "Sturm and Drang" in Europe it came to designate creative, subjective activity issuing from an existent but formless coagulation of ideas. Rousseau, and especially Herder, regarded language as the primary vehicle of such creative form-giving. More about this era can be read in Charles Taylor, *Hegel*, part I.

12. Edmund Husserl, *Ideen zu einer reinen Phänomenologie und phänomenologischen Philosophie*, 1950; *Ideas: General Introduction to Pure Phenomenology*, trsl. by W.R. Boyce Gibson, henceforth referred to as "Ideas, pp. German/English."

13. *Ideas*, p. 308/323.

14. Ibid, p. 310/325.

15. Ibid, p. 310/325.

16. Ibid, p. 312/327.

17. The word "as" makes all the difference for Levinas in his essay "Language and Proximity," (pp. 109–26) where he characterizes the function of the "as" as kerygmatic, i.e., as announcing the meaning of an object. In the word "as" Levinas sees thus indicated the arbitrariness inherent in the constitution of meaning that, rather than being empirically established by the object, is assigned by the subject.

18. *Ideas*, p. 122.

19. Ibid.

20. Ibid, p. 103/127.

21. Ibid, p. 162/182.

22. Ibid, p. 76/105.

23. Ibid, p. 79/107.

24. Emmanuel Levinas, *Totalité et Infini: Essai sur l'extériorité*, p. 224; translated by Alphonso Lingis, *Totality and Infinity*, p. 205. (Henceforth referred to as *"Totalité,"* p. French/English.)

25. In order to clarify the significance and difference between the concepts of language and speech, Levinas employs the Saussurian distinction between *"parole"* and *"langage."* Whereas the former designates communication itself, i.e. talks, conversations, prayers, etc., the latter designates the potential for communication, i.e. the fact that we have language.

26. Emmanuel Levinas, *Nine Talmudic Readings*, trsl. by Annette Aronowicz, Bloomington: Indiana University Press, 1990, p. 21.

27. The emphasis on language and speech can be paralleled if one looks at Franz Rosenzweig's introduction of grammar as revelation's organon in part II of, op. cit. Prior to creation, there exists a language that is prior to language. It is a logical language of archetypal words

"which lie hidden under each and every manifest (*"offenbaren"*) word as secret bases and which rise to the light in it" (p. 121/109). What was mute before and only palpable through an ideal language (*"Sprache"*), now turns into reality (*"Wirklichkeit"*) through grammar, and thus creates the human community in which the individual (*"das einzelne"*) remains a reality as well. For Rosenzweig redemption comes through liturgy with the suspension of language (*"Sprache"*) in favor of the gesture (*"Gebärde"*) where the individual will be taken up completely into the community of worshippers (326–30). Rosenzweig and Levinas go different ways at this point, most likely because Levinas has a very different concept of redemption in his philosophy.

28. *Totalité*, pp. 212/194–95.

29. Ibid. A good example for this is the silence of the psychoanalyst which the patient often feels to be overwhelming, since the former (through his or her reticence to speak, while simultaneously paying visual attention, i.e., by looking at the patient) gives the impression of silently judging the patient.

30. For the appropriateness of this term cf. note 1 in chapter 3 and the literature there cited.

31. Levinas gets his notion of desire from Hegel's *Phenomenology*. Here desire is the ever-active force which compels consciousness to go through different stages of self-identification and simultaneous transformations of its surrounding world. The difference for Levinas is that he attempts to circumvent the quality of struggle that Hegel's concept of desire implies. Levinas asserts, for example, that the other who imposes herself on me through that desire does so without any implication of violence. "The ethical presence is both other and imposes itself without violence" (*Totalité*, 242/219). "It is desire, teaching received, and the pacific opposition of discourse" (*Totalité*, p. 215/197). However, there can be no doubt that from the perspective of the "me" the struggle is not over. How else would one explain Levinas's references to the face's resistance to my powers, the idea of infinity as exceeding my powers (p. 213/196) and to the fact that " the other is the sole being I can wish to kill" (p. 216/198). These passages are examples for the dialectic relationship that exists between desire on the one and language on the other hand. Desire can only be there, because there already is a difference between the other and me which, as Levinas says, is established by language (i.e., language here refers to the more primordial sense still present in the French *"langage"*). Yet, in Levinas's words, it is in the face that this struggle can potentially come to an end: "The epiphany of the face is ethical. The face threatens the eventuality of a struggle (*"lutte"*)" (p. 218/199).

32. Richard A. Cohen, "Absolute Positivity and Ultra-Positivity," *The Question of the Other: Essays in Contemporary Continental Philosophy*,

ed. by Arlene B. Dallery and Charles E. Scott, pp. 35–47. Cohen's essay is generally good. However, he seems to emphasize the priority of *the ethical* as if that in itself already was *ethics*. He thus overlooks the fact that for Levinas the ethical is an epistemological category with a *potential* for ethics. In other words, nothing is won for the domain of ethics by the discovery that human beings are fundamentally directed towards the other. That by itself can only explain why we perceive the world around us without necessarily being part of it. The "more" of the face can only acquire practical ethical significance the moment we let it speak to us.

33. *Totalité*, pp. 218–19/200.

34. Ibid, p. 219/200.

35. Concerning the questions about the word "come" cf. chapter 6 of the second part of this book.

36. *Totalité*.

37. In *Autrement*, Levinas also refers to the relationship between phenomenology and the face. Here, however, he says that phenomenology defects into the face ("defectio" [lat.]: trash, reduction, disappearance, exhaustion). Although this seems to undermine my point that Levinas's epi-phenomenology of the face is the only real kind of phenomenology, I think that it is evident from everything that has been said so far that Levinas's position vis-a-vis phenomenology can by no means be understood as total rejection, but must be seen under the premise of re-formulation.

38. An interesting discussion of the priority of the face-to-face encounter can be found in Alphonso Lingis's essay "The Elemental Imperative," *Research in Phenomenology*, vol. 18, 1988, pp. 3–21. Lingis's contention is that, in order to perceive the command that issues from the other, one already has to be in a sensuous relationship with the world. There has to be a more elemental imperative that simply reaches out for the world. Whereas Levinas attempts to transcend this sphere of the elemental towards something exterior to it, as Lingis points out it is precisely this elemental form of the imperative that first creates an "eddy of subjectivity [which] first stirs in the night of the there-is" (p. 16).

39. *Totalité*, p. 230/209.

40. This can be taken to indicate the phenomenal background for Levinas's theory of the text, especially Scripture, as I develop it in chapter 1. It is precisely infinite perspectivalness inherent in the text but actualized through interpretation by the readers that makes revelation an infinite project.

41. *Totalité*, p. 240/218.

42. Ibid, p. 236/214.

43. *The Pentateuch and Rashi's Commentary: A Linear Translation*

into English by Rabbi Abraham Ben Isaiah and Rabbi Benjamin Sharf-man, Exodus 33, pp. 413–24.

44. Rashi's interpretation of this section goes even further in elid-ing the sense of impertinence that seems attached to Moses' second request and interprets God's answer to be something along the lines of "Glad you asked Moses, I needed to teach you the order of prayer any-way."

45. Possibly because the Hebrew word for "veil," "מַסְוֶה," comes from the Hebrew "מַסָּה," "temptation."

46. Interesting here that the Hebrew uses the preposition "בְּ" rather than "אֶל." Maybe this expresses already part of the mediated encoun-ter that the Israelites had with God.

47. Tamra Wright, et al., p. 173.

48. *Totalité*, p. 236/214.

49. Tamra Wright, et al., p. 176.

50. Emmanuel Levinas, "From Existence to Ethics," *Levinas Reader*, pp. 82–3.

51. Richard A. Cohen, *"Absolute Positivity and Ultra-Positivity,"* p. 39.

52. Note that both terms, "face" and "beholder," are metaphorical. The face is not material and the beholder is not a subject.

53. Chapter 2.

54. Schütz was born in Vienna in 1899. He studied with Weber and Husserl and left Austria to escape from the Nazis in 1939. He went to Paris for a year and from there came to the U.S. where he accepted a position at the New School for Social Research. Schütz's work is of interest for us, because his concern with the problematic of the other parallels Levinas's discussion. Furthermore, he focuses more than Levinas does on the consequent social applicability of his theory.

55. Edmund Husserl, *Cartesian Meditations*, p. 89.

56. Husserl, pp. 114–115.

57. Alfred Schütz, *The Phenomenology of the Social World*, p. 98.

58. Cp. Schütz, p. 103, 140, 163, 165.

59. Schütz, p. 103.

60. *Phenomenology*, p. 103.

61. Ibid, pp. 106–107.

62. Ibid, p. 113.

63. Ibid, p. 140.

64. Ibid, p. 143.

65. Ibid, p. 163.

66. Ibid, p. 163.

67. Schütz concedes that such an understanding is itself an ide-alization, since in everyday life such understanding would always be mediated by our actual understanding of the other's action and

thoughts. But as an ideal limit such thou-orientation has to be presupposed.

68. *Phenomenology*, p. 164.
69. Ibid, p. 167.
70. Ibid, p. 168.
71. Ibid, p. 178.

Notes to Chapter Five

1. Caputo, *Against Ethics*, p. 125.
2. Ibid, p. 126.
3. A good example of the results of such an asymmetrical reading is Richard Cohen's new book *Elevations: The Height of the Good in Rosenzweig and Levinas*. Included in the book is a chapter on the relationship between Derrida and Levinas. Cohen, a decided and unwavering disciple of Levinas's, labels this relationship "Derrida's (Mal) Reading of Levinas." Cohen, like many other adherents of Levinas and simultaneous critics of Derrida, makes the mistake of basing his interpretation on Derrida's earlier essay on Levinas "Violence and Metaphysics." Although this essay is written in a critical tone and certainly aiming at showing in which ways Levinas's text (*Totality and Infinity*) fails to establish the opening towards the other for which it is looking, Cohen's reading of Derrida as making "play of Levinas" (ft. 2, p. 306) is unfounded and superficial. Cohen reads Derrida as undermining Levinas's attempts to "invoke and increase responsibility" by increasing "the play of meaning or more precisely, [by increasing] the undecidability between responsible and playful meaning." (ibid) This reading simply overlooks a couple of important issues that relate to this particular text of Derrida's. The first and most important one is the fact that Derrida begins his text with an emphasis on the critical function of the question for ethics. It is the form of the question that invokes responsibility and Derrida shows in the essay that it is the answer, the response, that is lacking. Specifically the effort that Levinas makes with respect to naming that towards which we are responsible, viz. the other, is doomed in Derrida's eyes. However, the failure is not one of ethics but one of naming. In our attempt to name we are following the Greek *nomos*. Levinas, of course, is aware of this problem and tries to circumscribe the other in such a way that naming can be avoided. Derrida, however, points to the inevitable naming quality that any text centered around something unnamable must have. That is, in not naming the totally other, Levinas is still naming. Derrida, thus, is not critical of responsibility and ethics but of the attempt to name the absolute core of that responsibility. Cohen's critique of Derrida as being Heideggerian in his strategies is misleading. Certainly, for Cohen, simply

invoking the name of Heidegger is enough to categorize Derrida negatively. But, although Derrida's methodology is replete of Heideggerian turns, it is important to understand that Derrida is critical of Levinas in the same way that Adorno is critical of Heidegger in *Negative Dialektik*. Both Heidegger and Levinas make use of a language that mystifies and shrouds, yet awakenings a desire for something beyond this world. This in and of itself could be misread as a totalitarian move and therefore needs to be critiqued. Cohen's reading of Derrida could have benefited from a re-reading of "Violence and Metaphysics" based on some of Derrida's later work which we will discuss in the following chapters. More recently, Derrida's work on the gift and death further demonstrate the ethico-moral seriousness with which he approaches the play of responsibility.

4. Jacques Derrida, "En ce moment dans cet œuvre me voici," (1980) *Psyche: Inventions de l'autre*, pp. 159–203; trsl. by Ruben Berezdivin, "At this very Moment in this Work here I am," *Re-Reading Levinas*, ed. by Robert Bernasconi and Simon Critchley, pp. 11–51; henceforth referred to as "EM."

5. EM, 14.
6. Ibid, 13.
7. Ibid, 14.
8. Ibid.
9. Ibid.
10. Ibid, 16.
11. Ibid, 17.
12. Ibid.
13. Ibid.
14. Ibid.
15. Ibid, 12.
16. Ibid, 29.
17. Ibid, 19.
18. Ibid, 20.
19. Ibid, 29.
20. Ibid, 22.
21. Ibid, 24.
22. Ibid, 44.
23. Ibid.

Notes to Chapter Six

1. Derrida, *Of Grammatology*, p. 15/6.
2. *Of Grammatology*. For the applicability of Derrida's critique of writing and phonocentrism also cf. pp. 87–93 where he establishes explicitly the relationship between the different power-structures in the world and the possibility of access to the written sign.

3. On the question of the relationship between presence and the point and the question of temporality in the thought of Husserl see for example Timothy Stapleton, "Philosophy and Finitude: Husserl, Derrida and the end of Philosophy," *Philosophy Today*, Spring 1989, pp. 3–15.

4. In his 1989 dissertation Simon Critchley (op. cit.) asserts that deconstruction is always a deconstruction of a text. "The way of Derridian deconstruction, then, lies in the reading of texts, primarily philosophical texts" (ibid). This, unfortunately, sets the agenda in an entirely lopsided way, as if Derrida's approach was not also anchored in the problematic of understanding deconstruction as a possibly ethical approach to issues that deal with texts only on a secondary level. The fact that he can use texts in order to show the shortcomings, contradictions, and sometimes oppressiveness of a given tradition or system of thought has its origin not in the misleading notion that only texts can be deconstructed but in the fact that such traditions have caused the proliferation of an infinite amount of documents that all, in one way or another, affirm the tradition in its hierarchical superiority. Yet, what really gives unlimited power to a deconstructive approach are not philosophical texts but the regimentation of the sign that governs all human discourse and interaction.

5. Jacques Derrida, "Interpretations at War: Kant, the Jew, the German," *New Literary History*, pp. 39–95, henceforth referred to as "Interpretations at War."

6. Jacques Derrida, "Interpretations at War," pp. 39–95, esp. p. 58.

7. Interpretations at War, p. 41.

8. It would be a whole new study to investigate from where Husserl gets his inspiration. It is my own suspicion that his ties with neo-Kantianism were, indeed, much stronger than has been emphasized. It is known that he was on friendly terms with Paul Natorp, but that he did not think highly of Cohen. Yet, much in his thinking looks just like Cohen's analyses, if only with a more pronounced emphasis on epistemology rather than ethics as in Cohen.

9. Jacques Derrida, "'Genèse et structure' et la phénomenologie," *L'écriture et la différence*, 'Genesis and Structure' and Phenomenology," *Writing and Difference*, pp. 229–53/154–69; henceforth referred to as "Genesis and Structure," p. French/English."

10. Maurice Nathanson, *Edmund Huserl: Philosopher of Infinite Tasks*, p. 11, points out that "radical certitude must be phenomenology's method. The person who strives for such certitude must turn to himself as the locus of ultimate rigor. . . . Past any cheap 'subjectivism' and beyond all merely idiosyncratic attitudes." Nathanson here emphasizes a point that to my knowledge has been drastically neglected in the study of Husserl's phenomenology. This rigorous turn to the subjectivity of the philosopher, not as a last refuge for otherwise threatening nihilism, but as the foundation of anyone's philosophical insight has

had its ramifications all the way down to the present investigation. Both Derrida and Levinas are said to center their writing around an autobiographical focus. (Cf. Mark C. Taylor in *Tears*, and also J. Margolis in a conversation with me). From Nathanson's view-point the autobiographical element becomes understandable as a demand made by phenomenology on each true philosopher. Autobiography now is not only an idiosyncratic need for identity but becomes the founding epistemological principle of one's philosophy. Nathanson in fact quotes Husserl as saying that "anyone who seriously intends to become a philosopher must 'once in his life' withdraw into himself and attempt, within himself, *to overthrow and build anew* [my italics] all the sciences that, up to then, he has been accepting" (Nathanson, *Edmund Husserl*). Deconstruction, quite clearly, takes off from exactly this demand.

11. Genesis and Structure, p. 236/159.

12. Walter Benjamin, "Die Aufgabe des Übersetzers," *Illuminationen*, pp. 50–63; henceforth referred to as "Die Aufgabe."

13. A very good and insightful study of the relationship between Derrida and Husserl can be found in John D. Caputo, "The Economy of Signs in Husserl and Derrida," *Deconstruction and Philosophy: The Texts of Jacques Derrida*, ed. by John Sallis, pp. 99–114. Caputo's analysis of this relationship mainly supports my findings in this chapter, especially with regard to the status of the sign in Husserl's phenomenology and Derrida's attempt to reintroduce the sign into phenomenology itself by understanding it as the trace of the thing-itself, i.e., the only phenomenon that is epistemologically available. Caputo goes wrong, in my opinion, when he begins to read Derrida as the protagonist of a tradition-defying faction of philosophy (more prounced in Caputo's other essay, "Gadamer's Closet Essentialism: A Derridean Critique," *Dialogue and Deconstruction: The Gadamer-Derrida Encounter*, pp. 258–65). Although he is right when in the former essay he states that "what Derrida is after [is] . . . to rid us of idolatry before graven images, to remind us of the radical contingency and reformability of things . . ." he misses the point that Derrida is attempting to make, for the latter is precisely also affirming tradition. It is simply not enough just to describe one side (like Caputo does) and not see that that side is wholly dependent on the affirmation of a tradition without which Derrida's thought would have never developed. Derrida is only possible because of Gadamer. One might call this oppositional thinking, i.e. precisely the kind of thinking that Derrida attempts to reject. But I am not saying that Derrida is opposed to Gadamer (like Caputo does) and I am not saying that he is opposed to tradition (like Caputo does); I am saying that those oppositions are in a fundamental relationship with each other which makes naively divisive efforts futile. Furthermore, Caputo claims that, the "things themselves are woven

products." ("the Economy. . .," p. 111). Now, nowhere in Derrida have I been able to find a statement to that effect. The only constant reminder of significance for our question here is that the thing itself, like différance, like truth, like the sacred language, is inaccessible. But that does not say anything about the kind of thing that the thing in itself really is. If anything, what is woven is the text(s) that, for better or for worse, demonstrate that inaccessibility. Another, especially nice rebuttal of Caputo's attempt to win Derrida over for the anti-traditionalists is a passage in the essay "The Time of a Thesis: Punctuations," p. 42, where Derrida makes his position vis-a-vis tradition clear beyond all doubt. With respect to the transformation of university structures he says: "In this area I believe in transitions and negotiation — even if it may at times be brutal and speeded up — I believe in the necessity for a certain tradition, in particular for political reasons, that are nothing less than traditionalist, and I believe, moreover, in the indestructibility of the ordered procedures of legitimation, of the production of titles and diplomas and of the authorization of competence." More will have to be said about this passage in chapter 9 of this part. Derrida is being facetious and serious at the same time. Many readers of his texts, however, have yet to understand how he can be serious about such an assertion.

14. Jacques Derrida, *La Voix et le phénomène*; *Speech and Phenomena*, p. 4/5, (henceforth referred to as "*Speech*, p. French/English.")

15. Jacques Derrida, "Genesis and Structure," p. 232/157.

16. Edmund Husserl, *Formale und Transzendentale Logik*, English translation by Dorion Cairns, *Formal and Transcendental Logic*, so quoted in J. Derrida, *Speech and Phenomena*, p. 4/6.

17. Ibid, p. 4/6.

18. Ibid, p. 4/6.

19. J. Derrida, "Différance," p. 7/7. In "The Time of a Thesis: Punctuations," Derrida explains that "all of the problems worked on in the Introduction to the *Origin of Geometry* have continued to organize the work I have subsequently attempted," p. 39.

20. *Speech and Phenomena*, p. 5/7.

21. Ibid, p. 5/7. This was already discussed in Part I, chapt. 4.

22. Ibid, p. 6/8.

23. Ibid, p. 5/7.

24. Ibid, p. 10/11.

25. Ibid, p. 11/12.

26. Ibid, p. 13/13.

27. Ibid, p. 6/8.

28. Ibid, p. 13/14.

29. Ibid, p. 14/15.

30. Derrida, *Of Grammatology*, p. 22/11.

31. Ibid, p. 8/9.
32. Ibid, p. 8/9.
33. *Genesis and Structure*, p. 242/162.
34. *Genesis and Structure*, p. 250/167.
35. *Genesis and Structure*, p. 242/163.
36. It is interesting that not only Husserl but also Cohen himself started rethinking the systematic position of psychology over against philosophy. Presumably under the influence of Natorp he started lecturing on psychology. (Cf. Schwarzschild, "Introduction (to Herman Cohen's *Religion of Reason*)," unpublished essay.)
37. *Speech and Phenomena*, p. 79/87.
38. Ibid, p. 79/88.
39. Ibid, p. 117/104. Franz Rosenzweig, who is generally in agreement with Derrida on the question of the impossible present, makes an exception for the one situation in which I confess my love imperatively to my lover by saying "love me!" Rosenzweig explains: "The indicative has behind it the whole cumbersome rationalization of materiality, and at its purest therefore appears in the past tense. But the 'Love me!' is wholly pure and unprepared-for present tense, and not unprepared-for alone, but also unpremeditated." (*Stern*, p. 197/177) Rosenzweig sees thus inscribed the difference between "Gesetz" ("law") and "Gebot" ("commandment"). Whereas the former always appears in the indicative mode (i.e., a past that is still waiting for the future) the latter "knows only the moment" (*Stern*). It is tempting to apply this logic to the difference that Derrida makes between law and justice (for this see the following chapter). But the problematic of Rosenzweig's approach is the strong notion of phono-centrism that is woven through this passage. The English version only renders this insufficiently. But it is clear that the imperative's appeal to the present stems from the fact that "*Lautwerden und Entspringen sind beim Imperativ eins*" ("for emerging and finding voice are one and the same thing in the case of the imperative") (*Stern*). It is then clear that Rosenzweig merges the audible qualities of the imperative with its logical ones in order to arrive at what he calls "die Sofortigkeit des Gehorchens" ("the immediacy of obedience") (*Stern*). However, that it was especially phonocentrism that causes the mistake of believing in the possibility of presence is clearly the thrust of the first part of *Of Gramatology* ("This notion remains therefore within the heritage of that logocentrism which is also a phonocentrism: absolute proximity of voice and being, of voice and the meaning of being, of voice and the ideality of meaning.") and maybe at the heart of everything Derrida has to say about the possibility of presence.
40. Cf. the introduction to the translation of *Speech and Phenomena* by Newton Garver.

41. Derrida thus strikes a line here that is reminiscent of Hegel's reflection on the question of the immediacy or mediacy of a given object to sense-certainty. Hegel argues that although commonly we would assume that an object in front of us is given to us immediately within the confines of space and time, he can show that it is exactly the framework of space and time which is given as "here" and "now" (*"hier"* und *"jetzt"*) that indeed causes the mediacy of any given object to sense-certainty. Even though the "now" and the "here" both can be maintained (*"aufbewahrt"*) in their universality, their sense of immediacy with a respect to a specific time or place changes constantly and cannot be maintained in the same fashion. Hegel concludes that sense-certainty is nothing but the history of its movement (". . . *daß die Dialektik der sinnlichen Gewißheit nichts anderes als die einfache Geschichte ihrere Bewegung ihrer Erfahrung und die sinnliche Gewißheit selbst nichts anderes als nur diese Geschichte ist."*).

42. *Speech and Phenomena*, p. 4/6.

43. Ibid, p. 60/54.

44. Ibid, p. 9/10.

45. Ibid, pp. 31–32/29–30.

46. Ibid, p. 70. Derrida introduces the trace with explicit reference to Emmanuel Levinas and his most recent work (*Autrement*).

47. Jacques Derrida, "Des tours de Babel," *Psyche: Inventions de l'autre*, trsl. and ed. by Joseph F. Graham, "Des Tours de Babel," *Difference in Translation*, pp. 203–237/165–207; henceforth referred to as "Babel, p. French/English."

48. Walter Benjamin, "Die Aufgabe des Übersetzers," *Illuminationen*.

49. Babel, p. 203/165.

50. Voltaire, *Dictionnaire philosophique*, reprinted edition from 1700, Paris, 1969.

51. So quoted from Derrida, *Psyché*, p. 204/166.

52. Babel, p. 205/167.

53. Ibid, p. 220/187.

54. Ibid, pp. 228/195–96.

55. Ibid, pp. 233/202–203.

56. Ibid, p. 233/202.

57. It might be beneficial at this point to remember also that virtually the same structure that Benjamin suggests for the process of translation is what Bergson had, approximately forty years earlier, expressed in his *Matter and Memory* about the function of memory. At least one aspect of this memory-image, which is also asymptotically located between pure memory and pure perception, is that every part of it bears a date and is thus unrepeatable. In other words, every new experience adds another layer to the memory already accumulated. Bergson thus notes "at each repetition there is progress" that is to say the repetition

is never simply just a repetition. It includes an ever-increasing surplus. This became especially clear to me during a conversation with my friend and colleague Gereon Kopf who is presently working on a thesis on body-mind philosophy in relation to Bergson.

58. Die Aufgabe, p. 51.

59. Babel, p. 217/182.

60. Ibid, p. 218/184.

61. Ibid, p. 219/184.

62. Ibid, p. 224/191.

63. Ibid, p. 224/191.

64. Ibid, p. 233/202.

65. Ibid, p. 235/204.

66. Apocalyptic Tone, pp. 10/3–4.

67. Derrida also makes a couple of remarks about the possibility of thanking and gratitude in this context which should probably be read together with similar thoughts in his essay "En ce moment dans cet oeuvre me voici," At this point it should suffice to say that gratitude, like translations, are impossible, since they presuppose the possibility of a return to the giver/author of the gift/text. In that sense the giver/author will always remain other to my own efforts to respond.

68. Babel, p. 235/205.

Notes to Chapter Seven

1. Jacques Derrida, *D'un Tone Apocalyptique adopté Naguère en Philosophie*; "Of an Apocalyptic Tone Recently Adopted in Philosophy," *The Oxford Literary Review*, pp. 3–37; henceforth referred to as "Apocalyptic Tone, p. French/ English."

2. *Margins*, p. 123.

3. Ibid.

4. Ibid, p. 133.

5. Ibid, p. 134.

6. Ibid.

7. Ibid.

8. Ibid, p. 135.

9. Ibid.

10. For this cf. Gregory Dean Meyerson, "The Dialectic of Defeat: Domination and Liberation in Contemporary Critical Theory," p. 181: "[There is] no need for an apocalyptic break with the past since the apocalypse is always already at work, from the start. The apocalypse of the apocalyptic is that the apocalypse never comes." Although Meyerson is interpreting Derrida correctly on the infinite non-coming of the apocalypse, he fails to recognize that Derrida is attempting to show how the apocalypse precisely is something that does not come,

that cannot come but instead announces a coming. This coming is both an imperative that demands "Come!", as well as the movement of something that is coming towards me. In general Meyerson's study remains fairly superficial to Derrida's project (despite the analyses of many of Derrida's texts). Meyerson's main complaint about the writings of Derrida is that of perpetual contradiction. Sometimes, he charges, Derrida says "a" about a certain topic and then in his next essay he says "non-a" about it. What Meyerson is missing is that contradictions are only possible as part of the logic of binary oppositions which is precisely what Derrida is trying to undermine as an effect of logocentrism. In Derrida's thinking it has simply become impossible to say one thing about something while excluding the other as if it belonged to another realm. "a" and "non-a" belong to the same logical level and cannot be extricated from each other the way Meyerson would like to do it. Similarly, Meyerson complains about Derrida's constant use of the expression "il faut" (it is necessary; one must). Derrida's reflections regarding this topic can be read in the essay on the apocalyptic tone as well as in his essay on negative theology, "How not to speak." Derrida's point here is that no matter what is attempted to avoid the connection with essence, or else even if one deliberates on how not to speak, one has already begun to speak. This inevitable move, he says, is like a promise that was given before we had a chance to resist it. It is the promise given to the other to whom we will speak. Even remaining silent would just be another instance of such speaking. Différance, and we have seen this before, operates on the edge, between speaking and not speaking. *Is* there something between those two terms? The answer must be no, since from the stand-point of Being nothing can be found. But if we imagine speaking and not-speaking as two contiguous squares then the difference between them, right where they touch each other, becomes nonconceptualizable. Yet, and this is Derrida's point, it, albeit unavailable, first produces the possibility of the two squares, i.e. of speaking and nonspeaking. Viewed from this perspective, then, speaking and nonspeaking belong together as the product of a productive agent infinitely withdrawn. Also cf. Michael Ryan, *Marxism and Deconstruction: A Critical Articulation*, pp. 9ff.: "[In a binary] the second term in each case is inevitably made out to be external, derivative and accidental in relationship to the first, which is either an ideal limit or the central term of the metaphysical system. The reason why this is so, according to Derrida, is that the second term in each case usually connotes something that endangers the values the first term assures, values that connote presence, proximity, ownership, property, identity, truth conceived as conscious mastery, living experience, and a plenitude of meaning. The second term usually suggests the breakup of all these reassuring and empowering values, such terms as difference, absence, alteration, history, repetition, substitution, undecidability, and so on." Meyerson's remark is that such logic makes action impossible, because now oppositions have become impossible. However, Derrida is not saying that oppositions are impossible. Obviously in the case of speaking and nonspeaking we are in fact dealing with one. What is at stake is how the two sides of an opposition relate to each other. Whereas traditionally Western philosophy has considered opposites in terms of their mutual exclusiveness, his claim is that what seems mutually exclusive does, in fact, relate in a way that suggests that the allegedly oppositional terms derive from the same root. This can only be valuable for a philosophy that emphasizes ethics and action. The conjuring up of ethics' impossibility, in Meyerson's case as well in that of Derrida, is, simultaneously, an affirmation of ethics' relentless possibility.

11. Gilles Deleuze and Félix Guattari, *A Thousand Plateaus: Capitalism and Schizophrenia*, translation and foreword by Brian Massumi. The authors assume that history, philosophy, the history of truth, etc. all proceed in a fashion they call rhizomatic. Rhizoms are small roots with extremely erratic growth patterns. They grow for some time then die off and start growing again elsewhere.

12. Arnold Eisen, "Exile," *Contemporary Jewish Religious Thought: Original Essays on Critical Concepts, Movements and Thoughts*, ed. by Arthur A. Cohen and Paul Mendes-Flohr.

13. Eisen, Exile, p. 225.

14. Jacques Derrida, Edmond Jabès et la question du livre," *L'écriture et la différence*," pp. 99–117; "Edmond Jabès and the Question of the Book," *Writing and Difference*, pp. 64–78, (henceforth referred to as "Writing and Difference, French/English").

15. Writing and Difference, p. 103/67.

16. Ibid, p. 111/74.

17. Ibid, p. 104/68.

18. Ibid, p. 107/70.

19. Ibid, p. 101/66.

20. Ibid, p. 104/69.

21. Ibid, p. 102/67.

22. Ibid, p. 105/69.

23. Ibid, p. 104/68.

24. Immanuel Kant, "Von einem neuerdings in der Philosophie erhobenen vornehmen Ton," *Immanuel Kant: Werke in Zehn Bänden* (henceforth referred to as "Von einem vornehmen Ton").

25. In a conversation with Bob Gibbs about this particular feature of Kant's argumentation it became clear that he later reinstates the aesthetic personification of the moral law in his philosophy of religion. What he once rejected as "Isis" he here affirms as "Jesus."

26. In the original text this quote can be found in footnote A399: *"wozu auch die Versicherung kommt, daß es mit der Philosophie seit schon zweitausend Jahren ein Ende habe, weil 'der Stagirit für die Wissenschaft soviel erobert habe, daß er wenig Erhebliches mehr den Nachfolgern zu erspähen überlassen hat.'"*

27. Von einem vornehemen Ton, p. 389.

28. The German translation of Derrida's "Apocalyptic Tone" ("Von einem neuerdings erhobenen apokalyptischen Ton in der Philosophie," *Apokalypse*, trsl. by Michael Wetzel, pp. 9–91) reveals a misreading on Derrida's part concerning the concept of *"Entmannung."* Derrida writes: *"Bedenken Sie nun, daß Kant das Wort oder das Bild der Kastration oder genauer der 'Entmannung' zuvor als ein Beispiel für diese 'Analogien' und 'Wahrscheinlichkeiten' hinstellt, mit denen jene 'neuere mystisch-platonische Sprache' zum Zwecke der Manipulation Mißbrauch treibt"* [my italics]. Derrida's explanation hinges on the word *"Beispiel"* ("example") He seems to think that it is Kant's intention to use the image of castration as an example for the ways of mystagogical thinking. However, the German original of the Kant text makes it clear that it is the mystagogues themselves who fear truth's fate of castration in the case it is being *deprived* of its presentimental aspect.

29. Derrida argues that Kant's underlying assumption is that, similar to Freud's *"Bemächtigungstrieb,"* (the drive to appropriate) the mystagogues are trying to appropriate philosophy, i.e., the discourse on truth, for themselves. Kant actually specifically refers to the alchemists and the masons as some of the groups responsible for the confusion. He thereby corroborates a theme on which Umberto Eco picks up in his *Foucault's Pendulum.* The book entertains the suspicion that, for the last two-thousand years, certain groups, sometimes in the guise of alchemists, sometimes in the guise of the Masons, have attempted to take over the world by gaining access to a certain truth that would allow them to rule the world.

30. Cf. Apocalyptic Tone, p. 54/19.

31. Ibid.

32. Ibid, pp. 77–78/27.

33. Ibid, p. 71/23.

34. *Apocalypse of John*, 3:1–3.

35. It is interesting to remember in this context that Levinas as well uses the image of wakefulness to describe the disturbing impact that the other has on the the subject. In the case of insomnia, for example, which already expresses chronic wakefulness, the other is still actively awakening and disturbing the threatening monotony and sameness that accompanies insomnia. Levinas points to a being more awake than just being awake. The latter is a kind of being awake that, as he puts it, "is disturbed in the core of its formal or categorical

sameness by the *other*, which tears away at whatever forms a nucleus, a substance of the same, identity, a rest, a presence, a sleep." ("Reading and Revelation," p. 170).

36. The term "absent," of course, derives from the Latin "ab(s)esse" which means "off/away from being." I employ the term in this context, precisely to bring out the peculiar non-being structure that is implied in the issue of *venience*.

37. F. Rosenzweig, *Stern*, employs a similar constellation of language, primordial, holy-language, and silence ("Schweigen"). "*Schweigen*" constitutes the beginning as well as the end; cp. pp. 124/112 and 426/382. In the section on the holy language (pp. 334–36/301–302) he precisely interprets *Schweigen* as the other, the Ur-language, the lost old-holy language ("*verlorene altheilige Sprache*") which does not only signify the new linguistic situation of the Jew today but also points towards the disunity that has emerged between the Jew and his/her culture. In short, Rosenzweig, like Derrida, invokes the issue of exile, the wandering/erring Jew, who is to be displaced forever. Cf. also E. Wyschogrod, "Emmanuel Levinas and the Problem of Religious Language," *The Thomist: A Speculative Qarterly Review of Theology and Philosophy*, pp. 1–38, esp. p. 37 where she makes a similar claim about silence with reference to Levinas: "Thus, [for Levinas,] the telos of language would not lie in its very upsurge which is an act of violence but in something other than itself, in silence."

38. Cf. How not to Speak, pp. 559–61/28, 30.

39. Edmond Jabès, p. 116/78.

40. Ibid, pp. 107–108/71.

Notes to Chapter Eight

1. For Derrida's use of negations and privations, see Edith Wyschogrod, "How to Say No in French: Derrida and Negation in Recent French Philosophy," from forthcoming *Negation and Theology*, ed. Robert Scharlemann. This piece is instructive since it locates Derrida's own position on the boundaries of yet another neo-Kantian: Henri Bergson. Wyschogrod shows how Bergson's (and through Bergson also Deleuze) twofold understanding of the negation as 1) producing heterogeneity and as 2) privatively keeping this heterogeneity as one whole reappears in Derrida's concept of the khora, the place of God (and, one might add here, the apocalypse). My sense of her evaluation of the relationship between Derrida and Bergson, but also between Derrida and Levinas coincides with much of what I am suggesting in this chapter, with one important difference: Wyschogrod's reading of Derrida remains faithful to the by now established Derridean tradition that reads Derrida's work as a philosophical commentary on textuality and

everything that is included by it (semantics, semiotics, grammatology, phonology, etc.); cf. pp. 42, 46, esp. 54. I will return to this point in my last chapter. Suffice it to say here that it seems clear to me that Derrida's work *despite its textual appeal* is by no means just that. The text might perhaps serve as an appropriate paradigm for Derrida's understanding of the world. It may become appropriate at some point to call his work paratextual in order to emphasize the textual characteristics of an inquiry into something that resembles a text: the world. Almut Bruckstein in her recently finished dissertation, *Hermann Cohen (Characteristik der Ethik Maimons): A Reconstructive Reading*, comments many times on the relationship between Maimonides' and Cohen's concepts of negation and privation.

2. Z. Diesendruck, "Maimonides' Theory of the Negation of Privation," *PAAJR*, pp. 139–51; esp. pp. 139–41.

3. Louis Jacobs, "God," A.A. Cohen and Paul Mendes-Flohr, *Contemporary Jewish Religious Thought*, pp. 291–98.

4. I am leaving out the chapters in which he classifies the different kinds of attributes as well as the one where he explains the terms "likeness" and "difference" from the Aristotelian perspective. No attribute that we can possibly choose from our realm of experience will possibly match the essence of God. Maimonides shows that extensively in I:52 of the *Guide* where he lists the five groups of possible attributes, ruling out all of them but the last group. The first group is that of attributes as explanations of a thing's essence. Such attributes inappropriately describe God's essence because implied in them is a certain causality which assumes that there are "causes anterior" to God "by which, in consequence, He is defined." (p. 115) The second group of attributes is really only a subgroup of the first. It comprises those attributes which attempt to give a partial description of God's essence. They fail for the same reason the first group failed and in addition because they suggest that God's nature is of a composite kind which according to Maimonides is an "absurdity." (p. 115) The third group is the group of qualifying attributes or accidentia. Maimonides rejects this type of attributive discourse about God because it turns God into a substratum of those attributes. In other words, it assumes a distinction between God and God's qualities and thus creates a rupture withing God's nature. The fourth group is the group that attempts to relate God to a certain locality or time or both. Here again the crucial contention is the partialization of God's nature that would ensue if one agreed to such description. To say that God is in one place or at one certain time is to say that God is not at another. In consequence God's oneness would become questionable. The only type of attribute that Maimonides allows is that one which attributes actions to the essence in question. Yet, even here, the emphasis lies on the indivisibility of God's nature.

Differing actions on God's part do not imply that they are performed by different faculties or agencies within God. As actions, however, "this kind of attribute is remote from the essence of the thing of which it is predicated," (p. 119) The latter group, thus, can be seen as a useful type of attribute because of its difference from God's essence. God's actions stand without necessarily having to specify how and from where they were initiated.

5. *Guide*, I, 58, p. 134.

6. Diesendruck, p. 146, points out that the negated privation is really not just that but the privation of a privation (in our case the lack of a lack of something). The effect of such an attribution is that the attribute in question can be attributed to God in its infinite meaning without effecting what is said about God's indivisible essence.

7. *Guide*, p. 137.

8. *Religion*, p. 70/60.

9. Ibid, p. 71/61.

10. Ibid, p. 71/61.

11. Ibid, p. 71/61.

12. Ibid, p. 71/62.

13. Ibid, p. 46/39; here Cohen himself refers this understanding of God back to Maimonides' observation (which is again based on the latter's reading of the Book of Job) that "יש לו די להמצאם דברים זולחו" ("that he is sufficient in himself to bring forth the world").

14. Ibid, p. 74/64.

15. Ibid, p. 75/65.

16. *Stern*, pp. 23f./20f.

17. Ibid, p. 23/25.

18. Ibid, p. 23/25.

19. The view that in order to attain an unadulterated, pure concept of a thing, knowledge of something is preferrable to experiencing that something as a part of the world as a whole might strike one as fairly naive. That thinking, and thus also knowing, is part of the world and cannot be separated from it, is a suggestion that, although latently present since Husserl, didn't make its way into general philosophy until Heidegger's *Sein und Zeit* and then again with renewed force through the postmoderns. I will get back to this below in my discussion of Derrida's position. Suffice it to say here that it is a certain way of reading Kant that informs such naiveté. He asserts that it is possible to define, and then later work, within the limits of pure reason independently of the surrounding world. The catch with Rosenzweig is, of course, that Kant precisely ruled out the possibility of understanding God in that fashion. God remained noumenon and regulative idea. But it is just that kind of thinking that Rosenzweig is attacking here. To say that in the end God is nothing, a noumenon, is to neglect that this

nothing is already present to knowledge as the nothing of something and thus cannot be an absolute nothing anymore. This Rosenzweigian critique of Kant can be tracked down also in the beginning chapters of Book two and three of the first part of the *Stern*.

20. Ibid, p. 23/25.

21. Ibid, p. 24/26.

22. Cohen, "Die Urteile der Denkgesetze."

23. Jacques Derrida, "Comment ne pas parler: Dénégations," *Psyche*, trsl. by Ken Frieden, "How to avoid Speaking: Denials," ed. by Sanford Budick and Wolfgang Iser, *Languages of the Unsayable: The Play of Negativity in Literature and Literary Theory*, p. 595/62; (henceforth referred to as "How not to Speak, p. French/English.")

24. Jacques Derrida, "Différance," *Marges De La Philosophie; Margins of Philosophy*, trsl. by Alan Bass, p. 6/6; henceforth referred to as "Différance, p. French/ English."

25. Différance, p. 12/11.

26. David Wood & Robert Bernasconi (eds.), *Derrida and Différance*, p. 3.

27. Wood, *Derrida and Différance*, p. 85.

28. The problem of the "origin" finds various expressions in the discussion centered around the notion of différance. For this cf. Wood and Bernasconi, *Derrida and Différance*; esp. Brogan, pp. 32, 34, 36; Gayle Ormiston, "The Economy of Duplicity," pp. 44, 47; David Wood, "Différance and the Problem of Strategy," p. 66. Most commentators realize Derrida's reluctance to employ the concept of origin, yet fail to see, or maybe deliberately ignore, that Derrida remains purposely ambiguous about the issue. Brogan maybe comes closest when he says that, for Derrida, metaphysics originates in forgetting, "but the origin itself remains unthought. It cannot even be thought from within metaphysics, whose concepts of origin always come after and presuppose this originary origin." (p. 34)

29. Jacques Derrida, *De La Grammatologie*; trsl. by Gayatri Chakravorty Spivak, *Of Grammatology*, p. 38/23f. (henceforth referred to as "*Of Grammatology*, p. French/English").

30. *Of Grammatology*, p. 38/23.

31. "The original Discussion of 'Différance' (1968)," Wood, *Derrida and Différance*, p. 85.

32. So quoted from Wood, Ibid, p. 84.

33. Cp. previous chapter.

34. Différance, p. 6/6.

35. Différance, p. 6/6.

36. In other words, it surpasses what Heidegger calls the ontological difference ("ontologischer Unterschied"). For this cp. Walter

Brogan, "The Original Difference: Différance," in Wood, *Derrida and Différance*, pp. 31–41.

37. Jacques Derrida, "Lettre à un ami japonais," *Psyche*, "Letter to a Japanese Friend," in Wood, *Derrida and Différance*, p. 390/3.

38. How not to Speak, pp. 535–95/3–70.

39. Ibid, p. 595/62.

40. Ibid, p. 535/3.

41. This is somewhat confusing since the French translation of the essay is not "Comment ne pas dire" but "Comment ne pas parler." Derrida explains that he was asked for a preliminary title of the essay over the phone. "In a few minutes I had to improvise which I first did in my language: 'Comment ne pas dire . . .?'"

42. How not to Speak, p. 546/13.

43. Ibid, p. 547/14.

44. Ibid, p. 547/14.

45. Cp. also F. Rosenzweig's use of the term "Verbindung" in the *Stern*. Rosenzweig thinks the moment of the unification ("Vereinigung") is anticipated in the connection ("Verbindung") of the soul with the whole world (p. 261/234; unfortunately, Hallo's translation neglects to translate the German "Verbindung" adequately. He renders it as "universal fusion" and thereby blures the obvious connection with Cohen). Thus "Verbindung" turns into a preliminary term that describes status of the world as unredeemed, but directed towards redemption. Also p. 288/259 where Rosenzweig speculates that if humanity takes on the form of temporality in order to reach eternity then this path must be assured through an already existing "Verbindung." Also p. 335/302 shows the same characteristic usage of "Verbindung" this time as the relationship between the old holy language and the languages which the Jews speak nowadays.

46. How not to Speak, p. 552/20.

47. Ibid, p. 552/20.

48. Cf. part I, chapt 2.

49. Ibid, p. 553/21.

50. Ibid, p. 552/20.

51. Différance, p. 6/6.

52. The question how exactly one is supposed to think about différance is difficult to answer. In part those difficulties arise because of Derrida's own reservations concerning the use of the language of being. But also, the problem is how to think about something that is not something, i.e., something that rather must be described as the difference between two things as well as the temporal delay that occurs automatically between one thing and the other. Derrida, coming from structuralism, forces us to look at exactly that relationship — the differing/deferring connection between two things — as différance.

However, what is missing (yet, makes for an important part of structuralism) is the positivity with which structure is understood in it. For structuralism structure has being, it exists and hence can be evaluated scientifically, just the way any other science would investigate objects. The inherent problem of such an account of an object is that it is inevitably synchronic, i.e., it gathers into the present aspects of the object that really belong to its past or its future. The object, hence, cannot be understood as an object in time anymore, but is elevated out of the flux of time and turned into a theoretical static entity. Yet, Derrida does not want to look at differences as if they were nothing but an amalgam of static relationships. Structuralists made a good observation when they started looking at things by charting out the differences between them rather than looking at the things themselves. But the difficulty they ran into was their neglect of the temporal difference, the deferal, that is equally constitutive of a world of existents. This omission has to be cited when it comes to explaining the synchronic systematic character that structuralism left behind. Derrida seems to be suggesting that discourse on différance involves a close look at the differing/deferring space between things as something of a generative nature. In other words that space is not an absolute nothing; it rather is a productive nothing. The parallels with Rosenzweig's thinking are evident. Both thinkers conceive of the production of things as the affirmation of a not-nothing, i.e. the affirmation of a privation.

53. Différance, p. 6/6.

54. Levinas refers to this characteristic of language as its "quiddity."

55. The word "somehow" indicates the various attempts by different philosophers to account for what makes knowing possible. Husserl would have said that knowing happens through the ego's intentional approach to an object. Levinas agrees that it can happen that way, yet, he simultaneously rejects such a scheme since it makes conception of the other as other impossible. In other words, by remaining critical towards the relationship between the present tense and existence and by detaching différance from precisely this mechanism, Derrida expresses his reservations about a philosophy that is centered around a knowing subject.

56. Différance, p. 6/6. Derrida opts for a visible marker in addition to his verbal prohibitions to detach différance from the connection with the present: he erases the word "is."

57. Différance, p. 7/7.

58. On this cf. David Wood, "Différance and the Problem of Strategy," *Derrida and Différance*, pp. 63–71. Wood comments on Derrida's caution concerning the use of the word concept in reference to "différance" and points to various passages in Jacques Derrida, *Positions*, tr. by Alan Bass, Chicago: The University of Chicago Press, 1972,

p. 26ff. where Derrida talks about a "new concept of writing. This concept can be called gram or différance."

59. This translation of "diagram" is analogous to that of the Greek word "διαβαινω" which means "to walk through to the end." Generally, the prefix "dia-" can have two related meanings: 1. through, to the end. 2. division, separation. Both are applicable in our case. The division is that between origin and telos and the adverbial "to the end" designates the quality of the relationship *between* origin and telos.

60. Différance, p. 6/6.

61. Ibid, p. 7/7.

62. In how far Derrida's thinking has changed towards a more lenient, if not seeking, attitude with reference to the question of the telos, will be discussed below. Suffice it to say that at this point of his own reflective development (1968) he rejected the concept of telos as complicit with the spell of being, the system, and synchronic thinking in general.

63. Différance, p. 4/3.

64. Ibid, p. 7/7.

65. My Greek dictionary gives me fourteen different derivatives of the root-word "στρατεια." All of them are used in a military context, either to designate the army itself, the single soldier (the process of leading an army) their leader or in the sense of setting camp ("στρατο-πεδευομαι"). The French use of the word reflects almost exactly the same sense. The most general meaning I could find in the French, in *Pons: Micro Robert en Poche*, Paris: Klett, 1979, is *"Plan d'actions coordonnées."* Thus the Greek meaning of the word by itself indicates a meaning which Derrida refuses to accept or even inverts, viz. the coordination, the hierarchical notion that it carries along with it, in order to use the word in his context. However, the root "str-" can also be traced back to the Latin *"struere"* which carries the meanings of to streek, and to spread. Strategy thus indicates the spreading out of a plurality of details (soldiers). Strategy itself implies the sense of telos and origin without itself supplying it. It seems crucial that Derrida conjoins it with the term "adventurous," since that way he can undermine the above sense of coordination towards a more vagrant and aimless meaning. In "The Time of a Thesis: Punctuations," ed. by Alan Montefiore, *Philosophy in France Today*, p. 50, Derrida says about the term "strategy" that it "is a word that I have perhaps abused in the past" but that what he means when he uses the term is that "strategy is strategy without any finality; for this is what I hold and what in turn holds me in its grip, the aleatory strategy of someone who admits that he does not know where he is going." And in *Derrida and Différance*, p. 89, Derrida explains that when he talks about strategy he precisely does not refer to a homogenous stratefied entity, but to something that

is "irreducibly heterogeneous." And in "The Economy of Duplicity," Ibid, p. 43, Gayle L. Ormiston refers to Derrida's "'aleatory strategy' as (1) the simultaneous institution and effacement of support and structure; and (2) the play between attachment and detachment, between closure and breach, that is, the notion of *binding* (bander)."

66. How not to Speak, p. 536/4.

67. Ibid, p. 542/9.

68. Derrida, How not to Speak, p. 542/9.

69. Jacques Derrida, "Violence et métaphysique," *L'écriture et la différence*, transl. by Alan Bass, "Violence and Metaphysics," *Writing and Difference*, p. 168/114; (henceforth referred to as "Violence, p. French/English").

70. This is, of course, also Rosenzweig's demand when he introduces the reader to the three elements (God, man, world). In all three cases, Rosenzweig says, philosophy has failed to establish anything but negative certainty about what those things are.

71. Cp. my remarks about the logic of independence at the end of part I, chapt. 2.

72. Violence, p. 170/116.

73. Ibid, p. 170/115.

74. Jacques Derrida, "Edmond Jabès et la question du livre," *L'écriture et la différence . . ."* p. 116/78. This is how Derrida signs his essay on Edmond Jabès.

75. With respect to Sartre's work Derrida remarks in "The Ends of Man," *Margins*, p. 138/116 that even an atheism like that of Sartre "changes nothing in this fundamental structure" which consists in naming "the metaphysical unity between man and God, the relation of man to God, the project of becoming God as the project constituting human-reality."

76. Cf. the respective introductions to the three elements in Franz Rosenzweig, *Stern*, pp. 25/23, 44/41, 66/62.

77. André Chouraqui as quoted from Derrida, Apocalyptic Tone, p. 14/4.

78. *Guide*, pp. 113–14.

79. For this also cp. Mark C. Taylor, "The Eventuality of Texts," *Tears*, p. 167. With reference to Levinas's infinite he remarks: "This infinite is never inscribed *within* the text. Nor is it simply *outside* the text. The Other that cannot be reduced to the same is "inside" as an "outside" that renders text irreducibly event-ual by sending it into exile from itself." Although Taylor does not explicitly read the word "without" the way I suggest in the text, it seems obvious to me that he is describing the same idea. He also connects this reading with the topic of our previous chapter when he says that from this "internal" exile there is no return. The exilic text is errant; its reader/writer is a nomad.

It is another question if the use of the image of the wandering Jew is still an adequate mode of describing what Judaism is about today. Rosenzweig certainly also makes use of this image extensively (cp. *Stern*, p. 339/305), "in uns selbst schlugen wir Wurzel, wurzellos in der Erde, ewige Wanderer darum, doch tief verwurzelt in uns selbst in unserem eigenen Leib und Blut." Regarding this and other passages Norbert Samuelson pointed out to me that it is difficult not to recognize the latent anti-semitism that hides behind Rosenzweig's words. To characterize Jews as erring and as wanderers amounts to nothing but the kind of stereotyping that they have had to endure for two millennia. I find this criticism justified and worth considering. However, it seems that the Jewish community might not see eye to eye regarding this issue. Facing the problems that Israel is having because of its settlement policy on the West-Bank, it seems justified to say that the exile-problematic is not quite yet erased. Moreover, both Levinas and Derrida are after something that is larger than Judaism, their intention is to describe a certain epistemological condition, a transcendental condition of human thinking. Jewishness, and the image of the wandering Jew become metaphors that apply to any human being regardless of their ethnic and religious belonging.

Notes to Chapter Nine

1. *Religion*, p. 285.
2. *Stern*, pp. 305f., 318f.
3. *Religion*, p. 286.
4. Walter Benjamin, *Zur Kritik der Gewalt und andere Aufsätze*, Frankfurt.
5. Much of Derrida's work focuses on the state of college and university education in France and overseas. He is the co-founder of GREPH (Groupe de recherche de l'enseignement philosophique) and has published many essays and interviews on the topic of education such as *De l'esprit*, transl. by Geoffrey Bennington and Rachel Bowlby; *Of Spirit: Heidegger and the Question*. On Colleges and Philosophy: Jacques Derrida with Geoff Bennington. *Institute of Contemporary Arts, Documents 5*, 1986; "The Principle of Reason: The University in the Eyes of its Pupils," *Diacritics*; "Time of a Thesis: Punctuations." In Philosophy in France Today, ed. by Alan Montefiore.
6. *Margins*, p. 121.
7. Ibid.
8. Ibid, p. 123.
9. Ibid.
10. *Religion*, p. 357.

11. Ibid, p. 57.

12. Ibid, p. 338.

13. Walter Benjamin, "Über den Begriff der Geschichte," *Illuminationen*, pp. 251–262.

14. Stapleton, loc. cit., refers to this turn to the spatial, yet he takes this as an indication that the spatial in Derrida's thought is really only symbolic for the failure of the latter's attempt to move away from the metaphysics of presence: "For these classical concepts of spatial presence continue to constitute the horizon" (13). Stapleton fails to see that both the temporal and the spatial matrix that Derrida refers to reapeatedly in his work are recast into the neo-Kantian frame of messianism and khora which both, by virtue of their privative qualities and their ability to bring together good and bad infinity, exceed the notion of presence alltogether.

15. Apocalyptic Tone, p. 65.

16. The oxymoronic character of this formulation is intended and reflects several things at the same time: 1. gala as the root-word for both the unveiling and exiling of truth, 2. presentation as an ideal limit of the search for truth and 3. the desire for the truth that is implicit in the use of the term "gala."

17. Apocalyptic Tone, p. 77.

18. Ibid, pp. 83–84.

19. By employing the two different translations of the word event (German and English) the preceding quote signals different semantic strata that accompany the signficance of the place. The English "event" focuses on the event as that which comes out, which stands outside of the normal structures within which we live. The German "Ereignis" focuses on the event as that which provides us with a particular kind of proprietorship; it emphasizes the self — presence that inheres in the actual event.

20. How not to Speak, p. 20.

21. This is an important fact that Derrida does not get tired of repeating (cp. *Khora*, pp. 13–18; 65ff. etc; but also the whole scope of the essay "Force of Law"). The anti-mythic character of khora is the foundation for what Derrida, then, following Benjamin, can call justice.

22. *Khora*, p. 32.

23. Ibid, p. 33.

24. Ibid.

25. Ibid, p. 39.

26. Ibid, pp. 35–36.

27. Ibid, p. 95.

28. This is the basic idea to which Bob Gibbs's book *Correlations in Rosenzweig and Levinas* is devoted. Gibbs shows that Rosenzweig's

idea in the *Stern* was to render a sociological picture of the Jewish Community engaged in the annual cycle of ritual and liturgy. To be sure, the method with which Rosenzweig demonstrates the emergence of the community is markedly different form that of Derrida. Whereas for the former the community results from a Hegelian system that begins with a logic, moves through an analysis of linguistics and ends up with the social as the unified realm of Jewish existence, Derrida understands community as unified only in their disunity with the absolute.

29. For the following analysis of the relationship between Maimonidean and Aristotelian ethics compare Steven S. Schwarzschild, "Moral Radicalism and 'Middlingness' in the Ethics of Maimonides," *The Pursuit of the Ideal: Jewish Writings of Steven Schwarzschild*, ed. by Menachem Kellner, pp. 137–61.

30. We already discussed this question in chapter 4, part I, where we confronted Levinas's thinking with that of Alfred Schütz who, like Levinas, finds the core of the ethical relationship captured in the face-to-face relationship, and who, also like Levinas, finds the lack of a conceptualization of ethics in Husserl's phenomenology intolerable. Yet, for Schütz the face to face relationship was the *reciprocal* expression of the mutually manifested, nonreciprocal awareness of the other's stream of consciousness. In any reading of Derrida's work, however, the nonreciprocal is an almost self-evident premise of his descriptions of the exilic, apocalyptic, "negative," or progressive condition of human knowledge. The concept of nonreciprocality as the form of the ethical evolves from Derrida's thought with necessity and has been constitutive of his thinking from the earliest beginnings.

31. This is the locus of Derrida's essay on the gift ("En ce moment dans cette ouvrage me voici,") where he asserts the impossibility of a positive response to any gift since that would reaffirm a symmetrical relationship and thus compromise the position of the other to the point where he/she could not be identified as other anymore.

32. Jacques Derrida, "The Politics of Friendship," *The Journal of Philosophy*, July–Dec., no. 85, 1988, p. 636; henceforth referred to as "Friendship."

33. Friendship, p. 632.

34. Friendship, p. 637. The future anterior is a peculiar grammatical tense. It is rarely used in commonday colloquial speech. In the sentence "I will have finished the task by the time you come home," it is used to express the retrospective appreciation of the fulfillment of the task from a viewpoint that, at the time the sentence is said, still lies in the future. Colloquially, we would rather choose the passive future structure. "I will be finished with the task by the time you come around." Obviously, this reintroduces the copula "to be" and thus re-establishes a connection with being which at this point is undesirable, since it

would destroy the asymmetrical effect of the future anterior. It, more-over, emphasizes the passive over the active that is maintained in the future anterior and is consequently less appropriate to designate the act of friendship the way Derrida envisions it here.

35. Friendship, pp. 632–33.

36. Ibid, pp. 633–34.

37. Ibid, p. 633.

38. The prepositional qualification of responsibility (responsible to, for, and before) is a characteristic that Derrida analyzes along the lines of the nonreciprocal nature of any relationship. "One answers [is re-sponsible to] first *to* the other" then "one answers for oneself," and one answers before the other (638–39). Of these three, it is the responsibil-ity to the other that is prioritized in Derrida's reading, since it is the quality of singularity that is announced in it that passes through the law, i.e. through universality (640–41).

39. Jacques Derrida, "Force of Law: The 'Mystical Foundation of Authority'," *Cardozo Law Review: Deconstruction and the Possibility of Justice* (henceforth referred to as "Justice, p. French/English").

40. Justice, pp. 941–43.

41. Ibid, p. 943.

42. Ibid, p. 943.

43. Walter Benjamin, *Zur Kritik der Gewalt und andere Aufsätze*.

44. Justice, p. 1003.

45. Ibid, p. 1003.

46. Ibid, p. 943.

47. Ibid, p. 945.

48. Ibid, p. 929.

49. Ibid, p. 945.

50. Ibid, p. 947.

51. Ibid, p. 949.

52. Ibid, p. 951.

53. Ibid, p. 953.

54. Ibid, p. 955.

55. Ibid, p. 955.

56. Ibid, p. 957.

57. Ibid, p. 957.

58. Ibid, p. 961.

59. Ibid, p. 1015.

Notes to Conclusion

1. Cp. for example, Simon Critchley's, *The Ethics of Deconstruction*, or Zygmunt Bauman, *Postmodern Ethics*, Cambridge: Blackwell. There are even titles that, with great academic cunning, under the disguise

of fighting ethics, still propagate another kind of ethics; John Caputo, *Against Ethics: Contributions to a Poetics of Obligation with Constant Reference to Deconstruction.*

    2. Derrida in a conversation at a conference on Deconstruction and Phenomenology at Memphis State University, 1992.

    3. Loc. cit.

WORKS CITED

Benjamin, Walter. "Die Aufgabe des Übersetzers." *Illuminationen.* Frankfurt a.M.: Suhrkamp, 1977, 50–63.

Bergson, Henri. *Matter and Memory.* New York: Zone Books, 1991.

Bernasconi, Robert and David Wood, eds. *Derrida and Différance.* Evanston: Northwestern University Press, 1988.

———— and Simon Critchley. *Re-Reading Levinas.* Bloomington: Indiana University Press, 1991.

————. *The Provocation of Levinas.* New York: Routledge, 1988.

Boyarin, Daniel. *Intertextuality and the Reading of Midrash.* Bloomington: Indiana University Press, 1990.

Broome, Edwin C. "Ezekiel's Abnormal Personality." *JBL* 65 (1965): 277–92.

Bruckstein, Almut. *Hermann Cohen (Charateristik der Ethik Maimons): A Reconstructive Reading.* Unpublished Dissertation, Temple University, Philadelphia, 1991.

Caputo, John D. *Against Ethics: Contributions to a Poetics of Obligation with Constant Reference to Deconstruction,* Bloomington: Indiana University Press, 1993.

————. "The Economy of Signs in Husserl and Derrida." *Deconstruction and Philosophy: The Texts of Jacques Derrida.* Ed. by John Sallis. Chicago: Chicago University Press, 1987.

————. "Gadamer's Closet Essentialism: A Derridean Critique." *Dialogue and Deconstruction: The Gadamer-Derrida Encounter,* ed. by Diane P. Michelfelder and Richard E. Palmer. Albany: State University of New York Press, 1989, pp. 258–265.

Casper, Bernhard. "Denken im Angesicht des Anderen: Zur Einführung in das Denken von Emmanuel Levinas." *Verantwortung für den Anderen: Zum Werk von Emmanuel Levinas.* Hans Hermann Henrix (Hg.). Aachen: Einhard Verlag, 1984.

Cohen, Hermann. *Die Religion der Vernunft aus den Quellen des Judentums.* Wiesbaden: Fourier Verlag, 1988. Trsl. by Simon Kaplan,

Religion of Reason Out of the Sources of Judaism. New York: Frederick Ungar Publishing Company, 1971.

———. *Logik der Reinen Erkenntnis.* Berlin: Bruno Cassirer Verlag, 1914.

Cohen, Richard A. "Absolute Positivity and Ultra-Positivity." *The Question of the Other: Essays in Contemporary Continental Philosophy.* Ed. by Arlene B. Dallery and Charles E. Scott. Albany: State University of New York, 1989.

———. *The Height of the Good in Rosenzweig and Levinas.* Chicago: Chicago University Press, 1994.

Coward, Harold and Toby Foshay (eds.). *Derrida and Negative Theology.* Albany, SUNY, 1992.

Critchley, Simon. *The Ethics of Deconstruction: Derrida and Levinas.* Oxford: Blackwell, 1992.

Deleuze, Gilles and Felix Guattari. *A Thousand Plateaus: Capitalism and Schizophrenia.* Trsl. and foreword by Brian Massumi. Minneapolis: University Minnesota Press, 1988.

Derrida, Jacques. "Comment ne pas parler: Dénégations." *Psyché: Inventions de l'autre.* Paris: Galilée, 1987. Trsl. by Ken Frieden. "How to avoid Speaking: Denials." *Languages of the Unsayable: The Play of Negativity in Literature and Literary Theory.* Ed. by Sanford Budick and Wolfgang Iser. New York: Columbia University Press, 1989.

———. *De La Grammatologie.* Paris: Les Éditions De Minuit, 1967. *Of Grammatology.* Trsl. by Gayatri Chakravorty Spivak. Baltimore: The Johns Hopkins University Press, 1976.

———. *De l'esprit.* Paris: Éditions Galilée, 1987. Transl. by Geoffrey Bennington and Rachel Bowlby, *Of Spirit: Heidegger and the Question.* Chicago: University of Chicago Press, 1989.

———. "Des tours de Babel." *Psyche: Inventions de l'autre.* Paris: Éditions Galilée, 1987. Trsl. and ed. by Joseph F. Graham. "Des Tours de Babel." *Difference in Translation.* Ithaca: Cornell University Press, 1985.

———. *D'un Tone Apocalyptique adopté Naguère en Philosophie.* Paris: Éditions Galilée, 1983; "Of an Apocalyptic Tone Recently Adopted in Philosophy." *The Oxford Literary Review* 6, 2 (1984).

———. "En ce moment dans cet oeuvre me voici." (1980) *Psyche: Inventions de l'autre.* Paris: Galilée, 1987, pp. 159–203. Trsl. by Ruben Berezdivin, "At this very Moment in this Work here I am." *Re-Reading Levinas.* Ed. by Robert Bernasconi and Simon Critchley. Bloomington: Indiana University Press, 1991, 11–51.

———. "Force of Law: The 'Mystical Foundation of Authority'." *Cardozo Law Review: Deconstruction and the Possibility of Justice* 11 (July/August 1990).

———. "Interpretations at War: Kant, the Jew, the German." *New Literary History* 22 (1991): 39–95.

———. *La Voix et le phénomène.* Paris: Presses Universitaire de France, 1967. Trsl. by David B. Allison. *Speech and Phenomena.* Evanston: Northwestern University Press, 1973.

———. *L'écriture et la différence.* Paris: Éditions du Seuil, 1967. *Writing and Difference.* Trsl. by Alan Bass. Chicago: The Chicacgo University Press, 1978.

———. *Marges De La Philosophie.* Paris: Les Éditions De Minuit, 1972. *Margins of Philosophy.* Trsl. by Alan Bass. Chicago: The University of Chicago Press, 1982.

———. "Philosophie: Derrida l'insoumis." *Nouvel Observateur.* Paris (September 9, 1983).

———. *Positions.* Trsl. by Alan Bass. Chicago: The University of Chicago Press, 1972.

———. "On Colleges and Philosophy: Jacques Derrida with Geoff Bennington." *Institute of Contemporary Arts, Documents 5,* 1986.

———. "The Politics of Friendship." *The Journal of Philosophy* 85 (July–Dec. 1988).

———. "The Principle of Reason: The University in the Eyes of its Pupils." *Diacritics* (Fall 1983): 2–21.

———. "Time of a Thesis: Punctuations." *Philosophy in France Today.* Ed. by Alan Montefiore. Cambridge, UK: Cambridge University Press, 1983.

Descartes, René. *Discourse on Method: An Other Writings.* Trsl. and introduced by Arthur Wollaston. Baltimore: Penguin Books, 1960.

Diesendruck, Zevi. "Maimonides' Theory of the Negation of Privation." *PAAJR* VI (1934/35).

Eco, Umberto. *Foucault's Pendulum.* 1988.

Eisen, Arnold. "Exile." *Contemporary Jewish Religious Thought: Original Essays on Critical Concepts, Movements and Thoughts.* Ed. by Arthur A. Cohen and Paul Mendes-Flohr. New York: MacMillan, 1987.

Engelmann, Peter. "Jacques Derrida." *Philosophien.* Edition Passagen, 1985.

Eilberg-Schwarz, Howard. "Who's Kidding Whom?: A Serious Reading of Rabbinic Word Plays." *Journal of the American Academy of Religion* LV/4 (1988): 766–788.

Floyd Jr., Wayne. "To Welcome the Other: Totality and Theory in Levinas and Adorno." Unpublished paper, delivered at the *AAR* in New Orleans, 1988.

Forthomme, Bernard. *Une Philosophie de la Transcendance: La métaphysique d'Emmanuel Lévinas.* Paris: Librairie Philosophique J. Vrin, 1979.

Gadamer, Hans-Georg. *Truth and Method.* New York: Crossroads, 1985.

Gibbs, Robert B. *Correlations in Rosenzweig and Levinas.* Princeton: Princeton University Press, 1992.

———. "'Greek' in the 'Hebrew' Writings of Emmanuel Levinas." St. Louis University. Delivered at Academy of Jewish Philosophy, Wyncote, 1989.

Goldin, Judah. "The Freedom and Restraint of Aggadah." *Midrash and Literature.* Ed. by G.H. Hartman and S. Budick, New Haven: Yale Univ. Press, 1986.

Handelman, Susan. *Fragments of Redemption: Jewish Thought and Literary Theory in Benjamin, Scholem, and Levinas.* Bloomington: Indiana University Press, 1991.

Hegel, Georg Friedrich Wilhelm. *Phänomenologie des Geistes.* Frankfurt/a.M. 1970.

Heidegger, Martin. *Sein und Zeit.* Tübingen: Max Niemeyer Verlag, 1984.

Husserl, Edmund. *Cartesian Meditations.* Trsl. by Dorion Cairns. Boston: Martinus Nijhoff, 1982.

———. *Formale und Transzendentale Logik.* Halle: Max Niemeyer, 1929. Trsl. by Dorion Cairns. *Formal and Transcendental Logic.* The Hague: Martinus Nijhoff, 1969.

———. *Ideen zu einer reinen Phänomenologie und phänomenologischen Philosophie.* Haag: Martinus Nijhoff, 1950. *Ideas: General Introduction to Pure Phenomenology.* Trsl. by W.R. Boyce Gibson, New York: Macmillan, 1962.

———. *The Crisis of European Sciences and Transcendental Phenomenology: An Introduction to Phenomenological Philosophy.* Trsl. and with an Introduction by David Carr, Evanston: Northwestern University Press, 1970.

Hyppolite, Jean. *Genesis and Structure of Hegel's Phenomenology of Spirit.* Trsl. by Samuel Cherniak and John Heckman, Evanston: Northwestern Univ. Press, 1974.

Jacobs, Louis. "God." *Contemporary Jewish Religious Thought: Original Essays on Critical Concepts, Movements and Thoughts.* Ed. by Arthur A. Cohen and Paul Mendes-Flohr. New York: MacMillan, 1987, 291–298.

Kant, Immanuel. *Kritik der reinen Vernunft.* Werke, vols. 3–4. Darmstadt: WBG, 1968.

———. "Von einem neuerdings erhobenen vornehmen Ton in der Philosophie." *Werke,* vol. 5. Darmstadt: WBG, 1968

Kearney, Richard. "Jacques Derrida: Deconstruction and the Other." *Dialogues with Contemporary Thinkers: The Phenomenological Heritage.* Manchester: Manchester University Press, 1984, pp. 105–27.

Kierkegaard, Søren. *Philosophische Brocken: De Omnibus Dubitandum Est.* Gütersloh: GTB Siebenstern, 1981.

Klein, Ralph W. *Ezekiel: The Prophet and His Message.* Columbia, SC: University of South Carolina Press, 1988.

Köhler, Kaufmann. *Jewish Theology.* New York: Macmillan, 1923

Kugel, James A. "Two Introductions to Midrash." *Midrash and Literature.* Ed. by G.H. Hartman and S. Budick, New Haven: Yale Univ. Press, 1986.

Lacan, Jacques. *Écrits: A Selection.* Trsl. by Alan Sheridan. New York: W.W. Norton & Company, 1977.

Lauer, Quentin. *Phenomenology: Its Genesis and Prospect.* New York: Harper & Row, 1965.

Levinas, Emmanuel. *Autrement qu'être ou au-delà de l'essence.* 1974. Trsl. by Alphonso Lingis. *Otherwise than Being or Beyond Essence.* The Hague: Martinus Nijhoff Publishers, 1981.

———. *Collected Philosophical Papers.* Trsl. by Alphonso Lingis, Dordrecht, Boston, Lancaster: Martinus Nijhoff Publishers, 1987.

———. "Dieu et la philosophie." *De Dieu Qui Vient À l'Idée.* Paris: Librairie Philosophique, J. Vrin, 1982, 93–128. "God and Philosophy." Trsl. by Sean Hand. *The Levinas Reader.* Oxford, UK: Basil Blackwell, 1989, 166–90.

———. *Difficile Liberté.* Paris: Albin Michel, 1976. "Jewish Thought Today." *Difficult Freedom.* Trsl. by Sean Hand. Baltimore: The Johns Hopkins University Press, 1991.

———. *En découvrant l'existence avec Husserl et Heidegger.* Paris: Bibliothèque d'histoire de la philosophie, 1949.

———. *Ethics and Infinity: Conversations with Philippe Nemo.* Trsl. by Richard Cohen. Pittsburgh: Duquesne University Press, 1985.

———. "Fribourg, Husserl et la phénoménologie." *Revue d'Allemagne et des pays de langue allemande.* 5, 43 (1931).

———. "From Existence to Ethics." *The Levinas Reader.* Oxford, UK: Basil Blackwell, 1989, 82–3.

———. "Ideology and Idealism." *Modern Jewish Ethics: Theory and Practice.* Ed. by Marvin Fox. Institute for Judaism and Contemporary Thought: Ohio University Press, 1975.

———. "La Révélation Dans La Tradition Juive." *L'Au-Delà Du Verset: Lectures et Discours Talmudique.* Paris: Les Editions Minuit, 1982, 158–82.

———. "Revelation in the Jewish Tradition." Trsl. and ed. by Sean Hand. *The Levinas Reader.* Oxford, UK: Basil Blackwell, 1989, 190–211.

———. *La théorie de l'intuition dans la phénoménologie de Husserl.* Paris: Alcan, 1930.

———. *Méditations Cartésienne: Introduction à la phénoménologie par Edmund Husserl.* Paris: Bibliothèque de la Société française de Philosophie, 1931.

———. *Nine Talmudic Readings.* Trsl. by Annette Aronowicz. Bloomington: Indiana University Press, 1990.

———. "Phénoménologie (récension de Jahrbuch für Philosophie und phänomenologische Forschung)." *Revue Philosophique de la France et de l'Étranger.* CXVIII, 11–12, 414–20.

———. *Totalité et Infini: Essai sur l'extériorité.* Haag: Martinus Nijhoff, 1971. Trsl. by Alphonso Lingis, *Totality and Infinity.* Pittsburgh: Duquesne University Press, 1969.

Lingis, Alphonso. "The Elemental Imperative." *Research in Phenomenology* 18 (1988).

———. "The Origin of Infinity," *Research in Phenomenology.* 6 (1976).

MacDonald, Michael J. "Jewgreek and Greekjew: The concept of the trace in Derrida and Levinas." *Philosophy Today* (Fall 1991).

Maimonides, Moses. *Guide for the Perplexed.* Vols. I+II. Trsl. by Shlomo Pines. With an introduction by Leo Strauss. Chicago: The University of Chicago Press, 1963.

Meyerson, Gregory Dean. "The Dialectic of Defeat: Domination and Liberation in Contemporary Critical Theory." *Ph.D. Thesis.* Evanston: Northwestern University, 1989.

Nathanson, Maurice. *Edmund Huserl: Philosopher of Infinite Tasks.* Evanston: Northwestern University Press, 1973.

Néher, André. *The Exile of the Word.* Philadelphia: The Jewish Publication Society of America, 1981.

Norris, Christopher. *Derrida.* Cambridge Harvard University Press, 1987.

Olivetti, Marco M. "Philosophische Fragen an das Werk von Emmanuel Levinas." *Verantwortung für den Anderen und die Frage nach Gott: Zum Werk von Emmanuel Levinas.* Ed. by Hans Hermann Henrix, Aachen: Einhard Verlag, 1984, 42–70.

Peperzak, Adrian. "Phenomenology — Ontology — Metaphysics: Levinas Perspective on Husserl and Heidegger." *Man and World* 6 (1983): 113–27.

Rashi. *The Pentateuch and Rashi's Commentary: A Linear Translation into English by Rabbi Abraham Ben Isaiah and Rabbi Benjamin Sharfman.*

Rosenzweig, Franz. *Der Stern der Erlösung.* Haag: Martinus Nijhoff, 1976. Trsl. by William W. Hallo. *The Star of Redemption.* Notre Dame: Notre Dame Press, 1970.

Ryan, Michael. *Marxism and Deconstruction: A Critical Articulation.* Baltimore: The Johns Hopkins University Press, 1982.

Salusinszky, Imre. "Jacques Derrida." *Criticism in Society: Interviews with Jacques Derrida, Northrop Frye, Harold Bloom, Geoffrey Hartman, Frank Kermode, Edward Said, Barbara Johnson, Frank Lentricchia, J. Hillis Miller.* New York: Methuen, 1987, 11–24.

Samuelson, Norbert. "The Concept of Worship in Judaism." *Academy of Jewish Philosophy*, 1991.

Schütz, Alfred. *The Phenomenology of the Social World*. Trsl. by George Walsh and Frederick Lehnert, Evanston: Northwestern University Press, 1967.

Schwarzschild, Steven S. *The Pursuit of the Ideal: Jewish Writings of Steven Schwarzschild*. Ed. Menachem Kellner, Albany: Suny, 1990.

Seltzer, Robert. *Jewish People, Jewish Thought*. New York: MacMillan, 1980.

Stapleton, Timothy J. "Philosophy and Finitude: Husserl, Derrida and the end of Philosophy." *Philosophy Today* (Spring 1986).

Stern, David. "Midrash." *Contemporary Jewish Thought: Original Essays on Critical Concepts, Movements and Beliefs*. Ed. by A.A. Cohen and P. Mendes-Flohr, New York: Macmillan, 1987.

Strasser, Stephan. *Jenseits von Sein und Zeit: Eine Einführung in Emmanuel Levinas' Philosophie*. The Hague: Martinus Nijhoff, 1978.

Taylor, Charles. *Hegel*. Cambridge: Cambridge University Press, 1975.

Taylor, Mark. "How Not To Speak: Non-Negative Atheology." *Diacritics* 20, 4 (1990).

———. "The Eventuality of Texts." *Tears*. Albany: State University of New York Press, 1990.

Wyschogrod, Edith. "Interview with Emmanuel Levinas." 1982.

———. "Emmanuel Levinas and the Problem of Religious Language." *The Thomist: A Speculative Quarterly Review of Theology and Philosophy* XXXVI (January, 1972).

———. "How to Say No in French: Derrida and Negation in Recent French Philosophy." Forthcoming *Negation and Theology*. Ed. Robert Scharlemann, University of Virginia Press.

———. "The Moral Self: Emmanuel Levinas and Hermann Cohen." *Daat: a Journal of Philosophy* 4 (1980): 35–58.

Yount, Mark. "Two Reversibilities: Merleau-Ponty and Derrida." *Philosophy Today*. Summer 1990.

WORKS CONSULTED

Aeschlimann, Jean-Christophe (ed.). *Répondre d'autrui Emmanuel Lévinas*. Neuchâtel: Langages, 1989.

Anglet, Kurt. "Die Erschöpfung der Wörter: Jacques Derridas Abbruch der philosophischen Methodik." *Theologie und Philosophie* 64 (1989): 397–408.

Ash, Beth Sharon. "Jewish Hermeneutics and Contemporary Theories of Textuality: Hartman, Bloom, and Derrida." *Modern Philology:*

Journal Devoted to Reserach in Medieval and Modern Literature 85, 1 (August 1987): 65–80.

Beierwalter, Werner. *Visio Facialis*. München: Bayrische Akademie der Wissenschaften, 1988.

Boly, John R. "Nihilism Aside: Derrida's Debate over Intentional Models." *Philosophy and Literature* 9 (October 1985): 152–65.

Burgraeve, Roger. *E. Levinas: Une bibliographie primaire and secondaire*. Leuven: Peeters, 1990.

Caputo, John D. "Beyond Aestheticism: Derrida's Responsible Anarchy." *Research in Phenomenology* 18 (1988): 59–73.

———. "Mysticism and Transgression: Derrida and Meister Eckhart." (Unpublished essay).

———. "Derrida and Theology." (Unpublished essay).

Ciaramelli, Fabio. *Transcendence et éthique: Essai sur Emmanuel Levinas*. Brussells: Editions Ousia, 1989.

Cohen, Richard A. *Face to Face with Levinas*. Albany: State University of New York Press, 1986.

———. "The Face of Truth in Rosenzweig, Levinas, and Jewish Mysticism." Daniel Guerriera (ed.). *Phenomenology of the Truth Proper to Religion*. Albany: Suny Press, 1990. 175–201.

Culler, Jonathan. *On Deconstruction: Theory and Criticism after Structuralism*. Ithaca, NY: Cornell University Press, 1982.

Dallery, Arlene and Charles E. Scott. *The Question of the Other: Essays in Contemporary Continental Philosophy*. Albany: State University of New York Press, 1989.

Defaux, Gerard. "Against Derrida's Dead Letter": Christian Humanism and the Valorization of Writing." *French Forum* 13 (May 1988): 167–85.

Derrida, Jacques. *Du droit à la philosophie*. Paris: Galilée, 1990.

———. *Aporias*. Stanford: Standford University Press, 1993.

———. *Dissemination* Trsl. and with an introduction by Barbara Johnson. Chicago: The University of Chicago Press, 1981.

——— and Geoffrey Bennington. *Jacques Derrida*. Mars: Éditions du Seuil, 1991.

———. *Specters of Marx: The State of the Debt, the Work of Mourning, & the New International*. London: Routledge, 1994.

———. *Spurs: Nietzsche's Styles*. Trsl. by Barbara Harlow. Chicago: TheUniversity of Chicago Press, 1979.

———. *The Archeology of the Frivolous: Reading Condillac*. Trsl. and with and introduction by John P. Leavey, Jr. Lincoln and London: University of Nebraska Press, 1973.

———. *The Ear of the Other: Texts and Discussions with Jacques Derrida*. Lincoln and London: University of Nebraska Press, 1985.

———. *The Gift of Death*. Chicago: University of Chicago Press, 1995.

———. *The Other Heading: Reflections on Today's Europe*. Bloomington: Indiana University Press, 1992.

———. *The Postcard: From Socrates to Freud and Beyond*. Trsl. by Alan Bass. Chicago: The University of Chicago Press, 1987.

———. "Restitution of Truth to Size." *Research in Phenomenology* (1978).

Edmundson, Mark. "The Ethics of Deconstruction." *Michigan Quarterly Review* 27, 4 (Fall 1988): 622–43.

Evans, J. Claude. *Strategies of Deconstruction*. Minneapolis: University of Minnesota Press, 1991.

Faulconer, James E. "Protestant and Jewish Styles of Criticism: Derrida and His Critics." *Literature and Belief*. 45–66.

Felperin, Howard. *Beyond Deconstruction: The Uses and Abuses of Literary Theory*. Oxford: Clarendon Press, 1985.

Fischer, Michael. "Critical Discussion: 'Wittgenstein and Derrida'." Review Article. *Philosophy and Literature* 10 (April 1986): 93–97.

Frank, Manfred. "La Loi du Langage et l'Anarchie du Sens à Propos du Débat Searle-Derrida." *Revue Internationale de Philosophie* 151 (1984): 396– 421.

Gasché, Rodolphe. *The Tain of the Mirror: Derrida and the Philosophy of Reflection*. Cambridge, Mass: Harvard University Press, 1986.

Grathoff, Richard (ed.). *Philosopher's in Exile: The Correspondence of Alfred Schütz and Aron Gurwitsch, 1939–1959*. Trsl. by J. Claude Evans. Foreword by Maurice Nathanson. Bloomington: Indiana University Press, 1989.

Hirsch, David H. *The Deconstruction of Literature: Criticism after Auschwitz*. Hanover and London: University Press of New England, 1991.

Hoy, David. "Jacques Derrida." Quentin Skinner. *The Return of Grand Theory in the Human Sciences*. Cambridge: Cambridge University Press, 1985.

Jay, Gregory S. "Values and Deconstructions: Derrida, Saussure, Marx." *Cultural Critique* 8 (Winter 87–88): 153–96.

Kern, Iso. *Husserl and Kant*. Den Haag: Martinus Nijhoff, 1964.

Krupnick, Mark. *Displacement: Derrida and After*. Bloomington: Indiana Univ. Press, 1983.

Lingis, Alphonso. *Libido: The French Existential Theories*. Bloomington: Indiana University Press, 1985.

Louch, Alfred. "Critical Discussion: 'Does Deconstruction Make Any Difference? Poststructuralism and the Defense of Poetry in Modern Criticism'." Review Article. *Philosophy and Literature* 10 (October 1986): 325–33.

Levinas, Emmanuel. *Le temps et l'autre*. Paris: Fata Morgana, 1979.

———. *Du sacreé au saint: Cinq nouvelles lectures talmudique*. Paris: Les Éditions de Minuit, 1977.

———. *De dieu qui vient à l'idée*. Paris: Librairie Philosophique J. Vrin, 1982.

Lingis, Alphonso. "The Perception of Others." *Research in Phenomenology* 2, (1972): 45–62.

Lyotard, Jean-François. *The Differend: Phrases in Dispute*. Minneapolis: University of Minnesota Press, 1983.

Matt, Peter von. *Fertig ist das Angesicht: Zur Literaturgeschichte des menschlichen Gesichts*. München: Hanser, 1983.

Meyerson, Gegory Dean. *Dialectic of Defeat: Domination and Liberation in Contemporary Political Theory*. Ph.D. Thesis. Evanston: Northwestern University Press, 1989.

Nehemas, Alexander. "How to Understand Jacques Derrida: Truth and Consequences." *The New Republic* (Oct. 5, 1987): 31–36.

Norris, Christopher. *The Deconstructive Turn: Essays in the Rhetoric of Philosophy*. New York: Methuen, 1983.

———. "Home Thoughts From Abroad: Derrida, Austin, and the Oxford Connection." *Philosophy and Literature* 10 (April 1986): 1–25.

———. "On Derrida's Apocalyptique Tone: Textual Politics and the Principle of Reason." *Southern Review* 19 (March 1986): 13–30.

Ristat, Jean (ed.). *Lucette Finas, Sarah Kofman, Roger Laporte, Jean-Michel Rey: Écarts: Quatre essais à propos de Jacques Derrida*. Paris: Librairie Arhème Fayard, 1973.

Rorty, Richard. "Two Meanings of Logocentrism." Paper given at Conference for the 'Philosophy of the Human Studies. Sponsored by the *Greater Philadelphia Philosophy Consortium*. October 1, 1988.

Sallis, John. *Deconstruction and Philosophy: The Texts of Jacques Derrida*. Chicago: The Chicago University Press, 1988.

Samuelson, Norbert. "Issues for Jewish Philosophy: Jewish Philosophy in the 1980's (1+2). *Academy for Jewish Philosophy*. Elkins Park, 1980/81.

Scholes, Robert. "Deconstruction and Communication." *Critical Inquiry* (Winter 1988): 278–95.

Schumann, Karl. *Husserl Chronik: Denk- und Lebensweg Edmund Husserls*. Den Haag: Martinus Nijhoff, 1977.

Searle, John R. "Reiterating the Differences: A Reply to Derrida."

Siebers, Tobin. "Ethics in the Age of Rousseau: From Lévi-Strauss to Derrida." *MLN* 100, 4 (September 1985): 758–79.

Silverman, Hugh J. "Self-Decentering: Derrida Incorporated." *Research in Phenomenology* (1978).

Taureck, Bernhard. *Französische Philosophie im 20. Jahrhundert: Analysen Texte, Kommentare*. Reinbek bei Hamburg: Rohwolt, 1988.

Taylor, Mark. *Altarity*. Chicago: The University of Chicago Press, 1987.

Viscardi-Murray, Lorraine. "The Constitution of the Alter Ego in Husserl's Transcendental Phenomenology." *Research in Phenomenology* 15 (1985): 177–91.

White, Stephen K. *Political Theory and Postmodernism*. Cambridge: Cambridge University Press, 1991.

Willet, Cynthia. "Tropics of Desire: Freud and Derrida." *Research in Phenomenology* 22 (1992).

Wyschogrod, Edith. *Saints and Postmodernism: Revisioning Moral Philosophy*. Chicago: The University of Chicago Press, 1990.

———. "God and 'Being's Move' in the Philosophy of Emmanuel Levinas." *The Journal of Religion* 62, 2 (April 1982): 145–55.

Ziarek, Krzysztof. "Semantics of Proximity: Language and the Other in the Philosophy of Emmanuel Levinas." *Research in Phenomenology* 19 (1989): 213–47.

INDEX

Abraham, Isaac and Jacob, 78, 98, 126
Absolutism, 3, 6, 25, 185–86, 286
Adam and Eve, 98, 191
Agency, 90–109, 210
Alterity, 110, 114, 148–49, 210, 291
Anti-semitism, 10, 15, 18, 27, 300–01n37, 300n35
Apocalypse: Derrida on, 180, 183–89, 199, 201–08, 212–13, 228, 257, 296; and différance, 254, 257–58; as epistemological condition, 192–93; and ethics, 208–11; and exile, 189–91; Kant on, 199–202; Meyerson on, 332–34n10; in translation, 186–89; and truth, 204–05, 208
"Apocalypse of John," 202–03
Aristotle, 198, 215, 243
Artaud, Antonin, 11
Atheism, 222–24

Babel, story of, 158, 172–80
Bataille, Henry, 11
Being, 34, 39, 182, 192, 220–21, 232, 237–38, 269, 311n19
Benjamin, Walter: on Babel, 176–80, 254; Derrida on, 177–80, 260–61, 293; on language, 188; philosophy of, 5, 250–57; works by: "Die Aufgabe des Übersetzers," 157, 172; "Kritik der Gewalt," 253; "Über den Bergriff der Geschichte," 260
Bible. See also Old Testament, New Testament, Scripture, Torah: books of: Deuteronomy, 125–26; Exodus, 124; Genesis, 126, 172–74, 190; Job, 98; and ethics, 52, 54; Levinas on, 31–32, 48–49, 126–27; and phenomenology, 49
Blanchot, Maurice, 11, 15, 208
Blondel, Maurice-Édouard, 15
Boyarin, Daniel, 47, 304–05n34

Cain and Abel, 98, 191
Camus, Albert, 11
Caputo, John, 140–41, 299n34, 328–29n13
Chouraqui, André, 5, 240–41
Christianity, 20, 49, 52, 106
Cogito, 118–22
Cohen, Hermann: on community, 64–65, 76, 104–05; compared to Spinoza, 319n2; and Derrida, 154–55, 201, 212–13, 236,

244, 250; on différance, 224–25; on ethics, 61, 69–74, 77, 84–85, 232, 252; on Ezekiel, 103–06; on God, 63–65, 67–71, 85, 98, 157, 179–80, 212, 231, 244, 309–10n11, 311n19; on infinity, 66–67, 259; on Judaism, 61; and Kant, 5, 17–18, 64, 154–55, 180, 184; and Levinas, 56, 60–62, 71, 80–83, 85–86, 89, 105–06, 155; on mathematics, 221–22; and monotheism, 5, 57, 60, 62, 70–71, 127, 251; philosophy of, 24–25, 56, 83, 149, 220–21, 325n3; on privation, 65–67; and Rosenzweig, 62, 73–77, 80–83, 221, 229; works by: *Die Urteile de Denkgesetze*, 223; *Humanity and the Idea of Messiah*, 251; *Religion of Reason*, 63–64, 250; *Strafgericht Gottes*," 259
Community: aspects of, 26, 132, 316n32; and biblical interpretation, 54; Cohen on, 64–65, 76, 104–05; Derrida on, 267–68, 277; of the face, 111–13; and friendship, 276–77; and Jewish tradition, 267–68; and law, 26, 278; Levinas on, 25, 29, 111, 123; and neighbor, 90, 98, 290; and responsibility, 109, 268–69, 296; Schütz on, 135–36
Copula, 217–18, 242–43, 346–47n34
Correlation, 67–69
Creation, 63–67, 155, 190, 220–21, 223, 251, 313n47
Critique of Pure Reason (Kant), 184

Darwin, Charles, 248
David, Catherine, 9
de Man, H., 19, 246
Deconstruction: and Derrida, 6–7, 151–52, 175, 187, 225, 260, 279–80, 327n4; and Judaism, 11; and Maimonides, 255; and negative theology, 254–57; scope of, 8, 18, 23–24, 187, 246–50, 286, 301n39
Deleuze, Gilles, 185, 334n11
Derrida, Jacques: on absolute, 4, 185–86; and adventurous, 236–37; on apocalypse, 180, 183–89, 199, 201–08, 212–13, 228, 257, 296; on Babel, 158, 172–75, 176–78; on Benjamin, 177–80, 260–61, 293; biography of, 9–12, 21–22; central concepts of, 22–23; and Cohen, 154–55, 201, 212–13, 236, 244, 250; on community, 267–68, 277; conference on, 181, 332–34n10;

critique of Levinas, 6–7, 21, 25–26, 145–48, 232; and deconstruction, 6–7, 151–52, 175, 187, 225, 260, 279–80, 327n4; on différance, 212–13, 232–33, 236–39, 255–56, 266, 292, 340–41n32; on ethics, 1–3, 5–8, 22, 180, 207, 242–43, 295; on exile, 192–93, 196; and foundationalism, 22–23; on friendship, 275–77; on God, 143, 224; Habermas on, 297–98n1; and to Hegel, 3–4, 20–21; on Heidegger, 181; on human beings, 181–83; on Husserl, 26, 154–65, 168–69, 171–72, 180, 257; infinite, 183, 267; influences on, 2–3, 11–12; and Judaism, 5, 8–11, 18–19, 141–43, 186, 193, 196, 205–06, 296, 298n7; on Kant, 154–55, 184–85, 199–202; Kearney on, 19; on khora, 266–67; and language, 151–53, 161, 168, 170, 179, 183–84, 187–89, 209–10, 231; on law, 277–78; and Levinas, 5, 16–18, 142–44, 150, 205–09, 274; on Levinas, 6–7, 21; on Maimondies, 217–18, 244–45, 268–69; Meyerson on, 332–34n10; on negative theology, 26, 158, 214, 223–28, 238–40, 244; and negativity, 3, 14; on phenomology, 156–59, 161, 167–68, 170; and politics, 12–13; and promise, 230–32; as Reb Rida, 240, 343n74; on responsibility, 156, 273–74; on Rosenzweig, 154–55; on strategic, 236–37; on theology, 272; on translation, 176–77; on truth, 150, 180, 194, 200–03, 257, 265; works by: "At This Very Moment In This Work Here I Am," 143, 146; "Des Tours de Babel," 157, 172–73, 180; "Deutschtum and Juden," 244; "Différance," 5, 214, 228, 254, 272, 295; "D'un tone apocalyptique adopté naguère en philosophie," 181, 335n28; "En Ce Moment Dans Cette Ouvrage Me Voice," 25; "Ends of Man," 258; "Genesis and Structure and Phenomenology," 156, 165; "How not to Speak," 230; "Letter to a Japanese Friend," 225; "Of an Apocalyptic Tone Recently Adopted in Philosophy," 186–87, 272; "On Humanism," 181; "Philosophy and Anthropology," 181; "Speech and Phenomena," 26; "The Ideality of the Literary Object," 12; "The Politics of Friendship," 275; "Time of a Thesis: Punctuations," 12; *Writing and Difference, Of Grammatology*, 5, 151, 164, 225, 330n39

Descartes, René, 18, 58, 87, 89, 91
Dictionnaire philosophique (Voltaire), 174
Diesendruck, Z., 214–15
Différance: and apocalypse, 254, 257–58; Cohen on, 224–25; Derrida on, 212–14, 232–33, 236–39, 255–56, 266, 292, 340–41n52; meaning of, 238, 241, 243; and responsibility, 273–78; and truth, 234–38
Dilthey, Wilhelm, 113
Dionysius, 229, 232, 237
Dualism, 74–76

Eckhart, Meister, 229, 237
Ego, 38–40, 93, 95, 131–32, 156, 160–62
Eisen, Arnold, 190–91, 194, 196
Engelmann, Peter, 10
Epiphany, 112, 121, 128–29, 149
Epistemology. *See* Philosophy
Espace vital: and Derrida, 153; and Judaism, 28, 45, 57; and Levinas, 24, 31, 55–57, 153–54, 205, 245, 290; and reading, 27–29, 45, 111
Ethics: and apocalypse, 208–11; and Babel story, 172–80; Bible as model, 52, 54; Cohen on, 61, 69–74, 84–85, 232, 252; and commandments, 94; Derrida on, 1–3, 5–8, 22, 180, 207, 242–43, 295; and face, 128–30; and finite, 61; and fragmentation, 107–09; and freedom, 83, 87–88; and friendship, 277; function of, 112, 114, 209, 247–50; and God, 57, 60–62, 65–71, 76, 79, 87, 180, 212–13, 269; and human beings, 1–2, 41–42, 57–60, 70–71, 76, 100, 206; and infinite, 61, 172; and Judaism, 30, 57; Kant on, 94, 198–99; Levinas on, 1–2, 7–8, 22, 28–29, 35, 41, 55, 58–60, 81–84, 87, 90–96, 105, 108–09, 122, 128, 206–07, 210, 294–96, 308n3; and Midrash, 24–25, 50–54; responsibility of, 93, 268–69; Rosenzweig on, 71–72; and theology, 90, 191
Etymology. *See* Language
Exile: as apocalypse, 189–93; Derrida on, 192–93, 196, 205–08; hermmeneutics of, 205–08; and Jews, 27–28, 189–93, 205–07, 336n37, 343–44n79; meaning of, 189–91, 193–96, 204, 207–09, 268, 296
Expression, 114–16, 121
Ezekiel: Cohen on, 103–06; and God, 96–102, 109; Levinas on, 25, 89–90, 96–102, 106; Rashi on, 96; responsibility of, 95–102, 107, 290; significance of, 101–03, 316–19n35

Face-to-face: and cogito, 120–22; and community, 111–13; and ethics, 128–30; Levinas on, 111–13, 121–22, 135, 323n37; metaphor of, 128; and relationship, 133–34; Schütz on, 136–37
Finite: and ethics, 61; and God, 50; and human beings, 56, 79; and infinite, 24, 71, 76, 79–82, 90, 92, 99
Fragmentation, 90, 93, 107–09, 316–17n33
Free will, 64, 83, 98
Freedom, 53–54, 83, 86–88, 97, 121, 162,

290, 295
Friendship, 275–78, 293, 346–47n34

Gibbs, Robert, 300n35, 307–08n2
God: and being, 232, 237, 269, 311n19;
Cohen on, 63–65, 67–71, 98, 157, 179–80,
212, 231, 244, 309–10n11, 311n19; and
commandments, 25, 155, 189, 240; and
creation, 63, 220–21, 223; Derrida on,
143; and ethics, 57, 60–62, 65–70, 77, 79,
87, 180, 212–13, 269; and Ezekiel, 96–102,
109; face of, 124–26; and human beings,
49, 51–53, 61, 64, 68–69, 73–75, 79–81,
83–84, 96–102, 155, 191, 215–18, 240–
41; as infinite, 28, 51, 58–68, 81, 212,
223, 239, 309n10; in Judaism, 20, 47, 70,
81; and knowledge, 46, 88–90; Levinas
on, 28–29, 50, 57, 78, 86–88, 123–24, 150,
194; and Moses, 50, 124–28, 139; name
of, 148, 179, 241; and negative theology,
66, 68; obedience to, 37–38, 50–55; origin
of, 65–67, 88; and philosophy, 78–79, 137;
resisting of, 97–99; Rosenzweig on, 73–
74, 222–23; in scripture, 37–38, 48–50,
99, 102, 145; and transcendence, 35; as
truth, 6, 74–75, 265–66, 286; Voltaire
on, 174; and world, 24, 67, 205, 214, 218,
220, 309–10n11
Good, 2, 81–82, 93–95, 121, 126, 252
Greek, 10, 11, 112, 188
Groupe de Recherches sur
l'Enseignement Philosophique (GREPH),
13–14, 344n5
Guattari, Félix, 185, 334n11

Habermas, Jürgen, 297–98n1
Halakha, 46, 53, 268
Hebrew: and Babel, 179; and exile, 194–96;
translation of, 44, 124–25, 188–89, 206,
304n28
Hegel, Georg Wilhelm: Derrida compared
to, 2–3, 20–21; and Levinas, 30–32, 36,
85, 91, 93; and phenomenology, 139, 193,
332n31; philosophy of, 18, 20, 33, 59, 106,
316–17n33; Rosenzweig on, 60, 72; on
truth, 72
Heidegger, Martin: Derrida on, 181; and
language, 152; and Levinas, 15–16, 29,
33–34, 91; philosophy of, 19, 24, 110,
182, 234–35, 338–39n19; and Sartre, 11
Hermeneutic movement, 34, 113
Holy Spirit. See God
Human beings: Derrida on, 181–83; and
desire, 59–60, 98, 138; and ethics, 1–2,
41–42, 57–60, 70–71, 76, 100, 206; as
existence of, 259; as finite, 56; and free
will, 98; and genealogy, 173; and God, 49,
51–53, 61, 64, 68–69, 73–75, 79–81, 83–

84, 96–102, 155, 191, 215–18, 240–41; and
infinite, 56, 80–81, 92; and reason, 8, 55,
67, 136–38, 259; thinking of, 26, 87–88,
186; and truth, 26, 208–09
Husserl, Edmund: on Babel, 175–76; on
cogito, 118, 122; and constitution of other,
130–32; Derrida on, 26, 154–165, 168–
69, 171–72, 257; and expression, 115–16;
and Kant, 116–18, 154, 177–79, 184; and
language, 152, 161–64; Lauer on, 113; and
Levinas, 15–17, 25, 29–30, 33, 114, 118–
22, 140; and metaphysics, 158–61, 172;
and phenomenology, 29–30, 36, 39, 110,
112–14, 117, 120, 130–32, 140, 152, 156,
164–71, 175, 182, 275, 327–28n9, 328–
29n13; philosophy of, 5, 11, 24, 94, 114–
17, 154, 170–71, 175–76, 234–35, 308n4,
320n9; and Sartre, 11; and Schütz, 130,
132, 136–37; and scientific research, 113–
18, 156–58; and transcendental
knowledge, 131–32, 156; works by: Ideas,
114–15, 118; "The Cogito as 'Act.' The
Modal Form of Marginal Actuality," 118
Hyppolite, Jean, 39

Individuality, 103–05
Infinite: and being, 237–38, 261, 308n4;
Cohen on, 66–67, 259; Derrida on, 183,
267; desire of, 80–81; and ethics, 61; and
finite, 24, 71, 76, 79–82, 90, 92, 99; God
as, 28, 51, 58–68, 223, 239, 309n10; and
human beings, 56, 80–81, 92; and hyper-
essentiality, 237; Levinas on, 58–59, 71, 120
Isis, 198–99, 334n25
Israel, Israelites, 99–101, 124–26, 128, 189
Israelitische Lehrbil dungsanstalt für den
Westen, 16

Jabès, Edmond, 5, 192–93, 205–06, 296
Jacobs, Louis, 216
Jerusalem, 211, 229–30
Jewish, Jews, Judaism: and deconstruction, 11, 246; and Derrida, 5, 8–11, 18–19,
141–43, 193, 196, 205–06, 296, 298n7;
and espace vital, 28, 45, 57; and ethics,
30, 57; and exile, 27–28, 189–93, 336n37,
343–44n79; on God, 20, 47, 70, 81; and
Levinas, 4, 8–9, 14–16, 18, 28–30, 44–49,
78–79, 141–43, 205–06, 296; and messianism, 252–53; Modern, 47–48; and
monotheism, 21, 57, 60, 62, 142, 253; and
Moses, 128; Orthodox, 47; persecution
of, 9–10, 15, 246; philosophy of, 4–5, 192–
94, 300n35, 309n10, 345–46n28; and
rabbis, 28, 45–46, 240; and scripture, 28,
44–46, 193; and tradition, 52, 61–63,
123–29, 188–89, 267–68, 289–90
Joyce, James, 11

Judaism. *See* Jewish, Jews, Judaism
Judgment, 66, 210, 251
Justice, 121, 246, 259, 278–83

Kant, Immanuel: and apocalypse, 199–202;
Cohen compared to, 5, 17–18, 64, 154–55,
180, 184; Derrida on, 154–55, 184–85,
199–202; and ethics, 94, 198–99; Husserl
compared to, 116–18, 177–79, 184; and
language, 164–67; Levinas on, 32, 35–
36, 85–86, 91; philosophy of, 18, 29, 32–33,
58–59, 106, 196–201, 334*n*25, 338–39*n*19;
and postmodernism, 184–85; works by:
Critique of Judgment, 320*n*8; *Critique of
Pure Reason,* 184
Kearney, Richard, 10, 19
Khora: and community, 26; Derrida on,
266–67, 345*n*14; and messianism, 246,
250; as place, 264–67; and space, 150,
261–67; and time, 263–64
Knowledge, 84–85, 88–90, 191, 216, 251, 269
Kugel, James, 47, 305*n*34

Lacan, Jacques, 316–18*n*35
Language: and Babel, 173–75, 178; Benjamin on, 188; definition of, 41, 119, 172,
195, 243–44; and Derrida, 151–53, 161,
168, 170, 179, 183–84, 187–89, 209–10,
231; and exile, 189–90, 193; and Heidegger, 152; and Husserl, 161–64, 172;
and Kant, 164–67; and Levinas, 3–4, 32,
38–46, 91, 118–19, 146–47, 188, 303*n*15;
and meaning, 91–92, 152–53, 167–71,
180, 195, 213–14; as text, 38–44, 158,
192–93; and truth, 233
Lauer, Quentin, 113
Law, 246, 278–83
Levinas, Emmanuel: on being, 34;
biography of, 14–16, 21–22; Caputo on,
140–41; and Cohen, 56, 60–62, 71, 80–83,
85–86, 89, 105–06, 155; on community,
25, 29, 111, 123; critics of, 107–08; and
Derrida, 5, 16–18, 142–44, 150, 205–09,
274; Derrida's critique of, 6–7, 21, 25–
26, 145–48, 232; on Descartes, 91; on
ego, 39–40; on *espace vital,* 24, 31, 55–56,
153–54, 205, 245, 290; on essentialism,
1–2; on ethics, 1–2, 22, 28–29, 35, 41, 55,
58–60, 81–84, 87, 90–96, 105, 108–09,
122, 128, 138, 206–07, 210, 294–96,
308*n*3; on Ezekiel, 25, 89–90, 96–102, 106;
on fragmentation, 90, 93; on freedom, 85–
86; on God, 28–29, 50, 57, 78, 86–88, 123–
24, 150, 194; on goodness, 121; and Hegel,
30–32, 36, 85, 91, 93; and Heidegger,
15–16, 29, 33–34, 91; and Husserl, 15–
16, 25, 29–30, 33, 95, 114, 118–22, 140;
on independence, 83; on infinity, 58–59,

71, 80–81, 120, 332*n*31; and Judaism, 4,
8–9, 14–16, 18, 28–30, 44–49, 61, 78–79,
141–43, 186, 205–06, 296; on Kant, 29,
31, 35–36, 85–86, 91; on knowledge, 84–
85; and language, 3–4, 32, 38–46, 91, 118–
19, 146–47, 188, 303*n*15; on materiality,
37; and metaphysics, 129; on monotheism,
57, 62, 77, 123–24, 127, 137; on obedience,
53–54; and phenomenology, 10–11, 16,
25, 33–37, 39–40, 106–07, 110–14, 118–20,
121–23, 129–30, 138–39; on responsibility,
273–74; and Rosenzweig, 60, 80–83, 123,
306*n*55; and to Schütz, 137–39; on scripture, 31–32, 37–38, 44–50, 126–27, 138,
145, 149; and subjectivity, 29–28, 35–37;
works by: *Autrement qu'etre ou au-dela
de l'essence,* 50, 97, 106, 323*n*37; *Being
and Time,* 15; "God and Philosophy," 60,
98, 210; *La theorie de l'intution dans la
phenomenologie de Husserl,* 15; "Language
and Proximity," 321*n*17; *Otherwise Than
Being,* 15, 147; *Reality and its Shadow,*
42; "Revelation and the Jewish Tradition,"
27, 29–30, 96; *Totality and Infinity,* 16,
21, 120, 123, 145, 325*n*3; "Violence and
Metaphysics," 6, 144–45, 300*n*37,
313*n*42, 326*n*3

Maimonides, Moses: and deconstruction,
255; Derrida on, 217–18, 244–45, 268–
69; and medieval philosophy, 5; and
monotheism, 60–61, 216, 243, 309*n*10,
337–38*n*4; and negative theology, 211,
214–20, 229, 242, 296, 309*n*10; and
phenomenology, 268–71
Mandela, Nelson, 246
Mark, Karl, 13, 248
Materiality, 37, 40, 67–69, 129
Mathematics, 221–22, 234, 292
Messianic, Messiah, Messianism, 245,
246–254, 257–62
Metaphysics, 57–58, 129, 158–61, 166,
171–72, 240, 246, 258, 306*n*1
Meyerson, Gregory Dean, 332–34*n*10
Midrash, 24–25, 28–29, 30, 47–48, 50–54,
55, 304–05*n*34
Monotheism: Cohen on, 5, 57, 70–71, 127,
251; and ethics, 71; and inspiration, 86–
87; and Judaism, 20, 57, 60, 62, 142, 189,
253; Levinas on, 57, 62, 77, 123–24, 127,
137; Maimonides on, 60–61, 309*n*10;
Rosenzweig on, 57, 84; and theology, 90
Moses, 50, 98, 124–28, 139
Mystagogues, 198–99, 200–201, 335*n*28
Mysticism, 189, 222–23

Negative theology: and deconstruction,
254–57; Derrida on, 26, 158, 210–11,

214, 223–28, 238–40, 244; and God, 66,
68; insight of, 214, 242, 268; and Jewish
thought, 214–17; and Maimonides, 211,
214–20, 229, 242, 296, 309n10;
Rosenzweig on, 222–23
Neher, André, 97
New Testament, 196, 202–03
Nietzsche, Friedrich Wilhelm, 171, 185
Nouvel Observateur, 9, 11

Obedience, 37–38, 50–56, 90
"Of God, That He Exists" (Descartes), 58
Ontology, 91, 99, 234–35, 243, 307n2, 309–
10n11

Parain, Brice, 226–27
Parmenides (Plato), 78, 215, 302n11
Pensées (Pascal), 96
Phenomenology: definition of, 49, 112, 181,
189, 274, 294; Derrida on, 156–59, 161,
167–68, 170; and face, 108–18; Hegel on,
139, 193, 332n31; and Husserl, 29–30, 36,
39, 110, 112–14, 117, 120, 130–32, 140,
152, 156–59, 164–71, 175, 182, 275,
327–28n9, 328–29n13; and Levinas, 10–
11, 16, 25, 33–37, 39–40, 106–07, 110–14,
118–20, 121–23, 129–30, 138–39; and
Maimonides, 269–71; Schütz on, 132,
135–36, 138
Philosophy: death of, 186; foundation of,
275; and God, 78–79; purpose of, 186, 199;
and subjectivity, 37; transcendental, 166
Plato, 154, 160, 215, 229, 264, 266, 302n11
Ponge, Francis, 11
Postmodernism, 2, 22, 59, 184–85, 285–86,
330n35
Presence, 152–54, 159, 166
Present, 156–57, 168–71, 177
Prévenance, 202–05, 212–13, 241, 261, 265
Privation, 65–67, 79–82, 232, 243, 255–56,
260
Proximity, 92–95

Racism, 9–10, 12–13
Rashi, 96, 124, 126, 324n44
Reason, 36, 47–48, 55, 67
Religion of Reason (Cohen), 63–64
Revelation, 27, 37–38, 46–51, 52–55, 76,
100, 149, 289
Rosenzweig, Franz: and Cohen, 62, 73–77,
80–83, 221, 229; Derrida on, 154–55; on
ethics, 71–72; on finite, 76; on God, 73–74,
222–23; on Hegel, 60, 72; and independence, 83; on Judaism, 61, 300n35; and
Levinas, 60, 62, 80–83, 123, 306n55; and
monotheism, 57, 62, 84; on negative theology, 222–23; philosophy of, 5, 24, 321–
22n27, 330n39, 338–39n19, 340n45; on

truth, 73–76, 82; works by: *Stern,* 62–63
Rousseau, Jean, 154

Sanctification, 72–74
Sartre, Jean-Paul, 11, 343n75
Schütz, Alfred, 5, 130, 132–39, 324n54,
346n30
Science, 113–18, 154–58, 198, 218, 248,
257, 262, 295
Scripture. *See also* Bible, Torah, 25, 28, 31,
37, 42–50, 99–102, 145, 149, 193, 289
Shlomo Ytizhaqi. *See* Rashi
Sin, 64, 103–06, 126, 189
Sinai, 46, 128, 139
Spinoza, Baruch, 319n2
Stern, David, 47, 305n34
Stream of (lived) consciousness, 133–34
Structure, 2, 153
Subjectivity, 29–38, 46, 55, 93–94, 105–08,
114, 274
Submission, 92–95

Talmud, 10–11, 46, 69
Telos. *See also* Truth, 77, 158, 170, 182–86,
209–13, 234, 236, 258
Telos and Origin, 155–57, 168, 234–36,
255, 264, 278, 291–92
Theology, 47, 90, 191, 222, 233, 244–45, 272
"Third Meditation" (Descartes), 87
Timaeus (Plato), 266
Torah, 28, 38 42–48, 52, 54
Transcendence. *See also* metaphysics, 18–19,
26, 35, 54, 131–32, 162, 169–70, 175, 232
Translation, 173–80, 186–89, 254
Truth: and apocalypse, 204–05, 208; definition of, 39, 73–16, 177, 209; Derrida on,
150, 176–77, 180, 194, 200–03, 265; and
différance, 234–38; God as, 6, 74–74, 265–
66, 286; Hegel on, 72; and humanity, 26,
39, 182, 208–09; Kant on, 196–97; and
language, 233; and reality, 74–76; Rosenzweig on, 73–76, 82; and sanctification,
72–73; and theology, 233
Tsar Alexander II, 15
Tsar Nicholas II, 15

Violence, 8, 152, 171, 182, 248, 257, 278–
79, 291
Voltaire, 174

Werblowsky, J. Zwi, 252–53
Western culture, 30, 55, 81, 171, 185, 257,
290–94
World: downfall of, 252; and God, 24, 67,
205, 214, 218, 220; and language, 153;
structure of, 169
Wyschogrod, Edith, 44, 302n12, 336–37n1

Zionism, 16, 189